A SUBTLER MAGICK

THE WRITINGS AND PHILOSOPHY OF H. P. LOVECRAFT

S.T. JOSHI

Wildside Press
Berkeley Heights, NJ · 1999

A SUBTLER MAGICK

by S.T. Joshi

Published by:

Wildside Press
PO Box 45
Gillette, NJ 07933-0045

ISBN: 1-880448-61-4

THIRD EDITION

CONTENTS

DEDICATION

To the Memory of

FRANK BELKNAP LONG, JR.

INTRODUCTION

When I wrote the first version of this book, *H. P. Lovecraft*, in the summer of 1981, Lovecraft research was in the midst of a renaissance: with the emergence of such scholars as Dirk W. Mosig, Donald R. Burleson, and others who were consolidating the earlier researches of Fritz Leiber, George T. Wetzel, and Matthew H. Onderdonk, the study of Lovecraft seemed to be progressing by leaps and bounds. The purpose of my anthology, *H. P. Lovecraft: Four Decades of Criticism* (1980), was really nothing more than to codify the best of this earlier work; but its appearance seems to have triggered new work as well. Just as the first edition of this book was published, such diverse scholars as Steven J. Mariconda, Will Murray, and Robert M. Price were revolutionizing the field in various ways; Burleson, Peter Cannon, Barton L. St. Armand, David E. Schultz, and others were continuing to add their own substantial contributions; and the emergence of my corrected editions of Lovecraft's texts from Arkham House allowed still more precise and detailed scholarship to emerge.

All this work was brought to a culmination by the H. P. Lovecraft Centennial Conference in August 1990. The published proceedings of that conference, as well as the anthology of original essays issued at about the same time (*An Epicure in the Terrible*, edited by David E. Schultz and myself), may well represent a sort of pinnacle in the criticism and recognition of Lovecraft. It is certainly not the case that Lovecraft studies will, or should, ever reach a stage of completion, and one of course hopes that his life, work, and thought will constantly be subjected to reinterpretation; but we have now reached the stage where many of the basic facts needed for a sound analysis of Lovecraft are available, and it is now the responsibility of scholars to make use of these facts in order to produce ever more subtle and profound studies of the man and his work.

I have certainly benefited from the work of all my colleagues in the field, and I welcome the chance to write a book such as this. I am myself surprised at the degree to which my views on Lovecraft have changed over the past decade, and I trust that readers will find this book to be virtually a new work rather than merely a patched-up version of the original. Indeed, aside from the initial chapter and a few small portions of others, this version has been written entirely afresh, without even consultation of the original. The generous amount of space allowed by my publisher for this edition has also freed my hand considerably to discuss points in the depth and detail they require. Accordingly, I have not only expanded but entirely restructured this book, and I hope that it now paints a more accurate picture of the development of Lovecraft's work over his career.

As I write this book I am also in the midst of writing a full-length biography of Lovecraft. I have naturally drawn from that work-in-progress, but the quite different focus of this book should make it stand independently of the other. But work on the biography makes me still more convinced of the essential unity and integrity of Lovecraft's life and work, and I hope that I have conveyed that unity and integrity here.

The debt I owe to my colleagues should be obvious, and I should also like to thank Marc A. Michaud, James Turner, and other of my friends and associates for their support of my work over the last two decades. Steven J. Mariconda has read a draft of this book and has as always supplied illuminating comments.

—S. T. Joshi
New York City

AN H. P. LOVECRAFT CHRONOLOGY

1890 (20 August) Howard Phillips Lovecraft is born at 454 Angell St. in Providence, RI, son of Winfield Scott Lovecraft and Sarah Susan Phillips.

1890 (through 1893) Lovecraft and his parents reside at various locales in Massachusetts (Dorchester, 1890-92?; Dudley, summer 1892; Auburndale, 1892-93?) as father, Winfield Scott Lovecraft, pursues business interests.

1893 April 25: Hospitalization of Lovecraft's father at Butler Hospital in Providence; Lovecraft and his mother, Sarah Susan Lovecraft, return to family home at 454 Angell St.

1897 First writings in fiction ("The Noble Eavesdropper") and poetry ("The Poem of Ulysses").

1898 Discovers Edgar Allan Poe. Voluminous writing of stories ("The Secret Cave," "The Mystery of the Grave-Yard," "John the Detective"), some inspired by dime novels. Begins study of chemistry.
19 July: Death of Lovecraft's father. Lovecraft and mother spend summer in Westminster, Mass.
(through 1899, and 1902-03) Attendance at Slater Avenue School.

1899 4 March: Begins handwritten journal, *The Scientific Gazette* (to 1905), largely devoted to chemistry.

1902 Winter: Discovers astronomy, largely from books in library of maternal grandmother. Writes tales inspired by Jules Verne (non-extant).

1903 2 August: Begins *The Rhode Island Journal of Astronomy* (to 1907). Much scientific work in chemistry, astronomy, geography, history, mythology.

1904 28 March: Death of Lovecraft's maternal grandfather, Whipple Van Buren Phillips; family's subsequent financial collapse causes move to 598 Angell St. in Providence.

1904 (through 1908) Intermittent attendance at Hope Street High School.

1905 "The Beast in the Cave."

1906 (through 1908) Writes astronomy columns for *Pawtuxet Valley Gleaner* and *Providence Tribune*.

1908 Nervous breakdown causes Lovecraft to withdraw from high school. "The Alchemist."

1909 (through 1912) Takes correspondence course in chemistry; writes *A Brief Course in Inorganic Chemistry* (1910; non-extant).

1913 September: Literary controversy with John Russell in the letter columns of *Argosy* leads to Lovecraft's entry into amateur journalism (6 April 1914).

1914 (through 1923) Voluminous writing of essays, poetry, editorials, and reviews in the amateur press, mostly for the United Amateur Press Association (UAPA), but also later for the National Amateur Press Association (NAPA), which Lovecraft joins in 1917. Early amateur colleagues: Maurice W. Moe; Rheinhart Kleiner; W. Paul Cook; Samuel Loveman.
(through 1918) Writes astronomy column in *Providence Evening News*.

1915 April: First issue of Lovecraft's amateur journal, *The Conservative* (to July 1923; 13 issues in all).

1917 May: Attempts enlistment in Rhode Island National Guard and later in the U.S. army; through his mother's influence, he is rejected. June: "The Tomb," first fictional work after a nine-year hiatus.
(through 1918) Serves as President of the UAPA.

1919 March: Hospitalization of Lovecraft's mother at Butler Hospital.
"Beyond the Wall of Sleep," "The White Ship," "The Statement of Randolph Carter," and others.
September: Discovers work of Lord Dunsany.

1920 Begins correspondence with Frank Belknap Long, Jr.
Writes at least twelve stories, more than in any single year of his career, including "The Temple," "The Terrible Old Man," "Celephaïs," "From Beyond," "Nyarlathotep," "The Picture in the House," and others.

1921 "The Nameless City," "The Outsider," "The Music of Erich Zann," and others.
24 May: Death of Lovecraft's mother.
4 July: Meets Sonia Haft Greene at the NAPA convention in Boston.
(through 1922) Writes "Herbert West—Reanimator" to order for G. J. Houtain's *Home Brew* (first professional story appearance).

1922 6-12 April: First visit to New York City; meets Long, James F. Morton, and others. Aug.-Sept.: Travels to Cleveland to meet Samuel Loveman and Alfred Galpin; stops in New York City on return trip. "The Hound," "Hypnos," "The Lurking Fear" (for *Home Brew*).
August: Begins correspondence with Clark Ashton Smith.
17 December: Visits Marblehead, Mass., for the first time.

1923 Discovers work of Arthur Machen. "The Rats in the Walls," "The Festival," and others. Collaborations with C. M. Eddy, Jr. ("The Loved Dead" and others). Travels throughout New England (Salem, Marblehead, Newburyport, etc.).
October: "Dagon" (1917) first story published in *Weird Tales*.

1924 Discovers work of M. R. James and Algernon Blackwood.
3 March: Marries Sonia H. Greene and moves to Brooklyn, N.Y. Offered but refuses editorship of *Weird Tales*. Ghost-writes "Under the Pyramids" for Harry Houdini (published as "Imprisoned with the Pharaohs"). "The Shunned House."

1925 1 January: Sonia leaves to take job in Cleveland; Lovecraft moves to single-room apartment in Brooklyn Heights. Futile attempts to secure employment. "The Horror at Red Hook" (1-2 August), "He" (11 August), "In the Vault" (18 September).
(through 1927) "Supernatural Horror in Literature" written for W. Paul Cook's *The Recluse* (1927).

1926 17 April: Returns to Providence (10 Barnes St.), essentially ending marriage (divorce proceedings not undertaken until 1929). "The Call of Cthulhu," "Pickman's Model," "The Sil-

ver Key," and others. Begins correspondence with August Derleth.
(through 1927) *The Dream-Quest of Unknown Kadath.*

1927 August: Travels to Vermont, Maine, and elsewhere in New England. *The Case of Charles Dexter Ward*, "The Colour out of Space." Begins correspondence with Donald Wandrei.

1928 May-July: Spends summer in Brooklyn with Sonia as she tries to set up hat shop; extensive travels (Brattleboro, Vt.; Athol and Wilbraham, Mass.; Endless Caverns, Va.). "The Dunwich Horror."

1929 April-May: Extensive travels (Yonkers, N.Y.; Norfolk, Williamsburg, Richmond, Va.; New York City; New Paltz and Hurley, N.Y.).
(through 1930) "The Mound" (ghostwritten for Zealia Bishop), *Fungi from Yuggoth.*

1930 April-June: Travels (New York City; Charleston, S.C.; Richmond, Va.; Kingston and West Shokan, N.Y.; Athol and Worcester, Mass.). Begins correspondence with Henry S. Whitehead and Robert E. Howard. "The Whisperer in Darkness," "Medusa's Coil" (ghostwritten for Zealia Bishop).
August: Three-day excursion to Quebec. Writes lengthiest nonfiction work, *A Description of the Town of Quebeck* (Oct.-Jan. 1931).

1931 May-June: Travels (St. Augustine, Dunedin, Key West, Fla.; Savannah, Ga.; Charleston; Richmond; New York City). *At the Mountains of Madness*, "The Shadow over Innsmouth."

1932 May-July: Travels (New York City; Shenandoah Valley; Knoxville and Chattanooga, Tenn.; Natchez and New Orleans, La. [meets E. Hoffmann Price]). "The Dreams in the Witch House." Revises stories for Hazel Heald ("Out of the Aeons" and others).
3 July: Death of Lovecraft's elder aunt, Lillian D. Clark.
(through 1933) "Through the Gates of the Silver Key" (with E. Hoffmann Price).

1933 April: Begins correspondence with Robert Bloch.
15 May: Moves to 66 College St. with his younger aunt, Annie E. P. Gamwell. "The Thing on the Doorstep." Revises "Supernatural Horror in Literature" for incomplete serialization in *The Fantasy Fan* (Oct. 1933-Feb. 1935).

1934 April-July: Travels (Charleston; Savannah; St. Augustine; Fredericksburg, Va.; spends May-June with R. H. Barlow in De Land, Fla.).
(through 1935) "The Shadow out of Time."

1935 June-September: Travels (Fredericksburg; Charleston; New York City; spends June-Aug. with R. H. Barlow in De Land, Fla.). "The Haunter of the Dark."

1936 Brief correspondences with Willis Conover, Fritz Leiber, James Blish. R. H. Barlow visits Lovecraft in Providence (July-Sept.). "The Night Ocean" (with Barlow).

1937 15 March: Dies at Jane Brown Memorial Hospital in Providence. R. H. Barlow appointed literary executor.

1939 *The Outsider and Others* issued by Arkham House (August Derleth and Donald Wandrei).

I.

LIFE AND THOUGHT

A superficial glance at the life and thought of H. P. Lovecraft seems to reveal many inconsistencies and oddities: here was a self-proclaimed outsider in his time who professed to be happier in the periwig and small-clothes of the eighteenth century than in the garish modernity of the twentieth, yet who supported FDR and the New Deal; who worshipped Graeco-Roman civilization, colonial America, and Augustan England; who, though claiming to be an unswerving atheist and materialist, wrote tales of horror and fantasy wherein huge "gods" rule the cosmos; who, as he said, had the blood of Nordic warlords in his veins, yet was a sickly recluse for the first thirty years of his life; who wrote that blacks, Jews, and other racial and ethnic groups were either inferior to or incompatible with Anglo-Saxon civilization, yet who married a Russian Jew seven years his senior. Those critics who point out these "paradoxes" fail, however, to notice that Lovecraft himself, in his letters, did not feel that he was a "bundle of contradictions"[1] but repeatedly claimed that all his "oddities" could be reconciled by understanding a few central ideas and attitudes by which he led his life:

> ...I should describe mine own nature as tripartite, my interests consisting of three parallel and dissociated groups—(a) Love of the strange and the fantastic. (b) Love of abstract truth and of scientific logic. (c) Love of the ancient and the permanent. Sundry combinations of these three strains will probably account for all my odd tastes and eccentricities.[2]

It will be well, then, for us not to judge Lovecraft's life and character on our terms but on his; not to look at him from outside but to try to *get into* his mind and, by momentarily adopting his own attitudes, to see whether each of his actions and beliefs does or does not fall into a pattern. Only in this way can we begin to make a coordinated, sympathetic study of his life and, consequently, his work. The key term here is *sympathetic*, which does not refer to a simple condoning of all Lovecraft's actions and ideas, but rather—as with the Greek *sympatheia*, "a feeling together"—an analysis of Lovecraft from his own point of view and in the context of his times.

One critic has remarked that Lovecraft's life was "almost entirely without *incident*, yet rich in *detail*";[3] a statement that could apply to most individuals—whether they be authors, composers, scholars, or philosophers—who devote themselves to the life of the mind. It is, then, of the greatest importance to understand how the incidents of and influences upon Lovecraft's life helped to create his work. Few of us are able to realize how *distant* we are from Lovecraft's age, although he himself died only in 1937.

Born on August 20, 1890, in the home of his maternal grandfather at 454 (then 194) Angell Street in Providence, Rhode Island, Lovecraft early became susceptible to the environment in which he found himself. Interestingly for one who later identified himself so intimately with his native state, Lovecraft nearly ended up being a long-time resident of Massachusetts. A few months after his birth his parents returned to the home in Dorchester, Massachusetts, which they had been renting since their marriage in June 1889, as Lovecraft's father, Winfield Scott Lovecraft, pursued his career as a "commercial traveller" in the Boston area, probably for the Providence-based firm of Gorham & Co., Silversmiths. Lovecraft's earliest memories dated to the summer of 1892, when his parents vacationed in Dudley, Massachusetts. Later that summer the family moved temporarily into the home of the poet Louise Imogen Guiney (a friend of Lovecraft's mother, Sarah Susan Phillips) in Auburndale, and ended up spending the entire winter of 1892-1893 either at the Guiney home or, more likely (in spite of Lovecraft's testimony to the contrary), in rented quarters elsewhere in Auburndale. Lovecraft in any event had keen memories of the Guiney residence, with its huge friendly St. Bernard, the occasional visits of the aged Oliver Wendell Holmes, and his being forced to recite Mother Goose rhymes from the table-top.

Lovecraft was, as mentioned, on his way to being a resident of the Bay State, but the sudden illness of his father changed all the family's plans. Winfield Scott Lovecraft was stricken with a seizure of some sort in a hotel in Chicago in April 1893, and had to be brought back home in a straitjacket; he was admitted to Butler Hospital, an insane asylum in Providence, on April 25. The subsequent diagnosis was "paresis," at that time a catch-all term for a variety of neurological diseases, but it is now virtually certain that Winfield had syphilis. He remained at Butler Hospital until his death in July 1898; it is not likely that Lovecraft ever visited him there. The speculation—first broached by David H. Keller—that Lovecraft himself may have had congenital syphilis has been proven almost certainly false by an examination of Lovecraft's own medical records: when admitted to Jane Brown Memorial Hospital during his terminal illness in 1937, he was given a Wassermann test and tested negative.[4]

The immediate result of Winfield's illness was the abandonment of the home site the Lovecrafts had purchased in Auburndale and the return of Lovecraft and his mother to the family home in Providence. This home—a sprawling Victorian pile with barns, stables, and servants—was in the luxurious East Side of Providence, where the oldest and most respected families lived; not far from his home were the open fields of an as yet undeveloped countryside (now, of course, overrun by the expansion of the city), so that Lovecraft felt himself at once a part of the urban and the rural milieu. The city of Providence itself maintained abundant relics of colonial and late Georgian architecture, while the whole of New England—which Lovecraft would gradually explore during the course of his life—contained many pockets of antiquity where scarcely any touches of modernism intruded. From this early environment arose many of the attitudes destined to endure throughout his life: his love of New England landscape and architecture; his sense of "displacement" from his time, of being a "stranger in this century" (as he wrote in "The Outsider"); his desire to be a dignified country squire; and—for we must remember that Victoria was still Queen of England—his wish to maintain a Spartan decorum and dignity appropriate to an age that still distinguished the gentleman from the plebeian.

On his mother's side Lovecraft was descended from an old Rhode Island stock—the Phillips family—tracing its roots to the late seventeenth century; while his paternal ancestry was a British line (and we need look no further for the sources of his lifelong Anglophilia) that had left Devonshire in the early nineteenth century and settled in upstate New York. His own relatives—particularly his mother, maternal grand-father, and uncles—were by far the strongest influences upon his early development, since in his very early youth Lovecraft found little congeniality in the companionship of his peers.

Part of the reason for this circumstance was the precocity he displayed from his earliest years. He could speak by the age of one; could recite simple verse by two; was reading by four; had begun to write prose and verse by seven; and was learning Latin by eight or nine at the latest. At a time when mandatory public education did not exist, Lovecraft was allowed to stay at home and roam at will in the family library; he claimed to find fascination in the "black, windowless attic room"[5] where all the old books had been banished, and he probably learned more there than during his fitful attendance of the Slater Avenue School (1898-1899, 1902-1903).

The progression of his early interests reveals a mind already endowed with a keen sensitivity to a wide array of intellectual and imaginative stimuli. Grimm's *Fairy Tales* and the *Arabian Nights* had, by the age of five, helped to nurture his taste for fantasy; when he discovered the worlds of Greece and Rome at the age of six he began to gain that love of classicism—in its widest sense—which would form the core of his intellectual life; his love of clarity and dignity (as well as archaism) in writing was fostered by his reading of the greatest of the eighteenth-century poets and essayists by age eight; and his simultaneous discovery of chemistry (geography and astronomy followed by age twelve) led to the scientific rationalism that characterizes his philosophy. When Lovecraft was twelve he already had a complex intellectual and psychological character: the foundations for most of his attitudes and interests had been laid, and it was only a matter of time before they would find expression through fiction, essays, poetry, and letters.

Lovecraft's earliest writings date to around 1896 or 1897, in the form of fiction and poetry. His earliest story is the non-extant "The Noble Eavesdropper," which he describes as concerning "a boy who overheard some horrible conclave of subterranean beings in a cave."[6] This already suggests the tenor of his inclinations. Four other tales of the period 1898-1902 are extant, all of which are embarrassingly crude. Lovecraft claimed that these stories were influenced by Edgar Allan Poe, whom he had enthusiastically discovered in 1898: "Then I struck EDGAR ALLAN POE!! It was my downfall, and at the age of eight I saw the blue firmament of Argos and Sicily darkened by the miasmal exhalations of the tomb!"[7] The curious thing, however, is that these juvenile tales reveal not so much the influence of Poe as that of the dime novel. Lovecraft admits, late in life and a little sheepishly, that he had read dime novels as a youth, and such a story as "The Mystery of the Grave-Yard; or, A Dead Man's Revenge" is manifestly influenced by the dime or nickel novels of Old King Brady, Nick Carter, and other valiant detectives. It should be pointed out that the bulk of Lovecraft's juvenile fiction is wholly non-supernatural.

In fact, Lovecraft's poetry of the 1897-1902 period is far more technically polished than his contemporaneous fiction. The earliest existing poem is the "second edition" of "The Poem of Ulysses" (November 8, 1897), a delightful condensation in eighty-eight lines of the plot of Homer's *Odyssey*. Lovecraft wrote other paraphrases of ancient epic, but they do not survive. By 1902, when he produced the *Poemata Minora* (of which only the second of two volumes survives), he had not only mastered the standard meters in English (heroic couplet, Alexandrine, quatrain, iambic trimeter, etc.), but had achieved a startling diversity in subject-matter, from classical imitations (including the remarkable "Ovid's Metamorphoses" [1900?], a literal verse translation of the first eighty-eight lines of Ovid's epic) to humorous verse ("H. Lovecraft's Attempted Journey..." [1901]) to pensively philosophical lyrics ("On the Vanity of Human Ambition" [1902]). It is, therefore, in some ways not surprising that Lovecraft, up to the age of about thirty, fancied himself primarily a poet.

What forged his prose into the powerful and clear weapon it became in his maturity was not so much his discovery of Poe as the scientific writing he attempted shortly after his discovery of chemistry.

By 1902 he had written several small chemical treatises, as well as *Egyptian Myths*, *Early Rhode Island*, an *Antarctic Atlas*, and others. In 1903 the *Rhode Island Journal of Astronomy* and *The Scientific Gazette*[8] commenced weekly "publication" in handwritten hectographed copies. These delightful little journals are full of interesting matter: star charts, serial articles on the telescope, the moon, and other subjects, and—perhaps most entertaining of all—ads for various scientific and non-scientific paraphernalia or services, including the Providence Detective Agency (*i.e.*, Lovecraft and his boyhood friend, Chester P. Munroe) and the "Blackstone Military Band" (where Lovecraft played the zobo). But astronomy was the prime interest. Lovecraft's devotion to the science, and its importance in shaping his philosophical thought, is made evident in an essay of 1922:

> The most poignant sensations of my experience are those of 1896, when I discovered the Hellenic world, and of 1902, when I discovered the myriad suns and worlds of infinite space. Sometimes I think the latter event the greater, for the grandeur of that growing conception of the universe still excites a thrill hardly to be duplicated.[9]

The extent to which astronomy had captivated his interests is evidenced by the nine-volume *Science Library* (1904?), including small treatises on Galileo, the telescope, the moon, Saturn's rings, and the like. His fiction became influenced by these scientific studies as well, and Lovecraft reports writing several (non-extant) tales inspired by Jules Verne around 1902-1903.

It is appropriate to pause at the year 1904, for by this time much had happened in Lovecraft's personal life. The gloom in which the household was plunged by the illness of Winfield Scott Lovecraft was only augmented by the death of Lovecraft's maternal grandmother in January 1896; it was at this time that he became terrified by the mourning attire worn by the female members of his family, and as a result he began having hideous dreams of "night-gaunts" who would seize him by the stomach and take him on cosmic flights through space. Lovecraft's career as a great dreamer had begun, and dreams would either directly inspire his stories or be featured prominently in them. Lovecraft's maternal grandfather, Whipple Van Buren Phillips, was a fitting replacement for the father he never knew. A wealthy industrialist with interests both in Providence and in the far Northwest, Whipple encouraged Lovecraft in his literary endeavors—particularly in weird fiction—and in general assisted greatly in his intellectual maturation. In 1902 Dr. Franklin Chase Clark married Lovecraft's elder aunt, Lillian D. Phillips, and fostered Lovecraft's classical learning—Clark himself was a learned classicist who had translated Homer, Vergil, Lucretius, and others[10]—and purified his poetic idiom.

As mentioned, Lovecraft spent only two years between 1898 and 1903 at the Slater Avenue School; his perennial ill-health (probably nervous in origin at this time) prevented more extensive formal schooling. He did, however, slowly emerge from his solitude and developed friendships with the Munroe brothers, Chester and Harold, and other boys in the neighborhood. He and his friends turned the stable behind 454 Angell Street into an enormous and elaborate garden and railway yard. It was, perhaps, the most "normal" time of Lovecraft's boyhood.

The death of Whipple Phillips on March 28, 1904, and the subsequent collapse of his business, led not only to the sudden vanishment of much of the family's wealth, but—most importantly for Lovecraft—the loss of his birthplace. It is difficult for us to realize the degree to which Lovecraft, living before the age of rapid and ubiquitous travel, felt that "sense of place" which tied him not merely to New England but more intimately to the sites and scenes of his childhood. Lovecraft dates the beginning of the family's financial decline to 1900, at which time the coachman and all but one of the servants (whose names he still remembered twenty-five years later)[11] were gone; but the death of Whipple Phillips completed the collapse. The 454 Angell Street house was sold and Lovecraft and his mother were forced to move into smaller quarters at 598 Angell Street. This crushing blow brought Lovecraft for the first—and apparently almost the last—time to the brink of suicide: with his natal home gone and the possibly traumatic experience of high school ahead of him, the adolescent Lovecraft felt that he had little to live for, and on long bicycle rides considered immersing himself in the watery oblivion of the Barrington River. What stopped him—characteristically—was intellectual curiosity. Late in life Lovecraft described his sentiments at what was clearly a central turning-point in his life:

> Much of the universe baffled me, yet I knew I could pry the answers out of books if I lived and studied longer. Geology, for example. Just *how* did these ancient sediments and stratifications get crystallised and upheaved into granite peaks? Geography—just *what* would Scott and Shackleton and Borchgrevink find in the great white antarctic on their next expeditions...which I could—if I wished—live to see described? And as to history—as I contemplated an exit without further knowledge I became uncomfortably conscious of what I didn't know. Tantalizing gaps existed everywhere. When did people stop speaking Latin and begin to talk Italian and Spanish and French? What on earth ever happened in the black

> Middle Ages in those parts of the world other than Britain and France (whose story I knew)? What of the vast gulfs of space outside all familiar lands—desert reaches hinted of by Sir John Mandeville and Marco Polo.... Tartary, Thibet.... What of unknown Africa?[12]

So Lovecraft continued his literary and scientific pursuits. Both *The Rhode Island Journal of Astronomy* and *The Scientific Gazette*, which had been suspended even a few months before Whipple Phillips's death, were resumed, although the latter lasted only for another year or so. Meteorology emerged as a new interest, and a Providence Observatory was set up that issued daily weather forecasts which Lovecraft boasted were one-third more accurate than those of the local paper.

Lovecraft's experience at Hope Street High School proved to be unexpectedly pleasant, even though his attendance was still sporadic: he attended the 1904-1905 term, began the 1905-1906 term but left abruptly in November 1905 for unknown reasons (in a late letter he refers to a "near-breakdown"[13] of 1906, but its nature is not now ascertainable) and did not return until the 1906-1907 term, which he completed; he attended most of the 1907-1908 term but left on June 10, 1908, apparently at the very end of the term but prior to the completion of work necessary for a diploma.

Lovecraft's grades, especially in English and Latin, were not as high as one might have expected; perhaps he failed to apply himself in these areas, which he already knew thoroughly. He reports having great difficulty in mathematics, and he voluntarily repeated the last half of elementary algebra in the 1906-1907 term. He did not realize it at the time, but this failure at mathematics was to have an enormous impact on his subsequent career; and it may well have been a primary reason why he abruptly abandoned high school without a diploma in 1908. In a letter of 1916 he reports: "In 1908 I was about to enter Brown University, when my health completely gave way—causing the necessary abandonment of my college career."[14] This is a considerable equivocation: in fact, Lovecraft probably did not have enough credits to enter college even had he finished the 1907-1908 term; but he could not bring himself to admit (to others, at any rate) that he was, for all practical purposes, a high school dropout. Might his difficulty with mathematics been a causal factor? He implies as much in 1933:

> ...I was then intending to pursue *astronomy* as a career, and of course advanced astronomy is simply a mass of mathematics. That was the first major setback I ever received—the first time I was ever brought up short against a consciousness of my own limitations. It was clear to me that I hadn't brains enough

> to be an astronomer—and that was a pill I couldn't swallow with equanimity.[15]

In the end Lovecraft was (or should have been) grateful for this event, else he might have been known in future years as the author of competent but dry astronomical manuals rather than the weird fiction for which he is now achieving a tardy but universal fame.

Lovecraft's writings of his high school period are copious and diverse. Scientific writing still predominates, and Lovecraft could boast of achieving print prior to his sixteenth birthday. Several letters to the *Providence Journal* on astronomical subjects appeared in the summer of 1906, the first dating to June 3; impressively, Lovecraft also had a letter published in the *Scientific American* for August 15, 1906. By late summer of that year Lovecraft began writing astronomical articles for the *Pawtuxet Valley Gleaner* (a rural weekly in Phenix, Rhode Island) and the *Providence Tribune*; the former series continued at least into 1907 (although all copies of the paper after the end of 1906 appear to be lost), while the latter series ends abruptly in June 1908, exactly the time of Lovecraft's departure from school. Early drafts of many of these articles appeared in the *Rhode Island Journal of Astronomy*, which Lovecraft continued through 1907.

Many stories must have been written over this period—and we have hints of some lost tales including detective stories, horror tales, and scientific extravaganzas—but only two stories from the 1903-1908 period survived a purging of his fiction that Lovecraft undertook in 1908: "The Beast in the Cave" (1905) and "The Alchemist" (1908). Both tales reveal great promise, and it is inexplicable why Lovecraft would have decided to give up fiction-writing for nine years after writing the latter story. Lovecraft seemed on the verge of becoming a skillful fiction writer as well as a poet, essayist, and scientist.

But his breakdown of 1908 changed all that. For the next five years Lovecraft lapsed into a hermitry from which he rarely emerged. He reports that from 1909 to 1912 he pursued chemical interests, in part through a correspondence course,[16] but they led nowhere. A few pathetic issues of the *Scientific Gazette* and *Rhode Island Journal of Astronomy* were written in 1909, as if in a sort of regression to childhood; an astronomical notebook was kept between 1909 to 1914, although with large blank periods. Lovecraft, trapped in the hothouse atmosphere of 598 Angell Street with a mother who was becoming increasingly neurotic through financial worries and perhaps shame at the cause of her husband's death, seemed on his way to becoming the "eccentric recluse" that many mistakenly believe him to have been.

After several years devoted to scientific writing (including a lost treatise, *A Brief Course in Inorganic Chemistry* [1910]), Lovecraft returned around 1911 to poetry; his first published verse, the satire "Providence in 2000 A.D." (1912), saw him still attached to the poetic models of the late seventeenth and early eighteenth centuries (notably Samuel Butler, Dryden, Swift, Pope, Gray, and Johnson). Then, in late 1913, came the event that would transform Lovecraft and launch him permanently upon a career as man of letters. As early as 1905 he had begun to read some of the Munsey magazines, especially the *Argosy* and *All-Story*. A letter by Lovecraft to the editor of the *All-Story* published in the issue for March 7, 1914, proudly states that he had "read every number of your magazine since its beginning in January, 1905," going on to praise the very diverse work of Edgar Rice Burroughs, Zane Grey, Albert Payson Terhune, and other popular writers; it is noteworthy that a good many writers Lovecraft admits to enjoying were not weird fictionists, an indication that he read the entirety of these variegated fiction magazines.[17] Lovecraft elsewhere admits to reading other pulp magazines—*Popular Magazine*, the entire run of *Railroad Man's Magazine* (1906-1919),[18] etc.—meaning that he was consuming an enormous quantity of rather cheap popular fiction in addition to the classic literature, science, philosophy, and other work he must at this time have been reading.

But everything in the Munsey magazines was not to Lovecraft's taste. The sentimental love stories of one Fred Jackson particularly earned his wrath, and Lovecraft made no secret of his displeasure at Jackson's work in a letter published in the *Argosy* for September 1913. This letter had very unexpected consequences: the December 1913 issue was filled with letters from Jackson's supporters condemning Lovecraft, and a few who took his side. When one John Russell wrote a poetic squib against Lovecraft, the latter decided to respond in a medium he had long ago found congenial: the verse satire of the John Dryden ("Mac Flecknoe") and Alexander Pope (*The Dunciad*) variety. Lovecraft's piece is entitled *Ad Criticos*, and, of the four "books" he wrote of it, two were published in separate issues of the *Argosy* beginning in January 1914. The controversy raged on for months, Lovecraft and his fellow Jackson-haters always in a distinct minority, until finally the editor of the *Argosy* asked both Lovecraft and Russell to call a truce, which the two poets effected by writing a joint poem published in the October 1914 issue.

This whole incident would have been a mere interruption of Lovecraft's hermitry had not Edward F. Daas, official editor of the United Amateur Press Association (UAPA), noticed the controversy and invited both Lovecraft and Russell to join; both did so, although Russell only a year later. Lovecraft, after joining the UAPA in April 1914, very quickly rose to prominence in the organization, becoming both President (1917-1918) and Official Editor (1920-1922, 1924-1925), and issuing his own controversial journal, *The Conservative* (1915-1923; 13 issues). Through his work in amateurdom, Lovecraft came into contact with other members of similar or differing minds who would not only become lifelong associates (of whom the most important were Rheinhart Kleiner, James F. Morton, Maurice W. Moe, Alfred Galpin, Samuel Loveman, W. Paul Cook, and Frank Belknap Long), but, through steadily growing correspondence and ultimately personal contact, would help to bring Lovecraft out of his shell and broaden his tastes and attitudes. In a lecture, "What Amateurdom and I Have Done for Each Other" (1921), Lovecraft himself eloquently and accurately gauges the benefits of his lifelong amateur activity:

> In 1914, when the kindly hand of amateurdom was first extended to me, I was as close to the state of vegetation as any animal well can be...With the advent of the United I obtained a renewed will to live; a renewed sense of existence as other than a superfluous weight; and found a sphere in which I could feel that my efforts were not wholly futile. For the first time I could imagine that my clumsy gropings after art were a little more than faint cries lost in the unlistening void.[19]

Amateur journalism was exactly the right thing for Lovecraft at this critical juncture in his life. For the next ten years he devoted himself with unflagging energy to the amateur cause, and for the rest of his life he maintained some contact with it. For someone so unworldly, so sequestered, and—because of his failure to graduate from high school and become a scientist—so diffident as to his own abilities, the tiny world of amateur journalism was a place where he could shine.

Those "clumsy gropings after art" at this point still largely took the form of poetry, essays, and criticism. Lovecraft's poetry of the 1914-1917 period is almost wholly forgettable, and most of his amateur essays and criticism are as well; but the latter at least were instrumental in bringing suppleness and fluidity to his prose style and in exercising his controversial skills. Lovecraft, especially in *The Conservative*, was not hesitant to air his opinions on everything from amateur affairs (in particular his hostility to the rival organization, the National Amateur Press Association [NAPA], even though he himself joined it in 1917 and became its interim president in 1922-1923) to politics to literature to philosophy. His early views are very ill-formed, naive, and in many cases poorly reasoned, and the dogmatism and aggressiveness with which they are expressed does not endear Lovecraft to the modern reader; his lifelong racism is displayed in ugly remarks against blacks, Jews, and other non-Anglo-Saxons. I shall probe these views at a later stage, but it is to be noted that Lovecraft's exposure to individuals with opinions differing very sharply from his in the end proved beneficial in rendering him more tolerant; it was, however, a slow and imperfect metamorphosis.

By 1917 Lovecraft had already become a voluminous writer; but would he ever resume the writing of fiction? In 1915 he had said to G. W. Macauley, "I wish that I could write fiction, but it seems almost an impossibility."[20] Grudgingly he allowed his early tales, "The Beast in the Cave" and "The Alchemist," to be published in amateur journals; their warm reception, and in particular the encouragement of longtime amateur W. Paul Cook, finally incited Lovecraft to take up his fictional pen again. "The Tomb" and "Dagon" were written quickly in the summer of 1917, but even then he was slow to write fiction, and it was only his discovery of Lord Dunsany's work in the autumn of 1919 that gave his fiction-writing an emphatic stimulus. In 1920 he wrote more stories than in any single year of his career (at least twelve, perhaps fourteen), although they were all short and on the whole insubstantial. By 1921 Lovecraft's literary output had shifted dramatically: fiction and essays were of paramount importance, and his serious writing of poetry would vanish for nearly a decade until it revived fitfully at the end of 1929 with the production of the *Fungi from Yuggoth* and other verses.

Two important events in 1921 caused an overwhelming alteration in Lovecraft's personal life. First was the death of his mother on May 24 after two years' confinement at Butler Hospital following a nervous breakdown. There is scarcely any question that Lovecraft was tremendously attached to his mother; but her attitude toward him, and their relations over the fifteen years (1904-1919) they spent alone together at 598 Angell Street, are matters of greater doubt. That Susie Lovecraft had been deteriorating mentally for years is graphically depicted in a memoir by Clara L. Hess, a neighbor who knew both her and her son.[21] Hess speaks of Susie becoming disoriented on a streetcar, of her claiming to see strange monsters lurking in the bushes around her home, and—most tellingly—of her assertion that her son did not like to venture out during the day because of his "hideous" face. It is clear that Susie had developed a love-hate relationship with Lovecraft, perhaps because of her horror at the manner of her husband's death. There were other tensions: Lovecraft admits[22] that her opinion of amateurdom was not high and that she felt embarrassed at Lovecraft's complete immersion into it; and Lovecraft's quixotic attempt to enlist in the Rhode Island National Guard and, later, in the U.S. army in the summer of 1917[23]—which "prostrated" Susie and caused her to pull strings to have him rejected—can only have strained their relations further.

Nevertheless, Susie's death affected Lovecraft powerfully, and for weeks he seemed near the point of suicide: "Psychologically I am conscious of a vastly increased aimlessness and inability to be interested in events.... For some time I was unable to dress or be about—the shock affected my throat and motor nerves so that I could not each much or stand and walk with ease..."[24] Lovecraft actually recovered relatively quickly, and his later remarks that his general health began to improve dramatically at the age of thirty carry the covert suggestion that the death of his mother was in fact a liberating influence. The nervous problems that had plagued him in youth slipped away as he began to travel, and on his long walks through city and country he exhibited much greater vigor and energy than the friends who vainly and exhaustedly attempted to keep pace with him. From 1921 to 1924 he gradually widened his knowledge of New England through increasingly ambitious trips, culminating in the ecstatic discovery of Marblehead, Massachusetts, with its remarkable preservation of colonial atmosphere, on December 17, 1922.

The second event of 1921 seemed fortuitously to coincide with his mother's death: at the NAPA's national convention in Boston on July 2-4 he met Sonia Haft Greene, a Russian Jew and executive in a hat shop in New York City. After a three-year romance (not the first, apparently, for Lovecraft: there had been talk in amateur circles of some sort of involvement on his part with the beautiful amateur poet Winifred Virginia Jackson over the previous three years), the two married and settled in Sonia's spacious apartment in Brooklyn.

It is a commonplace among Lovecraft's biographers to remark that the marriage was doomed to failure, and Lovecraft's comment that the causes for the marriage's collapse were "98% financial"[25] are blithely brushed aside. The fact is that the reasons for the failed matrimonial attempt were a combination of "basic and essential diversities"[26] of character which only time could have brought out, combined with an unfortunate and unforeseen series of disasters—largely financial in nature—which beset the couple almost immediately upon their advent to New York. Sonia's hat shop went bankrupt, throwing her out of a job; Lovecraft was forced to look for a job, and tried valiantly at all manner of positions both suitable (editor/reviser for a newspaper or publishing house) and unsuitable (traveling salesman, bill collector). All his attempts, however, failed: Lovecraft had no background and had held no previous position; and the psychological trauma caused by his job-hunting attempts—understandable in one of such frail nervous condition and such notions of gentlemanly behavior as had been instilled in him since childhood—became a drain upon his mental state, and he could only flee to explore the remnants of antiquity left in the New York area "to get the taste out of my mouth."[27]

Sonia's own health gave way, and for a time she was in private sanitariums in Somerville, New Jersey, and Saratoga Springs, New York; no doubt she herself was under severe nervous strain over the couple's financial condition and over Lovecraft's pitiable inability to secure work. Finally she found a job with a department store in Cleveland, which compelled her to move there and visit New York only intermittently; accordingly, her large apartment at 259 Parkside Avenue was given up and Lovecraft, on the last day of 1924, moved into a cheap one-room flat at 169 Clinton Street in Brooklyn Heights, a dismal hovel filled with mice, unsavory tenants, and a general air of decrepitude. The situation was not helped by the robbery of this flat in May 1925, leaving Lovecraft with only the suit on his back. Gradually, the atmosphere of filth and decadence and the unfamiliar hordes of "aliens" began to oppress Lovecraft, and he took to avoiding even his many literary associates—Kleiner, Long, Loveman, George Kirk, Arthur Leeds, Everett McNeill, and other members of the Kalem Club (so called because their last names all began with K, L, or M). Toward the end of the year he began to hint to his aunts (to whom he had written constantly and voluminously ever since his arrival in New York) that a return to New England—perhaps first Boston, then Providence, that "Paradise to be regain'd at last"[28]—was in order; where exactly Sonia fit into these arrangements is not entirely clear. The invitation, however, only came early the next year, and Lovecraft has preserved an imperishable account of his return to Providence on April 17, 1926:

> Well—the train sped on, and I experienced silent convulsions of joy in returning step by step to a waking and tri-dimensional life. New Haven—New London—and then quaint Mystic, with its colonial hillside and landlocked cove. Then at last a subtler magick fill'd the air—nobler roofs and steeples, with the train rushing airily above them on its lofty viaduct—*Westerly*—in His Majesty's Province of RHODE ISLAND AND PROVIDENCE-PLANTATIONS! GOD SAVE THE KING!! Intoxication follow'd—Kingston—East Greenwich with its steep Georgian alleys climbing up from the railway—Apponaug and its ancient roofs—Auburn—just outside the city limits—I fumble with bags and wraps in a desperate effort to appear calm—THEN—a delirious marble dome outside the window—a hissing of air brakes—a slackening of speed—surges of ecstasy and dropping of clouds from my eyes and mind—HOME—UNION STATION—*PROVIDENCE!!!!*[29]

Maurice Lévy is correct in writing: "...this ecstatic return to his native land was in effect a return to the maternal breast. There is something moving in the account he gives of this mythical return to his home, something that betrays a vital, primordial experience."[30]

But again, the problem of Sonia had to be faced. Once Lovecraft was established in Providence, he absolutely ruled out any abandonment of his native city; and when she suggested relocating to Providence to set up a shop in the city, his aunts were equally firm: they could not "afford" to have a tradeswoman wife for their nephew in a city where they had a social reputation to maintain. We see here the clash of lingering Victorian tradition and the modern age at its clearest. We may find the aunts' behavior inexplicable, but they were behaving according to the standards by which they had led their entire lives. If Lovecraft is to be criticized, it is for his meek acquiescence in the whole situation, even though he on the whole sided more with Sonia than with his aunts. In fact, Lovecraft was not suitable for matrimony, and it is just as well that he was now able to resume the bachelor existence that he should never have given up two years before. The marriage was essentially over, although Sonia did summon Lovecraft back to Brooklyn in the summer of 1928 while she attempted (unsuccessfully, it appears) to set up a hat shop of her own; the next year divorce proceedings were finally undertaken.

The final eleven years of Lovecraft's life—spent at two homes on Providence's East Side, 10 Barnes Street (1926-1933) and the Samuel B. Mumford House (c. 1825) at 66 College Street (1933-1937), now moved to 65 Prospect Street—can be told briefly: Lovecraft did little but read, write, travel, and—in an interesting reversal from his younger years—tended to his two aunts, Lillian D. Clark (until her death in July 1932) and Annie E. Phillips Gamwell, destined to outlive him and to die only in 1941. Clearly Lovecraft was at the height of his literary powers: not only did he finish in 1927 the significant treatise, "Supernatural Horror in Literature" (begun in late 1925 for W. Paul Cook's *Recluse*), but he wrote some of his most impressive and best-known fiction: "The Call of Cthulhu" (1926), *The Dream-Quest of Unknown Kadath* (1926-1927), *The Case of Charles Dexter Ward* (1927), "The Colour out of Space" (1927), "The Dunwich Horror" (1928), "The Whisperer in Darkness" (1930), *At the Mountains of Madness* (1931), "The Shadow over Innsmouth" (1931), "The Shadow out of Time" (1934-1935), and others. His early health problems now largely relieved, he spent the bulk of each summer in ever-distant travels in search of antiquarian oases: Philadelphia, Washington, Richmond, Charleston (which became second only to Providence as his favorite city), Québec, St. Augustine, Natchez, New Orleans, and even Key West. He wrote long travelogues of these journeys, including "Observations on Several Parts of America" (1928), "Travels in the Provinces of America" (1929), "An Account of Charleston" (1930), and *A Description of the Town of Quebeck* (1930-1931), all written in an exquisite, tongue-in-cheek Georgian style entirely in accord with the subject-matter. The Québec travelogue is the single longest work ever written by Lovecraft.

Affording these trips was a minor miracle in itself, since Lovecraft's ever-increasing poverty led him to exercise severe economies in food (toward the end of his life he managed to feed himself on about $2.00 per week), travel expenses (he usually rode buses, frequently at night to avoid hotel bills), and lodging (usually at YMCAs or other cheap hostelries). For the fact is that Lovecraft never made any sort of steady income. The establishment in 1923 of the pulp magazine *Weird Tales* would seem to have promised a ready market for his work; his tales were indeed readily accepted by *Weird Tales*'s first editor, Edwin Baird, but not so readily by Baird's successor Farnsworth Wright. Lovecraft's early stories were well suited to the magazine, but as they became longer, more complex, and less in conformity with pulp standards (which sought action over atmosphere, simplicity over elaborateness in prose style, and familiar characters and happy endings instead of the faceless protagonists and grim and cheerless endings Lovecraft favored), they were more and more rejected. Lovecraft never succeeded in finding an alternative market to *Weird Tales*: he knew that his work would never be accepted in the "slick" magazines of the day, and although he submitted work to Harry Bates of the short-lived but better-paying *Strange Tales*, it was rejected because of Bates's emphasis on fast-paced action. Lovecraft scorned *Amazing Stories* after Hugo Gernsback paid him only a fifth of a cent per word for "The Colour out of Space," while his selling of *At the Mountains of Madness* and "The Shadow out of Time" to *Astounding Stories* in late 1935 were luckshots not likely to be repeated, given that relatively little of his work could classify as conventional science fiction. Meanwhile, book publishers (including Putnam's, Knopf, Vanguard Press, and Loring & Mussey) all considered but rejected proposed collections of his work. Lovecraft had always been sensitive to criticism and rejection, and notes that the unfavorable response to *At the Mountains of Madness* by both Farnsworth Wright and his colleagues "did more than anything else to end my effective fictional career."[31]

Lovecraft realized that, in spite of his lack of university education, he should have received training in some sort of clerical or other white-collar position that would have provided an income entirely separate from writing, so that he need not depend on the whims of the marketplace for the sale of his work:

> I made the mistake in youth of not realising that literary endeavour does not always mean an income. I ought to have trained myself for some routine clerical work...affording a dependable stipend yet leaving my mind free enough for a certain amount of creative activity—but in the absence of immediate need I was too damned a fool to look ahead. I seemed to think that sufficient money for ordinary needs was something which everyone had as a matter of course—and if I ran short, I "could always sell a story or poem or something." Well—my calculations were inaccurate![32]

Even the editorship of a magazine would have been a viable occupation for Lovecraft; and he has been criticized for not accepting the offer to edit *Weird Tales* when owner J. C. Henneberger offered it in early 1924. But he did not refuse it merely on the grounds that he did not care for the modernistic architecture of Chicago; instead, he was aware that Henneberger was $40,000 in debt, and there was no guarantee at all that *Weird Tales* would succeed and grant him a reliable income. In later years he wistfully hoped that he might edit a high-grade magazine devoted to weird fiction, but such a thing of course never came about.

Instead, Lovecraft fell into the occupation of reviser or ghost-writer. There were two disadvantages to this profession: first, it was too much like original writing, so that Lovecraft frequently did not have the time or mental energy to write stories of his own; and second, the low rates Lovecraft charged failed in the end to provide a sufficient income, especially when Lovecraft would frequently expend far more than the normal amount of time and effort on revising a work. It is pathetic to hear of him staying up sixty hours at a stretch in September 1936 to complete the revision of Anne Tillery Renshaw's mediocre textbook, *Well Bred Speech* (1936), especially since much of Lovecraft's work was not even included in the published version.

Lovecraft had begun revisory work as early as 1916, and it was a natural outgrowth of his amateur critical activity, especially his chairmanship of the Department of Public Criticism (1914-1917, 1918-1919). On several occasions he teamed up with other amateurs to form professional revisory services, such as the Symphony Literary Service (probably with Anne Tillery Renshaw) or, in the early 1920s, the Crafton Literary Service (with James F. Morton); but usually Lovecraft made arrangements with individuals for revision and ghostwriting. One of his earliest and most pestiferous clients was the itinerant lecturer David Van Bush, who published many books of pop psychology and utterly abysmal poetry in the 1920s, much of it apparently revised by Lovecraft. Around 1928 Lovecraft and Long placed an ad in *Weird Tales* for revision, and in this way got in touch with a number of authors who wished to write weird fiction. As a result, several of the tales Lovecraft ghostwrote for such clients as Zealia Bishop, Hazel Heald, and others are tantamount to original fiction, and a few of them can rank among his better tales. But the income generated from this activity was very irregular, and did little to alleviate the chronic poverty of his later years.

In effect, Lovecraft should have been a gentleman-author with an independent means of income, for he was manifestly unsuited to the life of a wage-earner. In his later years his ever-growing correspondence—which had already become sizable in his amateur years—became nearly unmanageable. While continuing correspondence with amateurs such as Kleiner, Morton, Galpin, and Loveman, he came into contact with other writers of weird fiction (Clark Ashton Smith, August

Derleth, Donald Wandrei, Robert E. Howard, Henry S. Whitehead), and, in the last few years of his life, with an enormous number of young fans and writers who sought his help and advice in writing (Robert H. Barlow, J. Vernon Shea, Robert Bloch, Duane W. Rimel, F. Lee Baldwin, Kenneth Sterling, Fritz Leiber, James Blish, Willis Conover). Lovecraft would spend hours a day "wrestling" with correspondence, writing ten-, twenty-, or thirty-page letters to individuals he had never met. In this way Lovecraft became a revered and beloved figure in the tiny worlds of amateur journalism and weird fiction.

It is therefore not surprising that his sudden death in early 1937 was met with shock and sadness throughout these communities. Sudden as it was, however, his death was perhaps not wholly unexpected. His fatal illness—cancer of the intestine and renal failure—had manifested itself so early as 1934, but Lovecraft had passed off the increasingly severe attacks as "bad digestion" or "grippe" and never sought medical treatment. Was it that he feared a fate similar to that of his mother, whose death was caused by complications following a gall bladder operation? We may never know; certainly poverty—both in terms of his inability to afford medical care and the very poor diet on which he subsisted—was a contributing factor. At any rate, a doctor was called in only in mid-February; on March 10 he was taken to Jane Brown Memorial Hospital, where he would die painfully five days later.[33] On March 18 he was laid in the Phillips family plot at Swan Point Cemetery, and only recently have separate markers—established by contributions from many Lovecraftians—been erected over his and his mother's graves. His is inscribed with the words: "I am Providence."[34]

In forty-six and one-half years Lovecraft wrote some of the most memorable fantasy fiction of this century, some powerful essays and poetry, and more letters than nearly anyone in the history of world literature. Lovecraft's life and character, however, cannot be so summarily dismissed; and we must now not merely explore some hitherto untouched or misunderstood facets of his personality, but also the philosophical thought upon which he himself claimed to base all his literary work.

The central tenet in what Lovecraft called his "cosmic indifferentism" is mechanistic materialism. The term postulates two ontological hypotheses: 1) the universe is a "mechanism" governed by fixed laws (although these may not all be known to human beings) where all entity is inextricably connected causally; there can be no such thing as chance (hence no free will but instead an absolute determinism), since every incident is the inevitable outcome of countless ancillary and contributory events reaching back into infinity; 2) all entity is material, and there can be no other essence, whether it be "soul" or "spirit" or any other non-material substance. Lovecraft evolved these ideas through a lifelong study of ancient and modern philosophy, beginning with the Greek Atomists (Leucippus and Democritus), their followers Epicurus and Lucretius (whose belief in free will Lovecraft was forced to abandon), and such modern thinkers as Ernst Haeckel, Thomas Henry Huxley, Friedrich Nietzsche, Bertrand Russell, and George Santayana. Lovecraft's metaphysical views seem to have solidifed around 1919, when he read Haeckel's *The Riddle of the Universe* (1899; English translation 1900) and Hugh Elliot's *Modern Science and Materialism* (1919).

Up to 1923 Lovecraft was content with this view, and indeed it was the view held by the most advanced thinkers of the nineteenth century. Then Einstein's theory of relativity, propounded initially in 1905 and the object of much scepticism in scientific and philosophical circles, received apparent confirmation from certain eclipse observations, and Lovecraft's entire conception of the universe seemed shaken:

> My cynicism and scepticism are increasing, and from an entirely new cause—the Einstein theory. The latest eclipse observations seem to place this system among the facts which cannot be dismissed, and assumedly it removes the last hold which reality or the universe can have on the independent mind. All is chance, accident, and ephemeral illusion—a fly may be greater than Arcturus, and Durfee Hill may surpass Mount Everest—assuming them to be removed from the present planet and differently environed in the continuum of space-time. There are no values in all infinity—the least idea that there are is the supreme mockery of all.[35]

Why this extreme reaction? What Einstein had shown is not merely that matter is simply one form of energy, but that mass is dependent upon rate of motion. This of course brought about the death-knell of conventional materialism, but Lovecraft gradually came to realize that a modified materialism could well be salvaged in spite (or even because) of Einstein. In 1929 Lovecraft concluded, correctly:

> The truth is, that the discovery of matter's identity with energy—and of its consequent lack of vital intrinsic difference from empty space—is *an absolute coup de grace to the primitive and irresponsible myth of "spirit." For matter, it appears, really is exactly what "spirit" was always supposed to be. Thus it is proved that wandering energy always has a detectable form*—that if it doesn't take the form of waves or electron-streams, *it becomes matter itself*; and that the

> absence of matter or any other detectable energy-form indicates *not the presence of spirit, but the absence of anything whatever.*[36]

As for Max Planck, whose quantum theory (first propounded in 1900) seemed to cast doubt upon the succession of cause and effect, rendering such assumptions merely the equivalent of statistical averages when applied to sub-atomic particles, Lovecraft came to terms with this also:

> What most physicists take the quantum theory, at present, to mean, is *not that any cosmic uncertainty exists* as to which of several courses a given reaction will take; but that in certain instances *no conceivable channel of information can ever tell human beings which courses will be taken*, or by what exact course a certain observed result came about.[37]

This is in fact an error, and the "uncertainty" posited by quantum theory does indeed inhere in sub-atomic particles; but Lovecraft was aware that phenomena on the atomic or molecular level are not subject to this uncertainty, and so remain as deterministic as they were before. It is still an unanswered question what role, if any, the "indeterminacy" (as Heisenberg termed it) of quantum theory has in human affairs. In all this speculation Lovecraft was keen on refuting two central metaphysical notions which he regarded as outmoded through the discoveries of nineteenth-century science, and which he maintained (correctly) were still outmoded even in the light of the revolutionary findings of modern physics: teleology (the belief that the universe is heading in a specified direction, specifically under the guidance of a governing deity) and the concept of the immaterial soul. Neither relativity nor the quantum theory have any significant effect upon the extreme improbability of both these conceptions, and Lovecraft ably defended his position on these two issues in the three *In Defence of Dagon* essays of 1921.

Teleology can take two forms, terrestrial (the idea that human or terrestrial life is evolving in some direction or toward some goal) and cosmic (the idea that the universe as a whole is so evolving). Lovecraft rejected both forms: it is not, of course, that he rejected Darwin's theory of evolution, but he refused to believe that the evolution of individual species inevitably leads in any given direction, especially since it is likely that all terrestrial life will end with the death of the sun; and certainly he saw no guiding force in the universe at large. Haeckel seemed so taken with the theory of evolution that he illegitimately applied it to the cosmos; and, curiously enough, Lovecraft's opponent in the *In Defence of Dagon* essays, a Mr. Wickenden, although a rigid theist, seemed to use evolution as a rhetorical ploy for much the same purpose. Lovecraft refutes him thoroughly:

> [Wickenden] sees a process of evolution in operation at one particular cosmic moment in one particular point in space; and at once assumes gratuitously that *all the cosmos* is evolving steadily *in one direction* toward a fixed goal. Moreover, he *feels* that it all must amount to something—he calls it a thing of "heroism and splendour"! So when it is shewn that life on our world will (relatively) soon be extinct through the cooling of the sun; that space is full of such worlds which have died; that human life and the solar system itself are the merest *novelties* in an eternal cosmos; and that all indications point to a gradual breaking down of both matter and energy which will eventually nullify the results of evolution in any particular corner of space; when these things are shewn, Mr. Wickenden recoils, and...cries out that it's all nonsense—it just *can't* be so!! But what of the actual probability, apart from man's futile wishes? If we cannot prove that the universe means *nothing*, how can we prove that it means *anything*—what right have we to invent a notion of purpose in the utter absence of evidence?[38]

The rejection of the notion of an immaterial soul also has as its foundation the theory of evolution. Lovecraft merely echoes Haeckel in his emphatic argument:

> One might ask, to the confounding of those who aver that men have "souls" whilst beasts have not,...just how the evolving organism began to acquire "spirit" after it crossed the boundary betwixt advanced ape and primitive human? It is rather hard to believe in "soul" when one has not a jot of evidence for its existence; when all the psychic life of man is demonstrated to be precisely analogous to that of other animals—presumably "soulless." But all this is too childish. When we investigate both ontogeny and phylogeny we find that man had both individually and racially evolved from the unicellular condition. Every man living was at the beginning of his life a single protoplasmic cell, whose simple reflex sensitiveness is the source of all the neural and psychic activity which later develops through increasing complexity of organisation. We can easily trace the whole process of development from the irritability of the simple cell-wall through various intermediate stages of spinal and

> ganglial activity to the formation of a true brain and finally to the manifestation of those complex functions which we know as intellect and emotion. This development occurs both pre-natally and post-natally in the individual, and can be followed with much exactitude. In the species, we can follow it hardly less exactly by means of comparative anatomy and biology.[39]

It is manifestly obvious that Lovecraft's materialism left no room for religion; indeed, his vision—as reflected both in his philosophy and in his fiction—is among the most secular of any writer of modern times, and this in spite of the creation of "gods" in his most celebrated tales. Lovecraft claimed to have dispensed with religion so early as the age of five,[40] but there is reason to doubt this. What is not in doubt is that his mature thought found religion simply to be an encumbrance to the proper conception of the universe:

> I certainly can't see any sensible position to assume aside from that of *complete scepticism tempered by a leaning toward that which existing evidence makes most probable.* All I say is that I think it is *damned unlikely* that anything like a central cosmic will, a spirit world, or an eternal survival of personality exist. They are the most preposterous and unjustified of all the guesses which can be made about the universe, and I am not enough of a hair-splitter to pretend that I don't regard them as arrant and negligible moonshine. In theory I am an *agnostic*, but pending the appearance of rational evidence I must be classed, practically and provisionally, as an *atheist*. The chances of theism's truth being to my mind so microscopically small, I would be a pedant and a hypocrite to call myself anything else.[41]

What Lovecraft uses here—and what he was compelled to do after absorbing relativity and quantum theory—is the notion of *probability*. Since it is logically impossible to prove that God does *not* exist, all one can do is to appeal to what we currently know about the constitution of the universe, and to evaluate whether the metaphysical claims of religion harmonize with it. To Lovecraft's mind they did not.

What Lovecraft felt to be a clinching argument in the matter of religion was the evidence from anthropology. Such works as John Fiske's *Myths and Myth-Makers* (1872) and Sir James George Frazer's *The Golden Bough* (1890) provided, to Lovecraft's mind, entirely convincing accounts of the natural *origin* of religious belief in primitive man:

> This matter of the explanation of "spiritual" feelings is really the most important of all materialistic arguments; since the explanations are not only overwhelmingly forcible, but so adequate as to shew that man could not possibly have developed without acquiring just such false impressions.[42]

Lovecraft expounds these explanations in a letter:

> Primarily, of course, men began to be religious and mystical because at intellect's dawn they knew no other way to explain the phenomena they saw around them, or to work off such residues of excess emotional energy as war and eroticism did not take care of. They could not understand any phenomenon without a cause as personal and purposeful as that which made the axe and club move in their own hands, or account for their vague emotions and dual life in dreams on any basis except that of a spirit-world paralleling theirs. That they attributed to Nature a set of human personalities which definite sentiments for or against themselves was only to be expected; and this formed of course an imperative reason for the gesture of worship—hortatory, propitiatory, laudatory, grateful, ecstatic, symbolic, or simply orgiastic. Believing themselves in the absolute sway of their nature-gods, primitive men of course quickly connected them with the systems of tribal polity which their stumbling experience had evolved—thus bringing into being the myth of morals and the legend of good and evil. Confusing wishes with hopes, and hopes with realities, they coined the idea of an immortality for the dream-bodies of themselves, their gods and cattle, their spears and clubs, their wives, and their food, clothing, and armaments. All the foundations of religion were laid, and in a perfectly natural and inevitable way. At that stage of existence, no other result of the contact of the human mind with Nature was possible.[43]

Lovecraft did not, however, become an evangelical atheist (as his colleague James F. Morton was for a time), for he had little faith that the mass of people could ever find emotional or intellectual satisfaction in an atheistic conception of the universe:

> My contention is that religion is still useful amongst the herd—that it helps their orderly conduct as nothing else could, and that it gives them an emotional satisfaction they could not get elsewhere. I don't say that it does either of these things as well as it used to do, but I do say that I believe nothing else could do them so well even now. The crude human animal is ineradicably superstitious, and there is every biological and historical reason why he should be. An irreligious barbarian is a scientific impossibility. Rationalistic conceptions of the universe involve a type of mental victory over hereditary emotion quite impossible to the undeveloped and uneducated intellect. Agnosticism and atheism mean nothing to a peasant or workman. Mystic and teleological personification of natural forces is in his bone and blood—he cannot envisage the cosmos (i.e., the earth, the only cosmos he grasps) apart from them. Take away his Christian god and saints, and he will worship something else.[44]

This passage may be of significance in elucidating the many "cults" who worship the gods of Lovecraft's fictional universe.

With cosmic teleology and religion firmly eliminated and determinism espoused, what possible ethical code could Lovecraft recommend on the human scale? There is, indeed, a problem with a determinist expounding a moral system at all, since determinism naturally implies the absence of free will and hence the absence of any fundamental moral culpability in any given action. Lovecraft evaded this dilemma (as most determinists, from Democritus onward, have done) by distinguishing between determinism and fatalism. Fatalism is an illegitimate extension of determinism in asserting that, since all things are determined, all human action is futile and we must simply give in to "fate." Lovecraft recognized this fallacy very early: "We have no specific destiny against which we can fight—for the fighting would be as much a part of the destiny as the final end."[45] Although this is Lovecraft's argument for determinism, in effect it could serve as his argument for a sort of free will also: since destiny is something that is enmeshed in the fabric of existence, it is for that reason undetectable; and we can continue engaging in any actions we please because those activities would be as much (or as little) a part of destiny as the failure to act. As Lovecraft wrote in "Some Causes of Self-Immolation" (1931):

> It was of course recognised by determinists that behind any proximate base must lie the general flux of the universe, be it simple or complex; that is, that in

> the last analysis each human act can be no less than the inevitable result of every antecedent and circumambient condition in an eternal cosmos. This recognition, however, did not prevent such thinkers from continuing to seek for the more proximate base or bases, and to speculate upon the immediate strings by which human puppets are moved.[46]

This notion of *proximate* causes—and its corollary, the recommendation of proximate values—is of the highest significance. Given that there is no absolute or objective morality (for this would imply teleology), Lovecraft nevertheless felt that certain values could be espoused purely on the human scale for the sake of individual self-realization and the smooth functioning of society:

> Now since man means nothing in the cosmos, it is plain that his only logical goal (a goal whose sole reference is *himself*) is simply the achievement of a reasonable equilibrium which shall enhance his likelihood of experiencing the sort of reactions he wishes, and which shall help along his natural impulse to increase his differentiation from unorganised force and matter. This goal can be reached only through teaching individual men how best to keep out of each other's way, and how best to reconcile the various conflicting instincts which a haphazard cosmic drift has placed within the breast of the same person. Here, then, is a practical and imperative system of ethics, resting on the firmest possible foundation and being essentially that taught by Epicurus and Lucretius.[47]

Such a position leads inevitably to an assertion on the relativity of values:

> Each person lives in his own world of values, and can obviously (except for a few generalities based on essential similarities in human nature) speak only for himself when he calls this thing "silly and irrelevant" and that thing "vital and significant," as the case may be. We are all meaningless atoms adrift in the void.[48]

This is all unexceptionable, but it gradually gives way to a much less defensible view. Lovecraft evolved the notion that he could best supply a sense of purpose to his existence by merging himself with the culture-stream in which he was born—specifically the Puritan-Victorian-Yankee heritage of colonial Rhode Island—even though he had rejected many of its intellectual bases (particularly religious belief). On occasion, however, he inconsistently recommended such an adherence to tradition for *everyone*, in spite of his acknowledgment of the relativity of values. Hence, in a letter clearly declaring that "'good' is a relative and variable quality," he goes on to say:

> Amidst this variability there is *only one anchor of fixity* which we can seize upon as the working pseudo-standard of "values" which we need in order to feel settled and contented—and that anchor is *tradition*, the potent emotional legacy bequeathed to us by the massed experience of our ancestors, individual or national, biological or cultural. Tradition means nothing cosmically, but it means everything locally and pragmatically because we have nothing else to shield us from a devastating sense of "lostness" in endless time and space.[49]

It is clear that tradition meant everything for Lovecraft, but not so clear why he felt it should mean everything for everyone else. In fact, he had passed through a phase of sophisticated cosmopolitanism in the early 1920s, only to reject it as both aesthetically and morally unfulfilling; but he should have realized that such a stance might well be fulfilling for others. In effect, Lovecraft was attempting to present a philosophical justification for many of the instinctive beliefs and emotional reactions that had been bred in him early in life—such things as class distinctions (always very deeply held by Lovecraft), "gentlemanly" attire and conduct, sexual repression (and such of its corollaries as extreme restraint in displays of affection and hostility to homosexuality), and scorn of metropolitanism, cosmopolitanism, and racial heterogeneity. Lovecraft attempts to justify these beliefs by an appeal to aesthetics:

> So far as I am concerned—I am an aesthete devoted to harmony, and to the extraction of the maximum possible pleasure from life. I find by experience that my chief pleasure is in symbolic identification with the landscape and tradition-stream to which I belong—hence I follow the ancient, simple New England ways of living, and observe the principles of honour expected of a descendant of English gentlemen. It is pride and beauty-sense, plus the automatic instincts of generations trained in certain conduct-patterns, which determine my conduct from day to day. But this is *not ethics*, because the same compul-

> sions and preferences apply, with me, to things wholly outside the ethical realm. For example, I never cheat or steal. Also, I never wear a top-hat with a sack coat or munch bananas in public on the street, because a gentleman does not do those things either. I would as soon do the one as the other sort of thing—it is all a matter of harmony and good taste—whereas the ethical or "righteous" man would be horrified by dishonesty yet tolerant of coarse personal ways.[50]

This is clever, but the appeal to aesthetics ends up sounding hollow given that Lovecraft's examples of violations of "good taste" rest fundamentally on social and not aesthetic bases.

The importance which Lovecraft attached to *culture* or *civilization*, and the preservation of it, is the foundation for his entire political philosophy. His politics underwent the most significant changes during the course of his life of any aspect of his thought; but the basic desire to maintain culture—and by "culture" he meant the ability of a given political unit or civilization to produce not only enduring art but also an harmonious *milieu* for those of the higher mental caliber—underlies all the changes. For the first forty years of his life Lovecraft felt that only aristocracy and oligarchy could produce sufficient leisure for the highest intellectual classes who always set the tone of a civilization: "I believe in an aristocracy, because I deem it the only agency for the creation of those refinements which make life endurable for the human animal of high organisation."[51] Influenced by Nietzsche, Lovecraft concluded that democracy is "a mere catchword and illusion of inferior classes, visionaries, and dying civilisations";[52] in the United States it

> ...gradually induced the notion of diffused rather than intensive development. Idealists wanted to raise the level of the ground by tearing down all the towers and strowing them over the surface—and when it was done they wondered why the ground didn't seem much higher, after all. And they had lost their towers![53]

In the end, however, Lovecraft became convinced that socialism could, if implemented properly, maintain as high a level of culture as aristocracy. This change occurred very gradually, and required a reversal of opinion on several fundamental points. In particular, Lovecraft in his early years still adhered to the naive view that capitalism rewarded pure intellect or aesthetic accomplishment—that the producers of art and culture would receive the proper monetary fruits of their labor. Late in life he realized his error:

> But the chief indictment of a capitalistic ideal is perhaps something deeper even than humanitarian principle—something which concerns the profound, subtle, and pervasive hostility of capitalism, and of the whole essence of mercantilism, to all that is finest and most creative in the human spirit....business and capital are the fundamental enemies of human worth in that they exalt and reward the *shrewdly acquisitive* rather than the *intrinsically superior and creative.*[54]

There is an aesthetic corollary to this notion: in a capitalistic democracy whose citizens are on the whole poorly educated but capable of influencing the production of art by their sheer numbers and their purchasing power, there will inevitably result a cleavage between "high" and "low" art, with the latter dominating the market and the available resources of the mass of society:

> Bourgeois capitalism gave artistic excellence and sincerity a death-blow by enthroning cheap *amusement-value* at the expense of that *intrinsic excellence* which only cultivated, non-acquisitive persons of assumed position can enjoy. The determinant market for written, pictorial, musical, dramatic, decorative, architectural, and other heretofore aesthetic material ceased to be a small circle of truly educated persons, but became a substantially larger...circle of mixed origin numerically dominated by crude, half-educated clods whose systematically perverted ideals (worship of low cunning, material acquisition, cheap comfort and smoothness, worldly success, ostentation, speed, intrinsic magnitude, surface glitter, etc.) prevented them from ever achieving the tastes and perspectives of the gentlefolk whose dress and speech and external manners they so assiduously mimicked. This herd of acquisitive boors brought up from the shop and the counting-house a complete set of artificial attitudes, oversimplifications, and mawkish sentimentalities which no sincere art or literature could gratify—and they so outnumbered the remaining educated gentlefolk that most of the purveying agencies became at once reoriented to them. Literature and art lost most of their market; and writing, painting, drama, etc. be-

> came engulfed more and more in the domain of *amusement enterprises.*[55]

What is the solution? Could it perhaps be the socialism that Lovecraft scorned when he saw the cultural devastation of the Russian Revolution in 1917? Yes, but it would be a very modified, non-Marxist socialism. Lovecraft came to see that his brand of socialism was, in theory, similar to aristocracy:

> ...what I used to respect *was not aristocracy, but a set of personal qualities which aristocracy then developed better than any other system ...a set of qualities, however, whose merit lay only in a psychology of non-calculative, non-competitive disinterestedness, truthfulness, courage, and generosity fostered by good education, minimum economic stress, and assumed position,* AND JUST AS ACHIEVABLE THROUGH SOCIALISM AS THROUGH ARISTOCRACY.[56]

Lovecraft's socialism, evolved as the Great Depression wreaked economic havoc in the 1930s, involved minimization of private profit, state control of important services and utilities, unemployment insurance and old age pensions, and full employment by means of artificial restriction of working hours. The greater leisure time accruing under this system could be utilized in increasing the general education and aesthetic responsiveness of the populace, so that art could once again resume its function as purveyor of aesthetic sincerity rather than cheap amusement.

In the political sphere, however, Lovecraft had very different ideas. If *economic wealth* must, if society is to escape a revolt of the permanently unemployed, be distributed more equitably amongst the many, then *political power* should be correspondingly limited to the few. Given his lifelong hostility to democracy and his justifiably low opinion of the intelligence of the masses, it was logical that Lovecraft would come to conclude that the complexity of government in a technological age rendered it impossible for any but experts to have a real grasp of the political situation; hence only technicians would be elected by a limited voting body consisting only of those individuals who could pass certain intellectual and psychological tests. In this way Lovecraft created his theory of "fascistic socialism"—a concept expounded not merely in his later letters and essays (especially "Some Repetitions on the Times" [1933]) but also in his fiction.

Did Lovecraft really believe that such a system could come about, and that FDR's New Deal was about to make it a reality? It certainly appears so, and he seemed entirely unaware that the New Deal was really a very conservative movement intended merely to salvage democracy and capitalism by means of governmental supervision (not control) of business and stop-gap measures to ease unemployment. But if, toward the end of his life, Lovecraft liked to envision a socialist utopia on the horizon, in his earlier years he manifestly saw little hope for a civilization where the machine was becoming the dominant force:

> But nothing good can be said of that cancerous machine-culture itself. It is not a true civilisation, and has nothing in it to satisfy a mature and fully developed human mind. It is attuned to the mentality and imagination of the galley-slave and the moron, and crushes relentlessly with disapproval, ridicule, and economic annihilation any sign of actually independent thought and civilised feeling which chances to rise above its sodden level. It is a treadmill, squirrel-trap culture—drugged and frenzied with the hasheesh of industrial servitude and material luxury. It is wholly a material body-culture, and its symbol is the tiled bathroom and steam radiator rather than the Doric portico and the temple of philosophy. Its denizens do not live or know how to live.[57]

What is the civilized person to do save to keep aloof from the throng and immerse himself in the culture-stream of the past? For Lovecraft this meant plunging intellectually and aesthetically into Graeco-Roman antiquity and eighteenth-century England; not only because he had grown immeasurably fond of these periods of Western culture, but because the latter age "was the *final* phase of that perfectly unmechanised aera which as a whole gave us our most satisfying life."[58] The nineteenth century (especially in the England of Victoria) was simply a "mistake"[59]—a "desert of illusions, pomposities, and hypocrisies"[60] whose only virtues were its "manners and conceptions of life as a fine art."[61] The twentieth century, recoiling from the hypocrisy and repression of the nineteenth, had gone too far in radicalism—hence Lovecraft's distaste for avant-garde architecture, music, literature, manners, and politics. Lovecraft espoused the theory of a "decline of the West" years before he read Spengler's monumental treatise, and his attitudes had been reached independently of his later readings of Joseph Wood Krutch (*The Modern Temper*), Bertrand Russell, and George Santayana.

It is again the desire to preserve culture that in part accounts for Lovecraft's racism. The America of Lovecraft's day was experiencing an enormous flood of immigration, and no longer from "Anglo-Saxon" peoples (England, Ireland, Germany, Scandinavia), but from those of Eastern Europe and Asia; a circumstance that naturally engendered feelings of unease amongst old-time Yankees. Lovecraft's early views on race are extremely ignorant and intolerant, and his naive belief in the *biological* superiority of the "Teuton" or the "Aryan" make sad reading. Gradually he was forced to yield on the point, even if grudgingly: "Biologically, the Nordic is probably not superior to the best Mediterranean stock, or the unbroken and now almost extinct Semitic white stock...."[62] But he maintained to the end of his life the biological inferiority of blacks, and recommended an absolute color line in respect to intermarriage.

Lovecraft's racism is certainly the most controversial aspect of his philosophical thought, and he has been roundly condemned for it; but critics have failed to examine his views in the proper historical context and to focus on the exact point at which Lovecraft's beliefs are open to criticism. It is not his desire to maintain an homogeneous Anglo-Saxon culture in America or his requiring foreigners to shed their own cultural heritage and adopt that of the dominant population that should be the subject of censure. As for the first point, Lovecraft is as justified in seeking homogeneity of culture as many of us today are in seeking diversity and heterogeneity; these are simply two different ways to conceive of the makeup of a society, and there are virtues and drawbacks to both. Neither conception can be regarded as intrinsically superior to the other. As for the second point, in Lovecraft's time it was commonly believed that immigrants would "assimilate" themselves to the prevailing culture, and Lovecraft was by no means exceptional in making this a necessity for social acceptance of foreigners. Many people have noted the apparent paradox of Lovecraft's prejudice against Jews on the one hand and his friendship with Samuel Loveman and his marriage to Sonia Greene on the other; but there is no paradox, for Lovecraft welcomed Loveman and Sonia because he felt that they were exactly the sort of assimilated aliens he could accept.

Where Lovecraft is in fact to be criticized is in his failure to maintain an open mind on the subject of race, in spite of the increasing anthropological and sociological evidence that was, throughout the early decades of the century, systematically destroying many of his cherished beliefs: that some races are superior or inferior to others; that races could even be identified coherently after millennia of intermixture; that the distinguishing "characteristics" of races are anything more than superficial stereotypes; and that cultures are ineradicably hostile to one another. Lovecraft, who readily changed his views on metaphysics, ethics, aesthetics, and politics as he encountered new information, failed to note that the racial theories he had absorbed from the Social Darwinists and other thinkers of the late nineteenth and early twentieth centuries had been entirely overthrown by 1930 and were regarded merely as wrong turns in the history of human thought. For a multiplicity of factors, Lovecraft was too keenly attached to his racist assumptions to give them up lightly. They remain a black mark on Lovecraft the man, the thinker, and the writer: not because most of us nowadays happen to disagree with them, but because they are simply false, and because they disfigure even some of his most distinguished works of fiction.

Lovecraft's aesthetics are a much more interesting and challenging component of his thought, and need to be examined with care. Early in life, as befits one who has absorbed classical antiquity and the Augustan age of English literature, Lovecraft was a devoted, even an extreme, classicist. Consider this statement in "The Case for Classicism" (1919):

> The literary genius of Greece and Rome, developed under peculiarly favourable circumstances, may fairly be said to have completed the art and science of expression. Unhurried and profound, the classical author achieved a standard of simplicity, moderation, and elegance of taste, which all succeeding time has been powerless to excel or even to equal. Indeed, those modern periods have been most cultivated, in which the models of antiquity have been most faithfully followed.[63]

This is a remarkable assertion: if the Graeco-Roman authors have "completed" the art of expression, all that is left for future generations to do is to imitate them; and indeed, Lovecraft attempted assiduously to do just that, in both prose and verse, at least through the late teens.

And yet, this classicism appeared to yield around 1919 to a radically different aesthetic theory: Decadence. The Decadent or Symbolist movement of the later nineteenth century was largely of French origin, but was popularized in England by such diverse figures as Oscar Wilde, Walter Pater, and the Pre-Raphaelites. The cardinal doctrine of the movement was "art for art's sake"—a defiance of the moral didacticism of the Victorian age. Once we realize this fact, and once we become aware that both the French Symbolists and the English aesthetes drew upon the critical theory of Poe as their foundation, we can come to understand why the movement might have had its attractions for Lovecraft. Poe's dictum that art has *beauty* for its goal whereas science must be devoted to *truth* was again a stick with which to beat the morally earnest Victorians, who were devoted to the ideal of art as an uplifter of the human race. All this struck a responsive chord in Lovecraft, for he had always scorned the nineteenth century and hearkened back to the previous century for his aesthetic stimulus. Lovecraft remained throughout his life as hostile to didacticism in art as any aesthete or Decadent.

Lovecraft's reading of Lord Dunsany—along with his friendship with such cosmopolitan aesthetes as Samuel Loveman and Frank Belknap Long—no doubt influenced this aesthetic shift. Despite its connections with his classicism, his new Decadent stance really was a significant change from his previous views; and, as his essay "Lord Dunsany and His Work" (1922) shows, he felt that such a stance was necessitated by the radical discoveries of modern science, which have

> ...proved an enemy to art and pleasure; for by revealing to us the whole sordid and prosaic basis of our thoughts, motives, and acts, it has stripped the world of glamour, wonder, and all those illusions of heroism, nobility, and sacrifice which used to sound so impressive when romantically treated.

What is the solution?

> It is then that we shall worship afresh the music and colour of divine language, and take an Epicurean delight in those combinations of ideas and fancies which we know to be artificial. Not that we can resume a serious attitude toward emotion—there is too much intellect abroad for that—but we can revel in the Dresden-china Arcadia of an author who will play with the old ideas, atmospheres, types, situations, and lighting effects in a deft pictorial way; a way tinged with affectionate reminiscence as for fallen gods, yet never departing from a cosmic and gently satirical realisation of the true microscopic insignificance of the man-puppets and their petty relations to one another.[64]

Lovecraft eventually came to repudiate, or at least significantly to modify, this view; and he did so largely because of certain events that occurred in his life. His New York period began with a heady cosmopolitanism that saw Lovecraft acting the part of the carefree sophisticate; but as the atmosphere of New York began steadily to wear away at him, Lovecraft came to realize that his New England heritage meant much more to him than he had believed. After he returned to Providence he saw that extreme classicism and extreme Decadence were both false trails:

> I can look back...at two distinct periods of opinion whose foundations I have successively come to distrust—a period before 1919 or so, when the weight of classic authority unduly influenced me, and another period from 1919 to about 1925, when I placed too high a value on the elements of revolt, florid colour, and emotional extravagance or intensity.[65]

The result was a renewed belief in the importance of tradition and heritage in art:

> I think an author strongly reflects his surroundings, and that he does best in founding his elements of incident and colour on a life and background to which he has a real and deep-seated relation. This may or may not be his native and childhood environment, but I think it is generally better so....[66]

Is it any wonder that the works he wrote upon his return to Providence from New York emphatically reflect this shift?—*The Dream-Quest of Unknown Kadath*, where Randolph Carter realizes that his "sunset city" is only "the sum of what [he] has seen and loved in youth"; *The Case of Charles Dexter Ward*, a paean to the historical richness of Providence; and the tales of his later period, each exploring with increased depth and subtlety the wonders and the terrors of his native New England. Clearly, Lovecraft had come home in more than a physical sense.

Nevertheless, Lovecraft's mature aesthetic thought amalgamates certain features from classicism and Decadence into a very sound and compelling view of the function of art and the artist. The basis is *pleasure*—the Epicurean ideal of rational intellectual pleasure and tranquillity; this means not that art is to provide a mere titillation of the senses, but is instead to fulfill a profound psychological need:

> False or insincere amusement is the sort of activity which does not meet the real psychological demands of the human glandular-nervous system, but merely affects to do so. Real amusement is the sort which is based on a knowledge of real needs, and which therefore hits the spot. *This latter kind of amusement is what art is*—and there is nothing more important in the universe.[67]

Despite the abstractness of the above, the sense is that only aesthetically sincere art can satisfy these "real psychological demands." This puts a great burden upon the creative artist, for his goal must not be the pandering of the herd with cheap, formula-ridden hackwork but instead must be *self-expression* in the profoundest sense. The artist must strive to capture those fleeting images of beauty or terror which clamor within him demanding an outlet. And because of Lovecraft's acceptance of Poe's truth/beauty distinction ("Poetry and art for *beauty*—but science and philosophy for truth,"[68] he dispensed with the didactic motive in art. This is not to say that art is to be philosophically vacuous: a profound artist cannot help but reflect his own vision of reality in one form or another, and we shall see that some of Lovecraft's tales are openly or primarily philosophical or moral in nature, while all his work directly or indirectly conveys the tenets of his own philosophy. The primacy of self-expression in art caused Lovecraft to repudiate the attempt to write for money; writing for money was for Lovecraft a paradox, or rather it was a *business* not associated with art at all: "It's a legitimate business, which somebody has got to do."[69] Indeed, it makes no difference whether a work of literature is even published after it is written, for its fundamental goal—"the mental and emotional satisfaction of self-expression"[70]—has already been achieved. "There are probably seven persons, in all, who really like my work; and they are enough," Lovecraft wrote in 1921. "I should write even if I were the only patient reader, for my aim is merely self-expression."[71]

This belief—instilled in him by his genteel upbringing, bolstered by his years in amateur journalism, and intellectualized as part of his general aesthetic theory—accounts for Lovecraft's "uncommercial" attitude toward his own work, an attitude that made him reluctant to submit his work to *Weird Tales* at all upon its founding, made him stick to *Weird Tales* as a market (in spite of half-hearted attempts to cultivate other pulp magazines) despite frequent rejections of his best work, made him feel (perhaps rightly) that *Weird Tales* had insidiously corrupted his style by causing his work to become too explicit and obvious, and made him unwilling to prepare either *The Dream-Quest of Unknown Kadath* or *The Case of Charles Dexter Ward* for book publication (and this despite several publishers' requests for novel-length work from his pen) because he was not convinced as to their merits. This attitude is the more remarkable and admirable since Lovecraft failed to compromise his high standards in the face of his abject poverty. That we, his readers, are vastly the beneficiaries of this aesthetic integrity is now abundantly clear not merely by the high accord granted to his work worldwide, but by the corresponding neglect and vacuity of the work of his colleagues who felt no such qualms about catering to the mob. Many critics have been exasperated at these attitudes of Lovecraft's, and would like to have seen him enjoy some of the success which his work, in its "posthumous triumph" (as L. Sprague de Camp aptly termed it), has enjoyed; but Lovecraft was willing to make personal sacrifices for the sake of his art, since it was not material profit but aesthetic sincerity that mattered most to him.

Lovecraft's aesthetic of weird fiction seems to have developed a few years after the resumption of his fiction-writing in 1917, and it is cogently addressed in the *In Defence of Dagon* essays of 1921, which anticipate the introduction to "Supernatural Horror in Literature" in presenting a noble defense of weird fiction as a viable form of expression. What Lovecraft has to face is the fact that weird fiction is such a cultivated taste: large numbers of people clearly have no fondness for it, and many even see it as "unhealthy" or unpleasant. Lovecraft makes all this a virtue: by dividing literature into three branches, romantic (an appeal to the emotions), realistic (an appeal to the intellect), and imaginative (a combination of both), he makes the clever rhetorical ploy that imaginative literature is a union of the best features of both the other types without their drawbacks. "Phantasy exists to fulfil the demands of the imagination; but since imagination is so much less widely diffused than are emotion and analytical reason, it follows that such a literary type must be relatively rare, and decidedly restricted in its appeal."[72] In "Supernatural Horror in Literature," he notes:

> The appeal of the spectrally macabre is generally narrow because it demands from the reader a certain degree of imagination and a capacity for detachment from every-day life. Relatively few are free enough from the spell of the daily routine to respond to rappings from outside, and tales of ordinary feelings and events, or of common sentimental distortions of such feelings and events, will always take first place in the taste of the majority; rightly, perhaps, since of course these ordinary matters make up the greater part of human experience. But the sensitive are always with us....[73]

In this way Lovecraft slyly implies that readers of imaginative literature are aesthetically superior to readers of realism or romanticism—they are more "sensitive" and imaginative. Accordingly, weird fiction is "a narrow though essential branch of human expression."[74]

Having defended the aesthetic worth of weird fiction, Lovecraft can proceed to define its precise nature. The most concise, if somewhat flamboyantly expressed, definition occurs in "Supernatural Horror in Literature":

> The true weird tale has something more than secret murder, bloody bones, or a sheeted form clanking chains according to rule. A certain atmosphere of breathless and unexplainable dread of outer, unknown forces must be present; and there must be a hint, expressed with a seriousness and portentousness becoming its subject, of that most terrible conception of the human brain—a malign and particular suspension or defeat of those fixed laws of Nature which are our only safeguard against the assaults of chaos and the daemons of unplumbed space.[75]

This is an intensely interesting statement, for many reasons. First, let us notice that it is explicitly metaphysical: weird fiction must present that very defiance of the "fixed laws of Nature" which Lovecraft, in his materialist philosophy, asserted so vigorously. Does this mean that Lovecraft was attempting to escape the implications of his materialism by way of weird fiction? Quite the reverse. Note the exact phrasing of his statement in "Notes on Writing Weird Fiction":

> I choose weird stories because they suit my inclinations best—one of my strongest and most persistent wishes being to achieve, momentarily, the *illusion* [my italics] of some strange suspension or violation of the galling limitations of time, space, and natural law which for ever imprison us and frustrate our curiosity about the infinite cosmic spaces beyond the radius of our sight and analysis.[76]

Lovecraft knows that the violation of natural law is only an illusion; in reality, natural law cannot be defied, but the human mind requires an imaginative outlet from these "galling limitations" with an *aesthetic* belief that such a defiance might be possible. This conception is clarified in a letter:

> If we can give ourselves even for rather a brief moment the illusory sense that some law of the ruthless cosmos has been—or could be—invalidated or defeated, we acquire a certain flush of triumphant emancipation comparable in its comforting power to the opiate dreams of religion. Indeed, religion itself is merely a pompous formalisation of fantastic art. Its disadvantage is that it demands an *intellectual* belief in the impossible, whereas fantastic art does not.[77]

The comparison with religion is telling: if Lovecraft actually attempted to believe in the literal reality of Cthulhu (as religious people believe in God), then he would simply feel foolish, since he knew that such an entity could not exist; rather, Cthulhu is a symbol for all those unknown aspects of the cosmos that may someday suddenly make themselves apparent to human beings.

Lovecraft's definition of weird fiction clearly rules out the possibility that non-supernatural horror—what is nowadays called "psychological suspense"—could ever be a component of the field. He makes a clear distinction between the weird tale and the "literature of mere physical fear and the mundanely gruesome."[78] Later remarks of his, however, represent not merely an equivocation on this point but in some ways a radical shift in his whole conception of the weird. As a starting-point we can begin with Lovecraft's dispute with August Derleth regarding the precise status of William Faulkner's superb tale of madness and necrophilia, "A Rose for Emily" (included in Dashiell Hammett's *Creeps by Night* [1931] along with a tale by Lovecraft):

> Manifestly, this is a dark and horrible thing which *could* happen, whereas the crux of a *weird* tale is something which *could not possibly happen.* If any unexpected advance of physics, chemistry, or biology were to indicate the *possibility* of any phenomena related by the weird tale, that particular set of phenomena would cease to be *weird* in the ultimate sense because it would become surrounded by a different set of emotions. It would no longer represent imaginative liberation, because it would no longer indicate a suspension or violation of the natural laws against whose universal dominance our fancies rebel.[79]

This is still in accordance with Lovecraft's banning of psychological suspense as a branch of the weird tale; but the sentence "If any unexpected advance..." leaves open the possibility that scientific progress might render some weird tales non-weird at some future date, when more natural laws are discovered than are currently known to human beings. Lovecraft is in effect heading in the direction of linking the weird to science, and hence to science fiction. A statement made slightly earlier than the above confirms the connection:

> The time has come when the normal revolt against time, space, and matter must assume a form not overtly incompatible with what is known of reality—when it must be gratified by images forming *supplements* rather than *contradictions* of the visible and mensurable universe. And what, if not a form of *non-supernatural cosmic art*, is to pacify this sense of revolt—as well as gratify the cognate sense of curiosity?[80]

This is a canonical utterance on Lovecraft's part, and it is really the key to the understanding of his entire later work. It is no accident that such tales as "The Colour out of Space," *At the Mountains of Madness*, and "The Shadow out of Time" were published in science fiction magazines; for they exactly present those "supplements rather than contradictions" that Lovecraft now felt was aesthetically necessary. A simple defiance of commonly held natural laws—especially by the use of stereotypical weird conventions such as the ghost, vampire, or werewolf—was now no longer credible: we know too much about the universe to credit such beings, even aesthetically, for a moment. Weird fiction must be "non-supernatural"—not in the manner of psychological suspense, but "cosmic" in the manner of science fiction. There must, however, still be an imaginative liberation involved, one that will come from those "supplements" to present-day science. These radical ideas are what help to make Lovecraft's later work so distinctive, and so important in the subsequent history of both weird fiction and science fiction. Throughout all these developments, cosmicism—as a philosophical conception (an awareness of the vastness of the universe), an ethical conception (a realization of the insignificance of the human race), and an aesthetic conception (the suggestion, through literature and art, of the boundless universe of unknown elements, entities, and phenomena)—remain constant, and show how Lovecraft's metaphysics, ethics, and aesthetics are all tightly knit into one unified philosophical outlook. The subsequent chapters of this book seek to demonstrate how his fiction is a systematic exposition of the basic components of that outlook.

II.

EARLY FICTION (1905-1921)

It is a pity that we do not have any of Lovecraft's fiction between "The Mysterious Ship" (1902) and "The Beast in the Cave" (1905); for the difference between the earlier tale—an entirely mediocre work even for a twelve-year-old—and the later one is little short of staggering. We know of several works Lovecraft was writing at this time—including a quasi-science-fiction tale, inspired by Jules Verne, about the dark side of the moon[1]—but none survive. We are left only to marvel at the remarkable sureness of touch revealed by a story Lovecraft wrote well before his fifteenth birthday, a tale which he himself later noted was the outcome of "some experimenting in fictional structure," so that he "achieved a new level of results."[2]

The first draft of "The Beast in the Cave" had, in fact, been written before he had left 454 Angell Street in the summer of 1904,[3] but the final draft was completed only in April 1905. Involving a man, lost in Mammoth Cave in Kentucky, who comes upon what appears to be an anomalous creature and, killing it, discovers it to be a man, it is a well-told, suspenseful story in spite of its stiff language. The mere fact that it is set in the present day (the back of the manuscript of the story announces it to be the first story in a proposed volume, *Tales of Terror*, in the subdivision: "Period—Modern") is notable for someone who still seemed (aside from his scientific interests) lost in the eighteenth century.

The tale broaches at least one significant theme that would dominate Lovecraft's later fiction—the possibility of reversal on the evolutionary scale. The "beast" of the story is nothing more than a man who, from years of solitude and lightlessness, has shed most of the tokens of his humanity, especially speech: he can no longer utter words but merely a "deep-toned chattering."[4] Indeed, when the narrator finally sees the entity for the first time, he takes it to be "an anthropoid ape of large proportions,"[5] clearly tying the story to the Darwin theory of evolution.

It should also be pointed out that "The Beast in the Cave" is non-supernatural; in fact, not a single one of Lovecraft's existing juvenile tales is supernatural. Like dime novels, many of these early stories suggest the supernatural but ultimately explain all events by natural, if at times implausible, means. Among Lovecraft's mature tales, however, there is not a single genuinely non-supernatural work (in the sense of a work based solely upon known natural laws), and his entire theory of weird fiction—which stresses the depiction of events "which could not possibly happen"—is founded upon the need for a supernatural or, at any rate, a supernormal scenario.

"The Alchemist" (1908) is also impressive, but in an entirely different way from "The Beast in the Cave." Here again we are in the modern period—no later than the nineteenth century—but the tale creates a very convincing atmosphere of medieval primitivism. This story may be Lovecraft's first genuinely supernatural tale, although even here the supernatural is manifested in a somewhat unexpected manner. The curse of the evil Charles le Sorcier for the death of his father, Michel Mauvais, follows the Comtes de C— down six centuries, and seems therefore to be a supernatural phenomenon; but it turns out that the deaths of the Comtes are mere murders. Supernaturalism, however, enters from a different direction when it is learned that the murderer is Charles le Sorcier himself, who has prolonged his life beyond normal bounds through sorcery. This tale bears the clear influence of the Gothic novels of the late eighteenth century, many of which Lovecraft had probably read by this time, if only in extracts.

These two tales are all that survive from Lovecraft's destruction of his fiction of 1903-1908. Not only is this a great tragedy—we again hear of several tantalizing tales which we would like to have, including "Gone—but Whither?," "The Picture," and an historical story about Rome—but it is still more tragic and inexplicable that Lovecraft abandoned fiction writing for nine years. Even when he resumed literary activity around 1911 and then entered amateur journalism in 1914, he remained convinced that his fiction was still worse than his poetry or essays, so that he devoted the bulk of his attention to these latter two bodies of work until at least 1920.

Aside from the encouragement of W. Paul Cook and others in 1917, Lovecraft seems to have given serious consideration to the resumption of fiction himself. Two books in his library—*Facts, Thought, and Imagination: A Book on Writing* by Henry Seidel Canby, Frederick Erastus Pierce, and W. H. Durham (1917), and *Writing the Short-Story* by J. Berg Esenwein (1909; rev. 1917)—were apparently obtained in 1917, and suggest that Lovecraft felt the need to ponder what contemporary authorities had to say on the art and craft of fiction. There is nothing in these books that can clearly be said to have influenced Lovecraft, but his mere acquisition of them at this time is indicative of a change—albeit still tentative—in the direction of his creative work.

As it is, the predominant influence on his early fiction—and, really, his entire fictional career—is Edgar Allan Poe. This is an unremarkable statement, and even unhelpful unless one specifies quite carefully what it was that Lovecraft saw in Poe's theory and practice of fiction-writing. It is clear that Lovecraft at the very outset accepted Poe's analysis of the function and import of the short story (as spelled out in such documents as the preface to *Tales of the Grotesque and Arabesque* [1840] and his review of Hawthorne's *Twice-Told Tales* [1842]); he himself summarizes them aptly in "Supernatural Horror in Literature": "...such things as the maintenance of a single mood and achievement of a single impression in a tale, and the rigorous paring down of incidents to such as have a direct bearing on the plot and will figure prominently in the climax."[6] All Lovecraft's stories—even his three short novels—adhere to this principle.

But Lovecraft found in Poe much more than a theoretical model; his actual tales—their style, texture, mood, and rhetorical effects—became deeply imbued in Lovecraft's mind and inevitably colored his work from the beginning. Indeed, in a sense it could be said that Lovecraft spent the rest of his life unconsciously striving to *escape* from the Poe influence. As late as 1930 Lovecraft was writing:

> Since Poe affected me most of all horror-writers, I can never feel that a tale starts out right unless it has something of his manner. I could never plunge into a thing abruptly, as the popular writers do. To my mind it is necessary to establish a setting & avenue of approach before the main show can adequately begin.[7]

This refers to Poe's penchant for introducing stories with several paragraphs of generalized commentary on the events to follow, so that the effect is almost like that of an essay; "The Premature Burial," in which this commentary occupies nearly the entire story, is the most extreme example of this device. Other features of Poe's work that are immediately recognizable in Lovecraft's are the dense, perhaps somewhat histrionic style, laced with archaic and recondite terms; an almost entire absence of "realistic" character portrayal, in place of which we find either characters in an aberrant mental state or colorless individuals whose only function is to serve as a conduit for the reader's perception of the weird; and the near-total absence of dialogue. This last feature is of some importance, for it is this—along with the compactly expository manner of narration—that produces that concise, intense atmosphere so readily detectable in Lovecraft's works, early and late, and facilitates the sense that every word has a clear and direct bearing on the outcome of the story.

"The Tomb" (1917),[8] the first tale Lovecraft wrote upon his resumption of fiction-writing, is not merely a textbook example of the Poe influence—more so, perhaps, than even the celebrated "The Outsider"—but is a surprisingly competent work of its own. Jervas Dudley, who "from earliest childhood" has been "a dreamer and a visionary," finds a tomb in a wooded hollow near his home, a tomb that houses the remains of a family, the Hydes, that had dwelt in a mansion nearby. This mansion had been struck by lightning and burned to the ground, although only one member of the family had perished in the flames. The tomb exercises an unholy fascination upon Dudley, and he haunts it for hours at a time. It is locked, but the door is "fastened *ajar* in a queerly sinister way by means of heavy iron chains and padlocks." He ultimately finds the key to the tomb and spends hours in it. Gradually he begins exhibiting various odd traits, in particular a knowledge of very ancient things that he could not possibly have learnt from books. Hitherto a recluse, he now shows signs of "ribald revelry," spouting a drinking song "never recorded in a book."

Dudley's parents, concerned about his increasingly odd behavior, now hire a "spy" to follow him. On one occasion Dudley thinks that this spy has seen him coming out of the tomb, but the spy tells his parents that Dudley had spent the night on the bower outside the tomb. Now convinced that he is under some sort of supernatural protection, Dudley frequents the tomb without fear or circumspection. One night, as thunder is in the air, he goes to the tomb and sees the mansion as it was in its heyday. A party is underway, and guests in powdered wigs are brought in by carriage. But a peal of thunder interrupts the "swinish revelry" and a fire breaks out. Dudley flees, but finds himself being restrained by two men. They maintain that he had spent the entire night outside the tomb, and point to the rusted and unopened lock as evidence. Dudley is put away in a madhouse. A servant goes to the tomb, breaks it open, and finds a porcelain miniature with the initials "J. H."; the picture could be of Dudley's twin. "On a slab in an alcove he found an old but empty coffin whose tarnished plate bears the single word '*Jervas*.' In that coffin and in that vault they have promised me I shall be buried."

The plot of "The Tomb" requires such detailed exposition because the story is for various reasons quite anomalous in Lovecraft's work. In the first place, there is genuine ambiguity as to whether the events are supernatural or psychological: is Jervas Dudley possessed by the spirit of his ancestor and lookalike, Jervas Hyde, or has he imagined the entire thing? Although Lovecraft remarked of both "The Tomb" and "Dagon" that they "are analyses of strange monomania, involving hallucinations of the most hideous sort,"[9] I think the supernatural explanation must ultimately prevail: Dudley's knowledge of the past is too detailed and otherwise inexplicable. The "hallucinations" to which Lovecraft refers probably involve Dudley's seeming participation in the events in the eighteenth century while possessed by his ancestor, especially the final scene involving the conflagration of the Hyde mansion; even here, however, "hallucinations" is not exactly the proper word, since the suggestion is that this is how the mansion actually burned down, and Dudley is witnessing it through the eyes of Hyde himself. The one remaining puzzle is the matter of the lock on the tomb, which really does seem to have remained unbroken. One can only assume that Dudley's body did in fact spend those nights on the bower but that his spirit entered the tomb.

The Poe influence enters in the unusual amount of psychological analysis devoted to the central character, who—as Lovecraft wrote of Poe's own protagonists—is "a dark, handsome, proud, melancholy, intellectual, highly sensitive, capricious, introspective, isolated, and sometimes slightly mad gentleman of ancient family and opulent circumstances."[10] Here, however, such psychological analysis—really self-analysis, since it is Dudley who tells the whole story in the first person—is necessary for the logic of the tale, since it is by the anomalous departures from his normal state of mind that we can gauge the insidious incursion of the soul of Jervas Hyde. This psychic possession, of course, is a telling sign of the Poe influence, and William Fulwiler is probably correct in thinking that Lovecraft had "Ligeia" in mind when writing this story. Fulwiler goes on to suggest plausibly that the use of the name Hyde is a tip of the hat to another celebrated tale of a *Doppelgänger*, Stevenson's *Dr. Jekyll and Mr. Hyde.*[11]

A few words may be said about the drinking song in "The Tomb." This poetical insertion may also have been derived from Poe, who included two of his finest poems ("The Conqueror Worm" and "The Haunted Palace") in two of his finest stories ("Ligeia" and "The Fall of the House of Usher"). Lovecraft's poem is not quite as vital to the logic of the tale as Poe's are, and in fact its inclusion could be regarded as something of an indulgence. It appears to have been written a few years before the story, as an attempt to outdo another unidentified writer's attempt at an eighteenth-century drinking song, and it bears the title "Gaudeamus" ("Let us delight"). No doubt Lovecraft was waiting for some suitable opportunity to use the piece; indeed, it is possible that it had some influence on the specific development of the tale.

"Dagon" (1917),[12] written probably less than a month after "The Tomb," is a very different sort of story; it too, however, is a commendable piece of work. A supercargo on a vessel during the Great War, the unnamed narrator is captured by a German sea-raider but escapes in a boat. One night he falls asleep, and awakes to find that an enormous subterranean land mass has been upheaved to the surface during the night. Walking along it after it dries, he comes upon "an immeasurable pit or canyon." Climbing down the side of the canyon, he notices an enormous object in the distance: it is a gigantic monolith "whose massive bulk had known the workmanship and perhaps the worship of living and thinking creatures." It bears a number of curious and repellent hieroglyphs and bas-reliefs, many of which depict bizarre aquatic creatures not known to science. But now a living creature emerges from the sea: "Vast, Polyphemus-like, and loathsome, it darted like a stupendous monster of nightmares to the monolith, about which it flung its gigantic scaly arms, the while it bowed its hideous head and gave vent to certain measured sounds." The narrator, his sanity shattered, flees, eventually finding himself in a San Francisco hospital. He intends to commit suicide after finishing his account.

The narrator of "Dagon" is not nearly as interesting as Jervas Dudley of "The Tomb," but this is by design; for the horror in this tale is purely external, and the narrator's function is merely to serve as the reader's eyes, ears, and mind in perceiving the events and their implications. Indeed, it is not the events themselves—hideous as they are—but these implications that are the most significant aspect of the story:

> I cannot think of the deep sea without shuddering at the nameless things that may at this very moment be crawling and floundering on its slimy bed, worshipping their ancient stone idols and carving their own detestable likenesses on submarine obelisks of water-soaked granite. I dream of a day when they may rise above the billows to drag down in their reeking talons the remnants of puny, war-exhausted mankind—of a day when the land shall sink, and the dark ocean floor shall ascend amidst universal pandemonium.

This passage is of consuming interest. Firstly, it has a poignancy no less than that of some portions of "The Tomb," but here the poignancy is derived not from the fate of a single individual but from the fate of all humanity. Secondly, the reflections on the political effects of the war, then at its height, is striking: the story was written only a few months after America's declaration of war against Germany in April 1917, and after Lovecraft's bootless attempt to enlist in May; and the mention of "puny, war-exhausted mankind" shows an awareness of the cultural and psychological devastation that the war is bringing in its wake. "The Tomb," although set in the modern age and in New England, has a much more antiquated feel and a more nebulous locale than "Dagon"; the initial pages of the latter tale establish the war context ably, and the clinically scientific descriptions of the newly risen land mass result in a tangible realism that would later become the hallmark of Lovecraft's work. Moreover, "Dagon" is the first tale of Lovecraft's early period to enunciate his "cosmic" perspective.

As we examine other stories of the 1917-1919 period—the little-known "A Reminiscence of Dr. Samuel Johnson" (1917); the dream-fantasy "Polaris" (1918); the lost "dime novel," "The Mystery of Murdon Grange" (1918); the slight collaborative tale "The Green Meadow" (1918 or 1919), written with Winifred Jackson; "Beyond the Wall of Sleep" (1919); the prose-poem "Memory" (1919); "The Transition of Juan Romero" (1919); "The White Ship" (1919); "The Doom That

Came to Sarnath" (1919); and "The Statement of Randolph Carter" (1919)—it becomes evident that Lovecraft was experimenting with a wide variety of styles and moods to see what best suited him. "A Reminiscence of Dr. Samuel Johnson" is, of course, not a weird tale at all, except in its tongue-in-cheek premise: the narrator, Humphry Littlewit, reveals that he was not born, as many believe, on August 20, 1890, but on August 20, 1690, and is now 228 years old. This delightful piece, perhaps the best comic story Lovecraft ever wrote, ably captures the flavor of the eighteenth century, and Lovecraft's thorough reading of Boswell's *Life of Johnson* and the works of Johnson himself is much in evidence. We know nothing about the actual content of "The Mystery of Murdon Grange" save that it was a dime novel of sorts—or perhaps a parody of the dime novel. It was included in Lovecraft's magazine *Hesperia*, a typewritten journal circulated in England and now lost. It is a work we would very much like to have. "Polaris," "The White Ship," "The Doom That Came to Sarnath," and "The Terrible Old Man" are better studied in the next chapter, dealing with the tales written under the influence of Lord Dunsany, even though "Polaris" was written more than a year before Lovecraft's first reading of Dunsany.

"Beyond the Wall of Sleep"[13] is an interesting tale, although not so much intrinsically as for its anticipation of several important themes in Lovecraft's later work. The story itself is quite mediocre. Joe Slater, a denizen of the Catskill Mountains, has all his life been afflicted with strange visions and sensations that cannot be passed off as simple dreams. One day in the year 1900 he viciously murders another man, but maintains that he was forced to do so to exact some nameless vengeance. An intern working at the mental institution where Slater is placed establishes a mental link with him through a "cosmic 'radio'" that he has devised, and he learns that Slater's mind has been occupied by an extraterrestrial entity which for some reason has a burning desire for revenge against the star Algol (the Daemon-Star). With the impending death of Slater, the entity will now be free to exact the vengeance it has always desired. On 22 February 1901 come reports of a celebrated nova near Algol, and we are left to infer that this event represents the fulfillment of the extraterrestrial entity's quest.

This is, clearly, Lovecraft's first science-fiction (or, since the genre was by no means well established at this time, proto-science-fiction) tale, but it is beset with difficulties of conception and treatment. No plausible account is given as to *why* the extraterrestrial entity finds itself trapped in Slater's body to begin with, and Lovecraft strangely seems not to feel that such an account is even necessary. One also wonders how he came to choose the locale of this tale, since he had not at this time visited the Catskills and would in fact never do so even in his later far-flung travels. It is possible that the locale was suggested to him by an amateur colleague, Jonathan E. Hoag, who lived not far from the region; but Lovecraft's real motivation was to provide the maximum contrast between a crude, ignorant, uncouth backwoods denizen and the cosmic being in his body. Lovecraft paints a harsh picture of the area and its inhabitants:

> [Slater's] appearance was one of the typical denizen of the Catskill Mountain region; one of those strange, repellent scions of a primitive colonial peasant stock whose isolation for nearly three centuries in the hilly fastnesses of a little-travelled countryside has caused them to sink to a kind of barbaric degeneracy, rather than advance with their more fortunately placed brethren of the thickly settled districts. Among these odd folk, who correspond exactly to the decadent element of "white trash" in the South, law and morals are non-existent; and their general mental state is probably below that of any other section of the native American people.

Lovecraft returns to this setting, for much the same reasons, in "The Lurking Fear" (1922).

"Beyond the Wall of Sleep," hampered as it is by clumsy and stilted language, vicious class-consciousness, and a failure to think through the ramifications of the plot, is nevertheless worthy on several counts. It, even more than "Dagon," is Lovecraft's first authentically cosmic story; for here we are concerned not merely with the world but with the universe. The nova Lovecraft chose as the focal point of the tale—and which was very likely the root inspiration for the story itself—was indeed a noteworthy incident (there have been only three significant novas since the eleventh century), even though it occurred just prior to his discovery of astronomy. Lovecraft ends the tale with a quotation taken directly from Garrett P. Serviss's *Astronomy with the Naked Eye* (1908).

The dream motif connects the tale to both "The Tomb" and "Polaris"; for what we have here again are not dreams as such but visions of some other realm of entity. Hence the narrator's rumination at the outset: "I have frquently wondered if the majority of mankind ever pause to reflect upon the occasionally titanic significance of dreams, and of the obscure world to which they belong." When the narrator concludes that "Sometimes I believe this less material life is our truer life, and that our vain presence on the terraqueous globe is itself the secondary or merely virtual phenomenon," one should not see this as a renunciation of Lovecraft's materialism but rather a confirmation of it from another direction: the "less material life" revealed by Slater's "dreams" is not less "real" than his diurnal existence on the earth;

rather, it is more "real" because it provides a tantalizing glimpse into cosmic realms normally withheld from human beings.

Lovecraft continues his experimentation in both subject-matter and setting with "The Transition of Juan Romero,"[14] a tale written in the autumn of 1919 but which he did not consider good enough for publication; it appeared only posthumously. It is, indeed, not an entire success. This account of some strange incident occurring in 1894 at the Norton Mine (somewhere in the Southwest, one imagines, although Lovecraft's narrator is not specific as to the exact location) is marred by indefiniteness of conception. Juan Romero, like Joe Slater, seems no more than an ignorant Mexican peasant, but the narrator thinks he may be descended from the Aztecs. One night Romero, as he pursues some "throb down in the ground" coming from a deep abyss near the mine, seems to be swallowed up by something in the abyss. The narrator peers over the edge of the abyss but coyly declares, *"but God! I dare not tell you what I saw!"* The next day the narrator and Romero are found in their bunks, with Romero having died in the night.

One wonders whether Lovecraft himself had any clear idea of what was down in the abyss, or what was causing that throbbing. In a late letter Lovecraft advised Duane W. Rimel on a critical point in story-conception: "A sort of general clarification *in your own mind* (not necessarily to be revealed in toto to the reader) of what is supposed to happen, & why each thing happens as it does, would produce a certain added convincingness worth securing."[15] In "The Transition of Juan Romero" Lovecraft himself has apparently failed to follow this recommendation.

A tale that is perhaps more interesting in its genesis than in its substance is "The Statement of Randolph Carter" (1919).[16] It is well known that this is an almost verbatim transcript of a dream experienced by Lovecraft in December 1919, with Samuel Loveman as Harley Warren and himself as Randolph Carter. It has frequently been ignored that this tale too is an experiment in a novel setting; for we are here apparently in Florida, as mentions of the "Gainesville pike" and the "Big Cypress Swamp" suggest. Warren himself is in other tales referred to as coming from South Carolina.[17] In any event, Warren leads Carter to an ancient cemetery, where they remove a slab that reveals a flight of stone steps leading downward into the earth. Warren forces Carter, because of his frail nerves, to remain on the surface; but he has conveniently brought along a sort of telephone set with a long cord so that the two can stay in touch. Warren descends into the crypt, and very quickly comes upon both wonders (*"God! If you could see what I am seeing!"*) and horrors (*"Carter, it's terrible—monstrous—unbelievable!"*). Like the narrator of "The Transition of Juan Romero," Warren coyly refuses to say what he has actually encountered, but in this case the ambiguity somehow succeeds. The ending is perhaps predictable, but still affecting. Carter is told by Warren to "beat it" and escape the horrors he has discovered, but as he is wavering on the surface wondering whether or not to descend, another voice—"deep; hollow; gelatinous; remote; unearthly; inhuman; disembodied"—utters through the telephone: *"YOU FOOL, WARREN IS DEAD!"*

We have three separate phenomena to deal with in discussing this story: the dream itself; the initial transcript of the dream (as recorded in a letter of December 1919); and the story. It should not be assumed naively that the three are in any sense identical, and interesting points of variance can be detected between the transcript and the story. Nevertheless, if we can accept Lovecraft's testimony on the matter (and there is no compelling reason to doubt it), this dream was remarkable for its coherence and cumulative power. Of course, the creature who makes that final utterance is very ill-defined, and Lovecraft was merely attempting to reproduce the sensation he experienced in the dream. Later he would learn to incorporate dreams and dream-phenomena more subtly into his work.

"The Temple" (1920)[18] picks up the theme of "Dagon" in using the Great War as a backdrop. A German submarine commander finds that his crew is strangely affected after an odd piece of ivory carving is taken on board following the destruction of a British freighter. Eventually the submarine becomes disabled from the crazed actions of the crew, most of whom die or are executed; the commander is left alone, drifting to the bottom of the ocean and finding there the remains of a vast underwater city with an enormous temple hollowed out of the solid rock. "Confronted at last with the Atlantis I had formerly deemed largely a myth," the commander leaves his craft to explore the temple, from which a strange phosphorescent glowing is visible, even though he knows he is going to his death.

This is Lovecraft's longest early story, but it barely escapes mediocrity. The incredibly clumsy and obvious satire on the German commander (who refers frequently to the "English pig-dogs," "my own German will," and the like) is a serious drawback, but gradually the scenario develops its own interest and we gain sympathy for the German—or, at least, a shared fascination with him in regard to the mystery he is facing. It is not entirely clear whether we are literally to consider the underwater realm to be Atlantis; but one of the most suggestive statements made in the story relates to the sculptures seen on the buildings of the city: "The art is of the most phenomenal perfection, largely Hellenic in idea, yet strangely individual. It imparts an impression of terrible antiquity, as though it were the remotest rather than the immediate ancestor of Greek art." There are two important implications here: first, that the race that built the underwater city was a true *civilization* as highly evolved intellectually and aesthetically as our own, and perhaps even more so; and second, that this civilization may have been the ultimate originator of all human culture on the surface. These implications are not developed in "The Temple," but they will be elaborated upon at length in some of Lovecraft's later tales.

"Facts concerning the Late Arthur Jermyn and His Family" (1920)[19] indirectly picks up on this theme, while at the same time continuing the exploration of exotic realms that we have seen as a dominant trait in Lovecraft's early short stories. The tale is set in England, but the true focus is the Congo, where in the eighteenth century Sir Wade Jermyn conducted some highly peculiar explorations and wrote a book that "earn[ed] him much ridicule," *Observations on the Several Parts of Africa*. Ever since Sir Wade brought home a mysterious wife from Africa (who later returned there on a subsequent expedition), the Jermyn line has displayed marked mental and physical abnormalities, culminating in the middle of the nineteenth century with Sir Robert Jermyn, who killed his entire family except a two-year-old grandson when he learned something from a fellow explorer to the Congo. Arthur Jermyn, although physically repulsive, seeks to restore the family's reputation by continuing Sir Wade's explorations; but when a nameless "object" is brought back by a Belgian explorer to Jermyn House, Arthur Jermyn goes out to the moor and calmly sets himself aflame. The "object" is nothing less than a female white ape which bears around its neck a locket with the Jermyn coat of arms. She is Sir Wade's lost wife.

"Arthur Jermyn" is nothing less than a sort of horrific *Origin of Species*: it seeks to make very real and very horrible the Darwinian notion that most of us have come to accept with a certain equanimity: that we are descended from apes. But I believe the implications of this story are far broader than merely a loathsome ancestral taint upon a single family; consider the celebrated and resounding opening statement:

> Life is a hideous thing, and from the background behind what we know of it peer daemoniacal hints of truth which make it sometimes a thousandfold more hideous. Science, already oppressive with its shocking revelations, will perhaps be the ultimate exterminator of our human species—if separate species we be—for its reserve of unguessed horrors could never be borne by mortal brains if loosed upon the world. If we knew what we are, we should do as Sir Arthur Jermyn did; and Arthur Jermyn soaked himself in oil and set fire to his clothing one night.

This *generalized* statement is not compatible with a *single* case of miscegenation. The critical phrase in this passage is the clause "if separate species we be"; for the thrust of the story is to demonstrate that *all human beings* (and not just the Jermyns) are not a separate species from a certain type of ape. What Sir Wade discovered in the Congo was the remains of a "prehistoric *white* [my italics] civilisation," a civilization made up of "creatures half of the jungle and half of the impiously aged city...things that might have sprung up after the great apes had overrun the dying city." Sir Wade's wife herself proves to be "a mummified white ape of some unknown species, less hairy than any recorded variety, and infinitely nearer mankind—quite shockingly so." In other words, all (white) civilization has sprung up from this ancient Congo race of ape-humans; and although the rest of us do not have the taint quite as directly as the Jermyns do, we are nonetheless forced to confess to our ultimate descent from these creatures. The dethronement of human self-importance—the shattering of the belief that we are a wholly "separate species" that can be clearly marked off, intellectually or morally, from the rest of creation—is the fundamental point of "Arthur Jermyn." Later tales will make this point still more exhaustively, but "Arthur Jermyn" is a quiet little triumph for enunciating the idea powerfully and compactly.

A different type of degeneration is exhibited in "The Picture in the House" (1920).[20] Here a lone bicyclist riding in the "Miskatonic Valley" is forced to take shelter in a ramshackle house that appears deserted but proves to be tenanted by a huge, white-haired, but apparently harmless and ignorant backwoods denizen. The narrator had already found himself fascinated by an ancient book in the man's house, Pigafetta's *Regnum Congo*, and it appears to be the man's favorite book. He finds especial pleasure in one plate in the book, which "represented in gruesome detail a butcher's shop of the cannibal Anziques." The man waxes eloquent in his crude patois about the delight this picture gives him, to the point that it makes him "*hungry fer victuals I couldn't raise nor buy.*" Although he denies that he ever acted upon this desire, a red drop that falls from the ceiling—clearly coming from the floor above—belies his statement. At that moment the house is struck by lightning, although the narrator implausibly manages to survive and tell his tale.

There is more to this story than what Colin Wilson called "a nearly convincing sketch of sadism,"[21] although the portrayal of the hideous cannibal is indeed effective:

> "Killin' sheep was kinder more fun—but d'ye know, 'twan't quite *satisfyin'*. Queer haow a *cravin'* gits a holt on ye—...They say meat makes blood an' flesh, an' gives ye new life, so I wondered ef 'twudn't make a man live longer an' longer ef *'twas more the same*—"

That last statement is the key to the story; for what we have here is not merely a cannibal but one who has prolonged his life unnaturally by means of cannibalism. When the man mentions one Ebenezer Holt who had "'traded me thet [book] in 'sixty-eight'," the narrator ponders deeply: he knows of no such individual save someone who lived before the Revolution. In other words, the cannibal has been alive from at least the early eighteenth century to the year 1896, when the story takes place. We do not know how the Terrible Old Man (see next chapter) has extended his life beyond normal bounds, but here it is human flesh that has done the trick. In a strange sense, however, this individual cannot be deemed a case of degeneration: he has, indeed, degenerated *morally*, but in his anomalously prolonged life he becomes superhuman, as the narrator dimly realizes when he first glimpses him:

> His face, almost hidden by a long beard which grew high on the cheeks, seemed abnormally ruddy and less wrinkled than one might expect; while over a high forehead fell a shock of white hair little thinned by the years. His blue eyes, though a trifle bloodshot, seemed inexplicably keen and burning. But for his horrible unkemptness the man would have been as distinguished-looking as he was impressive.

"The Picture in the House" is otherwise notable in Lovecraft's work for its introduction of the town of Arkham, although here it is merely alluded to in passing. I shall consider the development of Lovecraft's fictional New England topography at a later stage.

Lovecraft continues to span the globe in search of horror in "The Nameless City" (1921),[22] which takes us to Arabia. Here an archaeologist seeks an accursed city of which "Abdul Alhazred the mad poet dreamed on the night before he sang his unexplainable couplet":

> That is not dead which can eternal lie,
> And with strange aeons even death may die.

And so the mad Arab is introduced to the Lovecraft canon, although he is not yet the author of the *Necronomicon*; he would be so credited only in "The Hound" (1922). But this is not the focal point of the story. The archaeologist has come upon the remains of a strange city whose "*proportions* and *dimensions*" he does not like: it does not seem to be built by or for human beings. Later he encounters a hall lined with cases containing the most bizarre creatures:

> To convey any idea of these monstrosities is impossible. They were of the reptile kind, with body lines suggesting sometimes the crocodile, sometimes the seal, but more often nothing of which either the naturalist or the palaeontologist ever heard. In size they approximated a small man, and their fore legs

> bore delicate and evidently flexible feet curiously like human hands and fingers.

The narrator convinces himself that these are mere totem-beasts conceived by the city's inhabitants, and that the bas-reliefs depicted on the walls—which feature these creatures and not human beings—are a sort of allegory of the city's history. But these comforting illusions are swept away when a vast horde of these creatures rushes by him. The implication is clear: the city was built by these loathsome beings, and is still inhabited by them.

"The Nameless City" is more significant historically than intrinsically: it is in fact a very poor story—histrionic, wildly overwritten, verbose—but it introduces themes and motifs that Lovecraft would use to much better advantage later. Once again, as in "Dagon," "The Temple," and "Arthur Jermyn," we are concerned with a non-human *civilization* that poses a threat to the dominance of humanity; but more than any physical danger, it is its mere existence that causes a *mental* perturbation because we have been shown that a wholly alien species exists that is in no sense inferior to us. The tracing of the city's history through bas-reliefs would be used much more effectively in *At the Mountains of Madness*.

"The Moon-Bog" (1921)[23] takes us to Ireland; but as this tale was written to order for an amateur gathering on St. Patrick's Day, Lovecraft does not seem to have chosen the setting of his own accord, nor has he done anything especially distinctive with it. This is one of the most conventional supernatural tales in the Lovecraft corpus. It tells the story of Denys Barry, who comes from America to reclaim his ancestral estate in Kilderry, but also wishes to drain the bog there for commercial purposes. The spirits of the bog wreak vengeance on him, wafting him away on a moonbeam. This tale too is somewhat overwritten, and its elementary moral—do not meddle with the forces of Nature—and its working out of a very naive supernatural revenge motif do not give it a high place even among Lovecraft's early tales. It is unlikely that the setting was inspired by the example of Dunsany, especially since Dunsany was not writing about Ireland at this stage of his career. Curiously, however, the basic premise of "The Moon-Bog" is indeed elaborated upon, with tremendous richness and complexity, in Dunsany's later novel, *The Curse of the Wise Woman* (1933). It is, of course, scarcely to be imagined that Lovecraft's tale inspired Dunsany, but the parallelism is intriguing.

We have hitherto seen that many of Lovecraft's early stories seek to convey elements of his developing cosmic philosophy, in particular the notion that humanity is by no means the dominant force on this planet and, by extension, in the universe. The relative absence of conventional supernaturalism already points to his later abandonment of supernaturalism as a component of his weird work, and also underscores his materialism by depicting entities and scenarios that are logically conceivable rather than actually contrary to natural law.

Other tales of this period more clearly reflect Lovecraft's metaphysical and political philosophy. "From Beyond" (1920)[24] is one such example, although it is one of his poorest stories. A mad scientist, Crawford Tillinghast, has devised a machine that will "break down the barriers" between our feeble and incomplete senses and the "real" world. Tillinghast maintains: "'We shall overleap time, space, and dimensions, and without bodily motion peer to the bottom of creation.'" As he begins conducting an experiment for his skeptical friend, the latter at one point sees a "pale, outré colour or blend of colours which I could neither place nor describe"; Tillinghast tells him it is ultra-violet, otherwise invisible to the human eye. Later, hideous shapeless creatures resembling animated jelly are seen occupying every bit of space in the room; at one point "I felt the huge animate things brushing past me and occasionally *walking or drifting through my supposedly solid body*." The narrator, alarmed at something Tillinghast says or does, fires his revolver; it hits the machine, destroying it. Tillinghast is found dead of apoplexy.

This confused and poorly written tale nevertheless suggests powerful conceptions that will, as with so many of Lovecraft's early tales, be developed more adeptly later. The fundamental notion of the story is the limitation of the senses, as enunciated by Tillinghast:

> "What do we know...of the world and the universe about us? Our means of receiving impressions are absurdly few, and our notions of surrounding objects infinitely narrow. We see things only as we are constructed to see them, and can gain no idea of their absolute nature. With five feeble senses we pretend to comprehend the boundlessly complex cosmos, yet other beings with a wider, stronger, or different range of senses might not only see very differently the things we see, but might see and study whole worlds of matter, energy, and life which lie close at hand yet can never be detected with the senses we have."

This entire conception is almost certainly derived from Hugh Elliot's *Modern Science and Materialism* (1919). Note one passage in particular:

> Let us first ask why it is that all past efforts to solve ultimate riddles have failed, and why it is that they must continue to fail. It is, in the first place, due to the fact that all knowledge is based on sense-impressions, and cannot, therefore, go beyond what the

> senses can perceive. Men have five or six senses only, and these are all founded on the one original sense of touch. Of these five or six senses, the three of most importance for the accumulation of knowledge are those of sight, hearing, and touch. By these senses we are able to detect three separate qualities of the external Universe. Now, supposing that we happened to have a thousand senses instead of five, it is clear that our conception of the Universe would be extremely different from what it now is. We cannot assume that the Universe has only five qualities because we have only five senses. We must assume, on the contrary, that the number of its qualities may be infinite, and that the more senses we had, the more we should discover about it.[25]

The mention of ultra-violet in "From Beyond" also has an exact corollary in Elliot, as does the idea that what we take to be solid matter (including our own bodies) is largely empty space.

Elliot nonetheless did not believe that the limitations of human sense-organs was a barrier to a fairly dogmatic materialism; Lovecraft came to have greater doubts on the matter, but still believed that materialism was the most *probable* theory of the universe, all things considered. The notion of breaking down the "barriers" that prevent our perception of the "true" nature of the universe was nevertheless a fascinating one, and Lovecraft made it a cornerstone of his aesthetic of the weird. When, in the passage quoted earlier from "Notes on Writing Weird Fiction," he speaks of the "galling limitations of time, space, and natural law which for ever imprison us and frustrate our curiosity about the infinite cosmic spaces beyond the radius of our sight and analysis," it is clear that those "limitations" are the limitations of the senses, since a "limitation of time" in the literal sense is meaningless. Even the notion of presenting "supplements rather than contradictions" of known phenomena is really another way of presenting (from an aesthetic or imaginative point of view) some putative expansion of our sense-apparatus so that these "supplements" can be perceived. All this is only nebulously and crudely touched upon in "From Beyond," but the nucleus is there. And, of course, the idea of some unplaceable color or blend of colors makes us immediately think of that masterpiece of the weird, "The Colour out of Space."

At this time Lovecraft also used the prose-poem as another means of conveying certain facets of his philosophy. "Memory" (1919),[26] at 300 words the shortest story Lovecraft ever wrote, does little more than convey the ephemerality and future extermination of mankind. A Genie asks a "Daemon of the Valley" who were the creatures who once inhabited a deserted and ruined valley. The Daemon, who is Memory, replies: "These beings were like the waters of the river Than, not to be understood. Their deeds I recall not, for they were but of the moment. Their aspect I recall dimly, for it was like to that of the little apes in the trees. Their name I recall clearly, for it rhymed with that of the river. These beings of yesterday were called Man."

"Ex Oblivione" (1920 or 1921)[27] is rather more significant, and sustains a very striking atmosphere of pathos. The narrator, wearied by the "ugly trifles of existence," retreats into dream. There he finds a "little gate in [a] mighty wall" from which "there would be no return," but he cannot find the latch to the gate. Then, "one night in the dream-city of Zakarion," he finds a moldy papyrus that tells of what lies beyond the gate, some sages declaring that it is a realm of wonders, others maintaining that only horror and disappointment await one there. The narrator renews his efforts to find the latch of the gate, increasing his intake of dream-inducing drugs. One night the gate swings open; the narrator sees "neither land nor sea, but only the white void of unpeopled and illimitable space." He dissolves into the "native infinity of crystal oblivion," knowing that he has attained perfect happiness at last.

This simple yet exquisitely told fable (which bears conceptual affinities to the Dunsanian story "Celephaïs") does nothing more than to emphasis the tedium of life and the perfect peace to be found in death—a yearning that occasionally comes upon every intelligent mind. This tale is among the first to betray evidence of Lovecraft's Decadent sensibilities, something we will find emerging more emphatically in tales of a somewhat later period.

"Nyarlathotep" (1920)[28] is another prose-poem, and perhaps the best of them all; indeed, despite its brevity it can stand as one of Lovecraft's most potent vignettes. Its burden is nothing less than the overthrow of civilization. Although the tale is narrated in the first person, we learn at the very outset that more than the fate of a single individual is involved: "To a season of political and social upheaval was added a strange and brooding apprehension of hideous physical danger..." It is at this point that Nyarlathotep "came out of Egypt." He maintains that he has "risen up out of the blackness of twenty-seven centuries," and he conducts strange public exhibitions involving peculiar instruments and scenes displayed upon a cinema screen. In one of these scenes "I saw hooded forms amidst ruins, and yellow evil faces peering from behind fallen monuments." These exhibitions affect the people oddly, and they begin milling about "into curious involuntary formations." The narrator sees a tram-car knocked over on its side; looking at the horizon, he sees one of three towers missing and the second in ruins. The tale itself seems to dissolve into madness: "A sickened, sensitive shadow writhing in hands that are not hands, and whirled blindly past ghastly midnights of rotting creation, corpses of dead worlds with sores that were cities, charnel winds that brush the pallid stars and make them flicker low." And behind it all are "the blind, voiceless, mindless gargoyles whose soul is Nyarlathotep."

It is difficult to interpret precisely the symbolism of this evocative prose-poem, especially since much of the imagery is very likely derived from the dream on which it was based. Nevertheless, the dominant imagery is that of decay and destruction—of the human mind, of society, and of the universe itself (one of Nyarlathotep's cinema-scenes is of "the world battling against blackness; against the waves of destruction from ultimate space"). Nyarlathotep himself seems here to be a symbol for the destructive powers inherent in science. Later tales present Nyarlathotep in many different guises, both physical and metaphorical, to the degree that one is forced to question whether Lovecraft had any concrete or unified notion of exactly what Nyarlathotep is or stands for.

In a provocative recent article Will Murray has made a case that the Nyarlathotep of this prose-poem is based upon Nikola Tesla, the half-brilliant, half-charlatanic scientist and inventor who gave demonstrations involving "death-rays," light-shows, and the like at the turn of the century.[29] This is a highly likely theory, although there is much more to Nyarlathotep even in this work than merely an echo of Tesla; in particular, the Egyptian connection, which Lovecraft would emphasize in Nyarlathotep's later appearances, is absent in regard to Tesla. Nevertheless, this is one example of the frequency and subtlety with which Lovecraft incorporated contemporary scientific phenomena into his work. We will encounter many more such examples in later tales, and they should banish permanently the notion that Lovecraft was an eighteenth-century fossil with no interest in, or awareness of, his own time.

In this first phase of Lovecraft's fiction-writing career, experimentation is the keynote: experiments in setting, from the Pacific Ocean ("Dagon") to the Atlantic Ocean ("The Temple") to Africa ("Arthur Jermyn") to Arabia ("The Nameless City"); experiments in narrative tone, from Poe-esque psychological horror ("The Tomb") to languid prose-poetry ("Ex Oblivione") to realistic supernatural horror ("The Statement of Randolph Carter") to proto-science-fiction ("Beyond the Wall of Sleep"); experiments in scope, from cosmic horror ("Dagon," "Nyarlathotep") to the horror inspired by repellent individuals ("The Picture in the House"). It bears repeating that Lovecraft was still writing considerably more poetry and essays than fiction during this period, and would continue to do so for several more years. But the shift in his creative range can be gauged by noting that in 1920 he wrote at least twelve, and perhaps fourteen, stories (including two collaborations and one lost tale, "Life and Death"), the most he would ever write in his entire career. Also indicative of this shift is his commencement of a commonplace book as a repository of plot-germs, images, and themes. This commonplace book was probably begun in late 1919 or (more likely) early 1920; and although it was maintained to the end of Lovecraft's life, by far the greater number of entries date to 1920-1923. The majority of entries were never in fact used, and other entries appear only as minor elements in tales of very different focus and import; but the mere existence of this document points to Lovecraft's belief that fiction might ultimately be his dominant creative mode.

While most of the tales of this period are competent and effective, none ranks among Lovecraft's greatest stories. In many of them, however, are contained nuclei—in theme, conception, or image—of those later masterpieces which give him his well-deserved place in weird fiction. Lovecraft is one of the few writers in all literature whose most insignificant writings hold some modicum of interest, if only from a biographical perspective. By the middle of 1921, as Lovecraft was attempting to recover from the shattering blow of the death of his mother, he was ready to commence a stronger, more substantial vein of fiction-writing, and for the remaining sixteen years of his life his work would systematically gain in depth and richness as he continued to expand his vision, add to his life experiences, and gain a better understanding both of himself and of the world. Few authors have displayed so uniform a progression from mere competence to unexcelled brilliance.

III.

THE "DUNSANIAN" TALES (1919-1921)

Edward John Moreton Drax Plunkett, 18th Baron Dunsany (1878-1957), was born twelve years before Lovecraft and would outlive him by twenty years; he would write many times more fiction than Lovecraft, as well as poetry, plays, essays, reviews, and other matter that ought to grant him a significant place in Irish and fantasy literature. But today he is virtually forgotten as an Irish writer, and in the realm of weird fiction is acknowledged only as a significant forerunner of such later writers as J. R. R. Tolkien, Ursula K. Le Guin, and others. But in many ways Dunsany's literary achievement exceeds Lovecraft's, and he remains one of the most unrecognized authors of modern times.

And yet, in 1919 the situation was very different. Dunsany's first book, *The Gods of Pegana* (1905), had been issued at his own expense, but never again would he have to pay for the publication of his work. That volume, along with his other early books—the story collections *Time and the Gods* (1906), *The Sword of Welleran* (1908), *A Dreamer's Tales* (1910), *The Book of Wonder* (1912), *Fifty-One Tales* (1915), *The Last Book of Wonder* (1916), and *Tales of Three Hemispheres* (1919); and the play collections *Five Plays* (1914) and *Plays of Gods and Men* (1917)—represent the most remarkable body of work in the history of fantasy fiction, and their unexpected *succès d'estime* established Dunsany as a unique and much sought-after voice in Ireland, England, and America of the late teens. A Dunsany craze swept America around 1916, aided by the issuance of his books by the Boston firm of John W. Luce; in that year Dunsany became the only playwright ever to have five plays simultaneously produced on Broadway.

It is difficult to specify in brief compass the principal characteristics of Dunsany's early work, to say nothing of the novels, tales, and plays he wrote during the remaining four decades of his career; but Dunsany himself provides a few clues as to the basic import of all his work in *Patches of Sunlight*, as he recounts how at an early age he saw a hare in a garden:

> If ever I have written of Pan, out in the evening, as though I had really seen him, it is mostly a memory of

> that hare. If I thought that I was a gifted individual whose inspirations came sheer from outside earth and transcended common things, I should not write this book; but I believe that the wildest flights of the fancies of any of us have their homes with Mother Earth....[1]

Lovecraft would have been taken aback by this utterance, since it was precisely the apparent *remoteness* of Dunsany's realm—a realm of pure fantasy with no connection with the "real" world—that initially captivated him; and, strangely enough, Lovecraft came to express dissatisfaction at what he thought was the "dilution" of this otherworldliness in Dunsany's later work, when in fact his own creative writing of the 1920s and 1930s was on a path quite similar to Dunsany's in its greater topographical realism and evocation of the wonders and terrors of Nature.

But many readers can be excused for seeing the early work of Dunsany in this light, since its superficial exoticism appeared to signal it as virtually the creation of some non-human imagination. The realm of Pegana (which is featured in *The Gods of Pegana* and *Time and the Gods*, and in those volumes only) is wholly distinct from the "real" world; the first sentence of *The Gods of Pegana*—"Before there stood gods upon Olympus, or even Allah was Allah, had wrought and rested Mana-Yood-Sushai"—seems to refer to the *temporal* priority of Dunsany's creator god Mana-Yood-Sushai to the Graeco-Roman or Islamic gods, but beyond this citation there is no allusion to the "real" world at all. Dunsany himself, in his autobiography, remarks that his early tales were written "as though I were an inhabitant of an entirely different planet,"[2] something Lovecraft no doubt found very captivating, given his own cosmicism; but Dunsany could not keep this up for long, and already by *The Sword of Welleran* the real world has entered, as it would continue increasingly to do in his later writing. Indeed, it could be said that the uneasy mingling of the real and the unreal in *The Sword of Welleran* and *A Dreamer's Tales* produces some of the most distinctive work in Dunsany's entire canon.

Lovecraft must have heard of Dunsany well before reading him in 1919; but he reports that he was slow to read the Irish writer because he had been recommended to him "by one whose judgment I did not highly esteem."[3] This person was Alice M. Hamlet, an amateur journalist from Massachusetts; it was clearly at her urging that Lovecraft read his first Dunsany, *A Dreamer's Tales*[4] (not *The Gods of Pegana*, as some have believed), about a month prior to hearing Dunsany lecture at the Copley Plaza in Boston on October 20, 1919. This lecture was a part of Dunsany's triumphant American tour of 1919-1920, when he received the sort of adulation only rock musicians and sports figures receive today. Although Dunsany himself treats the Boston lecture with brevity in his own autobiography (*While the Sirens Slept*, 1944), Lovecraft dwells at length on it in a letter to Rheinhart Kleiner, stressing Dunsany's lofty stature (he was over six feet tall), his polished English accent, and the fact that after the lecture "Dunsany was encircled by autograph-seekers. Egged on by her aunt, Miss Hamlet almost mustered up courage enough to ask for an autograph, but weakened at the last moment.... For mine own part, I did not need a signature; for I detest fawning upon the great."[5]

Lovecraft read the bulk of Dunsany's hitherto published work, purchased his own copies of much of it, and continued to read Dunsany's later novels and tales (although with gradually diminishing enthusiasm) as they appeared through the 1920s and 1930s. He wrote two poems on his new mentor, one very mediocre ("To Edward John Moreton Drax Plunkett, Eighteenth Baron Dunsany" [1919]) and the other quite evocative ("On Reading Lord Dunsany's *Book of Wonder*" [1920]). In late 1922 he wrote a lecture, "Lord Dunsany and His Work," for an amateur journalism gathering.

What strikes us, however, about Lovecraft's seven or eight "Dunsanian" tales of the 1919-1921 period is that—in spite of Lovecraft's own testimony that his own creativity was completely submerged under the influence of Dunsany—many of his "borrowings" are in relatively insignificant external details. Some of these borrowings are, indeed, very obvious: the throne "wrought of one piece of ivory" in "The Doom That Came to Sarnath" clearly echoes Dunsany's throne "carved of one solid piece" in "Idle Days on the Yann" (in *A Dreamer's Tales*); the "dark wanderers" mentioned in "The Cats of Ulthar" are similar to the "Wanderers...a weird, dark tribe" from "Idle Days on the Yann"; and so on. Of course, the general fantastic atmosphere of "gods and men" is surely something that was influenced by Dunsany's example. One wonders, however, whether even this is something that Lovecraft might have come upon independently even if he had never read Dunsany; for we now must confront the seeming anomaly represented by the story "Polaris" (1918).[6]

This story was clearly written a full year or more before Lovecraft ever read Dunsany, and Lovecraft himself once noted that it was a striking instance of "parallelism in atmosphere, artificial nomenclature, treatment of the dream theme, etc."[7] This poignant brief tale treats of a man who appears to dream that he is initially a disembodied spirit contemplating some seemingly mythical realm, the land of Lomar, whose principal city Olathoë is threatened with attack from the Inutos, "squat, hellish, yellow fiends." In a subsequent "dream" the narrator learns that he has a body, and is one of the Lomarians. He is "feeble and given to strange faintings when subjected to stress and hardships," so is denied a place in the actual army of defenders; but he is given the important task of manning the watch-tower of Thapnen, since "my eyes were the keenest of the city." Unfortunately, at the critical moment

Polaris, the Pole Star, winks down at him and casts a spell so that he falls asleep; he strives to wake up, and finds that when he does so he is in a room through whose window he sees "the horrible swaying trees of a dream-swamp" (*i.e.*, his "waking" life). He convinces himself that "I am still dreaming" and vainly tries to wake up, but is unable to do so.

It should be noted, however, that this tale is not a "dream fantasy": the protagonist is not dreaming but rather has been possessed by a distant ancestor; in this sense the tale bears a thematic similarity to the earlier "The Tomb." Nevertheless, what is most remarkable about the story is its seeming anticipation of the Dunsanian mode long before Lovecraft ever read Dunsany. There are, perhaps, some ways to account for this anticipation. It is possible that he was drawing upon the prose-poems of Poe (especially "Silence—a Fable," "Shadow—a Parable," and "The Colloquy of Monos and Una"), which create a dream-like atmosphere through rhythmical prose and invented names. What is more, Lovecraft's letters make clear that the story was in some sense the outcome of a controversy on religion he was conducting with the theist Maurice W. Moe in the summer of 1918. What Lovecraft is keen on establishing is the "distinction between dream life and real life, between appearances and actualities."[8] Moe was maintaining that belief in religion is useful for social and moral order regardless of the question of its truth or falsity. As a counterargument, Lovecraft relates the following dream he had:

> Several nights ago I had a strange dream of a strange city—a city of many palaces and gilded domes, lying in a hollow betwixt ranges of grey, horrible hills.... I was, as I said, aware of this city visually. I was in it and around it. But certainly I had no corporeal existence.... I recall a lively curiosity at the scene, and a tormenting struggle to recall its identity; for I felt that I had once known it well, and that if I could remember, I should be carried back to a very remote period—many thousand years, when something vaguely horrible had happened.[9]

This is, clearly, the nucleus of "Polaris." Lovecraft continues in his letter to draw a conclusion from the dream: "...according to your pragmatism that dream was as real as my presence at this table, pen in hand! If the truth or falsity of our beliefs and impressions be immaterial, then I am, or was, actually and indisputably an unbodied spirit hovering over a very singular, very silent, and very ancient city somewhere between grey, dead hills." This *reductio ad absurdum* is reflected a little impishly in the story:

> ...I now desired to define my relation to [the scene], and to speak my mind amongst the grave men who conversed each day in the public squares. I said to myself, "This is no dream, for by what means can I prove the greater reality of that other life in the house of stone and brick south of the sinister swamp and the cemetery and the low hillock, where the Pole Star peers into my north window each night?"

The fact that the narrator at the end seems permanently confused between the real and the waking world (actually his present life and his past incarnation) may be a final tweaking of Moe's nose on the need to maintain such distinctions in real life.

"Polaris" is a quiet little triumph of prose-poetry, its incantatory rhythm and delicate pathos sustaining it in spite of its brevity. Critics have carped on a possible plot defect—why would the narrator, given to spells of fainting, be appointed the sole sentry in the watch-tower in spite of his keen eyes?—but only hard-headed literalists would see this as a significant flaw.

"The White Ship"[10]—written probably in November 1919 and the first of Lovecraft's avowed "Dunsanian" tales—is instructive in showing how Lovecraft kept a degree of independence in the fundamental philosophical message of a tale whose external features indeed owe much to Dunsany. This tale is frankly an allegory (something Dunsany almost never wrote save in some of the brief prose-poems in *Fifty-One Tales*) involving Basil Elton, a lighthouse-keeper who one day "walk[s] out over the waters...on a bridge of moonbeams" to a White Ship that has come from the South, captained by an aged bearded man. They sail to various fantastic realms: the Land of Zar, "where dwell all the dreams and thoughts of beauty that come to men once and then are forgotten"; the Land of Thalarion, "the City of a Thousand Wonders, wherein reside all those mysteries that man has striven in vain to fathom"; Xura, "the Land of Pleasures Unattained"; and finally Sona-Nyl, in which "there is neither time nor space, neither suffering nor death." Although Elton spends "many aeons" there in evident contentment, he gradually finds himself yearning for the realm of Cathuria, the Land of Hope, beyond the basalt pillars of the West, which he believes to be an even more wondrous realm than Sona-Nyl. The captain warns him against pursuing Cathuria, but Elton is adamant and compels the captain to launch his ship once more. But they discover that beyond the basalt pillars of the West is only a "monstrous cataract, wherein the oceans of the world drop down to abysmal nothingness." As their ship is destroyed, Elton finds himself on the platform of his lighthouse. The White Ship comes to him no more.

The surface plot of this story is clearly derived from Dunsany's "Idle Days on the Yann"; but that story is merely one of fantastic adventure, where a ship sails down the river Yann and encounters all manner of wonders along the voyage, with no attempt at any metaphorical or allegorical interpretation. Lovecraft, conversely, is making a philosophical point that is close to his own ethical position. The land of Sona-Nyl embodies the perfect Epicurean state, whereby all pain is eliminated and the fear of death is banished. In rejecting this realm Basil Elton brings upon his head a justified doom—not death, but sadness and discontent. The non-existence of Cathuria is anticipated by the land of Thalarion: this realm embodies all those "mysteries that man has striven in vain to fathom," and therein "walk only daemons and mad things that are no longer men"; such mysteries are not meant to be penetrated, and the hope of penetrating them (Cathuria is the Land of Hope) is both vain and foolish.

"The White Ship," like "Polaris," is also not a dream-fantasy. Both Dunsany's early tales and Lovecraft's Dunsanian imitations are carelessly referred to as dream-stories, but only a few by either author can be so designated. "Idle Days on the Yann" is one of them: the narrator tells his ship-captain that he comes "from Ireland, which is of Europe," feeling that this laborious circumlocution is necessary on the chance that the crew have not heard of such a place; but it is of no use: "the captain and all the sailors laughed, for they said, 'There is no such place in all the land of dreams'." But in most of Dunsany's stories, there is no clear distinction between dream and reality: the fantasy realm of Pegana *is* the "real" world, for there is no other. We will also find that this is the case in most of Lovecraft's tales; if anything, Lovecraft follows up dim suggestions in Dunsany that these fantastic realms have a *temporal* priority to the "real" world—*i.e.*, that they existed in the distant past of the known world. "Polaris" already makes this clear. In "The White Ship" we do not know where the North Point lighthouse is, but the implication is that it exists in the real world; and yet, the realms visited by the White Ship are so patently symbolic that no suggestion of their actual existence is made, or is even required by the logic of the tale.

"The Doom That Came to Sarnath" (1919)[11] is less philosophically interesting than "The White Ship," but it too is something more than a mere pastiche. On the surface this tale tells of the land of Mnar, where "ten thousand years ago" stood the ancient stone city of Ib, near a vast still lake, and populated by beings "not pleasing to behold"—flabby, green, voiceless creatures with bulging eyes. Ib was destroyed by the men of Sarnath, who were "dark shepherd folk." Afterward Sarnath flourishes greatly, becoming "the wonder of the world and the pride of all mankind." On the thousandth year after the destruction of Ib an enormous festival is held to commemorate the event, but amidst the celebrations Sarnath is overrun by "a horde of indescribable green voiceless things with bulging eyes, pouting, flabby lips, and curious ears," and is destroyed.

What seems like a tale of tit-for-tat vengeance becomes something more on analysis. Sarnath, it is very clear, brings doom upon itself by its flamboyant display of wealth. It furthermore becomes increasingly artificial in its design, aping the natural world but in fact repudiating it. Each house in Sarnath has a "crystal lakelet," parodying the actual "vast still lake" where Sarnath had consigned the ruins of Ib. The gardens of Sarnath defy the seasons: "In summer the gardens were cooled with fresh odorous breezes skilfully wafted by fans, and in winter they were heated with concealed fires, so that in those gardens it was always spring." Interestingly, in light of Lovecraft's own racism, the men of Sarnath have clearly killed the creatures of Ib out of simple race prejudice ("with their marvelling was mixed hate, for they thought it not meet that beings of such aspect should walk about the world of men at dusk"), and Lovecraft suggests that their doom was well merited.

Although "The Doom That Came to Sarnath" echoes many of Dunsany's stories of dooms that befall individuals, cities, or entire civilizations, it also exhibits the degree to which Lovecraft's prose style was fundamentally dissimilar to that of his mentor. Consider the following passage:

> Many were the pillars of the palaces, all of tinted marble, and carven into designs of surpassing beauty. And in most of the palaces the floors were mosaics of beryl and lapis-lazuli and sardonyx and carbuncle and other choice materials, so disposed that the beholder might fancy himself walking over beds of the rarest flowers.

It never seems to have occurred to Lovecraft that Dunsany achieved his most striking effects not through dense, adjective-laden passages like this—which are more reminiscent of Wilde's fairy tales—but through a staggeringly bold use of metaphor. Consider that quixotic quest by King Karnith Zo and his army to lay siege to Time:

> But as the feet of the foremost touched the edge of the hill Time hurled five years against them, and the years passed over their heads and the army still came on, an army of older men. But the slope seemed steeper to the King and to every man in his army, and they breathed more heavily. And Time summoned up more years, and one by one he hurled them at Karnith Zo and at all his men. And the knees of the army stiffened, and the beards grew and turned grey....[12]

This passage also displays Dunsany's powerful use of paratactic construction, or the failure to subordinate clauses. There is more to this style than merely the old joke of beginning every sentence with "And": its true function is to create a sense of simple linearity, typical of myth and other early narratives (including the King James Bible, the dominant influence on Dunsany's prose style), as opposed to the syntactic construction typical of classical prose. Lovecraft, raised on both Graeco-Roman literature and its imitators in the English Augustan age, could never achieve this sort of transparent simplicity. Later, of course, he would harness his dense syntactic style to achieve textural richness in his tales of the real world.

"The Terrible Old Man" (1920)[13] is not generally considered a Dunsanian story, and indeed it is not in the sense of being a tale set in an imaginary realm or in the past. We are here very clearly situated in present-day New England, but the tale nevertheless is likely derived from some of Dunsany's work. The story takes place in Kingsport, the first of Lovecraft's mythical New England towns; but it was only when he came upon the town of Marblehead, Massachusetts, in December 1922 and subsequently wrote "The Festival" (1923) that Kingsport became a clear fictional analogue of Marblehead. Right now we know only that it is the residence of the Terrible Old Man, a preternaturally aged individual who seems harmlessly eccentric: he is very feeble, spends much of his time apparently talking to bottles with lead pendulums suspended in them, and pays for his few wants with ancient Spanish gold. It is this last item that entices Angelo Ricci, Joe Czanek, and Manuel Silva, whose profession is thievery, to "pay a call" on the old man to see if they can persuade him to part with that gold. Ricci and Silva enter the house while Czanek waits in the car outside; soon hideous screams are heard, and Czanek, who is rather tender-hearted, hopes that his colleagues have not been forced to do physical harm to the old man. Soon he sees the figure of the Terrible Old Man leaning on a cane at his doorway, summoning him. Later three unidentifiable bodies are found washed in by the tide.

Once again we have a simple case of bad people getting their due; in this instance, however, Lovecraft seems clearly to have borrowed the basic plot from Dunsany's "Probable Adventure of the Three Literary Men" (in *The Book of Wonder*), which is written in exactly the arch and ponderous style of "The Terrible Old Man." Recent commentators have tried to deny the racism seemingly evident in the tale, but such an attempt is futile: Ricci, Czanek, and Silva (Italian, Polish, and Portuguese, respectively) each represent one of the leading minorities in Providence at the time, and it is hard to deny that Lovecraft took satisfaction in dispatching them. It is true that his wry comment ("They were not of Kingsport blood; they were of that new and heterogeneous alien stock which lies outside the charmed circle of New-England life and traditions") has a certain double-edged quality, satirizing the social restrictiveness of old-time New England Yankees as well as the influx of foreigners into the area; but the racist overtones of the entire story cannot be ignored.

The next of Lovecraft's "Dunsanian" tales is "The Tree" (1920); but this story is regarded as Dunsanian only for want of any other category in which to place it. It is Lovecraft's only tale set in ancient Greece, that realm he came to love in youth and continued to admire throughout his life. Dunsany rarely used ancient Greece as a setting for stories, but he did do so in two plays: *Alexander* (written in 1912, but not published until *Alexander and Three Small Plays* [1925], hence not read by Lovecraft until after he had written "The Tree") and *The Queen's Enemies* (published separately in 1916 and included the next year in *Plays of Gods and Men*), a delightful and celebrated play about Queen Nitokris of Egypt and the hideous (but not supernatural) vengeance she carries out upon her enemies. It was one of the works Dunsany read at the Boston lecture that Lovecraft attended.

"The Tree"[14] treats of two famous sculptors, Kalos and Musides, who are asked by the Tyrant of Syracuse to compete in the building of a statue of Tyché for his city. The two artists are the best of friends, but are very different in character: whereas Musides "revelled by night amidst the urban gaieties of Tegea," Kalos remains at home in quiet contemplation. The two begin working on their respective statues; but Kalos gradually takes ill, and in spite of Musides's constant nursing eventually dies. Musides wins the contest by default, but both he and his lovely statue are weirdly destroyed when a strange olive tree growing out of Kalos's tomb suddenly falls upon Musides's residence. The clear implication of the tale is that Musides, in spite of his friendship for his friend, has poisoned Kalos and suffers supernatural revenge.

The story's relative lack of vital connection to Dunsany's work can be gauged by the fact that the basic plot was evolved at least a year before Lovecraft ever read Dunsany. In an August 1918 letter to Alfred Galpin, Lovecraft outlines the plot of "The Tree," saying that it had already by that time been "long conceived but never elaborated into literary form";[15] he postponed writing the story because he evidently felt that Galpin's own tale "Marsh-Mad" (published in Galpin's amateur journal *The Philosopher* for December 1920) had pre-empted him by utilizing the "living tree" idea. The only feature absent from this plot-germ is the Grecian setting, which may conceivably have been suggested by Dunsany. Otherwise, the story is really an elementary exercise in divine justice, as well as a disquisition on the proper conduct for an artist (and, by extension, all human beings). One can sense Lovecraft's clear approval of the quiet lifestyle of Kalos and censure of Musides's "wild" life, so similar to that of the bohemians Lovecraft always despised:

> I have no respect or reverence whatever for any person who does not live abstemiously and purely—I can like him and tolerate him, and admit him to be a social equal as I do Clark Ashton Smith and Mortonius and Kleiner and others like that, but in my heart I feel him to be my inferior—nearer the abysmal amoeba and the Neanderthal man—and at times cannot veil a sort of condescension and sardonic contempt for him, no matter how much my aesthetick and intellectual superior he may be.[16]

The Grecian setting for "The Tree" is handled quite deftly, and it is possible to pinpoint the exact period in which the story must have taken place (between 371 and 353 B.C.).[17] "Kalos" means "fair" or "handsome" in Greek, while "Musides" means "son of the Muse(s)"; Tyché means "chance," and there was an actual cult of Tyché in fourth-century B.C. Greece. Lovecraft's absorption of Greek history in youth has paid good dividends here.

"The Cats of Ulthar" (1920)[18] always remained one of Lovecraft's favorite stories, probably because of the emphasis on cats. This tale owes more to Dunsany than many of his other "Dunsanian" fantasies. The narrator proposes to explain how the town of Ulthar passed its "remarkable law" that no man may kill a cat. There was once a very evil couple who hated cats and who brutally murdered any that strayed on their property. One day a caravan of "dark wanderers" comes to Ulthar, among which is the little boy Menes, owner of a tiny black kitten. When the kitten disappears, the heartbroken boy, learning of the propensities of the cat-hating couple, "prayed in a tongue no villager could understand." That night all the cats in the town vanish, and when they return in the morning they refuse for two entire days to touch any food. Later it is noticed that the couple has not been seen for days; when at last the villagers enter their house, they find two clean-picked skeletons.

Here again the "moral" is extremely elementary, and one can sense Lovecraft's rich satisfaction at the loathsome fate suffered by the evil cat-killing couple. As with several of his other Dunsanian tales, it borrows its vengeance motif and ponderous tone from *The Book of Wonder*.

It would be some months before Lovecraft produced another Dunsanian tale, but it would be both one of his best and most significant in terms of his later work. "Celephaïs" (1920)[19] (the dieresis over the "*i*" is frequently omitted) tells the story of Kuranes, who has a different name in waking life and who escapes the prosy world of London by dream and drugs. In this state he comes upon the city of Celephaïs, in the Valley of Ooth-Nargai. It is a city of which he had dreamed as a child, and there "his spirit had dwelt all the eternity of an hour one summer afternoon very long ago, when he had slipt away from his nurse and let the warm sea-breeze lull him to sleep as he watched the clouds from the cliff near the village." It is a realm of pure beauty:

> When he entered the city, past the bronze gates and over the onyx pavements, the merchants and camel-drivers greeted him as if he had never been away; and it was the same at the turqoise temple of Nath-Horthath, where the orchid-wreathed priests told him that there is no time in Ooth-Nargai, but only perpetual youth. Then Kuranes walked through the Street of Pillars to the seaward wall, where gathered the traders and sailors, and strange men from the regions where the sea meets the sky.

But Kuranes awakes in his London garret and finds that he can return to Celephaïs no more. He dreams of other wondrous lands, but his sought-for city continues to elude him. He increases his intake of drugs, runs out of money, and is turned out of his flat. Then, as he wanders aimlessly through the streets, he comes upon a cortege of knights who "rode majestically through the downs of Surrey," seeming to gallop back in time as they do so. They leap off a precipice and drift softly down to Celephaïs, and Kuranes knows that he will be its king forever. Meanwhile, in the waking world, the tide at Innsmouth washes up the corpse of a tramp, while a "notably fat and offensive millionaire brewer" buys Kuranes's ancestral mansion and "enjoys the purchased atmosphere of extinct nobility."

This tale is somewhat embarrassingly similar in conception to Dunsany's "The Coronation of Mr. Thomas Shap" (in *The Book of Wonder*). There a small businessman imagines himself the King of Larkar, and as he continues to dwell obsessively on (and in) this imaginary realm his work in the real world suffers, until finally he is placed in the madhouse of Hanwell. It is one of the few instances where Lovecraft has borrowed the entire theme of a story from Dunsany; and yet, it is a theme that was close to Lovecraft's heart as well, so that perhaps the borrowing is entirely or largely subconscious. The thrust of the story is nothing less than an escape from the "groans and grating / Of abhorrent life" (as he put it in the poem "Despair") into a realm of pure imagination—one which, nevertheless, is derived from "the nebulous memories of childhood tales and dreams." The man who in January 1920 wrote "Adulthood is hell"[20] had found in Dunsany a model for the glorious re-creation of those memories of youth for which he would yearn his entire life.

"Celephaïs" is a gorgeously evocative prose-poem that ranks close to the pinnacle of Lovecraft's Dunsanian tales. But it will gain added importance for the contrast it provides to a much later work superficially (and only superficially) in the Dunsanian vein, *The Dream-Quest of Unknown Kadath*. This novel, written after Lovecraft's New York experience, exhibits a marked, almost antipodal, alteration in Lovecraft's aesthetic of beauty, and when Kuranes reappears in it he and his imagined realm will take on a very different cast.

"The Quest of Iranon" (1921)[21] may be the most beautiful of all Lovecraft's Dunsanian fantasies, although in later years he savagely condemned it as mawkish. A youthful singer named Iranon comes to the granite city of Teloth, saying that he is seeking his far-off home of Aira, where he was a prince. The men of Teloth, who have no beauty in their lives, do not look kindly on Iranon, and force him to work with a cobbler. He meets a boy named Romnod, who similarly yearns for "the warm groves and the distant lands of beauty and song." Romnod thinks that nearby Oonai, the city of lutes and dancing, might be Iranon's Aira. Iranon doubts it, but goes there with Romnod. It is indeed not Aira, but the two of them find welcome there for a time. Iranon wins praises for his singing and lyre-playing, and Romnod learns the coarser pleasures of wine. Years pass; Iranon seems to grow no older, as he continues to hope one day to find Aira. Romnod eventually dies of drink, and Iranon leaves the town and continues his quest. He comes to "the squalid cot of an antique shepherd" and asks him about Aira. The shepherd looks at Iranon curiously and says:

> "O stranger, I have indeed heard the name of Aira, and the other names thou hast spoken, but they come to me from afar down the waste of long years. I heard them in my youth from the lips of a playmate, a beggar's boy given to strange dreams, who would weave long tales about the moon and the flowers and the west wind. We used to laugh at him, for we knew him from his birth though he thought himself a King's son."

At twilight an old, old man is seen walking calmly into the quicksand. "That night something of youth and beauty died in the elder world."

The poignancy of this story, along with its simple but powerful message—the loss of hope—make it unique in Lovecraft's work. There is perhaps a certain sentimentality—as well as the suggestion of social snobbery, since Iranon cannot bear the revelation that he is not a prince but only a beggar's boy—but the fundamental message is etched with great poignancy and delicacy. In a sense, "The Quest of Iranon" is a mirror-image of "Celephaïs": whereas Kuranes dies in the real world only to escape into the world of his childhood imaginings, Iranon dies because he is unable to preserve the illusion of the reality of those imaginings. Aside from its musical language, "The Quest of Iranon" bears no influence of any specific work by Dunsany, and may be the most original of Lovecraft's Dunsanian imitations.

Lovecraft's final explicitly Dunsanian story is "The Other Gods" (1921).[22] The "gods of earth" have forsaken their beloved mountain Ngranek and betaken themselves to "unknown Kadath in the cold waste where no man treads"; they have done this ever since a human being from Ulthar, Barzai the Wise, attempted to scale Mt. Ngranek and catch a glimpse of them. Barzai was much learned in the "seven cryptical books of Hsan" and the "Pnakotic Manuscripts of distant and frozen Lomar," and knew so much of the gods that he wished to see them dancing on Mt. Ngranek. He undertakes this bold journey with his friend, Atal the priest. For days they climb the rugged mountain, and as they approach the cloud-hung summit Barzai thinks he hears the gods; he redoubles his efforts, leaving Atal far behind. But his eagerness turns to horror. He thinks he actually sees the gods of earth, but instead they are "'The *other* gods! The *other* gods! The gods of the outer hells that guard the feeble gods of earth!'" Barzai is swept up ("'Merciful gods of earth, *I am falling into the sky!*'") and is never seen again.

"The Other Gods" is a textbook example of hubris (overweening pride), and not an especially interesting one. Dunsany had already treated the matter several times in his own work; in "The Revolt of the Home Gods" (in *The Gods of Pegana*) the humble home gods Eimes, Zanes, and Segastrion declare: "We now play the game of the gods and slay men for our pleasure, and we be greater than the gods of Pegana." But, even though they be gods, they suffer a dismal fate from the gods of Pegana.

"The Other Gods" is somewhat more interesting in that it establishes explicit links with other of Lovecraft's "Dunsanian" fantasies—characters, cities, and other details are taken from several previous works. This sort of linkage had, in fact, been occurring all along, and leads to two conclusions: first, that the Dunsanian tales (now including "Polaris," since "The Other Gods" cites the Pnakotic Manuscripts and Lomar, first mentioned in that tale) occupy a single imagined realm; and second, that that realm does not exist in a dreamworld or an imagined universe, but in the distant past of the earth. This latter conclusion is very evident from many mentions in all the stories considered here. A reference in "Polaris" to "Six and twenty thousand years" dates that story to 24,000 B.C. Other tales follow this pattern: Ib (in "The Doom That Came to Sarnath") stood "when the world was young"; "The Other Gods," by mentioning Lomar and Ulthar, incorporates the latter (and by extension the entire story "The Cats of Ulthar") into the earth's prehistory; and "The Quest of Iranon," by mentioning Lomar in conjunction with the cities named in "The Doom That Came to Sarnath," does the same (recall also the final sentence: "That night something of youth and beauty died in the *elder world*"). Only "The

White Ship" (clearly an allegory) and "Celephaïs" (in which dream and reality are starkly contrasted) stand outside this tightly knit web of stories. We shall, of course, see this sort of interconnectedness becoming increasingly evident in Lovecraft's later stories set in the real world as well, although it is probably going too far, as one critic has done,[23] to refer to Lovecraft's entire fictional work as one large novel. Nevertheless, the degree of intertextuality—going well beyond thematic or philosophical unity—is remarkable.

An examination of Dunsany's early tales and plays reveals many thematic and philosophical similarities with Lovecraft: cosmicism (largely restricted to *The Gods of Pegana*); the exaltation of Nature; hostility to industrialism; the power of dream or imagination to transform the mundane world into a realm of gorgeously exotic beauty; the awesome role of Time in human and divine affairs; and, of course, the evocative use of language. It is scarcely to be wondered at that Lovecraft felt for a time that Dunsany had said all he had wished to say in a given literary and philosophical direction.

From this perspective, it is a little odd that only one of Lovecraft's Dunsanian tales—"The Other Gods"—evokes that cosmicism which Lovecraft felt to be the keynote of Dunsany's early work. He would assert hyperbolically in "Supernatural Horror in Literature" that Dunsany's "point of view is the most truly cosmic of any held in the literature of any period,"[24] although later he would modify this opinion considerably. Perhaps Lovecraft felt at this time that Dunsany had conveyed his cosmicism so effectively in *The Gods of Pegana* that he could not hope to equal it, so that he chose to imitate Dunsany's more "human" tales instead.

What, then, did Lovecraft learn from Dunsany? The answer may not be immediately evident, since it took several years for the Dunsany influence to be assimilated, and some of the most interesting and important aspects of the influence are manifested in tales that bear no superficial resemblance to Dunsany. For now, however, one lesson can be summed up in Lovecraft's somewhat simple-minded characterization in "Supernatural Horror in Literature": "Beauty rather than terror is the keynote of Dunsany's work."[25] Whereas, with the exceptions of "Polaris" and such non-weird ventures as "A Reminiscence of Dr. Samuel Johnson," Lovecraft's experiments in fiction up to 1919 had been entirely within the realm of supernatural horror, he was now able to diversify his fictional palette with tales of languorous beauty, delicacy, and pathos. To be sure, horror is present as well; but the fantastic settings of the tales, even given the assumption that they are occurring in the earth's prehistory, cause the horror to seem more remote, less immediately threatening.

More to the point, Lovecraft learned from Dunsany how to enunciate his philosophical, aesthetic, and moral conceptions by means of fiction, beyond the simple cosmicism of "Dagon" or "Beyond the Wall of Sleep." The relation between dream and reality—dimly probed in "Polaris"—is treated exhaustively and poignantly in "Celephaïs"; the loss of hope is pensively etched in "The White Ship" and "The Quest of Iranon"; the perfidy of false friendship is the focus of "The Tree." Lovecraft found *Time and the Gods* "richly philosophical,"[26] and the whole of Dunsany's early—and later—work offers simple, affecting parables on fundamental human issues. Lovecraft would in later years express his philosophy in increasingly complex ways as his own fiction gained in breadth, scope, and richness.

It can scarcely be denied—in spite of his own assertions to the contrary—that Lovecraft's "Dunsanian" fantasies are far more than mechanical pastiches of a revered master: they reveal considerable originality of conception while being only superficially derived from Dunsany. It is true that Lovecraft might never have written these tales had he not had Dunsany's example at hand; but he was, even at this early stage, an author who was searching for things of his own to say, and in Dunsany's style and manner he merely found suggestive ways to say them. Interestingly, Dunsany himself came to this conclusion: when Lovecraft's work was posthumously published in book form, Dunsany came upon it and confessed that he had "an odd interest in Lovecraft's work because in the few tales of his I have read I found that he was writing in my style, entirely originally & without in any way borrowing from me, & yet with my style & largely my material."[27] Lovecraft would have been grateful for the acknowledgment.

IV.

REGIONAL HORROR (1921-1926)

"The Outsider" (1921)[1] has frequently been taken to be emblematic of Lovecraft's early work, and perhaps his work as a whole: it was the title story of his first major collection, and its poignant line "I know always that I am an outsider; a stranger in this century and among those who are still men" has been thought to apply to Lovecraft himself, the "eccentric recluse" who repudiated the twentieth century for the safe, rational haven of the eighteenth. We have already seen how this conception may be a serious misconstrual of Lovecraft the man and thinker, but "The Outsider" nevertheless holds a special place in his canon, and perhaps rightly, for it is a haunting and inexhaustibly interpretable story. For a variety of reasons, however, I hesitate to rank it among his greatest works, and it may also be quite unrepresentative of the tales of this period.

The plot of this story scarcely needs to be retold. The first-person narrator, a mysterious individual raised in a spectral castle that never admits the sun, gains so burning a desire to see the light of day that he scales the tallest tower of the castle, thinking that there if anywhere he might see the open sky; instead, he finds only the solid ground. Stunned by the revelation, he proceeds along an unused path and comes upon a mansion where a fancy-dress ball is taking place. As he enters through a window, the guests flee in terror as from the sight of some hideous monster. The narrator thinks he sees the monster out of the corner of his eye, but he ultimately learns that he is instead looking in a mirror.

On the face of it, the tale makes little sense. If we are to imagine the Outsider's castle as being underground, how is it that he occasionally goes out into the "endless forest" that surrounds it? And even if the castle had no mirrors, thereby preventing the Outsider from seeing himself, surely he could have looked down at himself and seen his "eaten-away and bone-revealing outlines," as he does in the mirror at the end. Realizing these implausibilities, and taking into consideration the epigraph from Keats's *Eve of St. Agnes* (which speaks of a Baron and "all his warrior-guests" who were "long be-nightmared"),

William Fulwiler has conjectured that we are to regard "The Outsider" as a dream or nightmare.[2]

The story does have some further intricacies of plot, however. What are we to make of the fact that the park through which the Outsider proceeds on his way to the gaily lit mansion is "maddeningly familiar, yet full of perplexing strangeness"? What of the fact that, in the mansion itself, "some of the well-known towers were demolished; whilst new wings existed to confuse the beholder"? When the Outsider enters the mansion and sees the guests, "Some of the faces seemed to hold expressions that brought up incredibly remote recollections." All these hints, along with the narrator's emergence from his tower into an apparent mausoleum, make clear that the Outsider is himself a remote ancestor of the current occupants of the mansion. Even this notion is fraught with difficulties, for we must either assume that the Outsider has either awakened from the dead or has somehow maintained a conscious existence all along.

But we can easily overlook these conceptual difficulties and relish the atmosphere of the tale. Although it is somewhat overwritten and hyperbolic, it contains some memorable lines and passages; the following may be symptomatic of Lovecraft's "purple prose," but in the context of the story it is undeniably effective:

> I cannot even hint what it was like, for it was a compound of all that is unclean, unwelcome, abnormal, and detestable. It was the ghoulish shade of decay, antiquity, and desolation; the putrid, dripping eidolon of unwholesome revelation; the awful baring of that which the merciful earth should always hide. God knows it was not of this world—or no longer of this world—yet to my horror I saw in its eaten-away and bone-revealing outlines a leering, abhorrent travesty on the human shape; and in its mouldy, disintegrating apparel an unspeakable quality that chilled me even more.

There can scarcely be any doubt that the above, as with the tale as a whole, is Poe-inspired. Lovecraft himself admitted that the story "represents my literal though unconscious imitation of Poe at its very height,"[3] and August Derleth frequently claimed for "The Outsider" the dubious distinction that it could easily be mistaken for a lost story by Poe. The opening paragraphs of the tale seem very deliberately to be based upon the opening of "Berenice," and the scene at the end seems to be a sort of mirror-image of "The Masque of the Red Death," where the Red Death is seen traversing the rooms of a gaudily decorated mansion; the anomalous life-in-death of the central figure clearly brings "Facts in the Case of M. Valdemar" to mind. As for the central image of the monster seeing himself in the mirror, a number of possible literary influences have been put forth: Colin Wilson has suggested Wilde's fairy tale, "The Birthday of the Infanta," George Wetzel has taken note of Nathaniel Hawthorne's "Fragments from the Journal of a Solitary Man" (in which a man dreams that he sees himself in a picture-window and notes with horror that he has been walking the street in his shroud), and there is a scene in Mary Shelley's *Frankenstein* in which the monster looks in a pond and is horrified at his own reflection.[4] But this image is so elementary that no conscious literary influence need be postulated, and Lovecraft may well have derived it independently.

Nevertheless, the tale is worth examining as other than a mere pastiche. A biographical interpretation is very tempting, and would be much augmented if it could be ascertained that the tale was written just after the death of Lovecraft's mother on May 24, 1921; but the exact date of writing of "The Outsider" has not been established, and we can only say that it was written after "The Moon-Bog" (March) and before "The Other Gods" (August 14). It is very attractive to think of the Outsider as reflecting Lovecraft's own self-image—the self-image of one whose mother seemed to make frequent mention to others of her son's "hideous face." Indeed, the Outsider's desperate attempt to escape from the castle that has served as his home for (as he believes) his entire lifetime could be an echo of Lovecraft's own desire to escape the increasingly stifling clutches of his increasingly disturbed mother, with whom he had lived alone since 1904.

But a biographical interpretation would be too restrictive, and the tale can bear many other types of interpretation. Dirk W. Mosig has written a fine paper examining "The Outsider" from biographical, psychological, philosophical, and cultural perspectives,[5] and each of these has value. The poignant line, "it were better to glimpse the sky and perish, than to live without ever beholding day," employs the common symbol—used frequently in Lovecraft—of light as knowledge and darkness as ignorance, and perhaps echoes Lovecraft's own belief on the mixed blessings of scientific enquiry: "To the scientist there is the joy in pursuing truth which nearly counteracts the depressing revelations of truth."[6]

If "The Outsider" has considerable merit, it is still hampered by conceptual difficulties, excessive derivativeness, an unfortunate reliance on overheated prose, and a "surprise" ending that cannot be much of a surprise to many readers. And in its very nebulous topographical setting—no place names of any sort appear in the story, and we could be in New England, England, Europe, or almost any other ancient realm—it contradicts that tendency toward increasing *precision* in setting which will prove to be the principal unifying feature of the tales of this period.

"The Music of Erich Zann" (1921)[7] is a good example of this tendency. Lovecraft does not need to mention Paris for us to realize that we are in the French capital; and yet, while the Parisian locale is vividly evoked, Lovecraft is careful to maintain sufficient ambiguity for the supernatural to enter. "I have examined maps of the city with the greatest care, yet have never again found the Rue d'Auseil," the narrator declares, suggesting that a zone of unreality has somehow lodged itself into a very real locale. This is exactly the type of thing we will find in Lovecraft's later tales, although there the intrusion of the unreal, the irrational, and the fantastic will be still more subtle than it is here. In spite of Lovecraft's later remarks on the subtlety and restraint of the tale, "The Music of Erich Zann" is still a little crude and obvious in its depiction of landscape. Consider the following:

> The houses were tall, peaked-roofed, incredibly old, and crazily leaning backward, forward, and sidewise. Occasionally an opposite pair, both leaning forward, almost met across the street like an arch; and certainly they kept most of the light from the ground below. There were a few overhead bridges from house to house across the street.

This is, in effect, *too bizarre* for a tale purportedly set in the real world. Conversely, the actual weird phenomenon—whatever it is that lies beyond the window of Erich Zann's garret room—is too nebulous in its nature and import. Zann's weird viol-playing somehow "holds the undimensioned worlds at bay" (as Lovecraft would write in *Fungi from Yuggoth*), but we never know what or how or why: Zann's scribbled manuscript—"a full account...of all the marvels and terrors which beset him"—conveniently flies out the window, and the narrator's own glimpse out the window reveals nothing more than "the blackness of space illimitable; unimagined space alive with motion and music, and having no semblance to anything on earth." While Lovecraft is perhaps to be praised for this sort of vagueness—especially when his later tales are open to the opposite criticisms of obviousness and explicitness—one senses that a little more clarification might have been in order. Again, as with "The Transition of Juan Romero," it appears that Lovecraft himself may not have had a clear idea of the nature of the supernatural phenomenon in this tale.

Nevertheless, "The Music of Erich Zann" is one of Lovecraft's early triumphs for its sustained atmosphere of incomprehensible weirdness, its evocative capturing of the sense of bizarrerie latent in ancient places, and in its characterization of Zann—at once a poignant and a vaguely horrifying figure. Robert M. Price's analysis of the story—interpreting Zann as a satyr-figure whose soul returns at the end to those outer spheres where he actually belongs—seems very apt.[8]

Lovecraft had by no means abandoned the pure fantasy as a vehicle for probing philosophical and aesthetic concerns; "Hypnos"

(1922)[9] is one such example. Although this tale is purportedly set in "hoary Kent," it really takes the cosmos—or the human mind—as its backdrop. The narrator, a sculptor, claims to have found a "friend" who leads him on spectacular cosmic voyagings through dream, and who perishes as a result of offending the "mocking and insatiate Hypnos, lord of sleep," being left only as a perfectly sculpted bust carved in marble.

Our first query regarding "Hypnos" is the reliability of the narrator's account: is he telling the truth? is he self-deluded? did he ever have a friend at all, or did he merely hallucinate such a person? I do not believe it is possible to answer any of these questions definitively, and indeed there may be no great difference one way or the other. Let us consider first the supernatural explanation.

Under this view, the narrator's friend really did exist and really did suffer the fate attributed to him. What this friend sought to do was to utilize dream as a vehicle for some sort of physical or mental domination. He had, according to the narrator, "designs whereby the earth and the stars would move at his command, and the destinies of all living things be his." This is, as in "The Other Gods," a textbook case of hubris, and the individual rightly summons his own doom as a result.

If we adopt the psychological explanation, we are in a surprisingly similar situation. Under this view, it was the narrator himself who entertained such "designs" about universal domination, and he has created an imaginary friend to slough off responsibility from himself. Note how, after noting his friend's "designs," he harriedly adds: "I affirm—I swear—that I had no share in these extreme aspirations." From this perspective, the narrator may seem to be an instance of split personality.

The fundamental point of "Hypnos," however, is the relation of "dreams" and reality, and in this sense it continues a theme we have already seen in "The Tomb," "Beyond the Wall of Sleep," "Celephaïs," and other tales. For here again we are dealing not with mundane dreams but with some sort of visions that allow access to other realms of entity. The narrator declares that his and his friend's studies

> ...were of that vaster and more appalling universe of dim entity and consciousness which lies deeper than matter, time, and space, and whose existence we suspect only in certain forms of sleep—those rare dreams beyond dreams which come never to common men, and but once or twice in the lifetime of imaginative men.

What these studies reveal is that "The cosmos of our waking knowledge, born from such an universe as a bubble is born from the pipe of a jester, touches it only as a bubble may touch its sardonic source when sucked back by the jester's whim." In other words, these dreams, like those of Joe Slater in "Beyond the Wall of Sleep," are glimpses of a supra-reality beyond our mundane sphere. "Hypnos," indeed, shares many points of detail with that earlier story: whereas Slater was possessed by an interstellar being situated somewhere near Algol, the narrator of "Hypnos" becomes fearful of the star Corona Borealis; just as Slater claims that he "would soar through abysses of emptiness, *burning* every obstacle that stood in his way,"[10] the narrator and his friend tell of "rushing aërially along shocking, unlighted, and fear-haunted abysses, and occasionally *tearing* through certain well-marked and typical obstacles."

Another of the important themes in "Hypnos"—as Steven J. Mariconda has demonstrated in a brilliant recent paper[11]—is the relation of art and reality. It is no accident that the narrator is a sculptor; for what he seeks to do is to experience, *physically* rather than merely aesthetically, that expansion of vision which Lovecraft saw as the prime function of art. In a letter Lovecraft claims that each artist's vision is so unique that a reader's understanding of many different works of art will produce a widened conception of the universe and even, ultimately, an "approach to *the mystic substance of absolute reality itself*."[12] But whereas such a goal is, as an aesthetic gesture, harmless, the protagonist of "Hypnos" seeks to fulfill it in actual life, thereby bringing merited destruction upon himself and his friend.

"Hypnos" is a powerful little vignette that deserves greater attention for its subtlety, power, and philosophical richness. The vagueness of the supernatural phenomena here is a triumph of restraint: we never learn exactly what it is that the narrator and his friend saw and experienced in their voyagings through space; we never know what force turned that friend into marble; and we can never be sure whether that friend existed at all outside the narrator's own mind. These tantalizing hints and ambiguities allow "Hypnos" to be an endlessly interpretable tale whose exact import will remain just beyond reach.

Lovecraft returns to England in a somewhat more realistic way in "The Hound" (1922) and "The Rats in the Walls" (1923). These are, indeed, virtually the last of Lovecraft's tales to be set outside the American continent, and both are notable, although for very different reasons. Both "Hypnos," with its epigraph from Baudelaire, and "The Hound" (1922)—which, as Steven J. Mariconda has demonstrated,[13] is clearly derived from the work of J.-K. Huysmans—are prime documents in Lovecraft's aesthetic shift from classicism to Decadence.

"The Hound,"[14] moreover, is obviously a self-parody—or, at the very least, a parody of the wild, histrionic, uncontrolled blood-and-thunder novels and tales that had already become hackneyed by Lovecraft's day. The escapades of St. John and his nameless friend, the narrator, are so broadly overwritten and bombastic that one can only suspect Lovecraft's tongue firmly in his cheek in the writing of this story.

Various obvious literary influences—several references to Huysmans; the repeated mentions of "the faint deep-toned baying of some gigantic hound," clearly a nod to Sir Arthur Conan Doyle's *The Hound of the Baskervilles*; the mention of "the damned thing," a tip of the hat to Ambrose Bierce—point in this same direction.

St. John and the narrator, true to their Decadent instincts, are "wearied with the commonplaces of a prosaic world." They have tried everything, but to no avail: "The enigmas of the symbolists and the ecstasies of the pre-Raphaelites all were ours in their time, but each new mood was drained too soon of its diverting novelty and appeal." It turns out that "only the sombre philosophy of the decadents"—specifically Baudelaire and Huysmans, both mentioned by name—can appease them for a time, but even this proves only temporary. Finally they resort to "that hideous extremity of human outrage" called grave-robbing. The doom they suffer when they rob a particularly redoubtable grave of a supposed ghoul in Holland, from which they take an amulet in the shape "of a crouching winged hound," is the core of this intentionally hysterical narrative.

If analyzed logically, there is in "The Hound" (as in "The Temple," although quite unintentionally there) an *excess* of supernaturalism that would make the story preposterous if it were intended seriously. It is true that the supernatural incidents are more integrated here than in "The Temple," but such statements as "Less than a week after our return to England, strange things began to happen" and, a little later, "Bizarre manifestations were now too frequent to count" are a clear tip-off to the parodic nature of the story. And yet, the story gains a certain power in its maniacal way, and—so long as one realizes that Lovecraft has *chosen* to write the tale in this manner—one can derive considerable guilty pleasure out of it. Some of the prose is filled with elaborate rhetorical devices—alliteration, stream-of-consciousness, prose-poetic rhythm—that Lovecraft would continue to refine in later works. Here is the last paragraph:

> Madness rides the star-wind...claws and teeth sharpened on centuries of corpses...dripping death astride a bacchanale of bats from night-black ruins of buried temples of Belial.... Now, as the baying of that dead, fleshless monstrosity grows louder and louder, and the stealthy whirring and flapping of those accursed web-wings circles closer and closer, I shall seek with my revolver the oblivion which is my only refuge from the unnamed and unnamable.

The regional element, which we will see to be increasingly dominant in the tales of this period, enters "The Hound" in a somewhat circuitous way. The story was inspired by Lovecraft's visit in September 1922 to the Dutch Reformed Church in Brooklyn, an exquisite eighteenth-century edifice flanked by an eerie and crumbling cemetery full of Dutch graves. Lovecraft actually chipped off a piece of one ancient gravestone, and ruminated on the consequences of his act: "who can say what *thing* might not come out of the centuried earth to exact vengeance for his desecrated tomb?"[15] But rather than setting the tale in a now unglamorous section of Brooklyn, he set the tale in Holland itself. To be sure, Lovecraft's utter lack of first-hand experience of Holland or neighboring England (site of the two protagonists' manor-house) makes his landscape descriptions vague to the point of fantasy; but "The Hound" is still of some importance in showing how real locales were increasingly impelling the creation of Lovecraft's weird tales. Lovecraft was by no means done with purely fantastic settings—as the very brief fragment of a purported novel, "Azathoth,"[16] and the prose-poem "What the Moon Brings,"[17] both written in the summer of 1922, attest—but topographical realism was becoming more and more of a desideratum in his work.

"Herbert West—Reanimator" can perhaps be considered in this light, even though this episodic story is surely one of Lovecraft's poorest fictional works and is of importance only in being his first professionally published tale. It was written for a wretched magazine, *Home Brew*, founded by an amateur associate, George Julian Houtain, who managed to get other amateurs—including James F. Morton and Rheinhart Kleiner—to contribute poetry, essays, and fiction to the venture. It is frequently overlooked that *Home Brew* was principally a humor magazine—a point made abundantly clear by the somewhat risqué limericks that are placed as fillers at the end of some episodes of the two stories Lovecraft wrote for the "vile rag."[18] And yet, Houtain wished Lovecraft to write a six-part horror story, to be titled "Grewsome Tales," and specifically asked him to be as unrestrained as possible: "Houtain said, 'You can't make them too morbid,' and I have taken him at his word!"[19] Lovecraft reports in a letter. He goes on to complain frequently, and with a certain masochistic relish, about the degradation of writing a story of this sort:

> Now this is manifestly inartistic. To write to order, and to drag one figure through a series of artificial episodes, involves the violation of all that spontaneity and singleness of impression which should characterise short story work. It reduces the unhappy author from art to the commonplace level of mechanical and unimaginative hack-work.[20]

Certainly, "Herbert West—Reanimator"[21]—written over at least a seven- or eight-month period, from fall 1921 to summer 1922—is structurally weak in its need to recapitulate the plot of the preceding episode in every successive segment. One in fact wonders why Lovecraft even felt the need to do this, since Houtain himself provided brief headnotes to each story that could easily have been fleshed out as actual synopses, as is customary in serials. Nevertheless, it becomes clear that each segment is intended to build upon its predecessor, and that the final episode harks back to the very earliest segment and brings the entire series to a relatively unified conclusion. Despite the length of time taken in its writing—unusual for a story of only moderate length—"Herbert West—Reanimator" was manifestly conceived as a single entity rather than as a string of unrelated episodes.

The various attempts by Dr. Herbert West, graduate of the Miskatonic University Medical School in Arkham (and this is the first time that that celebrated institution of higher learning is cited in Lovecraft's work), to reanimate the dead seem superficially derived from a venerable literary ancestor, Mary Shelley's *Frankenstein*; but in fact West's actual procedure in reanimation (revivification of entire bodies) is very different from that of Victor Frankenstein, who has assembled a composite body from disparate human fragments. Only at a very late stage in West's adventures does he resort to this sort of piecemeal assemblage, and by this time the tale has lapsed into clear self-parody. Indeed, it is possible that Lovecraft *began* writing the story with a (moderately) straight face, but that as he perceived the increasing absurdity and grotesqueness of the plot, he gave up the attempt at a "serious" work of art. It is difficult not to detect parody in a late tableau:

> I can still see Herbert West under the sinister electric light as he injected his reanimating solution into the arm of the headless body. The scene I cannot describe—I should faint if I tried it, for there is madness in a room full of classified charnel things, with blood and lesser human debris almost ankle-deep on the slimy floor, and with hideous reptilian abnormalities spouting, bubbling, and baking over a winking bluish-green spectre of dim flame in a far corner of black shadows.

Like Crawford Tillinghast of "From Beyond," Herbert West is one more representative of the already hackneyed mad scientist. Lovecraft would later refine this trope considerably by introducing learned men of science whose inventions or researches unwittingly release hideous monstrosities that threaten the very fabric of the universe; but here we are on a very much lower level.

Also like "From Beyond," "Herbert West—Reanimator" introduces philosophical conceptions close to Lovecraft's own beliefs, even if at times flippantly. West believes "with Haeckel that all life is a chemical and physical process, and that the so-called 'soul' is a myth"; as such, his attempts to reanimate the dead are—since the distinction between living and dead matter is not regarded as at all absolute in mechanistic materialism—theoretically possible. Toward the end, however, this idea is taken to such absurd extremes that parody must again be suspected. West, having clearly succeeded—after a fashion—in proving the truth of his mechanistic theories by reanimating the dead, now ventures further:

> He had wild and original ideas on the independent vital properties of organic cells and nerve-tissue separated from natural physiological systems...Two biological points he was exceedingly anxious to settle—first, whether any amount of consciousness and rational action be possible without the brain, proceeding from the spinal cord and various nerve-centres; and second, whether any kind of ethereal, intangible relation distinct from the material cells may exist to link the surgically separated parts of what has previously been a single living organism.

This latter idea is, of course, an utter contradiction of materialism, and is something Lovecraft himself would never have countenanced.

There is topographical realism of a kind in one or two of the episodes. Five of the six segments are set, nominally, in New England—either in imaginary Arkham or the very real, if tiny and obscure, town of Bolton, Massachusetts. It cannot be said that there is much genuine evocation of the landscape in any of these episodes, but the second one offers an interesting sociological aside. Dr. Allan Halsey, dean of the medical school, is branded as a "product of generations of pathetic Puritanism" whose "intellectual sins" include "Ptolemaism, Calvinism, anti-Darwinism, anti-Nietzscheism, and every sort of Sabbatarianism and sumptuary legislation." All this is vaguely like Lovecraft's general complaints (especially in later life) of the social, political, and intellectual conservatism of old-time Yankees, and even brings to mind Lovecraft's remarks in *In Defence of Dagon* upon a reactionary article published in a 1915 issue of the *Atlantic Monthly*: "There is no real argument of importance in the harangue of the anonymous author, but the atmosphere of sorrow at the passing of the old illusions makes the whole complaint an absorbing human document."[22]

"Herbert West—Reanimator" has gained undesirable fame by serving as the basis for several lurid and equally self-parodic films by Stuart Gordon. It is, to be sure, not an utterly contemptible piece of work, and as humor it succeeds occasionally, perhaps better than Lovecraft knew. Its elementary tit-for-tat vengeance motif—all West's reanimated specimens come back to tear him to pieces and carry the fragments of his body off to some nameless charnel gulf—is a little less than inspiring, even if intended comically, and no one should judge Lovecraft on the basis of this one tale; but Lovecraft has certainly written worse.

"The Lurking Fear" (1922) can also be considered as fostering regionalism, even though it returns to the Catskill mountains that had served as the setting of "Beyond the Wall of Sleep"—a region that Lovecraft never saw at first hand. And yet, the sense of the reality of Tempest Mountain and the neighboring areas is very evident. This story—the second and, mercifully, the last serial tale written for Houtain's *Home Brew*, which folded shortly after "The Lurking Fear" appeared there—suffers, like its predecessor, from the requirement of a startling climax at the end of each of the four episodes; but there is at least some advance in technique in the absence of awkward repetitions and in a greater sense of overall unity. This tale too can be read as partially a self-parody, especially at the end when Lovecraft unleashes a wild, flamboyant prose-poetry that brings the story to a suitably demoniacal climax; but, like "The Hound," these histrionics somehow work to create an effect that many seem to regard as prototypically "Lovecraftian."

"The Lurking Fear"[23] introduces more of a mystery element than we have seen in earlier tales. In attempting to ascertain why "Fear had lurked on Tempest Mountain for more than a century," and how to account for a recent tragedy in which dozens of ignorant squatters in the region had been killed by a creature whom the denizens can only label a demon and which seems somehow to be connected with the evilly reputed Martense mansion at the summit of the mountain, the narrator acts as a virtual detective in sifting through evidence and forming theories. He discusses the matter with a colleague, Arthur Munroe:

> We did...deem ourselves justified in assuming that it was a living organism highly susceptible to electrical storms; and although certain of the stories suggested wings, we believed that its aversion for open spaces made land locomotion a more probable theory. The only thing really incompatible with the latter view was the rapidity with which the creature must have travelled in order to perform all the deeds attributed to it.

It is that "incompatible" bit of evidence that finally leads the narrator to understand the truth after further investigation: the entire mountain is riddled with tunnels that house not one creature but an entire race of hideous, apelike entities—the degenerate offspring of generations of inbreeding by the Martense family.

The narrator finally pieces the entire puzzle together by means of historical research. With strange poignancy he utters at one point:

"History, indeed, was all I had after everything else ended in mocking Satanism." This makes one think of a much later utterance in a letter: "The past is *real*—it is *all there is*."[24] This notion of understanding the past in order to come to terms with the present is a vital motif in much of Lovecraft's fiction, and its introduction in the third segment of "The Lurking Fear" gives that tale an importance that redeems many of its other flaws. The narrator has come to realize that the history of the Martense clan, from the late seventeenth century to the present, is a central clue to the solution of the mystery of Tempest Mountain, and this segment is narrated with that sober, scientific air which will become increasingly evident in Lovecraft's later tales.

And yet, like "The Hound," "The Lurking Fear" provides abundant pleasures of a lesser variety in its deliberately unrestrained prose. Who but Lovecraft could have written the following?

> Shrieking, slithering, torrential shadows of red viscous madness chasing one another through endless, ensanguined corridors of purple fulgurous sky... formless phantasms and kaleidoscopic mutations of a ghoulish, remembered scene; forests of monstrous overnourished oaks with serpent roots twisting and sucking unnamable juices from an earth verminous with millions of cannibal devils; mound-like tentacles groping from underground nuclei of polypous perversion...insane lightning over malignant ivied walls and daemon arcades choked with fungous vegetation....

Later the narrator piquantly takes care to "destroy certain overnourished trees whose very existence seemed an insult to sanity." Lovecraft has been roundly abused for this pull-out-all-the-stops prose; but such criticisms ignore the clear self-parody of many such passages. One should merely let this wave of imagery and language wash over one, keeping in mind that Lovecraft always reserves such tableaux for the critical climactic scenes of his tales and unfailingly prepares the reader emotionally for them by a careful and atmospheric build-up that in later works extends over the length of an entire novelette or short novel.

Less than a year after finishing "The Lurking Fear" Lovecraft wrote "The Rats in the Walls" (1923), and the exponential leap in quality is staggering. It is clearly the best of Lovecraft's fictional works prior to 1926; and in its rich texture, complexity of theme, and absolute perfection of short-story technique it need not fear comparison even with "The Fall of the House of Usher" or any other of Poe's masterpieces.

The plot of "The Rats in the Walls"[25] is deceptively simple. A Virginian of British ancestry, Walter Delapore, decides to spend his latter years in refurbishing and occupying his ancestral estate in southern England, Exham Priory, whose foundations go disturbingly far back in time, to a period even before the Roman conquest of the first century A.D. Delapore spares no expense in the restoration, and proudly moves into his estate on July 16, 1923. He has reverted to the ancestral spelling of his name, de la Poer, in spite of the fact that the family has a very unsavory reputation with the local population—a reputation for murder, kidnapping, witchcraft, and other anomalies extending back to the first Baron Exham in 1261. Associated with the house or the family is the "dramatic epic of the rats—the lean, filthy, ravenous army which had swept all before it and devoured fowl, cats, dogs, hogs, sheep, and even two hapless human beings before its fury was spent."

All this seems merely conventional ghostly legendry, and de la Poer pays no attention to it. But shortly after his occupancy of Exham Priory, odd things begin to happen; in particular, he and his several cats seem to detect the scurrying of rats in the walls of the structure, even though such a thing is absurd in light of the centuries-long desertion of the place. The scurrying seems to be descending to the basement of the edifice, and one night de la Poer and his friend, Capt. Edward Norrys, spend a night there to see if they can elucidate the mystery. De la Poer wakes to hear the scurrying of the rats continuing "*still downward*, far underneath this deepest of sub-cellars," but Norrys hears nothing. They come upon a trap-door leading to a cavern beneath the basement, and decide to call in scientific specialists to investigate the matter. As they descend into the nighted crypt, they come upon an awesome and horrific sight—an enormous expanse of bones: "Like a foamy sea they stretched, some fallen apart, but others wholly or partly articulated as skeletons; these latter invariably in postures of daemoniac frenzy, either fighting off some menace or clutching some other forms with cannibal intent." When de la Poer finds that some bones have rings bearing his own coat of arms, he realizes the truth—his family has been the leaders of an ancient cannibalistic witch-cult that had its origins in primitive times—and he experiences a spectacular evolutionary reversal:

> Curse you, Thornton, I'll teach you to faint at what my family do!...'Sblood, thou stinkard, I'll learn ye how to gust...wolde ye swynke me thilke wys?... *magna Mater! Magna Mater!...Atys...Dia ad aghaidh 's ad aodann...agus bas dunach ort! Dhonas 's dholas ort, agus leat-sa!...Ungl...ungl...rrrlh... chchch...*

He is found bending over the half-eaten form of Capt. Norrys.

Many of the surface details of this story are taken from other works. The Gaelic portions of Delapore's concluding cries ("*Dia ad aghaidh...*") are cribbed from Fiona Macleod's superb story, "The Sin-Eater" (which Lovecraft read in Joseph Lewis French's 1920 anthology, *The Best Psychic Stories*); while some of the legendry about rats and other features are derived from S. Baring-Gould's compilation *Curious Myths of the Middle Ages* (1869).[26] And yet, "The Rats in the Walls" is one of many stories that demonstrates how fundamentally original and dynamic in theme and conception Lovecraft's stories remain even when many superficial points owe their origin to external sources.

The central theme of the story—hereditary degeneration—is found in much of Lovecraft's fiction, and it achieves its apogee here. We have already seen how the past can reach out and affect the present in the cases of psychic possession by an ancestor in "The Tomb" and "Polaris"; more pertinently, degeneration caused by unwholesome inbreeding is the source of horror in "The Lurking Fear," while miscegenation is the focus of "Arthur Jermyn" and, later, "The Shadow over Innsmouth" (1931). Here we have a case of pure atavism: de la Poer (who unwittingly anticipates his reversion to type by the resumption of the ancestral spelling of his name) has the blood of his cannibal ancestors in him, even though the scientific sobriety of the first three-quarters of his narrative seeks to convince us—and himself—otherwise; but the final confronting of the inescapable truth of his ancestors' practices causes an instant reversion to primitive apedom.

What is remarkable about "The Rats in the Walls" is its convincing portrayal of vast gulfs of history in a narrative about 8000 words in length. Later tales such as *At the Mountains of Madness* (1931) and "The Shadow out of Time" (1934-1935) will utilize tens of thousands of words to suggest the passing of countless millennia, but "The Rats in the Walls" performs the feat by the use of simple rhetorical devices such as polysyndeton, or reduplication of conjunctions ("...trying to keep for the nonce from thinking of the events which must have taken place there three hundred, or a thousand, or two thousand, or ten thousand years ago"), spectacular analogies ("huge stone bins older than Rome"), and the marshalling of scientific terms ("Those nightmare chasms choked with the pithecanthropoid, Celtic, Roman, and English bones of countless unhallowed centuries!"). Indeed, the condensation of historical time is not merely a rhetorical device but the central theme of the entire story.

Lovecraft the Anglophile captures the English setting of the tale with notable felicity, although with some puzzling errors. The town nearest to Exham Priory is given as Anchester, but there is no such town in England. Lovecraft must have been thinking either of Ancaster in Lincolnshire or (more likely) Alchester in the southern county of Oxfordshire. Perhaps this is a deliberate alteration; but then, what do we make of the statement that "Anchester had been the camp of the Third Augustan Legion"? Neither Alchester nor Ancaster were the sites of legionary fortresses in Roman Britain; what is more, the Third

Augustan Legion was never in England at all, and it was the Second Augustan Legion that was stationed at Isca Silurum (Caerleon-on-Usk) in what is now Wales. This is a strange error for Lovecraft to have made, and he repeats it in the fragment "The Descendant" (1926?).[27] Even if this is a deliberate change, it is too clearly at variance with the known facts to be plausible.

Criticism has been directed to the unlikelihood of the first-person narrator de la Poer's soberly erudite tone at the beginning and his increasing frenzy at the end, since all the facts of the case are being presented as a flashback while de la Poer is in a lunatic asylum. This device is common in Lovecraft's first-person narratives, which are almost always being told after the fact; but the criticism seems excessively pedantic. It could even be thought that de la Poer's very deliberate air of scientific or historical verisimilitude ("Exham Priory had remained untenanted, though later allotted to the estates of the Norrys family and much studied because of its peculiarly composite architecture") is a psychological defense-mechanism whereby he is attempting to shield himself from the truth of the loathsome acts he commits at the end of the narrative. The psychological acuity of the portrayal of de la Poer is singular for Lovecraft, and we feel a keen sense of pathos mingled with horror as we watch his pitiable decline into atavistic madness.

"The Unnamable" and "The Festival," Lovecraft's two other original stories of 1923, return to New England in their different ways. The former is a very slight tale, but could be thought of as a sort of veiled justification for the type of weird tale he was at this time evolving; much of it, in fact, reads like a treatise on aesthetics. It has gone relatively unnoticed that "The Unnamable"[28] is the second story to involve Randolph Carter, even though he is referred to only once as "Carter." The tale takes place in an "old burying ground" in Arkham, where Carter and his friend Joel Manton (clearly based upon Lovecraft's friend Maurice W. Moe) are discussing the horror tales that Carter has written. Through Manton, Lovecraft satirizes the stolid bourgeois objections to the weird—as contrary to probability, as not based on "realism," as extravagant and unrelated to life—that he no doubt received on many occasions in the amateur press, as for instance in the responses to his work in the Transatlantic Circulator of 1921 (which led to the first coherent enunciation of his theory of the weird in the *In Defence of Dagon* papers). The narrator paraphrases Manton's views:

> It was his view that only our normal, objective experiences possess any aesthetic significance, and that it is the province of the artist not so much to rouse strong emotion by action, ecstasy, and astonishment, as to maintain a placid interest and appreciation by accurate, detailed transcripts of every-day affairs.

This, and the rest of the passage, testify to Lovecraft's absorption of Decadent aesthetics and his revulsion from Victorian standards of mundane realism. The mention of "ecstasy" may reflect his reading, around this time, of Arthur Machen's treatise on aesthetics, *Hieroglyphics: A Note upon Ecstasy in Literature* (1902), which, although not accepting it in its entirety, he found stimulating in its championing of literature that frees itself from the commonplace. Manton's objection to supernaturalism in literature, in spite of the fact that he "believ[es] in the supernatural much more fully than I," is a snide reference to Maurice W. Moe's theism: anyone who believes in an omnipotent God and in the divinity of Jesus Christ can scarcely object to the depiction of the supernatural in fiction! More seriously, the passage suggests Lovecraft's later awareness (in a letter already quoted in the opening chapter) that the aesthetic acceptance of the supernatural in fiction is much more preferable to the intellectual acceptance of the supernatural in religion. The rest of "The Unnamable"—in which Manton scoffs at the very idea of something being termed "unnamable" but later encounters just such an entity in the burying ground—does not require much comment.

Aside from its interesting aesthetic reflections, "The Unnamable" fosters that sense of the lurking horror of New England history and topography which we have already seen in "The Picture in the House," and which would become a dominant topos in Lovecraft's later work. The tale is set in Arkham, but the actual inspiration for the setting—a "dilapidated seventeenth-century tomb" and, nearby, a "giant willow in the centre of the cemetery, whose trunk has nearly engulfed an ancient, illegible slab"—is the Charter Street Burying Ground in Salem, where just such a tree-engulfed slab can be found. This itself is a little anomalous, in its suggestion that Arkham is to be identified with Salem, an identification that did not genuinely occur until around 1931. Later in the story Lovecraft records various "old-wives' superstitions," some of which are taken from Cotton Mather's *Magnalia Christi Americana* (1702), of which he owned an ancestral first edition. As in "The Picture in the House," Lovecraft's attempt to find horror in the seventeenth century is manifest: "...no wonder sensitive students shudder at the Puritan age in Massachusetts. So little is known of what went on beneath the surface—so little, yet such a ghastly festering as it bubbles up putrescently in occasional ghoulish glimpses."

One of those glimpses is presented in "The Festival" (1923),[29] which for the sustained modulation of its prose can be ranked as a virtual 3000-word prose-poem. It is well known that the tale was ultimately inspired by Lovecraft's visit to Marblehead in December 1922, although it is a little odd that it took nearly a year (and several further trips there) for his impressions to solidify in the form of a weird tale. Marblehead was—and, in large part, still is—an exquisite haven of colonial antiquity, and no one need wonder at Lovecraft's raptures at stumbling upon by accident in the late afternoon snow:

> I came to Marblehead in the twilight, and gazed long upon its hoary magick. I threaded the tortuous, precipitous streets, some of which an horse can scarce climb, and in which two waggons cannot pass. I talked with old men and revell'd in old scenes, and climb'd pantingly over the crusted cliffs of snow to the windswept height where cold winds blew over desolate roofs and evil birds hovered over a bleak, deserted, frozen tarn. And atop all was the peak; Old Burying Hill, where the dark headstones clawed up thro' the virgin snow like the decay'd fingernails of some gigantick corpse.
>
> Immemorial pinnacle of fabulous antiquity!... How compleatly, O Mater Novanglia, am I moulded of thy venerable flesh and as one with thy century'd soul![30]

The fact that, years later, he would still refer to his first sight of Marblehead as "the most powerful single emotional climax experienced during my nearly forty years of existence"[31] attests to the imperishable impression it made on him—it was as if he had gone back in time, and thereby momentarily achieved exactly that "illusion of some strange suspension or violation of the galling limitations of time, space, and natural law" which he later stated in "Notes on Writing Weird Fiction" to be his desideratum in fiction.

Although it is only in "The Festival" that the mythical town of Kingsport (first cited in "The Terrible Old Man") is definitively identified with Marblehead, Lovecraft makes it clear that the seventeenth-century past is not in fact the true source of horror in the tale; in rhythmical, alliterative prose Lovecraft suggests a horror of much older lineage: "It was the Yuletide, that men call Christmas though they know in their hearts it is older than Bethlehem and Babylon, older than Memphis and mankind." The Christian holiday is a mere veneer for a much older festival that reaches back to the agricultural rhythms of primitive man—the winter solstice, whose passing foretells the eventual reawakening of the earth in spring.

The narrator follows a course along the old town that can be traversed to this day. He passes by the old cemetery on the hill, where (in a literal borrowing from his letter of nearly a year previous) "black gravestones stuck ghoulishly through the snow like the decayed fingernails of a gigantic corpse," and makes his way to a house with an overhanging second story (a house clearly identifiable in the central square of Marblehead). There he encounters the past embodied in both furnishings and inhabitants:

> He beckoned me into a low, candle-lit room with massive exposed rafters and dark, stiff, sparse furniture of the seventeenth century. The past was vivid there, for not an attribute was missing. There was a cavernous fireplace and a spinning-wheel at which a bent old woman in loose wrapper and deep poke-bonnet sat back toward me, silently spinning despite the festive season.

For Lovecraft, the eighteenth-century rationalist, the seventeenth century in Massachusetts—dominated by the Puritans' rigid religion, bereft of the sprightliness of the Augustan wits, and culminating in the psychotic horror of the Salem witchcraft trials—represented an American "Dark Age" fully as horrifying as the early medieval period in Europe he so despised. Religion—seen by Lovecraft as the overwhelming of the intellect by emotion, childish wish-fulfilment, and millennia of pernicious brainwashing—proves to be the source of terror in "The Festival," whose culminating scene occurs in what is in reality an exquisite early eighteenth-century church in Marblehead (St. Michael's Episcopal Church in Frog Lane). But Lovecraft sees this Christian edifice as a mere façade for rituals of much older provenance; and when the band of townspeople descend robotically down a "trap-door of the vaults which yawned loathsomely open just before the pulpit," we can see both a relationship to "The Rats in the Walls" (where also a physical descent symbolizes a descent into the archaic past) and an indication of the superficiality of Christianity's formalization of primitive festivals from the depths of prehistory.

The conclusion of "The Festival"—marred by the luridness of grotesque winged creatures who carry off each of the celebrants on their backs—is not commensurate with its mesmeric opening and middle sections; but its evocation of the centuried past, in prose as fluid, restrained, and throbbingly vital as Lovecraft ever wrote, will always give this tale a high place amongst his lesser works.

Lovecraft's move to New York in the spring of 1924 did not put an immediate end to what might be called the Novanglicization of his fictional work. Lovecraft wrote only five stories during his two years in New York, three of them in a period of six weeks in August and September 1925; of these five, three are indeed set in New York, but the other two return to New England for their locales. That Lovecraft did not write more fiction in this period is not surprising: his time was largely occupied with bootless attempts at finding work, weekly meetings of the Kalem Club and many other day, evening, or sometimes all-night sessions with his "gang" of friends, voluminous letters to his aunts, research on "Supernatural Horror in Literature," amateur affairs, and other matters—not to mention intermittent gestures at being a husband, a difficult task for the lifelong bachelor Lovecraft, especially in light of Sonia's breakdowns in health.

Nevertheless, the first story of his New York period, "The Shunned House" (1924),[32] reverts to Providence for its setting. There is an obvious psychological explanation for this—if he could not be in Providence in person, he could at least be there for the duration of a tale—and indeed "The Shunned House" is the first story to draw upon the history rather than merely the topography of Providence. The tale—based upon the same house at 135 Benefit Street which had served as the inspiration for the poem "The House" (1919), and in which his aunt Lillian Clark had briefly resided—becomes somewhat bogged down in the chronicling of the Harris family over the generations, as the narrator and his uncle Elihu Whipple (clearly modelled upon Lovecraft's own beloved uncle, Dr. Franklin Chase Clark) attempt to account for the peculiar number of deaths in the house. They are very anxious to make clear that "the house was never regarded by the solid part of the community as in any real sense 'haunted'," as if in this way Lovecraft could avoid the suggestion that his story was merely a conventional "haunted house" tale. It is, indeed, not that, for no ghost or other such figure from hackneyed spectral lore appears; and when the creature causing the deaths is finally identified as a sort of psychic vampire, the justification for such a seemingly stereotyped spook is highly significant in terms of Lovecraft's own evolving conception of weird fiction:

> We were not...in any sense childishly superstitious, but scientific study and reflection had taught us that the known universe of three dimensions embraces the merest fraction of the whole cosmos of substance and energy. In this case an overwhelming preponderance of evidence from numerous authentic sources pointed to the tenacious existence of certain forces of great power and, so far as the human point of view is concerned, exceptional malignancy. To say that we actually believed in vampires or werewolves would be a carelessly inclusive statement. Rather must it be said that we were not prepared to deny the possibility of certain unfamiliar and unclassified modifications of vital force and attenuated matter; existing very infrequently in three-dimensional space because of its more intimate connexion with other spatial units, yet close enough to the boundary of our own to furnish us occasional manifestations which we, for lack of a proper vantage-point, may never hope to understand....
>
> Such a thing was surely not a physical or biochemical impossibility in the light of a newer science

> which includes the theories of relativity and intra-atomic action....

This is one of the most critical passages in Lovecraft's early tales; for it embodies virtually all the conceptions we will find in letters of the 1930s enunciating his later aesthetic of the weird as "images forming *supplements* rather than *contradictions* of the visible and mensurable universe."[33] In this sense, "The Shunned House"—despite its evocation of the centuries-old history of Providence—may be thought of as Lovecraft's first authentic science fiction story, in its attempt to account for the anomalous creature in terms of advanced science rather than primitive myth. The fact that the entity is dispatched by the use of sulphuric acid rather than a stake through the heart emphasizes this point.

"The Shunned House" is itself, however, not entirely satisfying as a tale; its historical section is dry and long-winded, and its conclusion, in which the vampire is destroyed by acid and utters a "hideous roar" (a scenario which may or may not have been inspired by Arthur Conan Doyle's "When the World Screamed"), borders upon the bathetic. But as an evocation of Lovecraft's home town it offers a foretaste of the much greater capturing of Providence history in *The Case of Charles Dexter Ward*.

By August of 1925 Lovecraft—having lived for seven months in a dingy one-room apartment in a run-down section of Brooklyn—could no longer shield himself from the grinding realities of New York, and he felt compelled to express his loathing of the city in the form of fiction. He states explicitly to Frank Belknap Long, a lifelong New Yorker, that "The Horror at Red Hook" "represents at least an attempt to extract horror from an atmosphere to which you deny any qualities save vulgar commonplaceness"[34]—a remark that makes clear that the topographical and social conditions of his environment were becoming increasingly important sources for his weird tales.

And yet, "The Horror at Red Hook"[35] is one of Lovecraft's great failures. This tale of the horrors that a police detective, Thomas Malone, finds in the seedy Red Hook section of Brooklyn is little more than a tired rehash of hackneyed demonology and a viciously racist story that transmogrifies the immigrants of the area into the members of an evil cult on the underside of American civilization seeking to overthrow the pure-blooded and pure-minded white citizens to whom this territory supposedly belongs. Lovecraft portrays the social landscape in clearly racial terms:

> Red Hook is a maze of hybrid squalor near the ancient waterfront opposite Governor's Island...The population is a hopeless tangle and enigma; Syrian, Spanish, Italian, and negro elements impinging upon one an-

> other, and fragments of Scandinavian and American belts lying not far distant.

The loaded terms "hybrid squalor" and "hopeless tangle and enigma" suggest that the very process of racial integration is an abomination; and the most curious feature is the mention of "American belts," since even Lovecraft cannot fail to be aware that white Americans are, by and large, the most "hybrid" of all individuals. From this perspective, the figure of Robert Suydam—an aristocrat of old Dutch ancestry who appears to be the leader of the motley gang of foreigners—is of the greatest importance: he is a traitor both to his class and to his race, for as a high-born member of the civilization that originally colonized the area he has no business "loitering on the benches around Borough Hall in conversation with groups of swarthy, evil-looking strangers."

Craftily, Suydam comes to realize that his clandestine activities must be masked by a façade of propriety; so he cleans up his act, foils the attempts of relatives to deem him legally incompetent by ceasing to be seen around those evil foreigners, and as a final coup marries Cornelia Gerritsen, "a young woman of excellent position" whose wedding attracts "a solid page from the Social Register." In all this there is a rather tart satire (entirely unintended by Lovecraft) on the meaninglessness of class distinctions. The wedding party following the ceremony, held aboard a steamer at the Cunard Pier, ends in horror as the couple are found horribly murdered and completely bloodless. Incredibly, officials follow the instructions written on a sheet of paper, signed by Suydam, and insouciantly hand his body over to a suspicious group of men headed by "an Arab with a hatefully negroid mouth."

From here the story takes a still more pulpish turn, and we are taken into the basement of a dilapidated church that has been turned into a dance-hall, where horrible rites to Lilith are being practised by loathsome monstrosities. The corpse of Suydam, miraculously revivified, resists being sacrificed to Lilith but instead somehow manages to overturn the pedestal on which she rests (with the result that the corpse sends "its noisome bulk floundering to the floor in a state of jellyish dissolution"), thereby somehow ending the horror. All this time detective Malone merely watches from a convenient vantage-point, although the sight so traumatizes him that he is forced to spend many months recuperating in a small village in Rhode Island.

Such is the tale, one of the clearest instances of the deleterious effect on Lovecraft's writing a tale with *Weird Tales* manifestly in mind. Much of the magical mumbo-jumbo was copied wholesale from the articles on "Magic" and "Demonology" from the 9th edition of the *Encyclopaedia Britannica*, which Lovecraft owned; in a later letter he attempts to supply a translation of the Graeco-Hebraic formula, committing embarrassing errors in the process.[36] Even the perfervid rhetoric which in other tales provides such harmless enjoyment here comes off sounding forced and bombastic:

> Here cosmic sin had entered, and festered by unhallowed rites had commenced the grinning march of death that was to rot us all to fungous abnormalities too hideous for the grave's holding. Satan here held his Babylonish court, and in the blood of stainless childhood the leprous limbs of phosphorescent Lilith were laved.

How the atheist Lovecraft could provide a satisfactory explanation for "cosmic sin" and the presence of Satan would be an interesting question; and the burden of this passage, as of the story as a whole, is the dread of being overwhelmed and "mongrelised" by those foreigners who by some miracle are increasingly ousting all the sturdy Anglo-Saxons who founded this great white nation of ours. Lovecraft cannot help ending the story on a note of dour ponderousness ("The soul of the beast is omnipresent and triumphant"), and with a transparent indication that the horrors that were seemingly suppressed by the police raid will recur at some later date: the final scene shows Malone overhearing a "swarthy squinting hag" indoctrinating a small child in the same incantation he heard earlier in the tale. It is a fittingly stereotyped ending for a story that does nothing but deal in stereotypes—both of race and of weird fictional imagery.

"He,"[37] the story Lovecraft wrote only ten days after "The Horror at Red Hook," is a rather different proposition. Although marred by the same sort of lurid conclusion that spoils "The Festival," it much more effectively conveys Lovecraft's feelings for New York because it is so clearly personal and heart-felt. Lovecraft told Donald Wandrei bluntly: "If you want to know what I think of New York, read 'He'."[38] How can an autobiographical interpetation of the poignant opening be resisted?

> My coming to New York had been a mistake; for whereas I had looked for poignant wonder and inspiration in the teeming labyrinths of ancient streets that twist endlessly from forgotten courts and squares and waterfronts to courts and squares and waterfronts equally forgotten, and in the Cyclopean modern towers and pinnacles that rise blackly Babylonian under waning moons, I had found instead only a sense of horror and oppression which threatened to master, paralyse, and annihilate me.... [But I] still refrained from going home to my people lest I seem to crawl black ignobly in defeat.

One wonders how Sonia reacted to that first line.

The narrator—like Lovecraft himself throughout his New York period—seeks to banish the dreariness of the city, with its "squat, swarthy strangers with hardened faces and narrow eyes," by seeking the few antiquarian havens not overwhelmed by the "noxious elephantiasis of climbing, spreading stone," especially in the Greenwich Village section of lower Manhattan. On one such excursion the narrator encounters an elderly man who claims to be able to show him much more obscure wonders of the past than are commonly known. Much of the journey taken by the narrator and his antiquated companion can be followed today (the inner courtyard where the climax of the tale occurs can be clearly identified as one existing at 93 Perry Street), but it is of vital importance to Lovecraft's purpose that at some point the trail should become cloudy and mysterious:

> ...we squeezed through interstices, tiptoed through corridors, clambered over brick walls, and once crawled on hands and knees through a low, arched passage of stone whose immense length and tortuous twistings effaced at last every hint of geographical location I had managed to preserve.

In this way is effected a transition from the known to the unknown—which, in Lovecraft, is so often equivalent to a transition from the present to the past. Once the threshold separating reality from fantasy, from the streets of a geographically precise area to the labyrinths of a land of wonder, is crossed, anything can happen.

The leader makes his way to a private estate where he apparently dwells, an estate that seems to have escaped the ravages of time. And when the man reveals himself ("in full mid-Georgian costume from queued hair and neck ruffles to knee-breeches, silk hose, and the buckled shoes I had not previously noticed"), he seems perhaps a harmless eccentric, but one who likewise has managed to shield himself from the present. His speech—full of those archaic terms that Lovecraft himself so loved to utilize in some of his articles and letters, and which he learned from a lifetime of readings in eighteenth-century literature—again seems innocuously quaint; but things take a different turn when he tells the story of his "ancestor" who "'flouted the sanctity of things as great as space and time, and...put to strange uses the rites of sartain half-breed red Indians once encamped upon this hill'." He then leads the narrator to a window, where in a succession of fantastic visions he reveals glimpses of past and future New York. The latter is cataclysmic:

> I saw the heavens verminous with strange flying things, and beneath them a hellish black city of giant

> stone terraces with impious pyramids flung savagely to the moon, and devil-lights burning from unnumbered windows. And swarming loathsomely on aërial galleries I saw the yellow, squint-eyed people of that city, robed horribly in orange and red, and dancing insanely to the pounding of fevered kettle-drums, the clatter of obscene crotala, and the maniacal moaning of muted horns whose ceaseless dirges rose and fell undulantly like the waves of an unhallowed ocean of bitumen.

Note those "yellow, squint-eyed people": Maurice Lévy's nasty pun, "Evil is embodied only by coloured people,"[39] once again lays bare Lovecraft's racism. But, although this scene at the window is very likely derived from an analogous scene in Dunsany's *The Chronicles of Rodriguez* (1922),[40] it is an effective depiction of the frenzied future that we are now ourselves experiencing. Lovecraft should have ended the story here rather than tacking on a ridiculous conclusion wherein ghosts of those Indians whom the eighteenth-century squire killed come to destroy him hideously; but the imagery of a future gone mad nevertheless remains potent. And the very final scene—where the narrator, who has managed to survive the experience, reports that he has now "gone home to the pure New England lanes up which fragrant sea-winds sweet at evening"—is as unmistakable an instance of wish-fulfilment as one is likely to find.

"Cool Air,"[41] written probably in February 1926, is the last and perhaps the best of Lovecraft's New York stories. Set in the brownstone at 317 West 14th Street where Lovecraft's friend George Kirk had his bookshop and residence,[42] the tale is a compact exposition of pure physical loathsomeness. The narrator, having "secured some dreary and unprofitable magazine work" in the spring of 1923, finds himself in a run-down boarding-house whose landlady is a "slatternly, almost bearded Spanish woman named Herrero" (in fact, Lovecraft's Clinton Street landlady was Mrs. Burns, an Irishwoman) and occupied generally by low-life except for one Dr. Muñoz, a cultivated and intelligent retired medical man who is continually experimenting with chemicals and indulges in the eccentricity of keeping his room at a temperature of about 55° by means of an ammonia cooling system. The narrator is impressed by Muñoz:

> The figure before me was short but exquisitely proportioned, and clad in somewhat formal dress of perfect cut and fit. A high-bred face of masterful though not arrogant expression was adorned by a short iron-grey full beard, and an old-fashioned pince-nez shielded the full, dark eyes and surmounted an

> aquiline nose which gave a Moorish touch to a physiognomy otherwise dominantly Celtiberian. Thick, well-trimmed hair that argued the punctual calls of a barber was parted gracefully above a high forehead; and the whole picture was one of striking intelligence and superior blood and breeding.

Muñoz, clearly, embodies Lovecraft's ideal type: a man who belongs both to the aristocracy of blood and the aristocracy of intellect; who is highly learned in his field but also dresses well. We are, therefore, meant to sympathize wholly with Muñoz's plight, especially as he is clearly suffering from the effects of some horrible malady that struck him eighteen years ago. When, weeks later, his ammonia cooling system fails, the narrator undertakes a frantic effort to fix it, at the same time enlisting "a seedy-looking loafer" to keep the doctor supplied with the ice that he repeatedly demands in ever-larger amounts. But it is to no avail: when the narrator finally returns from his quest to find air-conditioner repairmen, the boarding-house is in turmoil; and when he enters the room, he sees a "kind of dark, slimy trail [that] led from the open bathroom to the hall door" and that "ended unutterably." In fact, Muñoz died eighteen years before and had been attempting to keep himself functioning by artificial preservation.

There are no transcendent philosophical issues raised by "Cool Air," but some of the gruesome touches are uncommonly fine. When at one point Muñoz experiences a "spasm [that] caused him to clap his hands to his eyes and rush into the bathroom," we are clearly to understand that his excitement has caused his eyes nearly to pop out of his head. There is, to be sure, a perhaps deliberate undercurrent of the comic in the whole story, especially when Muñoz, now holed up in a bathtub full of ice, cries through his bathroom door, "More—more!"

Interestingly, Lovecraft later admitted that the chief inspiration for the tale was not Poe's "Facts in the Case of M. Valdemar" but Machen's "The Novel of the White Powder,"[43] where a hapless student unwittingly takes a drug that reduces him to "a dark and putrid mass, seething with corruption and hideous rottenness, neither liquid nor solid, but melting and changing before our eyes, and bubbling with unctuous oily bubbles like boiling pitch."[44] And yet, one can hardly deny that M. Valdemar, the man who is kept alive for months by hypnosis and who collapses "in a nearly liquid mass of loathsome—of detestable putridity,"[45] was somewhere in the back of Lovecraft's mind in the writing of "Cool Air." This story, much more than "The Horror at Red Hook," is Lovecraft's most successful evocation of the horror to be found in the teeming clangor of America's only true megalopolis.

In September 1925 Lovecraft returned to New England in a brief and insignificant tale, "In the Vault,"[46] whose central situation was suggested by Lovecraft's amateur colleague C. W. Smith, editor of the *Tryout*. This entirely unmemorable story—inexplicably included by August Derleth in Lovecraft's *Best Supernatural Stories* (1945) and accordingly embalmed amongst much greater tales—is the simple account of a careless village undertaker, George Birch, who decides to economize on coffins by cutting off the ankles of an evil but tall individual named Asaph Sawyer and cramming the body into a coffin originally designed for the diminutive Matthew Fenner. But when Birch finds himself trapped in the receiving-tomb one spring night and is forced to erect a pyramid of coffins to escape through the transom, his feet collapse through the topmost coffin and his ankles suffer curious but severe injuries: they exhibit teeth-marks whose source is unmistakably the corpse of Asaph Sawyer.

This childishly simple-minded vengeance tale (one character even notes platitudinously, "An eye for an eye!") is wholly unredeemed by virtues of style, conception, or atmosphere. The strangely flat, clumsily cynical narrative tone is perhaps meant to recall Ambrose Bierce, as is the literal graveyard humor of the piece as a whole; but the story utilizes the supernatural revenge motif too obviously and uninterestingly to be in any way notable. Even the New England setting is not captured very efficaciously: in spite of the narrator's blunt declaration of a "bucolic Yankee setting" for the tale, we have few specific intimations of New England topographical or social features.

Indeed, "In the Vault" is not merely the last of Lovecraft's tales that is not based upon some quite precise New England location (that is, among those tales that are in fact set in New England), but virtually the last of his purely supernatural narratives. From this time on, Lovecraft would elaborate upon the suggestive hints found in "The Shunned House" and conceive of scenarios whose explicit supernaturalism is significantly qualified by appeals to advanced astrophysics and the high probability that very different natural laws exist in those gulfs of space to which we have no access. It would, however, require Lovecraft's ecstatic return to Providence in the spring of 1926, and his subsequent realization of the importance of his New England heritage to his psychological and aesthetic makeup, to effect the much deeper probings into New England landscape, society, and history that we find in the tales of his final decade.

For now, the tales of this period adequately display Lovecraft's sensitivity to his environment, whether it be New England or New York. Increasingly abandoning English settings of which he had no first-hand knowledge (although managing even these more ably here—as in "The Rats in the Walls"—than in his earlier works), Lovecraft came more and more to adhere to that oldest of writers' adages: "Write what you know." Whether there was any specific event or influence that led him in this direction seems unlikely. Donald R. Burleson[47] points out that Lovecraft appears to have read the work of Nathaniel Hawthorne quite thoroughly around 1920, but Jason C. Eckhardt,[48] noting the relative absence of distinctive evocations of New England in Lovecraft's fiction between "The Picture in the House" (1920) and "The Festival" (1923), correctly doubts whether Hawthorne's example alone could have provided Lovecraft the impetus to draw upon his native heritage. Lovecraft's actual travels throughout New England only began in earnest in the 1921-1923 period, as did his investigations of New England history, architecture, and social customs. In any event, it is clear that he was gradually coming to realize the potentialities for horror inherent in the New England locale, and in later tales that horror would be inextricably mingled with a heartfelt love of the old traditions of the region that had given him birth and from which he throughout his life drew the strength to live.

V.

THE MAJOR FICTION: FIRST PHASE (1926-1930)

1. The Repudiation of Dunsanianism

Lovecraft's return from New York inspired a tremendous outburst of fiction-writing such as he never experienced before or since: within a period of six to eight months he wrote "The Call of Cthulhu" (1926), "Pickman's Model" (1926), "The Silver Key" (1926), "The Strange High House in the Mist" (1926), *The Dream-Quest of Unknown Kadath* (1926-1927), *The Case of Charles Dexter Ward* (1927), and "The Colour Out of Space" (1927). It is clear that Lovecraft's creative energies had been blocked by the atmosphere of New York and by his increasing depression and despair at being trapped—perhaps permanently—in the metropolis. Now that he had returned to the land of his birth, those energies were not only released but his work gained in depth, substance, and maturity. New York had not been all bad: it had been a painful experience, but one that made many things—about himself and about the world—clearer to Lovecraft. W. Paul Cook's memorable summation—"He had been tried in the fire and came out pure gold"[1]—is true in many more ways than one.

One of the ways in which Lovecraft's work and thought developed in tandem was in his attitude toward the fantastic. The Dunsanianism that was the hallmark of his 1919-1921 period appears to reemerge in a startling fashion in several tales of 1926, notably the dream-fantasy *The Dream-Quest of Unknown Kadath*; but when read closely, these tales in reality present a repudiation of Dunsanianism—or, more precisely, of what Lovecraft imagined Dunsany to represent. In the first flush of his discovery of Dunsany, Lovecraft revelled in what appeared to be the purely otherworldly quality in Irish writer's fiction—the invented gods, the imagined realms whose only metaphysic is Oscar Wilde's imperishable dictum, "The artist is the creator of beautiful things,"[2] the apparent scorn of the mundane and the ordinary. We have already seen that this is itself a misconstrual of Dunsany's true aims as a writer; but it led Lovecraft to abandon supernatural realism in those handful of tales we call "Dunsanian." And, as we have seen, this view affected his aesthetics as well; for, conjoined with his momentary

Decadent phase, Dunsanianism led Lovecraft to believe that the only way to salvage art in an age whose scientific discoveries have shattered so many previous illusions about life is to "take an Epicurean delight in those combinations of ideas and fancies which we know to be artificial," as he put it in "Lord Dunsany and His Work." For what, in Lovecraft's view, does Dunsany do?

> He creates a world which has never existed and never will exist, but which we have always known and longed for in dreams. This world he makes vivid not by pretending that it is real, but by exalting the quality of unreality and suffusing his whole dream-universe with a delicate pessimism drawn half from modern psychology and half from our ancestral northern myths of Ragnarok, the Twilight of the Gods.[3]

This is, as I say, not what Dunsany sought to do at all, but at this time it suited Lovecraft to think so. Returning home after two years spent in an alien environment made Lovecraft more aware than ever of his "roots" as a New England Yankee. *The Dream-Quest of Unknown Kadath* seems anything but an instantiation of this awareness, but it is exactly that.

It is scarcely worthwhile to pursue the rambling plot of this short novel, which in its continuous, chapterless meandering consciously resembles not only Dunsany (although Dunsany never wrote a long work exactly of this kind) but William Beckford's *Vathek* (1786); several points of plot and imagery also bring Beckford's Arabian fantasy to mind.[4] Lovecraft resurrects Randolph Carter, previously used in "The Statement of Randolph Carter" (1919) and "The Unnamable" (1923), in a quest through dreamland for his "sunset city," which is described as follows:

> All golden and lovely it blazed in the sunset, with walls, temples, colonnades, and arched bridges of veined marble, silver-basined fountains of prismatic spray in broad squares and perfumed gardens, and wide streets marching between delicate trees and blossom-laden urns and ivory statues in gleaming rows; while on steep northward slopes climbed tiers of red roofs and old peaked gables harbouring little lanes of grassy cobbles.[5]

This certainly sounds—except for some odd details at the end—like some Dunsanian realm of the imagination; but what, in fact, does Carter discover as he leaves his hometown of Boston to make a laborious excursion through dreamland to the throne of the Great Ones who dwell in an onyx castle on unknown Kadath? Nyarlathotep, the messenger of the gods, tells him in a passage as moving as any in Lovecraft:

> "For know you, that your gold and marble city of wonder is only the sum of what you have seen and loved in youth. It is the glory of Boston's hillside roofs and western windows aflame with sunset; of the flower-fragrant Common and the great dome on the hill and the tangle of gables and chimneys in the violet valley where the many-bridged Charles flows drowsily. These things you saw, Randolph Carter, when your nurse first wheeled you out in the springtime, and they will be the last things you will ever see with eyes of memory and of love....
>
> "These, Randolph Carter, are your city; for they are yourself. New-England bore you, and into your soul she poured a liquid loveliness which cannot die. This loveliness, moulded, crystallised, and polished by years of memory and dreaming, is your terraced wonder of elusive sunsets; and to find that marble parapet with curious urns and carven rail, and descend at last those endless balustraded steps to the city of broad squares and prismatic fountains, you need only to turn back to the thoughts and visions of your wistful boyhood."[6]

We suddenly realize why that "sunset city" contained such otherwise curious features as gables and cobblestoned lanes. And we also realize why it is that the various fantastic creatures Carter meets along his journey—gugs, ghasts, ghouls, moonbeasts, zoogs—touch no chord in us: they are not meant to. They are all very charming, in that "Dresden-china" way Lovecraft mistook Dunsany to be; but they amount to nothing because they do not correspond to anything in our memories and dreams. So all that Carter has to do—and what he does in fact do at the end—is merely to wake up in his Boston room, leave dreamland behind, and realize the beauty to be found on his doorstep:

> Birds sang in hidden gardens and the perfume of trellised vines came wistful from arbours his grandfather had reared. Beauty and light glowed from classic mantel and carven cornice and walls grotesquely figured, while a sleek black cat rose yawning from hearthside sleep that his master's start and shriek had disturbed.[7]

Carter's revelation is brilliantly prefigured in an earlier episode in which he meets King Kuranes, the protagonist of "Celephaïs" (1920). In that story Kuranes, a London writer, had dreamt as a child of the realm of Celephaïs, which is indeed a land of otherworldly beauty; at the end of the story his body dies but his spirit is somehow transported to the land of his dreams. Carter meets him in Celephaïs, but he finds that Kuranes is not quite as happy as he thought he would be:

> It seems that he could no more find content in those places, but had formed a mighty longing for the English cliffs and downlands of his boyhood, where in little dreaming villages England's old songs hover at evening behind lattice windows, and where grey church towers peep lovely through the verdure of distant valleys.... For though Kuranes was a monarch in the land of dream, with all imagined pomps and marvels, splendours and beauties, ecstasies and delights, novelties and excitements at his command, he would gladly have resigned forever the whole of his power and luxury and freedom for one blessed day as a simple boy in that pure and quiet England, that ancient, beloved England which had moulded his being and of which he must always be immutably a part.[8]

It has frequently been conjectured that *The Dream-Quest of Unknown Kadath* is the carrying out of Lovecraft's old novel idea "Azathoth" (1922); but while this may be true superficially in the sense that both works seem to center around protagonists venturing on a quest to some wondrous land, in reality the novel of 1926 presents a reversal of the novel idea of 1922. In the earlier work—written at the height of Lovecraft's Decadent phase—the unnamed narrator "travelled out of life on a quest into the spaces whither the world's dreams had fled"; but he does this because "age fell upon the world, and wonder went out of the minds of men."[9] In other words, the narrator's only refuge from prosy reality is the world of dream. Carter thinks that this is the case for him, but at the end he finds more value and beauty in that reality—transmuted, of course, by his dreams and memories—than he believed.

Of course, *The Dream-Quest of Unknown Kadath* is full of delightful tableaux of wonder, fantasy, and even horror that make it a very engaging work; such scenes as Carter being wafted from the moon back to the earth on the bodies of legions of cats, his encounter with the dreaded high-priest not to be named on the plateau of Leng, and of course his climactic appearance in Kadath before Nyarlathotep are triumphs of fantastic imagination. A certain whimsy and even flippancy lend a distinctive tone to the novel, as in Carter's grotesque encounter with his old friend Richard Upton Pickman (whose first appearance, of course, was in "Pickman's Model," written a month or so before the novel), who has now become a full-fledged ghoul:

> There, on a tombstone of 1768 stolen from the Granary Burying Ground in Boston, sat the ghoul which was once the artist Richard Upton Pickman. It was naked and rubbery, and had acquired so much of the ghoulish physiognomy that its human origin was already obscured. But it still remembered a little English, and was able to converse with Carter in grunts and monosyllables, helped out now and then by the glibbering of ghouls.[10]

The Dream-Quest of Unknown Kadath also seeks to unite most of Lovecraft's previous "Dunsanian" tales, making explicit references to features and characters in such tales as "Celephaïs," "The Cats of Ulthar," "The Other Gods," "The White Ship," and others; but in doing so it creates considerable confusion. In particular, it suddenly transfers the settings of these tales into the dreamworld, whereas those tales themselves had manifestly been set in the dim prehistory of the real world. Lovecraft, of course, is under no obligation to adhere to earlier conceptions in such matters, but it does not seem as if he has thought through the precise metaphysical status of the dreamworld, which is full of ambiguities and paradoxes.[11] It is not likely that Lovecraft would have done much to iron out these difficulties in a subsequent revision, for he clearly regarded the work merely as "useful practice for later and more authentic attempts in the novel form,"[12] writing it not only without thought of publication but without any real desire to tie up all the loose ends. In later years he repudiated the work, refusing several colleagues' desires to prepare a typed copy of the manuscript until finally R. H. Barlow badgered Lovecraft to send the text to him. Barlow typed about half the novel, and it was not published until *Beyond the Wall of Sleep* (1943).

"The Silver Key" is a conscious sequel to the *Dream-Quest*, even though it was written in the fall of 1926, well before the completion of the novel in late January 1927. (This fact alone should destroy previous hypotheses that Lovecraft had not planned out the *Dream-Quest* before writing it.) In "The Silver Key"[13] Randolph Carter, now thirty, has "lost the key of the gate of dreams," and therefore seeks to reconcile himself to the real world, which he now (a little oddly) finds prosy and aesthetically unrewarding. He tries all manner of literary and physical novelties until one day he does find the key—or, at any rate, a key of silver in his attic. Driving out in his car along "the old remembered way," he goes back to the rural New England region of his childhood and, in some magical and wisely unexplained manner, finds himself transformed into a nine-year-old boy. Sitting down to dinner with his aunt Martha, Uncle Chris, and the hired man Benijah Corey, Carter finds perfect content as a boy who has sloughed off the tedious complications of adult life for the eternal wonder of childhood.

"The Silver Key" is a peculiar story that has very little to do with Dunsany except perhaps in its use of fantasy for philosophical purposes. And yet, one further fascinating and subtle connection may exist. Carter, having lost the dreamworld, resumes the writing of books (recall that he was a writer of horror tales in "The Unnamable"); but it brings him no satisfaction:

> ...for the touch of earth was upon his mind, and he could not think of lovely things as he had done of yore. Ironic humour dragged down all the twilight minarets he reared, and the earthy fear of improbability blasted all the delicate and amazing flowers in his faery gardens. The convention of assumed pity spilt mawkishness on his characters, while the myth of an important reality and significant human events and emotions debased all his high fantasy into thin-veiled allegory and cheap social satire.... They were very graceful novels, in which he urbanely laughed at the dreams he lightly sketched; but he saw that their sophistication had sapped all their life away.

This is a perfect encapsulation of Lovecraft's own attitude toward Dunsany's later work, which he believed to be lacking in the childlike wonder and high fantasy that characterized his early period. Consider a remark in a 1936 letter:

> As he [Dunsany] gained in age and sophistication, he lost in freshness and simplicity. He was ashamed to be uncritically naive, and began to step aside from his tales and visibly smile at them even as they unfolded. Instead of remaining what the true fantaisiste must be—a child in a child's world of dream—he became anxious to show that he was really an adult good-naturedly pretending to be a child in a child's world.[14]

What "The Silver Key" really is, of course, is a very lightly fictionalized exposition of Lovecraft's own social, ethical, and aesthetic philosophy. It is not even so much a story as a parable or philosophical diatribe. He attacks literary realism—

> He did not dissent when they told him that the animal pain of a stuck pig or dyspeptic ploughman in real life is a greater thing than the peerless beauty of Narath

> with its hundred carven gates and domes of chalcedony...

conventional religion—

> ...he had turned to the gentle churchly faith endeared to him by the naive trust of his fathers...Only on closer view did he mark the starved fancy and beauty, the stale and prosy triteness, and the owlish gravity and grotesque claims of solid truth which reigned boresomely and overwhelmingly among most of its professors...It wearied Carter to see how solemnly people tried to make earthly reality out of old myths which every step of their boasted science confuted...

and bohemianism—

> ...their lives were dragged malodorously out in pain, ugliness, and disproportion, yet filled with a ludicrous pride at having escaped from something no more unsound than that which still held them. They had traded the false gods of fear and blind piety for those of licence and anarchy.

Each one of these passages, and others throughout the story, has its exact corollary in Lovecraft's letters. It is rare that Lovecraft so bluntly expressed his philosophy in a work of fiction; but "The Silver Key" can once again be seen as an affirmation of his own evolving beliefs and his definitive repudiation of Decadence even as a literary theory. Carter's return to childhood may perhaps exemplify a much earlier statement of Lovecraft's—"Adulthood is hell"[15]—but in reality his return is not so much to childhood as to ancestral ways, the one means Lovecraft saw of warding off the sense of futility engendered by the manifest truth of man's insignificance in the cosmos.

This point is made still clearer by Kenneth W. Faig, Jr.'s discovery that "The Silver Key" is in part a fictionalized account of the visit Lovecraft and his aunt Annie E. P. Gamwell took to ancestral sites in Foster, Rhode Island, in October 1926,[16] a visit that was itself a reprise of visits made in 1896 and in 1908 with his mother.[17] Details of topography, character names (Benijah Corey is surely an adaptation of Benejah Place, the owner of the farm across the road from the place where Lovecraft stayed), and other similarities make this conclusion unshakable. Just as Lovecraft felt the need, after two rootless years in New York, to restore connections with the places that had given him and his family birth, so in his fiction did he need to announce that, henceforth, however far his imagination might stray, it would always return to New England and look upon it as a source of bedrock values and emotional sustenance.

"The Strange High House in the Mist,"[18] written on 9 November 1926, is the last of Lovecraft's avowedly Dunsanian tales, and shows that the Dunsany influence had now been thoroughly internalized so as to allow for the expression of Lovecraft's own sentiments through Dunsany's idiom and general atmosphere. Indeed, the only genuine connections to Dunsany's work may perhaps be in some details of the setting and in the manifestly philosophical, even satiric purpose which the fantasy is made to serve.

We are now again in Kingsport, a city to which Lovecraft had not returned since "The Festival" (1923), the tale that first embodied his impressions of Marblehead and its magical preservation of the tokens of the past. North of Kingsport "the crags climb lofty and curious, terrace on terrace, till the northernmost hangs in the sky like a grey frozen wind-cloud." On that cliff is an ancient house inhabited by some individual whom none of the townsfolk—not even the Terrible Old Man—have ever seen. One day a tourist, the "philosopher" Thomas Olney, decides to visit that house and its secret inhabitant; for he has always longed for the strange and the wondrous. He arduously scales the cliff, but upon reaching the house finds that there is no door on this side, only "a couple of small lattice windows with dingy bull's-eye panes leaded in seventeenth-century fashion"; the house's only door is on the *other* side, flush with the sheer cliff. Then Olney hears a soft voice, and a "great black-bearded face" protrudes from a window and invites him in. Olney climbs through the window and has a colloquy with the occupant:

> And the day wore on, and still Olney listened to rumours of old times and far places, and heard how the Kings of Atlantis fought with the slippery blasphemies that wriggled out of rifts in ocean's floor, and how the pillared and weedy temple of Poseidonis is still glimpsed at midnight by lost ships, who know by its sight that they are lost. Years of the Titans were recalled, but the host grew timid when he spoke of the dim first age of chaos before the gods or even the Elder Ones were born, and when only *the other gods* came to dance on the peak of Hatheg-Kla in the stony desert near Ulthar, beyond the river Skai.

Then a knock is heard at the door—the door that faces the cliff. Eventually the host opens the door, and he and Olney find the room occupied by all manner of wondrous presences—"Trident-bearing Neptune," "hoary Nodens," and others—and when Olney returns to Kingsport the next day, the Terrible Old Man vows that the man who went up that cliff is not the same one who came down. No longer does Olney's soul long for wonder and mystery; instead, he is content to lead his prosy bourgeois life with his wife and children. But people in Kingsport, looking up at the house on the cliff, say that "at evening the little low windows are brighter than formerly."

On various occasions Lovecraft admits that he had no specific locale in mind when writing this tale: he states that memories of the "titan cliffs of Magnolia"[19] in part prompted the setting, but that there is no house on the cliff as in the story; a headland near Gloucester which Lovecraft calls "Mother Ann,"[20] and which has not been precisely identified, also inspired the setting. There is also a passage in Dunsany's *Chronicles of Rodriguez* about the home of a wizard on the top of a crag which Lovecraft may have had in mind.[21] What this means is that Lovecraft metamorphosed the New England landscape in this story more than he did in his "realistic" tales, and did so for the purpose of augmenting the fantastic element: "The Strange High House in the Mist" contains little in the way of specific topographical description, and we are clearly in a never-never land where—anomalously for Lovecraft—the focus is on human character.

For the strange transformation of Thomas Olney is at the heart of the tale. What is its meaning? How has he lost that sense of wonder which had guided his life up to his visit to Kingsport? The Terrible Old Man hints at the answer: "somewhere under that grey peaked roof, or amidst inconceivable reaches of that sinister white mist, there lingered still the lost spirit of him who was Thomas Olney." The body has returned to the normal round of things, but the spirit has remained with the occupant of the strange high house in the mist; the encounter with Neptune and Nodens has been an apotheosis, and Olney realizes that it is in this realm of nebulous wonder that he truly belongs. His body is now an empty shell, without soul and without imagination: "His good wife waxes stouter and his children older and prosier and more useful, and he never fails to smile correctly with pride when the occasion calls for it." This tale could be read as a sort of mirror-image of "Celephaïs": whereas Kuranes had to die in the real world in order for his spirit to attain his fantasy realm, Olney's body survives intact but his spirit stays behind.

"The Strange High House in the Mist" is, as Lovecraft knew, "one of the last of the things I wrote in the semi-poetic Dunsany manner";[22] and it was only four years after writing it that he declared, "What I do *not* think I shall use much in future is the Dunsanian pseudo-poetic vein—not because I don't admire it, but because I don't think it is natural to me."[23] What a contrast to the "Dunsany *is myself*"[24] delusion in which Lovecraft indulged when first encountering the Irish fantaisiste! Lovecraft came to realize that he was "fundamentally a *prose realist* whose prime dependence is on the building up of atmosphere through the slow, pedestrian method of multitudinous suggestive detail & dark scientific verisimilitude";[25] and nearly all his subsequent works adopt this technique. It is no surprise that it is largely on them that his reputation currently and properly rests.

2. The Paean to Providence

It is remarkable that, almost immediately after completing *The Dream-Quest of Unknown Kadath* in late January 1927, Lovecraft plunged into another "young novel,"[26] *The Case of Charles Dexter Ward*. This work must have been written in a tremendous hurry, for Lovecraft announces it as "just finished" on 3 March.[27] At approximately 50,000 words, it is the longest piece of fiction Lovecraft would ever write. While it does betray a few signs of haste, and while he would no doubt have polished it had he made the effort to prepare it for publication, the fact is that Lovecraft felt so discouraged as to its quality—as well as its marketability—that he never made such an effort, and the work remained unpublished until four years after his death.

Perhaps, however, it is not so odd that Lovecraft wrote this work in a blinding rush nine months after his return to Providence; for the novel—the second of Lovecraft's major tales (after "The Shunned House") to be set entirely in the city of his birth—had been gestating for at least a year or more. In August 1925 Lovecraft was contemplating a novel about Salem;[28] but then, in September, he read Gertrude Selwyn Kimball's *Providence in Colonial Times* (1912) at the New York Public Library, and this rather dry historical work clearly fired his imagination, possibly leading to a uniting of the Salem idea (of which we know nothing) with a work about his hometown. But the literary lockjaw that Lovecraft suffered in New York could only be alleviated by a return to New England, and *The Case of Charles Dexter Ward*—which is nothing less than his paean to Providence—is the result.

The plot of the novel is relatively simple, although full of subtle touches. Joseph Curwen, a learned scholar and man of affairs, leaves Salem for Providence in 1692, eventually building a succession of elegant homes in the oldest residential section of the city. Curwen attracts attention because he does not seem to age much, even after the passing of fifty or more years. He also acquires very peculiar substances from all around the world for apparent chemical—or, more specifically, alchemical—experiments; and his haunting of graveyards does nothing to salvage his reputation. When Dr. John Merritt visits Curwen, he is both impressed and disturbed by the number of alchemical and cabbalistic books on his shelves; in particular, he sees a copy of Borellus with one key passage—concerning the use of the "essential Saltes" of humans or animals for purposes of resurrection—heavily underscored.

Things come to a head when Curwen, in an effort to restore his reputation, arranges a marriage for himself with the well-born Eliza Tillinghast, the daughter of a ship-captain under Curwen's control. This so enrages Ezra Weeden, who had hoped to marry Eliza himself, that he begins an exhaustive investigation of Curwen's affairs. After several more anomalous incidents, it is decided by the elders of the city—among them the four Brown brothers; Rev. James Manning, president of the recently established college (later to be known as Brown University); Stephen Hopkins, former governor of the colony; and others—that something must be done. A raid on Curwen's property in 1771, however, produces death, destruction, and psychological trauma amongst the participants well beyond what might have been expected of a venture of this sort. Curwen is evidently killed, and his body is returned to his wife for burial. Curwen is never spoken of again, and as many records concerning him as can be found are destroyed.

A century and a half pass, and in 1918 Charles Dexter Ward—Curwen's direct descendant by way of Curwen's daughter Ann—accidentally discovers his relation to the old wizard and seeks to learn all he can about him. Although always fascinated by the past, Ward had previously exhibited no especial interest in the *outré*; but as he unearths more and more information about Curwen—whose exact physical double he proves to be—he strives more and more to duplicate his ancestor's cabbalistic and alchemical feats. He undertakes a long voyage overseas to visit the presumable descendants of individuals with whom Curwen had been in touch in the eighteenth century. He finds Curwen's remains and, by the proper manipulation of his "essential Saltes," resurrects him. But something begins to go astray. He writes a harried letter to Dr. Marinus Bicknell Willett, the family doctor, with the following disturbing message:

> Instead of triumph I have found terror, and my talk with you will not be a boast of victory but a plea for help and advice in saving both myself and the world from a horror beyond all human conception or calculation.... Upon us depends more than can be put into words—all civilisation, all natural law, perhaps even the fate of the solar system and the universe. I have brought to light a monstrous abnormality, but I did it for the sake of knowledge. Now for the sake of all life and Nature you must help me thrust it back into the dark again.[29]

But, perversely, Ward does not stay for the appointed meeting with Willett. Willett finally does track him down, but something astounding has occurred: although still of youthful appearance, his talk is very eccentric and old-fashioned, and his stock of memories of his own life seems to have been bizarrely depleted. Willett later undertakes a harrowing exploration of Curwen's old Pawtuxet bungalow, which Ward had restored for the conducting of experiments; he finds, among other anomalies, all manner of half-formed creatures at the bottom of deep pits. He confronts Ward—whom he now realizes is no other than Curwen—in the madhouse in which he has been placed; Curwen attempts to summon up an incantation against him, but Willett counters with one of his own, reducing Curwen to a "thin coating of fine bluish-grey dust."[30]

This skeletonic summary cannot begin to convey the textural and tonal richness of *The Case of Charles Dexter Ward*, which in spite of the speed of its composition remains among the most carefully wrought fictions in Lovecraft's entire corpus. The historical flashback— occupying the second of the five chapters—is as evocative a passage as any in his work. To be sure, he has taken many details from the Kimball book and others he read or owned; but the chapter does much more than merely recycle odd bits of history—it mingles history and fiction in an inextricable union, breathing vivid life into the dry facts Lovecraft had gathered over a lifetime of study of his native region and insidiously inserting the imaginary, the fantastic, and the weird into the known historical record.

What, indeed, is the fundamental message of *The Case of Charles Dexter Ward*? To answer this question, we must first ascertain exactly what Curwen and his cohorts around the world were attempting to do by gathering up these "essential Saltes." Lovecraft makes the matter a trifle too clear in a passage toward the end—a passage which, one hopes, he might have had the good sense to omit in a revised version:

> What these horrible creatures—and Charles Ward as well—were doing or trying to do seemed fairly clear...They were robbing the tombs of all the ages, including those of the world's wisest and greatest men, in the hope of recovering from the bygone ashes some vestige of the consciousness and lore which had once animated and informed them.[31]

It is not, indeed, entirely clear how the tapping of human brains—even the "world's wisest and greatest"—would result in some scenario that might threaten "all civilisation, all natural law, perhaps even the fate of the solar system and the univese." Curwen occasionally speaks in notes and letters about calling up entities from "Outside ye Spheres"—including perhaps Yog-Sothoth, who is first mentioned in this novel—but these hints are so nebulous that not much can be made of them. There are further hints that Curwen in 1771 died not because of the raid by the citizenry but because he had raised some nameless entity and could not control it. Nevertheless, the basic conception of a Faustian quest for knowledge has led Barton L. St. Armand, one of the acutest commentators on the work, to declare: "The simple moral of *The Case of Charles Dexter Ward* is that it is dangerous to know too much, especially about one's own ancestors."[32]

Well, perhaps it is not so simple as that. By this interpretation, Ward himself becomes the villain of the piece; but surely it is Curwen who is the real villain, for it is he who conceived the idea of ransacking the world's brains for his own (rather unclear) purposes. Ward certainly does pursue knowledge ardently, and he certainly does resurrect Curwen's body; but it is false to say (as St. Armand does) that Curwen "possesses" Ward. There is no psychic possession—not, at least, of the obvious sort—here, as there is in "The Tomb" and as there will be again in "The Thing on the Doorstep" (1933). Curwen is physically resurrected, and when Ward proves unwilling to assist him in carrying out his plans, Curwen ruthlessly kills him and tries to pass himself off as Ward. And note Ward's defense of his actions in the letter to Willett, specifically the sentence: "I have brought to light a monstrous abnormality, but I did it for the sake of knowledge." This single utterance comprises Ward's (and Lovecraft's) justification: in the first part of the sentence Ward confesses to moral culpability; but the second part of the sentence is preceded by "but" because Ward (with Lovecraft) sees the pursuit of knowledge as intrinsically a good. Sometimes, however, that pursuit simply leads to unfortunate and unforeseen consequences. Ward was perhaps naive in thinking that his resurrection of Curwen would lead to no harm; but, as Willett himself says at the end: "...he was never a fiend or even truly a madman, but only an eager, studious, and curious boy whose love of mystery and of the past was his undoing."[33]

The Case of Charles Dexter Ward represents one of Lovecraft's few relative triumphs of characterization. Both Curwen and Ward are vividly realized—the latter largely because Lovecraft drew unaffectedly upon his own deepest emotions in the portrayal. Willett is not so successful, and on occasion he reveals himself to be somewhat pompous and self-important. After solving the case he makes the following ludicrous speech: "I can answer no questions, but I will say that there are different kinds of magic. I have made a great purgation, and those in this house will sleep the better for it."[34]

But St. Armand is nonetheless right in seeing Providence itself as the principal "character" of the novel. It would require a lengthy commentary to specify not only all the historical data Lovecraft has unearthed, but the countless autobiographical details he has enmeshed into his narrative. The opening descriptions of Ward as a youth are filled with echoes of Lovecraft's own upbringing, although with provocative changes; and Ward's ecstatic return to Providence after several years abroad can scarcely be anything but a transparent echo of Lovecraft's own return to Providence after two years in New York. The simple utterance that concludes this passage—"It was twilight, and Charles Dexter Ward had come home"[35]—is one of the most quietly moving statements in all Lovecraft's work. And it is of interest to note how Willett's complete eradication of Curwen stands in such stark contrast to Malone's obvious failure to eliminate the age-old horror in Red Hook: New York may be the haven of all horror, but Providence must at the end emerge cleansed of any evil taint. We will observe this occurring in many of Lovecraft's tales of Providence. In many ways *The Case of Charles Dexter Ward* is a refinement of "The Horror at Red Hook." Several features of the plot are borrowed from that earlier story: Curwen's alchemy parallels Suydam's cabbalistic activities; Curwen's attempt to repair his standing in the community with an advantageous marriage echoes Suydam's marriage with Cornelia Gerritsen; Willett as the valiant counterweight to Curwen matches Malone as the adversary of Suydam. Lovecraft has once again reverted to his relatively small store of basic plot elements, and once again transformed a mediocre tale into a masterful one.

It is certainly a pity that Lovecraft made no efforts to prepare *The Case of Charles Dexter Ward* for publication, even when book publishers in the 1930s were specifically asking for a novel from his pen; but we are in no position to question Lovecraft's own judgment that the novel was an inferior piece of work, a "cumbrous, creaking bit of self-conscious antiquarianism."[36] It certainly stands as one of his finest works, and emphasizes the message of *The Dream-Quest of Unknown Kadath* all over again: that Lovecraft is who he is because of his birth and upbringing as a New England Yankee. The need to root his work in his native soil became more and more clear to him as time went on, and it led to his gradual transformation of all New England as the locus of both wonder and terror.

3. The Lovecraft Mythos

We now come to the most controversial of H. P. Lovecraft's creations—what has come to be called the "Cthulhu Mythos." This subject does not appear to be conducive to impartiality or objectivity, and I do not make any such claims for my own remarks here. What it might be possible to do, however, is to lay down some basic *facts* that shall help to answer certain fundamental questions, namely: What is the Cthulhu Mythos? Is it anything at all? What did Lovecraft "mean" by it? What are its parameters and scope? To what degree can we regard other writers' contributions to it as valid or significant? I do not pretend to answer all these questions here, but I hope to shed some light on them in my remarks in the following two chapters and in the Conclusion.

Lovecraft could certainly not have been aware, when he wrote "The Call of Cthulhu" in the fall of 1926, that he had initiated a creation that would take on a life of its own and in a sense overwhelm or engulf all the rest of his work; but that he was doing something quite revolutionary, even in regard to his own development as a writer, is agreed by all. We can date the nucleus of the story all the way back to 1920, when Lovecraft had a dream of fashioning a bas-relief and presenting it to the curator of a museum of antiquities.[37] The story itself—with its title—had been fully conceived a year before its writing: on the evening of August 12-13 (one day after writing "He") Lovecraft stayed up all night to draft the plot or synopsis of the tale.[38] But again, it required his return to Providence to free his pen and actually write the tale.[39]

The plot of this well-known story scarcely needs recapitulation. The subtitle, "(Found Among the Papers of the Late Francis Wayland Thurston, of Boston)," announces that the text is an account written by Thurston of the strange facts he has assembled, both from the papers of his recently deceased grand-uncle, George Gammell Angell, and from personal investigation. Angell, a professor of Semitic languages at Brown University, had collected several peculiar pieces of data. First, he had taken extensive notes of the dreams and artwork of a young sculptor, Henry Anthony Wilcox, who had come to him with a bas-relief he had fashioned in his sleep on the night of March 1, 1925. The sculpture is of a hideous-looking alien entity, and Wilcox had reported that in the dream that had inspired it he had repeatedly heard the words "*Cthulhu fhtagn.*" It was this that had piqued Angell's interest, for he had encountered these words or sounds years before, at a meeting of the American Archaeological Society, in which a New Orleans police inspector named John Raymond Legrasse had brought in a sculpture very much like Wilcox's and claimed that it had been worshipped by a degraded cult in the Louisiana bayou which had chanted the phrase "*Ph'nglui mglw'nafh Cthulhu R'lyeh wgah'nagl fhtagn.*" One of the cult members had proffered a translation of this outlandish utterance: "In his house at R'lyeh dead Cthulhu waits dreaming." Legrasse had also interviewed one cultist, a mestizo named Castro, who had told them that Cthulhu was a vast being that had come from the stars when the earth was young, along with another set of entities named the Great Old Ones; he was buried in the sunken city of R'lyeh and would emerge when the "stars were ready" to reclaim control of the earth. The cult "would always be waiting to liberate him."[40] Castro points out that these matters are spoken of in the *Necronomicon* of the mad Arab Abdul Alhazred.

Thurston scarcely knows what to make of this bizarre material, but then by accident he finds a newspaper clipping telling of strange events aboard a ship in the Pacific Ocean; accompanying the article is a picture of another bas-relief very similar to that fashioned by Wilcox and found by Legrasse. Thurston goes to Oslo to talk with the Norwegian sailor, Gustaf Johansen, who had been on board the ship, but finds that he is dead. Johansen has, however, left behind an account of his experience, and this shows that he had actually encountered the dreaded Cthulhu as the city of R'lyeh emerged as the result of an earthquake; but, presumably because the stars are not "ready," the city sinks again, returning Cthulhu to the bottom of the ocean. But the mere existence of this titanic entity is an unending source of profound unease to Thurston because it shows how tenuous is mankind's vaunted supremacy upon this planet.

This tale certainly contains nearly all the elements that would be utilized in subsequent "Cthulhu Mythos" fiction by Lovecraft and others. It can scarcely be denied that there is something going on in many of the tales of Lovecraft's last decade of writing: they are frequently interrelated by a complex series of cross-references to a constantly evolving body of imagined myth, and many of them build upon features—superficial or profound as the case may be—found in previous tales. But certain basic points can now be made, although even some of these are not without controversy: 1) Lovecraft himself did not coin the term "Cthulhu Mythos"; 2) Lovecraft felt that *all* his tales embodied his basic philosophical principles; 3) the mythos, if it can be said to be anything, is not the tales themselves and not the philosophy behind the tales, but a series of *plot devices* utilized to convey that philosophy. Let us study each of these points further.

1. The term "Cthulhu Mythos" was invented by August Derleth after Lovecraft's death; of this there is no question. As early as 1931 he had actually suggested to Lovecraft that the term "Mythology of Hastur" be used to denote the phenomenon; Lovecraft tactfully rejected the idea, since "Hastur" (which was coined by Ambrose Bierce as a god of the shepherds and was borrowed by Robert W. Chambers, who however seems to refer to it as a place) does not figure at all prominently in Lovecraft's own tales, and because "it was really from Machen & Dunsany & others rather than through the Bierce-Chambers line, that I picked up my gradually developing hash of theogony—or daemonogony."[41] I shall return to this idea a little later. Lovecraft does, however, in this letter and elsewhere refer to "Cthulhuism & Yog-Sothothery," which is the closest he comes to giving his invented pantheon and related phenomena a name. Donald R. Burleson and I independently adopted the term "Lovecraft Mythos" around 1982 as a means of distinguishing it from "Cthulhu Mythos," since that term had presumably become corrupted by Derleth's repeated misinterpretations of Lovecraft's pseudomythology; but I am no longer certain whether this term has any genuine value. It may still be of some use in distinguishing the conceptions created by Lovecraft (or, at least, created within Lovecraft's lifetime) and those created later; although this sense of the term has now been confounded by Robert M. Price, who inexpli-

cably bestowed the title *Tales of the Lovecraft Mythos* (1992) to a volume collecting material mostly written after Lovecraft's time.

2. When Lovecraft claimed that "'Yog-Sothoth' is a basically immature conception, & unfitted for really serious literature,"[42] he may perhaps have been unduly modest, whatever he may have meant by "Yog-Sothoth" here. But as the rest of this letter makes clear, Lovecraft was utilizing his pseudomythology as one (among many) of the ways to convey his fundamental philosophical message, specifically cosmicism. This point is made clear in a letter written to Farnsworth Wright in July 1927 upon the resubmittal of "The Call of Cthulhu" to *Weird Tales* (it had been rejected upon initial submission):

> Now all my tales are based on the fundamental premise that common human laws and interests and emotions have no validity or significance in the vast cosmos-at-large. To me there is nothing but puerility in a tale in which the human form—and the local human passions and conditions and standards—are depicted as native to other worlds or other universes. To achieve the essence of real externality, whether of time or space or dimension, one must forget that such things as organic life, good and evil, love and hate, and all such local attributes of a negligible and temporary race called mankind, have any existence at all.[43]

This statement may perhaps not be capable of bearing quite the philosophical weight that some (including myself) have placed upon it: in spite of the very general nature of the first sentence, the bulk of the passage (and of the letter as a whole) is dealing with a fairly specific point of *technique* in regard to the weird or science fiction tale—the portrayal of extraterrestrials. What Lovecraft was combating was the already well-established convention (found in Edgar Rice Burroughs, Ray Cummings, and others) of depicting extraterrestrials as humanoid not merely in appearance but also in language, habits, and emotional or psychological makeup. This is why Lovecraft created such an *outré* name as "Cthulhu" to designate a creature that had come from the depths of space.

And yet, the passage quoted above maintains that *all* Lovecraft's tales emphasize cosmicism in some form or another. Whether this is actually the case is another matter, but at least Lovecraft felt it to be so. If, then, we segregate certain of Lovecraft's tales as employing the framework of his "artificial pantheon and myth-background,"[44] it is purely for convenience, with a full knowledge that Lovecraft's work is not to be grouped arbitrarily, rigidly, or exclusively into discrete categories ("New England tales," "Dunsanian tales," and "Cthulhu Mythos tales," as Derleth decreed), since it is transparently clear that these (or any other) categories are not well-defined or mutually exclusive in Lovecraft.

3. It is careless and inaccurate to say that the Lovecraft Mythos *is* Lovecraft's philosophy: his philosophy is mechanistic materialism and all its ramifications, and if the Lovecraft Mythos is anything, it is a series of plot devices meant to facilitate the expression of this philosophy. These various plot devices need not concern us here except in their broadest features. They can perhaps be placed in three general groups: a) invented "gods" and the cults or worshippers that have grown up around them; b) an ever-increasing library of mythical books of occult lore; and c) a fictitious New England topography (Arkham, Dunwich, Innsmouth, etc.). It will readily be noted that the latter two were already present in nebulous form in much earlier tales; but the three features only came together in Lovecraft's later works. Indeed, the third feature does not appreciably foster Lovecraft's cosmic message, and it can be found in tales that are anything but cosmic (*e.g.*, "The Picture in the House"); but it is a phenomenon that has exercised much fascination with readers, writers, and critics alike, and can still be said to be an important component of the Lovecraft Mythos. It is an unfortunate fact, of course, that these surface features have frequently taken precedence with readers (and even critics) rather than the philosophy of which they are symbols or representations; and many of those writers who have sought to "add" to the "Cthulhu Mythos" have similarly felt that the mere invention of some mythical god or book is sufficient to justify a tale. I shall have more to say about this point elsewhere.

It is now worth examining some of the misinterpretations foisted upon the Lovecraft Mythos by August Derleth as a prelude to examining what the Mythos actually meant to Lovecraft. These errors are readily acknowledged by most critics (although Robert M. Price has recently been making some futile and hyperventilated attempts to defend Derleth), so that not much time need be wasted on them. The errors can be summed up under three heads: 1) that Lovecraft's "gods" are elementals; 2) that the "gods" can be differentiated between "Elder Gods," who represent the forces of good, and the "Old Ones," who are the forces of evil; and 3) that the Mythos as a whole is philosophically akin to Christianity.

It does not require much thought to deem all these points absurd and ridiculous. The notion that the "gods" are elementals seems largely derived from the fact that Cthulhu is imprisoned under water and that he resembles an octopus, and is therefore supposedly a water elemental; but the facts that he clearly came from *outer space*, and that he is *imprisoned* in sunken R'lyeh, must make it obvious both that his resemblance to an octopus is fortuitous and that water is not his natural element. Derleth's attempt to make elementals of the other "gods" is still more preposterous: Nyarlathotep is arbitrarily deemed an earth elemental and Hastur (which is only mentioned in passing once in "The Whisperer in Darkness") is claimed to be an air elemental. Not only does this leave out what are, by all accounts, the two chief deities in Lovecraft's pantheon—Azathoth and Yog-Sothoth—but Derleth is then forced to maintain that Lovecraft "failed" in some inexplicable fashion to provide a fire elemental, in spite of the fact that he was (in Derleth's view) working steadily in the "Cthulhu Mythos" for the last ten years of his life. (Derleth came to Lovecraft's rescue by supplying Cthugha, the purportedly missing fire elemental.)

Derleth, himself a practising Catholic, was unable to endure Lovecraft's bleak atheistic vision, and so he invented the "Elder Gods" out of whole cloth to act as a counterweight to the "evil" Old Ones, who had been "expelled" from the earth but are eternally preparing to reemerge and destroy humanity. He seems to have taken a clue from *The Dream-Quest of Unknown Kadath* (which, paradoxically, he then refused to number among "tales of the Cthulhu Mythos"), whereby the god Nodens seems to take Randolph Carter's side (although actually doing nothing for Carter) against the machinations of Nyarlathotep. In any case, this invention of "Elder Gods" allowed him to maintain that the "Cthulhu Mythos" is substantially akin to Christianity, therefore making it acceptable to people of his conventional temperament. An important piece of "evidence" that Derleth repeatedly cited to bolster his claims was the following "quotation," presumably from a letter by Lovecraft:

> All my stories, unconnected as they may be, are based on the fundamental lore or legend that this world was inhabited at one time by another race who, in practising black magic, lost their foothold and were expelled, yet live on outside ever ready to take possession of this earth again.

In spite of its superficial similarity with the "All my stories..." quotation previously cited (of which Derleth was familiar), this quotation does not sound at all like Lovecraft—at any rate, it is entirely in conflict with the thrust of his philosophy. When Derleth in later years was asked to produce the actual letter from which this quotation was purportedly taken, he could not do so, and for a very good reason: it does not in fact occur in any letter by Lovecraft. It comes from a letter to Derleth written by Harold S. Farnese, the composer who had corresponded briefly with Lovecraft and who, evidently, severely misconstrued the direction of Lovecraft's work and thought very much as Derleth did.[45] But Derleth seized upon this "quotation" as a trump card for his erroneous views.

By now there is little need to rehash this entire matter: the work of such modern critics as Richard L. Tierney, Dirk W. Mosig, and others has been so conclusive that any attempt to overturn it can only seem comically reactionary. There is no cosmic "good vs. evil" struggle in Lovecraft's tales; there certainly are struggles between various extraterrestrial entities, but these have no moral overtones and are merely part of the history of the universe. There are no "Elder Gods" whose goal is to protect humanity from the "evil" Old Ones; the Old Ones were not "expelled" by anyone and are not (aside from Cthulhu) "trapped" in the earth or elsewhere. Lovecraft's vision is far less cheerful: humanity is *not* at center stage in the cosmos, and there is no one to help us against the entities who have from time to time descended upon the earth and wreaked havoc; indeed, the "gods" of the Mythos are not really gods at all, but merely extraterrestrials who occasionally manipulate their human followers for their own advantage.

This last point is worth examining specifically in relation to "The Call of Cthulhu," to which we can now finally return. The outlandish story about the Great Old Ones told to Legrasse by Castro speaks of the intimate relation between the human cult of Cthulhu worshippers and the objects of their worship: "That cult would never die till the stars came right again, and the secret priests would take great Cthulhu from His tomb to revive His subjects and resume His rule of earth."[46] The critical issue is this: is Castro right or wrong? The tale when read as a whole seems emphatically to suggest that he is wrong; in other words, that the cult has nothing to do with the emergence of Cthulhu (it certainly did not do so in March 1925, since that was the product of an earthquake), and in fact is of no importance to Cthulhu and his ultimate plans, whatever they may be. This is where Lovecraft's remark about the avoidance of human emotions as applied to extraterrestrials comes into play: the fact of the matter is that we scarcely know anything about the real motivations of Cthulhu, but his pathetic and ignorant human worshippers wish to flatter their sense of self-importance by believing that they are somehow integral to his ultimate resurrection, and that they will share in his domination of the earth (if, indeed, that is what he wishes to do).

And it is here that we finally approach the heart of the Lovecraft Mythos. Lovecraft's remark that it was Lord Dunsany "from whom I got the idea of the artificial pantheon and myth-background represented by 'Cthulhu,' 'Yog-Sothoth,' 'Yuggoth,' etc."[47] has either been misunderstood or ignored; but it is central to the understanding of what the pseudomythology meant to Lovecraft. Dunsany had created his artificial pantheon in his first two books (and only there), *The Gods of Pegana* (1905) and *Time and the Gods* (1906). The mere act of creating an imaginary religion calls for some comment: it clearly denotes some dissatisfaction with the religion (Christianity) with which the author was raised. Dunsany was, by all accounts, an atheist, although not quite so vociferous a one as Lovecraft; and his gods were, like Lovecraft's, *symbols* for some of his most deeply held philosophical beliefs.

In Dunsany's case, these were such things as the need for human reunification with the natural world and distaste for many features of modern civilization (business, advertising, and in general the absence of beauty and poetry in contemporary life). Lovecraft, having his own philosophical message to convey, used his imaginary pantheon for analogous purposes.

What Lovecraft was really doing, in other words, was creating (as David E. Schultz has felicitously expressed it)[48] an *anti-mythology*. What is the purpose behind most religions and mythologies? It is to "justify the ways of God to men."[49] Human beings have always considered themselves at the center of the universe; they have peopled the universe with gods of varying natures and capacities as a means of explaining natural phenomena, of accounting for their own existence, and of shielding themselves from the grim prospect of oblivion after death. Every religion and mythology has established some vital connection between gods and human beings, and it is exactly this connection that Lovecraft is seeking to subvert with his pseudomythology. And yet, he knew enough anthropology and psychology to realize that most human beings—either primitive or civilized—are incapable of accepting an atheistic view of existence, and so he peopled his tales with cults which in their own perverted way attempted to reestablish that bond between the gods and themselves; but these cults are incapable of understanding that what they deem "gods" are merely extraterrestrial entities who have no intimate relation with human beings or with anything on this planet, and who are doing no more than pursuing their own ends, whatever they may happen to be.

"The Call of Cthulhu" is a quantum leap for Lovecraft in more ways than one. It is, most emphatically, the first of his tales that can genuinely be termed cosmic. "Dagon," "Beyond the Wall of Sleep," and a few others had dimly hinted at cosmicism; but "The Call of Cthulhu" realizes the notion fully and satisfyingly. The suggestion that various phenomena all around the world—bas-reliefs found in New Orleans, Greenland, and the South Pacific, and carved by a Providence artist; anomalously similar dreams had by a wide variety of individuals—may all be insidiously linked to Cthulhu makes Thurston realize that it is not he alone who is in danger, but all the inhabitants of the globe. And the mere fact that Cthulhu still lives at the bottom of the ocean, even though he may be quiescent for years, decades, centuries, or millennia, causes Thurston to reflect poignantly: "I have looked upon all that the universe has to hold of horror, and even the skies of spring and the flowers of summer must ever afterward be poison to me."[50] It is a sentiment that many of Lovecraft's later narrators will echo.

From the cosmicism of "The Call of Cthulhu" to the apparent mundaneness of "Pickman's Model" (1926)[51] seems a long step backward; and while this tale cannot by any means be deemed one of

Lovecraft's best, it contains some features of interest. The narrator, Thurber, writing in a colloquial style very unusual for Lovecraft, tells why he no longer associates with the painter Richard Upton Pickman of Boston, who has in fact recently disappeared. He had maintained relations with Pickman long after his other acquaintances dropped him because of the grotesqueness of his paintings, and so on one occasion he was taken to Pickman's secret cellar studio in the decaying North End of Boston, near the ancient Copp's Hill Burying Ground. Here were some of Pickman's most spectacularly demonic paintings; one in particular depicts a "colossal and nameless blasphemy with glaring red eyes" nibbling at a man's head the way a child chews a stick of candy. A strange noise is heard, and Pickman harriedly maintains that it must be rats clambering through the underground tunnels honeycombing the area. Pickman, in another room, fires all six chambers of his revolver—a rather odd way to kill rats. After leaving, Thurston finds that he had inadvertently taken away a photograph affixed to the canvas; thinking it a mere shot of scenic background, he is horrified to find that it is a picture of the monster itself—"*it was a photograph from life.*"

No reader is likely to have failed to predict this conclusion, but the tale is more interesting not for its actual plot but for its setting and its aesthetics. The North End setting is—or, rather, was—portrayed quite faithfully, right down to many of the street names; but, less than a year after writing the story, Lovecraft was disappointed to find that much of the area had been torn down to make way for new development. But the tunnels he describes are real: they probably date from the colonial period and may have been used for smuggling. Lovecraft captures the atmosphere of hoary decay vividly, and in so doing he enunciates (through Pickman) his own views on the need for a long-established cultural heritage:

> "God, man! Don't you realise that places like that [the North End] weren't merely *made*, but actually *grew*? Generation after generation lived and felt and died there, and in days when people weren't afraid to live and feel and die.... No, Thurber, these ancient places are dreaming gorgeously and overflowing with wonder and terror and escapes from the commonplace, and yet there's not a living soul to understand or profit by them."

But "Pickman's Model" states other views close to Lovecraft's heart. In effect, it expresses, in fictionalized form, many of the aesthetic principles on weird fiction that Lovecraft had just outlined in "Supernatural Horror in Literature" (1925-1927). When Thurber declares that "any magazine-cover hack can splash paint around wildly and call it a nightmare or a Witches' Sabbath or a portrait of the devil," he is repeating the many censures found in letters about the need for artistic *sincerity* and a knowledge of the true foundations of fear in the production of weird art. Thurber continues:

> ...only the real artist knows the actual anatomy of the terrible or the physiology of fear—the exact sort of lines and proportions that connect up with latent instincts or hereditary memories of fright, and the proper colour contrasts and lighting effects to stir the dormant sense of strangeness.

This statement, *mutatis mutandis*, is Lovecraft's ideal of weird literature as well. And when Thurber confesses that "Pickman was in every sense—in conception and in execution—a thorough, painstaking, and almost scientific *realist*," he is reiterating his own recent abandonment of the Dunsanian prose-poetic technique for the "prose realism" that would be the hallmark of his later work.

"Pickman's Model," however, suffers from several flaws aside from its rather obvious plot. Thurber, although supposedly a "tough" guy who had been through the World War, expresses implausible horror and shock at Pickman's paintings: his reactions seem strained and hysterical, and make the reader think that he is not at all as hardened as he repeatedly claims he is. And the colloquial style is—as is the case with "In the Vault"—simply not suited to Lovecraft, and it is well that he subsequently abandoned it except for his ventures into New England dialect.

The last tale of Lovecraft's great spate of fiction-writing of 1926-1927 is "The Colour out of Space," written in March 1927. There can scarcely be a doubt that it is one of his great tales, and it always remained Lovecraft's own favorite. Here again the plot is too well known to require lengthy description. A surveyor for the new reservoir to be built "west of Arkham"[52] encounters a bleak terrain where nothing will grow; the locals call it the "blasted heath." The surveyor, seeking an explanation for the term and for the cause of the devastation, finally finds an old man, Ammi Pierce, living near the area, who tells him an unbelievable tale of events that occurred in 1882. A meteorite had landed on the property of Nahum Gardner and his family. Scientists from Miskatonic University who come to examine the object find that its properties are of the most bizarre sort: the substance refuses to grow cool, displays shining bands on a spectroscope that had never been seen before, and fails to react to conventional solvents applied to it. Within the meteorite is a "large coloured globule": "The colour...was almost impossible to describe; and it was only by analogy that they called it colour at all."[53] When tapped with a hammer, it bursts. The meteorite itself, continuing to shrink anomalously, finally disappears altogether.

Henceforth increasingly odd things occur. Nahum's harvest of apples and pears, though unprecedentedly huge in size, proves unfit to eat; plants and animals with peculiar mutations are seen; Nahum's cows start giving bad milk. Then Nahum's wife Nabby goes mad, "screaming about things in the air which she could not describe";[54] she is locked in an upstairs room. Soon all the vegetation starts to crumble to a greyish powder. Nahum's son Thaddeus goes mad after a visit to the well, and his other sons Merwin and Zenas also break down. Then there is a period of days when Nahum is not seen or heard from. Ammi finally summons up the courage to visit his farm, and finds that the worst has happened: Nahum himself has snapped, and he can only utter confused fragments:

> "Nothin'...nothin'...the colour...it burns...cold an' wet, but it burns...it lived in the well...suckin' the life out of everything...in that stone...it must a' come in that stone...pizened the whole place...dun't know what it wants...it beats down your mind an' then gits ye...can't git away...draws ye...ye know summ'at's comin', but 'tain't no use..."[55]

But that is all: "That which spoke could speak no more because it had completely caved in."[56] Ammi brings policemen, a coroner, and other officials to the place, and after a series of bizarre events they see a column of the unknown color shoot vertically into the sky from the well; but Ammi sees one small fragment of it return to earth. Now they say that the grey expanse of the "blasted heath" grows by an inch per year, and no one can say when it will end.

Lovecraft was entirely correct in calling this tale an "atmospheric study,"[57] for he has rarely captured the atmosphere of inexplicable horror better than he has here. First let us consider the setting. The reservoir mentioned in the tale is a very real one: the Quabbin Reservoir, plans for which were announced in 1926, although it was not completed until 1939. And yet, Lovecraft declares in a late letter that it was not this reservoir but the Scituate Reservoir in Rhode Island (built in 1926) that caused him to use the reservoir element in the story.[58] I cannot, however, believe that Lovecraft was not also thinking of the Quabbin—which is located exactly in the area of central Massachusetts where the tale takes place, and which involved the abandonment and submersion of entire towns in the region—when writing the tale. Whatever the case, the bleak rural terrain is portrayed with mastery, as its opening paragraph is sufficient to demonstrate:

> West of Arkham the hills rise wild, and there are valleys with deep woods that no axe has ever cut. There are dark narrow glens where the trees slope fantastically, and where thin brooklets trickle without ever having caught the glint of sunlight. On the gentler slopes there are farms, ancient and rocky, with squat, moss-covered cottages brooding eternally over old New England secrets in the lee of great ledges; but these are all vacant now, the wide chimneys crumbling and the shingled sides bulging perilously beneath low gambrel roofs.[59]

This is a refinement of the opening of "The Picture in the House" (1920), which might be thought to have piled on the horror—and the adjectives—a little too strongly; here greater restraint is shown, and the entire story could be regarded as one long but subdued prose-poem.

The key to the story, of course, is the anomalous meteorite. Is it—or the colored globules inside it—animate in any sense we can recognize? Does it house a single entity or many entities? What are their physical properties? More significantly, what are their aims, goals, and motives? The fact that we can answer none of these questions very clearly is by no means a failing; indeed, this is exactly the source of terror in the tale. As Lovecraft said of Machen's "The White People," "the *lack of anything concrete* is the *great asset* of the story."[60] In other words, it is precisely because we cannot define the nature—either physical or psychological—of the entities in "The Colour out of Space" (or even know whether they are entities or living creatures in any sense we can understand) that produces the sense of nameless horror. Lovecraft later maintained (probably correctly) that his habit of writing—even if unconsciously—with a pulp audience in mind had corrupted his technique by making his work too obvious and explicit. We will indeed find this problem in some later tales, but here Lovecraft has exercised the most exquisite form of artistic restraint in not defining the nature of the phenomena at hand.

It is, therefore, in "The Colour out of Space" that Lovecraft has most closely achieved his goal of avoiding the depiction of "the human form—and the local human passions and conditions and standards—...as native to other worlds or other universes." For it is manifest that the meteorite in "The Colour out of Space" must have come from some dim corner of the universe where natural laws work very differently from the way they do here: "It was just a colour out of space—a frightful messenger from unformed realms of infinity beyond all nature as we know it; from realms whose mere existence stuns the brain and numbs us with the black extra-cosmic gulfs it throws open before our frenzied eyes."[61] The chemical experiments performed on the object establish that it is *physically* unlike anything we know; and the utter absence of any sense of willful viciousness, destructiveness, or conventionalized "evil" in the object or the entities it contains similarly results in a *psychological* distancing from human or earthly standards. To be sure, the meteorite causes great destruction, and because some remnants of it are still on the planet, it will continue to do so; but who can say but that this is an inevitable product of the mingling of our world and its own? In order for an animate being to be morally culpable of "evil," it must be conscious that it is doing what is regarded as evil; but who can say whether the entities in "The Colour out of Space" are conscious at all? Nahum Gardner's poignant dying speech makes the matter clear: his simple utterance, "dun't know what it wants," puts the matter in a nutshell. We have no way of ascertaining the mental or emotional orientation of the anomalous entities, and as a result we cannot possibly apportion praise or blame to them by any conventional moral standards.

But Lovecraft has rendered the plight of the Gardner family inexpressibly poignant and tragic, so that although we cannot "blame" the meteorite for causing their deaths, we still experience a tremendous sense of sorrow mingled with horror at their fate. It is not merely that they have been physically destroyed; the meteorite has also beaten down their minds and wills, so that they are unable to escape its effects. When Ammi tells Nahum that the well water is bad, Nahum ignores him: "He and the boys continued to use the tainted supply, drinking it as listlessly and mechanically as they ate their meagre and ill-cooked meals and did their thankless and monotonous chores through the aimless days."[62] This single sentence is one of the most heart-rending and depressing moments in all Lovecraft.

"The Colour out of Space," first published in *Amazing Stories* (September 1927), is of course the first of Lovecraft's major tales to effect that union of horror and science fiction which would become the hallmark of his later work. It continues the pattern already established in "The Call of Cthulhu" of transferring "the focus of supernatural dread from man and his little world and his gods, to the stars and the black and unplumbed gulfs of intergalactic space," as Fritz Leiber ably termed it.[63] In a sense, of course, Lovecraft was taking the easy way out: by simply having his entities come from some remote corner of the universe, he could attribute nearly any physical properties to them and not be required to give a plausible explanation for them. But the abundance of chemical and biological verisimilitude Lovecraft provides makes these unknown properties very convincing, as does the gradually enveloping atmosphere of the tale. If there is any flaw in "The Colour out of Space," it is that it is just a little too long: the scene with Ammi and the others in the Gardner farmhouse is dragged out well beyond the requirements for the tale, and actually dilutes some of the tensity of atmosphere Lovecraft has so carefully fashioned. But beyond this slight (and debatable) flaw, "The Colour out of Space" is an achievement Lovecraft rarely, perhaps never, equalled.

It would be more than a year before Lovecraft would write another story (exclusive of revisions or of such whimsies as "History of the *Necronomicon*" [1927], his tongue-in-cheek history of the writing and publication of his mythical tome, or "Ibid" [c. 1928],[64] a hilarious send-up of the schoolboy's common error that *Ibid.* is an actual author); but in late summer of 1928 he wrote "The Dunwich Horror." This is, certainly, one of Lovecraft's most popular tales, but I cannot help finding serious flaws of conception, execution, and style in it. Its plot, too, is well known. In the seedy area of Dunwich in "north central Massachusetts"[65] live a small handful of backwoods farmers. One of these, the Whateleys, are the source of particular suspicion ever since the birth, on Candlemas 1913, of Wilbur Whateley, the offspring of his albino mother and an unknown father. Lavinia's father, Old Whateley, shortly after the birth makes an ominous prediction: "*some day yew folks'll hear a child o' Lavinny's a-callin' its father's name on the top o' Sentinel Hill!*"[66]

Wilbur grows up anomalously fast, and by age thirteen is already nearly seven feet tall. He is intellectually precocious also, having been educated by the old books in Old Whateley's shabby library. In 1924 Old Whateley dies, but manages to wheeze instructions to his grandson to consult "page 751 *of the complete edition*" of some book so that he can "open up the gates to Yog-Sothoth."[67] Two years later Lavinia disappears and is never seen again. In the winter of 1927 Whateley makes his first trip out of Dunwich, to consult the Latin edition of the *Necronomicon* at the Miskatonic University Library; but when he asks to borrow the volume overnight, he is denied by the old librarian Henry Armitage. He tries to do the same at Harvard but is similarly rebuffed. Then, in the late spring of 1928, Wilbur breaks into the library to steal the volume, but is killed by the vicious guard-dog. His death is very repulsive:

> ...it is permissible to say that, aside from the external appearance of face and hands, the really human element in Wilbur Whateley must have been very small. When the medical examiner came, there was only a sticky whitish mass on the painted boards, and the monstrous odour had nearly disappeared. Apparently Whateley had no skull or bony skeleton; at least, in any true or stable sense. He had taken somewhat after his unknown father.[68]

Meanwhile bizarre things are happening elsewhere. Some monstrous entity whom the Whateleys had evidently been raising in their home now bursts forth, having no one to feed or tend to it. It creates havoc throughout the town, crushing houses as if they were matchsticks. Worst of all, it is completely invisible, leaving only huge footprints to indicate its presence. It descends down into a ravine called the Bear's Den, then later comes up again and causes hideous devastation. Armitage has in the meantime been decoding the diary in cipher that Wilbur had kept, and finally learns what the true state of affairs is:

> His wilder wanderings were very startling indeed, including...fantastic references to some plan for the extirpation of the entire human race and all animal and vegetable life from the earth by some terrible elder race of beings from another dimension. He would shout that the world was in danger, since the Elder Things wished to strip it and drag it away from the solar system and cosmos of matter into some other plane or phase of entity from which it had once fallen, vigintillions of years ago.[69]

But he knows how to stop it, and he and two colleagues go to the top of a small hill facing Sentinel Hill, where the monster appears to be heading. They are armed with an incantation to send the creature back to the other dimension it came from, as well as a sprayer containing a powder that will make the thing visible for an instant. Sure enough, both the incantation and the powder work, and the entity is seen to be a huge, ropy, tentacled monstrosity that shouts, "HELP! HELP!... *ff—ff—ff*—FATHER! FATHER! YOG-SOTHOTH!"[70] and is completely obliterated. It was Wilbur Whateley's twin brother.

It should be evident even from this narration that many points of plotting and characterization in the story are painfully inept. Let us first contrast the *moral* implications of "The Dunwich Horror" with those of "The Colour out of Space." We have seen that it is nearly impossible to deem the entities in the earlier story "evil" by any conventional standard; but the Whateleys—especially Wilbur and his twin—are clearly meant to be perceived as evil because of their plans to destroy the human race. And yet, was it not Lovecraft himself who, five years earlier, had whimsically written the following to Edwin Baird of *Weird Tales*?:

> Popular authors do not and apparently cannot appreciate the fact that true art is obtainable only by rejecting normality and conventionality in toto, and approaching a theme purged utterly of any usual or preconceived point of view. Wild and "different" as they may consider their quasi-weird products, it remains a fact that the bizarrerie is on the surface alone; and that basically they reiterate the same old conventional val-

> ues and motives and perspectives. Good and evil, teleological illusion, sugary sentiment, anthropocentric psychology—the usual superficial stock in trade, all shot through with the eternal and inescapable commonplace.... Who ever wrote a story from the point of view that man is a blemish on the cosmos, who ought to be eradicated?[71]

This criticism applies perfectly to "The Dunwich Horror." What we have here is an elementary "good vs. evil" struggle between Armitage (representing humanity and the forces of "good") and the Whateleys (representing the extraterrestrials and the forces of "evil"). The only way around this conclusion is to assume that "The Dunwich Horror" is a parody of some sort; this is, indeed, exactly what Donald R. Burleson has done in an interesting essay,[72] pointing out that it is the Whateley twins (regarded as a single entity) who, in mythic terms, fulfill the traditional role of the "hero" much more than Armitage does (*e.g.*, the mythic hero's descent to the underworld is paralleled by the twin's descent into the Bear's Den), and pointing out also that the passage from the *Necronomicon* cited in the tale—"Man rules now where They [the Old Ones] ruled once; They shall soon rule where man rules now"[73]—makes Armitage's "defeat" of the Whateleys seem a mere temporary staving off of the inevitable. These points are well taken, but there is no evidence in Lovecraft's letters that "The Dunwich Horror" was meant parodically (*i.e.*, as a satire on immature readers of the pulp magazines) or that the figure of Armitage is meant anything but seriously.

Armitage is, indeed, clearly modelled upon Willett of *The Case of Charles Dexter Ward*: he defeats the "villains" by incantations, and he is susceptible to the same flaws—pomposity, arrogance, self-importance—that can be seen in Willett. Armitage is, indeed, the prize buffoon in all Lovecraft, and some of his statements—such as the melodramatic "*But what, in God's name, can we do*?"[74]—make painful reading, as does the silly lecture he delivers to the Dunwich folk at the end: "We have no business calling in such things from outside, and only very wicked people and very wicked cults ever try to."[75]

There are problems of plot, also. What, exactly, is the *purpose* of the "powder" Armitage uses to make the creature visible for an instant? What is to be gained by this procedure? It seems to be used simply to allow Lovecraft to write luridly about ropy tentacles and the like. Consider also Old Whateley's prediction about a child of Lavinia's calling to his father on Sentinel Hill: surely he did not have in mind the child calling for his father as he was being destroyed, but it is not clear in what other sense the statement is meant; it again seems designed merely to provide a purportedly clever foreshadowing of the ending. The spectacle of three small human figures—Armitage and his stalwart cohorts—waving their arms about and shouting incantations on the top of a hill is so comical that it seems incredible that Lovecraft could have missed the humor in it; but he seems to have done so, for this is presumably the climactic scene in the story.

What "The Dunwich Horror" did was, in effect, to make the rest of the "Cthulhu Mythos" (*i.e.*, the contributions by other and less skillful hands) possible. Its luridness, melodrama, and naive moral dichotomy were picked up by later writers (it was, not surprisingly, one of Derleth's favorite tales) rather than the subtler work embodied in "The Call of Cthulhu," "The Colour out of Space," and others. In a sense, then, Lovecraft bears some responsibility for bringing the "Cthulhu Mythos" and some of its unfortunate results down on his own head.

Lovecraft, of course, did indeed encourage the mutual borrowing that one finds increasingly in the tales of Clark Ashton Smith, Robert E. Howard, and others of this period, although he did so as a means of creating greater verisimilitude and as "background-material,"[76] not as the prime focus of the tales as occurs in the work of Derleth and his followers. Lovecraft himself begins this borrowing in "The Dunwich Horror" by noting John Dee's English translation of the *Necronomicon*, first cited as an epigraph by Frank Belknap Long in "The Space-Eaters" (written in 1927; published—without the epigraph—in *Weird Tales* for July 1928). This borrowing is of such a trivial sort—affecting only the use of imagined names, not fundamental themes or conceptions—that it seems captious to argue, as Will Murray has, that Lovecraft "lost control" of the Mythos in later years by failing to prevent his colleagues from using his own terms or of inventing their own.[77] One wonders how Lovecraft could feasibly have prevented such a thing: he was certainly in no position to tell Clark Ashton Smith or Robert E. Howard not to write a given story, and his own name-dropping of a book or god invented by a colleague was more in the spirit of fun than anything. Murray may perhaps be correct in thinking that the mythos was already becoming somewhat trivialized by these ever-increasing in-jokes; but Lovecraft's own stories, at any rate, remained—on the level of philosophical orientation—very much his own.

There is, conversely, no justification whatever for the belief (expressed by Robert M. Price and others) that Lovecraft was somehow "orchestrating" the development of the mythos. Not only is it clear that he himself was creating new terms and elements as the spirit moved him, without any advance planning, but he had little or nothing to do with other writers' inventions. It was Smith who invented the god Tsathoggua (in "The Tale of Satampra Zeiros" [1929]), and Lovecraft who borrowed the entity in "The Mound" (1929-1930) and other tales; to say, therefore, that Smith was "adding" to Lovecraft's mythos is a serious misconstrual of the facts, since Smith believed that other writers (including Lovecraft) were borrowing from *his* mythology. Lovecraft was not some sort of managing editor of a writers' group laying down the law what others should write; if some element created by one of his colleagues amused or intrigued him, he would adopt it. In later years Lovecraft gives the appearance of urging his younger associates to "add" to his mythos; but in reality he was merely providing encouragement to these literary novices, and he always took care to advise them to write *their own* stories, not merely slavish imitations of his. Lovecraft's own attempts at imitating Dunsany, Machen, and others had shown him the fundamental aesthetic emptiness of pastiche except as a formative influence.

In an important sense, indeed, "The Dunwich Horror" itself turns out to be not much more than a pastiche. The central premise—the sexual union of a "god" or monster with a human woman—is taken directly from Machen's "The Great God Pan"; Lovecraft makes no secret of the borrowing, having Armitage say of the Dunwich people at one point, "Great God, what simpletons! Shew them Arthur Machen's Great God Pan and they'll think it a common Dunwich scandal!"[78] The use of bizarre footsteps to indicate the presence of an otherwise undetectable entity is borrowed from Blackwood's "The Wendigo." Lovecraft was clearly aware of the number of tales featuring invisible monsters—Maupassant's "The Horla" (certain features of which had already been adapted for "The Call of Cthulhu"); Fitz-James O'Brien's "What Was it?"; Bierce's "The Damned Thing"—and derived hints from each of them in his own creation. The fact that Lovecraft on occasion borrowed heavily from previous sources need not be a source of criticism, for he ordinarily made exhaustive alterations in what he borrowed; but in this case the borrowings go beyond mere surface details of imagery to the very core of the plot.

"The Dunwich Horror" is, of course, not a complete failure. Its portrayal of the decaying backwoods Massachusetts terrain is vivid and memorable, even if a little more hyperbolic than that of "The Colour out of Space"; it is, moreover, largely the result of personal experience. Lovecraft admitted in later years that Dunwich was located in the area in south central Massachusetts around Wilbraham, an area he had visited earlier in the summer of 1928 when he stayed for two weeks with an old amateur colleague, Edith Miniter, in Wilbraham. Miniter, a tremendous fund of old New England folklore, told him of the very real legendry regarding whippoorwills (as psychopomps of the dead) still current amongst the populace, and Lovecraft makes several mentions of it in the story. But, if Wilbraham is roughly the setting for Dunwich, why does Lovecraft in the very first sentence of the story declare that the town is located in "*north* central Massachusetts"? Some parts of the locale are indeed taken from that region, specifically the Bear's Den, which is an actual ravine near Athol to which H. Warner Munn took Lovecraft in late June 1928.[79] The name Sentinel Hill is taken from a Sentinel Elm Farm in Athol.[80] Lovecraft has, in other words, *mingled* topographical impressions from various sites and coalesced them into a single imagined locale. We have already seen this phenomenon in the creation of Arkham: Miskatonic University is no doubt a fictionalization of Brown University in Providence, while the actual location and perhaps the name is taken from the east-central Massachusetts town of Oakham (later to be transferred to the coastal town of Salem). We will see it again in the case of Innsmouth.

A word should be said about the extensive use of New England dialect in the tale. How authentic is it? Did it ever actually exist? Consider a statement made in 1929:

> As for Yankee farmers—oddly enough, I hadn't noticed that the majority talk any differently from myself; so that I've never regarded them as a separate class to whom one must use a special dialect. If I were to say, "Mornin', Zeke, haow ye be?" to anybody along the road during my numerous summer walks, I fancy I'd receive an icy stare in return—or perhaps a puzzled inquiry as to what theatrical troupe I had wandered out of![81]

And yet, in the summer of 1928, when Lovecraft ventured up to Vermont to visit Vrest Orton, he writes to his aunt: "Whether you believe it or not, the rustics hereabouts *actually* say 'caow,' 'daown,' 'araound,' &c.—& employ in daily speech a thousand colourful country-idioms which we know only in literature."[82] That last remark is of great interest, for it suggests that Lovecraft's earlier use of the dialect—in, for example, "The Picture in the House" (1920)—was literarily inspired. What could have been the source? Jason C. Eckhardt[83] has made a powerful case that it is James Russell Lowell's poem-cycle *The Biglow Papers* (1848-1862), which contains a version of the dialect and a note that it was even then archaic in New England. This latter point is of some interest in regard to "The Picture in the House," in that it thereby becomes another subtle clue to the old rustic's preternatural age; but in "The Dunwich Horror" Lovecraft, having just discovered the dialect still existent—even if in Vermont and not in Massachusetts—felt no compunction in using it extensively as a means of augmenting the horror by having it expressed in the crude patois of ignorant peasants.

For those interested in following the surface details of the "Cthulhu Mythos," "The Dunwich Horror" offers much fodder for argument. That it builds in part upon "The Call of Cthulhu" and other tales is clear from the mentions of Cthulhu, Kadath, and other terms in the lengthy quotation from the *Necronomicon* in the story; but the term "Old Ones" is ambiguous, and it does not appear to refer to the "Great Old Ones" of "The Call of Cthulhu," nor is it clear whether Yog-

Sothoth—who never recurs as a major figure in any subsequent Lovecraft tale—is one of the Old Ones or not. Probably Lovecraft did not expect that his casually coined terms would be sifted and analyzed by later critics as if they were biblical texts, and he threw them off largely for the sake of resonance and atmosphere. Lovecraft, as will become manifestly evident, not only did not plan out all (or any) of the details of his pseudomythology in advance, but also had no concern whatever in altering the details of his pseudomythology when it suited him, never being bound by previous usage—something that later critics have also found infuriating, as if it were some violation of the sanctity or unity of a mythos that never had any sanctity or unity to begin with. It should also be pointed out that this is the only story that contains a lengthy extract from the *Necronomicon*; later writers have not been so reticent, but their bungling quotations—written with a lamentable lack of subtlety and (in Derleth's case especially) a pitiable ignorance of archaic diction—have resulted in the watering down of the potentially powerful conception of a book of "forbidden" knowledge.

A brief note as to the name Dunwich may be in order. It has been pointed out that there is a real town in England with this name—or, rather, that there *was* such a town on the southeast coast of the island, a town that suffered inexorable desertion as the sea washed away more and more of the coastal terrain on which it stood. It was the subject of Swinburne's memorable poem "By the North Sea" (although it is never mentioned by name there), and is cited in Arthur Machen's *The Terror* (1917). The curious thing, however, is that the English Dunwich is more similar to Lovecraft's decaying seaport of Innsmouth than it is of the inland town of Dunwich; nevertheless, it is likely enough that the name alone was indeed derived from this English counterpart. There are, of course, any number of towns in New England with the *-wich* ending (*e.g.*, Greenwich, one of the Massachusetts towns evacuated to make way for the Quabbin Reservoir).

Another year and a half would pass before Lovecraft commenced another original tale, although in this interval (1928-1930) he ghostwrote the significant tale "The Mound" (1929-1930) for Zealia Bishop and also wrote the *Fungi from Yuggoth* sonnet-cycle. But in February 1930 Lovecraft began "The Whisperer in Darkness." This story would be among the most difficult in its actual composition of any of his major tales, for it was "provisionally" finished in the summer but underwent extensive revision based, apparently, upon suggestions made by Bernard Austin Dwyer;[84] and Lovecraft did not complete the tale to his satisfaction until September. The result is a 25,000-word novelette—the longest of his fictions up to that time aside from his two "practice" novels—that conjures up the hoary grandeur of the New England countryside even more poignantly than any of his previous works, but which still suffers from some flaws of conception and motivation.

The Vermont floods of November 3, 1927, cause great destruction in the rural parts of the state, and also engender reports of strange bodies—not recognizably human or animal—floating down the flood-choked rivers. Albert N. Wilmarth, a professor of literature at Miskatonic University with a side interest in folklore, dismisses these accounts as standard myth-making; but then he hears from a reclusive but evidently learned individual in Vermont, Henry Wentworth Akeley, who not only confirms the reports but maintains that there is an entire colony of extraterrestrials dwelling in the region, whose purpose is to mine a metal they cannot find on their own planet (which may be the recently discovered ninth planet of the solar system, called Yuggoth in various occult writings) and also, by means of a complicated mechanical device, to remove the brains of human beings from their bodies and to take them on fantastic cosmic voyagings. Wilmarth is naturally skeptical of Akeley's tale, but the latter sends him photographs of a hideous black stone with inexplicable hieroglyphs on it along with a phonograph recording he made of some sort of ritual in the woods near his home—a ritual in which both humans and (judging from the highly anomalous buzzing voice) some utterly non-human creatures participated. As their correspondence continues, Wilmarth slowly becomes convinced of the truth of Akeley's claims—and is both wholly convinced and increasingly alarmed as some of their letters go unaccountably astray and Akeley finds himself embroiled in a battle with guns and dogs as the aliens besiege his house.

Then, in a startling reversal, Akeley sends him a reassuring letter stating that he has come to terms with the aliens: he had misinterpreted their motives and now believes that they are merely trying to establish a workable rapport with human beings for mutual benefit. He is reconciled to the prospect of his brain being removed and taken to Yuggoth and beyond, for he will thereby acquire cosmic knowledge made available only to a handful of human beings since the beginning of civilization. He urges Wilmarth to visit him to discuss the matter, reminding him to bring all the papers and other materials he had sent so that they can be consulted if necessary. Wilmarth agrees, taking a spectral journey into the heart of the Vermont backwoods and meeting with Akeley, who has suffered some inexplicable malady: he can only speak in a whisper, and he is wrapped from head to foot with a blanket except for his face and hands. He tells Wilmarth wondrous tales of travelling faster than the speed of light and of the strange machines in the room used to transport brains through the cosmos. Numbed with astonishment, Wilmarth retires to bed, but hears a disturbing colloquy in Akeley's room with several of the buzzing voices and other, human voices. But what makes him flee from the place is a very simple thing he sees as he sneaks down to Akeley's room late at night: "For the things in the chair, perfect to the last, subtle detail of microscopic resemblance—or identity—were the face and hands of Henry Wentworth Akeley."[85]

Without the necessity of stating it, Lovecraft makes clear the true state of affairs: the last, reassuring letter by "Akeley" was in fact a forgery by the alien entities, written as a means of getting Wilmarth to come up to Vermont with all the evidence of his relations with Akeley; the speaker in the chair was not Akeley—whose brain had already been removed from his body and placed in one of the machines—but one of the aliens, perhaps Nyarlathotep himself, whom they worship. The attempted "rapport" which the aliens claim to desire with human beings is a sham, and they in fact merely wish to enslave the human race; hence Wilmarth must write his account to warn the world of this lurking menace.

Our first order of business is to ascertain, if possible, exactly what the nature of Lovecraft's revisions in the story may have been. Steven J. Mariconda has studied the matter thoroughly, and his conclusions can be accepted with confidence. Frank Belknap Long, in a 1944 memoir, speaks of hearing Lovecraft read the tale to him in New York; although some parts of his account are clearly erroneous, there is perhaps a kernel of truth in Long's recollection of one point: "Howard's voice becoming suddenly sepulchral: 'And from the box a tortured voice spoke: "Go while there is still time—"'"[86] It is clear that this is at least one point on which Dwyer suggested revision: the "tip-off" (presumably by Akeley's brain from one of the canisters) is so obvious that it would dilute the purported "surprise" ending of the story (if indeed the story in this version ended as it did). It also appears that Dwyer recommended that Wilmarth be made a rather less gullible figure, but on this point Lovecraft does not seem to have made much headway: although random details seem to have been inserted to heighten Wilmarth's skepticism, especially in regard to the obviously forged final letter by "Akeley," he still appears spectacularly naive in proceeding blithely up to Vermont with all the documentary evidence he has received from Akeley. And yet, Wilmarth exhibits in extreme form what we have seen in many of Lovecraft's characters: the difficulty in believing that something supernatural or supernormal has occurred. Wilmarth, as a professor of literature, immediately detects the difference in style and tone in "Akeley's" last letter: "Word-choice, spelling—all were subtly different. And with my academic sensitiveness to prose style, I could trace profound divergences in his commonest reactions and rhythm-responses."[87] But he attributes this—not entirely implausibly—to the spectacular alteration in Akeley's consciousness that has resulted from his "rapport" with the aliens.

But "The Whisperer in Darkness" suffers from a somewhat more severe flaw, one that we have already seen in "The Dunwich Horror." Once again, in violation of Lovecraft's stated wish to discard conventional morality in regard to his extraterrestrials, he has endowed his aliens with common—and rather petty—human flaws and motivations. They are guilty of cheap forgery on two occasions—both in that last letter from "Akeley" and in an earlier telegram they had sent under Akeley's name to prevent Wilmarth from coming prematurely to Vermont; and on that occasion the aliens were so inept as to misspell Akeley's name, in spite of the fact that, as they themselves maintain, "Their brain-capacity exceeds that of any other surviving life-form."[88] Their gun-battle with Akeley takes on unintentionally comic overtones, reminiscent of shoot-outs in cheap western movies. When Wilmarth comes to the Akeley farmhouse, they drug his coffee to make him sleep; but he, disliking the taste, does not drink it, hence overhears parts of the colloquy that was not meant for his ears.

But whereas such flaws of conception and execution cripple "The Dunwich Horror," here they are only minor blemishes in an otherwise magnificent tale. "The Whisperer in Darkness" remains a monument in Lovecraft's work for its throbbingly vital evocation of New England landscape, its air of documentary verisimilitude, its insidiously subtle atmosphere of cumulative horror, and its breathtaking intimations of the cosmic.

Once again, the setting is founded upon actual travels Lovecraft made in Vermont; indeed, several paragraphs of his essay, "Vermont—A First Impression" (1927), have been incorporated wholesale into the story, but with subtle changes to augment the sense of unease and remoteness engendered by the locale. Lovecraft visited Vermont for the first time in the summer of 1927, returning in the summer of 1928. He did not actually witness the Vermont floods (a real event), but they received extensive coverage in newspapers throughout the East Coast, and Lovecraft no doubt heard some first-hand accounts of them from his several friends in Vermont, including Vrest Orton and Arthur Goodenough. Indeed, it seems as if Akeley's secluded farmhouse is a commingling of the Orton residence in Brattleboro and Goodenough's home farther to the north. The figure of Akeley seems in part based on one Bert Akley, a reclusive self-taught artist whom Lovecraft met in 1928. This remarkable fusion of fact and fiction, of personal experience and fantastic imagination, is one of the most distinctive features of Lovecraft's work as a whole.

Lovecraft's identification of his imagined planet Yuggoth (first cited, of course, in the *Fungi from Yuggoth*) with the recently discovered Pluto is certainly a piquant in-joke. The actual announcement of the planet's discovery was made some weeks after Lovecraft commenced writing the story, so that it cannot be said that the discovery—the only "new" planet found in Lovecraft's lifetime, and an astronomical event of major significance—actually inspired the tale; but his very adept and seamless incorporation of it into the fabric of his plot is a remarkable instance of opportunism.

"The Whisperer in Darkness" occupies a sort of middle ground in terms of Lovecraft's portrayal of extraterrestrials. So far we have seen aliens regarded as violent but "beyond good and evil" ("The Call of Cthulhu"), as utterly incomprehensible ("The Colour out of Space"), and as conventionally "evil" ("The Dunwich Horror"); "The Whisperer in Darkness" falls somewhere in between, asking us to express great horror at the aliens' physically *outré* form and properties (they cannot be photographed by regular cameras), their deceit and trickery, and, preeminently, their plans to remove human brains and take them off the earth in canisters. And yet, on this last point Lovecraft begins to waver a little. Wilmarth, after receiving the forged letter, ruminates:

> To shake off the maddening and wearying limitations of time and space and natural law—to be linked with the vast *outside*—to come close to the nighted and abysmal secrets of the infinite and the ultimate—surely such a thing was worth the risk of one's life, soul, and sanity![89]

Such a thing actually sounds rather appealing; and the interesting thing is that the utterance exactly parallels Lovecraft's own views as to the function of weird fiction: "I choose weird stories because...one of my strongest and most persistent wishes [is] to achieve, momentarily, the illusion of some strange suspension or violation of the galling limitations of time, space, and natural law."[90] But Wilmarth cannot sustain his enthusiasm for long. One of the encased brains in Akeley's room (a human being) tells him: "Do you realise what it means when I say I have been on thirty-seven different celestial bodies—planets, dark stars, and less definable objects—including eight outside our galaxy and two outside the curved cosmos of space and time?"[91] This is a spectacularly cosmic conception, and again a rather attractive one; but Wilmarth ultimately backs away in horror: "My scientific zeal had vanished amidst fear and loathing...."[92]

Later tales would carry the metamorphosis of alien races still farther, making them actual symbols or representations of humanity or of the future social and political evolution of the human race; it is an evolution of consuming interest that we shall study later.

"The Whisperer in Darkness" resembles "The Colour out of Space" more than "The Dunwich Horror" in its tantalizing *hints* of wonders and horrors beyond our ken, especially in such things as the fragmentary transcript of the ritual recorded by Akeley, the almost self-parodic dropping of countless "Mythos" names and terms as contained in one of Akeley's letters, the muffled colloquy heard at the end by Wilmarth (of which he himself remarks that "even their frightful effect on me was one of *suggestion* rather than *revelation*,"[93] and, especially, what the false Akeley tells him about the hidden nature of the cosmos.

"Never was a sane man more dangerously close to the arcana of basic entity,"[94] Wilmarth states, but then refuses to do more than tease the reader with some of what he learnt:

> I learned whence Cthulhu *first* came, and why half the great temporary stars of history had flared forth. I guessed—from hints which made even my informant pause timidly—the secret behind the Magellanic Clouds and globular nebulae, and the black truth veiled by the immemorial allegory of Tao.... I started with loathing when told of the monstrous nuclear chaos beyond angled space which the *Necronomicon* had mercifully cloaked under the name of Azathoth.[95]

If Lovecraft's later followers had exercised such restraint, the "Cthulhu Mythos" would not be quite the travesty it became.

The four years comprising Lovecraft's return to Providence from New York clearly represent the first phase of his most significant period of fiction writing. Two short novels, four novelettes, and several short stories (along with revisions and poetry, to be considered elsewhere) may perhaps not seem like much in contrast to more mechanically prolific pulpsmiths, but this relatively slim output—in conjunction with the equally slender work that followed in the next five years—has generated more popular interest and academic criticism than almost any other body of fiction in the history of weird literature. These tales are by no means without flaws, but their exponential increase in quality from the intermittently interesting but ultimately insubstantial work that preceded them shows that Lovecraft was approaching the pinnacle of his fiction-writing career.

VI.

THE MAJOR FICTION: SECOND PHASE (1931-1935)

The end of 1930 is in one sense a good place to pause in our discussion of the fiction of Lovecraft's final decade; for it was at the beginning of 1931 that he made one of his most prescient and provocative statements on the nature of weird fiction, and specifically of the type of weird fiction he himself was attempting to write. I have cited this statement in an earlier chapter, but it now requires more detailed analysis. The letter (to Frank Belknap Long, 27 February 1931) in which it is imbedded is one of the greatest documents of his entire literary career (it occupies more than fifty pages in the *Selected Letters*, and at that is clearly abridged), and at its core is the need to revitalize art in light of modern science, in particular the sciences of physics, biology, and psychology, which have fundamentally altered our attitude to ourselves and to the universe. Many formerly accepted beliefs—the belief that human beings are at the center of the cosmos; the belief that our mental and emotional processes are essentially straightforward and easily recoverable—have been irrevocably shaken in the light of Einstein, Planck, Freud, and others; so that art must now reshape itself to take cognizance of these new realities. Much of Lovecraft's thinking here was influenced by Joseph Wood Krutch's revolutionary book, *The Modern Temper* (1929), which laid bare the hollowness of previous attitudes toward art and life. In many ways Lovecraft anticipated Krutch's findings, and it was precisely because he and Krutch saw things so similarly that the book so affected him. The answer, for Lovecraft the writer of weird fiction, was to bring the weird tale "up to date" by abandoning any features that were definitely outmoded in light of present-day science. This meant much more than merely the abandonment of such things as the vampire (which had already been extensively modified and updated in "The Shunned House"), the ghost (which Lovecraft never used), and other such conventional myths:

> The time has come when the normal revolt against time, space, & matter must assume a form not overtly incompatible with what is known of reality—when it must be gratified by images forming *supplements*

> rather than *contradictions* of the visible & mensurable universe. And what, if not a form of *non-supernatural cosmic art*, is to pacify this sense of revolt—as well as gratify the cognate sense of curiosity?[1]

This may be the most important utterance Lovecraft ever made: the renunciation of the supernatural, as well as the need to offer supplements rather than contradictions to known phenomena, make it transparently clear that Lovecraft was now consciously moving toward a union of weird fiction and science fiction (although perhaps not the science fiction largely published in the pulp magazines of this time). Indeed, in formal terms nearly all of Lovecraft's work since "The Call of Cthulhu" *is* science fiction, if by that we mean that it supplies a *scientific justification* (although in some cases a justification based upon some hypothetical advance of science) for the purportedly "supernatural" events; it is only in Lovecraft's manifest wish to *terrify* that his work remains on the borderline of science fiction rather than being wholly within its parameters.

Lovecraft's work had been inexorably moving in this direction since at least the writing of "The Shunned House." Even in much earlier tales—"Dagon" (1917), "Beyond the Wall of Sleep" (1919), "The Temple" (1920), "Arthur Jermyn" (1920), "From Beyond" (1920), "The Nameless City" (1921), and even perhaps "Herbert West—Reanimator" (1921-1922)—Lovecraft had already provided pseudo-scientific rationales for weird events, and such things as *At the Mountains of Madness* (1931) and "The Shadow out of Time" (1934-1935) are only the pinnacles in this development. Pure supernaturalism had, in fact—aside from such minor works as "The Moon-Bog" (1921) and a few others—*never* been much utilized by Lovecraft.

What, then, do we make of a statement uttered less than a year after the one I have quoted above? "...the crux of a *weird* tale is something which *could not possibly happen*."[2] Here, certainly, "something which could not possibly happen" must be regarded as supernatural. But the context of this utterance must be examined with care. It was made in the course of a discussion with August Derleth regarding William Faulkner's "A Rose for Emily," that masterful story of necrophilia. Lovecraft, while admiring the story, was maintaining that it was not "weird" because necrophilia is a mundane horror that does not involve the contravention of natural law *as we know it*. The letter continues:

> If any unexpected advance of physics, chemistry, or biology were to indicate the *possibility* of any phenomena related by the weird tale, that particular set of phenomena would cease to be *weird* in the ultimate sense because it would become surrounded by a dif-

> ferent set of emotions. It would no longer represent imaginative liberation, because it would no longer indicate a suspension or violation of the natural laws against whose universal dominance our fancies rebel.

Lovecraft is carving out a very special position for his type of weird tale: it can neither be a mere *conte cruel* or a tale of physical gruesomeness (what is now termed "psychological suspense"), nor can it plainly violate *currently known* natural laws, as in standard supernatural fiction. In effect, Lovecraft is occupying a middle ground between work that is *too non-supernatural* (the *conte cruel*) and work that is *too supernatural* (tales of ghosts, vampires, witches, etc.). Only the intermediate ground—"non-supernatural cosmic art," art that presents accounts of phenomena not currently explainable by science—can offer possibilities for creative expression in this field, at least for Lovecraft.

As I have said, Lovecraft's fiction had been tending in this direction for some time, and "The Call of Cthulhu" initiates the most representative phase of his writing in this regard. Some interesting passages in that story are worth examining to show how Lovecraft is, as it were, trying to have his cake and eat it too—trying not to contradict the known facts of science but doing so in such a way as still to provide him that kick of "imaginative liberation" he sought. The narrator, Thurston, admits openly and frequently that he is a materialist; but then, toward the end of his account, he states: "My attitude was still one of absolute materialism, *as I wish it still were*"[3] (italics Lovecraft's). What could this mean? Is Lovecraft himself discarding his materialism? Hardly. What Thurston has discovered is at least one instance of some "violation of natural law" as he understands it—not so much the actual existence of Cthulhu but some of his properties, specifically his ability to control dreams and (as Johansen discovered) his ability to recombine disparate parts of himself. These things do not absolutely "contradict" natural law because Cthulhu, as a being from the remotest depths of space, may well be obeying the natural laws of his native region; but they contradict Thurston's *conception* of natural law, which is founded solely upon what happens on the earth.

At the Mountains of Madness, written in the first three months of 1931, is Lovecraft's most ambitious attempt at "non-supernatural cosmic art"; it is a triumph in every way. At 40,000 words it is Lovecraft's longest work of fiction save *The Case of Charles Dexter Ward*; and just as his other two novels represent apotheoses of earlier phases of his career—*The Dream-Quest of Unknown Kadath* the culmination of Dunsanianism, *Ward* the pinnacle of pure supernaturalism—so is *At the Mountains of Madness* the greatest of his attempts to fuse weird fiction and science fiction.

The Miskatonic Antarctic Expedition of 1930-1931, led by William Dyer (his full name is never supplied here but is given in "The Shadow out of Time"), begins very promisingly but ends in tragedy and horror. Spurred by a new boring device invented by engineer Frank H. Pabodie, the expedition makes great progress at sites on the shore of McMurdo Sound (on the opposite side of the Ross Ice Shelf from where Byrd's expedition had only recently camped). But the biologist Lake, struck by some peculiar markings on soapstone fragments he has found, feels the need to conduct a sub-expedition far to the northwest. There he makes a spectacular discovery: not only the world's tallest mountains ("Everest out of the running,"[4] he laconically radios back to the camp), but then the frozen remains—some damaged, some intact—of monstrous barrel-shaped creatures that cannot be reconciled with the normal evolution of this planet. They seem half-animal and half-vegetable, with tremendous brain-capacity and, apparently, with more senses than we have. Lake, who has read the *Necronomicon*, jocosely thinks they may be the Elder Things or Old Ones spoken of in that book and elsewhere, who are "supposed to have created all earth-life as jest or mistake."[5]

Later Lake's sub-expedition loses radio contact with the main party, apparently because of the high winds in that region. After a day or so passes, Dyer feels he must come to Lake's aid and takes a small group of men in some airplanes to see what has gone amiss. To their horror, they find the camp devastated—either by winds or by the sled dogs or by some other nameless forces—but discover no trace of the intact specimens of the Old Ones; they do come upon the damaged specimens "insanely" buried in the snow, and are forced to conclude that it is the work of the one missing human, Gedney. Dyer and the graduate student Danforth decide to take a trip by themselves beyond the titanic mountain plateau to see if they can find any explanation for the tragedy.

As they scale the immense plateau, they find to their amazement an enormous stone city, fifty to one hundred miles in extent, clearly built millions of years ago, long before there could have been any humans on the planet. Exploring some of the interiors, they are eventually forced to conclude that the city was built by the Old Ones. Because the buildings contain, as wall decorations, many bas-reliefs supplying the history of the Old Ones' civilization, they are able to learn that the Old Ones came from space some fifty million years ago, settling in the antarctic and eventually branching out to other areas of the earth. They built their huge cities with the aid of shoggoths—amorphous, fifteen-foot masses of protoplasm which they controlled by hypnotic suggestion. Unfortunately, over time these shoggoths gained a semi-stable brain and began to develop a will of their own, forcing the Old Ones to conduct several campaigns of resubjugation. Later other extraterrestrial races—including the fungi from Yuggoth and the

Cthulhu spawn—came to the earth and engaged in battles over territory with the Old Ones, and eventually the latter were forced back to their original Antarctic settlement. They had also lost the ability to fly through space. The reasons for their abandonment of this city, and for their extinction, are unfathomable.

Dyer and Danforth then stumble upon traces that someone dragging a sled had passed by, and they follow it, finding first some huge albino penguins, then the sled with the remains of Gedney and a dog, then a group of decapitated Old Ones, who had obviously come to life by being thawed in Lake's camp. Then they hear an anomalous sound—a musical piping over a wide range. Could it be some other Old Ones? Not stopping to investigate, they flee madly; but they simultaneously turn their flashlights upon the thing for an instant, and find that it is nothing but a loathsome shoggoth:

> It was a terrible, indescribable thing vaster than any subway train—a shapeless congeries of protoplasmic bubbles, faintly self-luminous, and with myriads of temporary eyes forming and unforming as pustules of greenish light all over the tunnel-filling front that bore down upon us, crushing the frantic penguins and slithering over the glistening floor that it and its kind had swept so evilly free of all litter.[6]

As they fly back to camp, Danforth shrieks out in horror: he has seen some further sight that unhinges his mind, but he refuses to tell Dyer what it is. All he can do is make the eldritch cry, "*Tekeli-li! Tekeli-li!*"

Once again the utter inadequacy of a synopsis of this short novel will be evident to every reader. In the first place, it cannot begin to convey the rich, detailed, and utterly convincing scientific erudition that creates the sense of verisimilitude so necessary in a tale so otherwise *outré*. Lovecraft was, of course, a lifelong student of the Antarctic: he had written small treatises on *Wilkes's Explorations* and *The Voyages of Capt. Ross, R.N.* as a boy, and had followed with avidity reports of the explorations of Borchgrevink, Scott, Amundsen, and others in the early decades of the century. Indeed, as Jason C. Eckhardt has demonstrated,[7] the early parts of Lovecraft's tale clearly show the influence of Admiral Byrd's expedition of 1928-1930, as well as other contemporary expeditions; I believe Lovecraft also found a few hints on points of style and imagery in the early pages of M. P. Shiel's great novel *The Purple Cloud* (1901; reissued 1930), which relates an expedition to the Arctic. But it is also Lovecraft's thorough knowledge of geology, biology, chemistry, physics, and natural history that lead to a passage like this:

> This was my first word of the discovery, and it told of the identification of early shells, bones of ganoids and placoderms, remnants of labyrinthodonts and thecodonts, great mososaur skull fragments, dinosaur vertebrae and armour-plates, pterodactyl teeth and wing-bones, archaeopteryx debris, Miocene sharks' teeth, primitive bird-skulls, and skulls, vertebrae, and other bones of archaic mammals such as palaeotheres, xiphodons, dinocerases, eohippi, oreodons, and titanotheres.[8]

Lovecraft's science in this novel is absolutely sound for its period, although subsequent discoveries have made a few points obsolete. In fact, he was so concerned about the scientific authenticity of the work that, prior to its first publication in *Astounding Stories* (February, March, and April 1936), he inserted some revisions eliminating an hypothesis he had made that the Antarctic continent had originally been two land masses separated by a frozen channel between the Ross and Weddell Seas—an hypothesis that had been proven false by the first airplane flight across the continent, by Lincoln Ellsworth and Herbert Hollick-Kenyon in late 1935.

Some impatient readers have found the scientific passages—especially at the beginning—excessive, but they are absolutely essential for establishing the atmosphere of realism (and also of the protagonists' rationality) that will make the latter parts of the novel insidiously convincing. *At the Mountains of Madness*, which avowedly presents itself as a scientific report, is the greatest instance of Lovecraft's dictum that "no weird story can truly produce terror unless it is devised with all the care & verisimilitude of an actual *hoax*."[9] Indeed, the narrator claims that even this account is a less formal version of a treatise that will appear "in an official bulletin of Miskatonic University."[10]

The real focal point of *At the Mountains of Madness* is the Old Ones. Indeed, although initially portrayed as objects of terror, they ultimately yield to the shoggoths in this regard; as Fritz Leiber remarks, "the author shows us horrors and then pulls back the curtain a little farther, letting us glimpse the horrors of which even the horrors are afraid!"[11] There is, however, even more to it than this. It is not merely that the Old Ones become the secondary "horrors" in the tale; it is that they cease, toward the end, to be horrors at all. Dyer, studying the history of the Old Ones—their colonization of the earth; their building of titanic cities on the Antarctic and elsewhere; their pursuit of knowledge—gradually comes to realize the profound bonds that human beings share with them, and which neither share with the loathsome, primitive, virtually mindless shoggoths. The canonical passage occurs near the end, as he sees the group of dead Old Ones decapitated by the shoggoth:

> Poor devils! After all, they were not evil things of their kind. They were the men of another age and another order of being. Nature had played a hellish jest on them...and this was their tragic homecoming.
>
> ...Scientists to the last—what had they done that we would not have done in their place? God, what intelligence and persistence! What a facing of the incredible, just as those carven kinsmen and forbears had faced things only a little less incredible! Radiates, vegetables, monstrosities, star-spawn—whatever they had been, they were men![12]

This triumphant conclusion is, however, prefigured in a number of ways. When Lake's decimated camp is discovered, it is evident to every reader (although Dyer cannot bring himself to admit it) that the destruction has been the work of the Old Ones. But are they morally culpable here? It is later ascertained that the immediate cause of the violence was a vicious attack upon them by the dogs of Lake's party (Dyer, trying to look at matters from the Old Ones' perspective, alludes to "an attack by the furry, frantically barking quadrupeds, and a dazed defence against them and the equally frantic white simians with the queer wrappings and paraphernalia."[13] Some of Lake's men have been "incised and subtracted from in the most curious, cold-blooded, and inhuman fashion"[14] by the Old Ones; but how is this different from the crude dissection Lake himself had attempted on one of the damaged specimens? Later, when Dyer and Danforth discover the sled containing the body of Gedney (a specimen which the Old Ones had taken with them), Dyer notes that it was "wrapped with patent care to prevent further damage."[15]

The most significant way in which the Old Ones are identified with human beings is in the historical digression Dyer provides, specifically in regard to the Old Ones' social and economic organization. In many ways they represent a utopia toward which Lovecraft clearly hopes humanity itself will one day move. The single sentence "Government was evidently complex and probably socialistic"[16] establishes that Lovecraft had himself by this time converted to moderate socialism. Of course, the Old Ones' civilization is founded upon slavery of a sort; and one wonders whether the shoggoths might be, in part, a metaphor for blacks. There is one tantalizing hint to this effect. Late in the novel the protagonists stumble upon an area that, as they learn later, has been decorated with bas-reliefs by the shoggoths themselves. Dyer reports that there is a vast difference between this work and that of the Old Ones—

> ...a difference in basic nature as well as in mere quality, and involving so profound and calamitous a

> degradation of skill that nothing in the hitherto observed rate of decline could have led one to expect it.
>
> This new and degenerate work was coarse, bold, and wholly lacking in delicacy of detail....[17]

Recall Lovecraft's remark (made less than a year earlier) on the decline of architecture in Charleston in the nineteenth century: "Architectural details became heavy and almost crude as negro craftsman replaced skill'd white carvers, though the good models of the eighteenth century were never wholly lost sight of."[18] But the identification of shoggoths and blacks is perhaps too nebulous and imprecise to be worth pressing.

The Old Ones, of course, are not human beings, and Lovecraft never makes us forget that in many ways—intellectual capacity, sensory development, aesthetic skill—they are vastly our superiors. Even this point may be capable of a sociocultural interpretation, for the Old Ones—who created all earth life—can perhaps be seen as analogous of the Greeks and Romans who, in Lovecraft's view., created the best phases of our own civilization. There are a number of similarities between the Old Ones and the ancients, slavery being only one of them. At one point an explicit parallel is drawn between the Old Ones and the Romans under Constantine.[19] One thinks of *In Defence of Dagon*: "Modern civilisation is the direct heir of Hellenic culture—all that we have is Greek"; and elsewhere in the same essay: "perhaps one should not wonder at *anything* Greek; the race was a super-race."[20] The Old Ones, too, are a super-race.

The exhaustive history of the Old Ones on this planet is of consuming interest, not only for its imaginative power but for its exemplification of a belief that Lovecraft had long held and which was emphasized by his reading in 1926 of Oswald Spengler's landmark volume, *The Decline of the West* (*Der Untergang des Abendlandes* [1918-1922; English translation 1926-1928]): the inexorable rise and fall of successive civilizations. Although the Old Ones are vastly superior to human beings, they are no less subject to the forces of "decadence" than other races. As Dyer and Danforth examine the bas-reliefs and piece together the history of their civilization, they can detect clear instances of decline from even greater heights of physical, intellectual, and aesthetic mastery.[21] No simplistic moral is drawn from this decline—there is, for example, absolutely no suggestion that the Old Ones are morally blameworthy for their creation of shoggoths as slaves, only regret that they were not able to exercise greater control over them and thereby subdue their rebelliousness—and it seems as if Lovecraft sees their decadence as an inevitable result of complex historical forces. As he had said as early as 1921, "No civilisation has lasted for ever, and perhaps our own is perishing of natural old age. If so, the end cannot well be deferred" (*In Defence of Dagon*).[22]

Not only have the Old Ones created all earth-life—including human beings—as a jest or mistake; they have done more: "It interested us to see in some of the very last and most decadent sculptures a shambling primitive mammal, used sometimes for food and sometimes as an amusing buffoon by the land dwellers, whose vaguely simian and human foreshadowings were unmistakable."[23] This must be one of the most misanthropic utterances ever made—the degradation of humanity can go no further. But, although the Old Ones had created all earth-life as "jest or mistake," it is later stated that "Nature had played a hellish jest" on those very Old Ones—first, perhaps, because they were annihilated by the shoggoths, and then because the few remnants of their species who had fortuitously survived to our age were revivified and suffered further horrors at the hands of the loathsome protoplasmic entities they have created. Human beings, accordingly, become merely the dupes of dupes, and Nature has the last laugh.

In terms of the Lovecraft Mythos, *At the Mountains of Madness* makes explicit what has been evident all along—that most of the "gods" of the mythos are mere extraterrestrials, and that their followers (including the authors of most of the books of occult lore to which reference is so frequently made by Lovecraft and others) are mistaken as to their true nature. Robert M. Price, who first noted this "demythologising" feature in Lovecraft,[24] has in later articles gone on to point out that *At the Mountains of Madness* does not, as he had earlier asserted, make any radical break in this pattern, but it does emphasize the point more clearly than elsewhere. The critical passage occurs in the middle of the novel, when Dyer finally acknowledges that the titanic city in which he has been wandering must have been built by the Old Ones: "They were the makers and enslavers of [earth] life, and above all doubt the originals of the fiendish elder myths which things like the Pnakotic Manuscripts and the *Necronomicon* affrightedly hint about."[25] The content of the *Necronomicon* has now been reduced to mere "myth." As for the various wars waged by the Old Ones against such creatures as the fungi from Yuggoth (from "The Whisperer in Darkness") and the Cthulhu spawn (from "The Call of Cthulhu"), it has been pointed out that Lovecraft has not consistently followed his earlier tales in his accounts of their arrival on the earth; but, as I have mentioned earlier, Lovecraft was not concerned with this sort of pedantic accuracy in his mythos, and there are even more flagrant instances of "inconsistency" in later works.

The casually made claim that the novel is a "sequel" to Poe's *Narrative of Arthur Gordon Pym* deserves some analysis. In my view, the novel is not a true sequel at all—it picks up on very little of Poe's enigmatic work except for the cry "Tekeli-li!," as unexplained in Poe as in Lovecraft—and the various references to *Pym* throughout the story end up being more in the manner of in-jokes. It is not clear that *Pym* even influenced the work in any significant way.

At the Mountains of Madness is not without a few small flaws. The wealth of information Dyer and Danforth manage to decipher from bas-reliefs strains credulity, as does the revival of the frozen Old Ones after millennia of some sort of cryogenic suspended animation. But the overwhelming scientific erudition in the novel, its breathtakingly cosmic sweep as it portrays millions of years of this planet's prehistory, and the harrowingly gripping conclusion with the emergence of the shoggoth—perhaps the most frightening moment in all Lovecraft, if not in all horror literature—cause this work to stand at the very summit of Lovecraft's fictional achievement, even higher than "The Colour out of Space." Is it any wonder that its rejection by *Weird Tales* in the summer of 1931, conjoined with the simultaneous rejection of a proposed collection of Lovecraft's work by G. P. Putnam's Sons, did, as Lovecraft confessed later, "more than anything else to end my effective fictional career"?[26]

Indeed, the remaining five or six years of that career were increasingly marred by self-doubt, discouragement at his previous work, lack of confidence in his ability to do what he really wished to do as a fiction writer, and a series of unsuccessful experiments at striking out in new directions. All these difficulties are manifested in the genesis—but not the final product—of Lovecraft's next tale, "The Shadow over Innsmouth," written in November and December of 1931. Lovecraft reports that his revisiting of the decaying seaport of Newburyport, Massachusetts (which he had first seen in 1923),[27] led him to conduct a sort of "laboratory experimentation"[28] to see which style or manner was best suited to the theme. Several attempts were made and discarded, and finally Lovecraft simply wrote the story in his accustomed manner, producing a 25,000-word novelette whose extraordinary richness of atmosphere scarcely betrays the almost agonizing difficulty Lovecraft experienced in its writing.

In "The Shadow over Innsmouth" the narrator, Robert Olmstead (never mentioned by name in the story, but identified in the surviving notes to the novel), a native of Ohio, celebrates his coming of age by undertaking a tour of New England—"sightseeing, antiquarian, and genealogical"[29]—and, finding that the train fare from Newburyport to Arkham (whence his family derives) is higher than he would like, is grudgingly told by a ticket agent of a bus that makes the trip by way of a seedy coastal town called Innsmouth. The place does not seem to appear on most maps, and many odd rumors are whispered about it. Innsmouth was a flourishing seaport up to 1846, when an epidemic of some sort killed over half the citizens; people believe it may have had something to do with the voyages of Captain Obed Marsh, who sailed extensively in China and the South Seas and somehow acquired vast sums in gold and jewels. Now the Marsh refinery is just about the only business of importance in Innsmouth aside from fishing off the shore near Devil's Reef, where fish are always unusually abundant. All the townspeople seem to have repulsive deformities or traits—which are collectively termed "the Innsmouth look"—and are studiously avoided by the neighboring communities.

This account piques Olmstead's interest as an antiquarian, and he decides to spend at least a day in Innsmouth, catching a bus in the morning and leaving for Arkham in the evening. He goes to the Newburyport Historical Society and sees a tiara that came from Innsmouth; it fascinates him more and more:

> It clearly belonged to some settled technique of infinite maturity and perfection, yet that technique was utterly remote from any—Eastern or Western, ancient or modern—which I had ever heard of or seen exemplified. It was as if the workmanship were that of another planet.[30]

Going to Innsmouth on a seedy bus run by Joe Sargent, whose hairlessness, fishy odor, and never-blinking eyes provoke his loathing, Olmstead begins exploration, aided by directions and a map supplied by a normal-looking young man who works in a grocery chain. All around he sees signs of both physical and moral decay from a once distinguished level. The atmosphere begins to oppress him, and he thinks about leaving the town early; but then he catches sight of a nonagenarian named Zadok Allen who, he has been told, is a fount of knowledge about the history of Innsmouth. Olmstead has a chat with Zadok, loosening his tongue with bootleg whiskey.

Zadok tells him an outrageous story about alien creatures, half fish and half frog, whom Obed Marsh had encountered in the South Seas. Zadok maintains that Obed struck up an agreement with these creatures: they would provide him with bountiful gold and fish in exchange for human sacrifices. This arrangement works for a while, but then the fish-frogs seek to mate with humans. It is this that provokes a violent uproar in the town in 1846: many citizens die and the remainder are forced to take the Oath of Dagon, professing loyalty to the hybrid entities. There is, however, a compensating benefit of a sort. As humans continue to mate with the fish-frogs, they acquire a type of immortality: they undergo a physical change, gaining many of the properties of the aliens, and then they take to the sea and live in vast underwater cities for millennia.

Scarcely knowing what to make of this wild tale, and alarmed at Zadok's maniacal plea that he leave the town at once because they have been seen talking, Olmsted makes efforts to catch the evening bus out of Innsmouth. But he is in bad luck: it has suffered inexplicable engine trouble and cannot be repaired until the next day; he will have to put up in the seedy Gilman House, the one hotel in the town. Reluctantly checking into the place, he feels ever-growing intimations of horror and menace as he hears anomalous voices outside his room and other strange noises. Finally he knows he is in peril: his doorknob is tried from the outside. He begins a frenetic series of attempts to leave the hotel and escape the town, but at one point is almost overwhelmed at both the number and the loathsomeness of his pursuers:

> And yet I saw them in a limitless stream—flopping, hopping, croaking, bleating—surging inhumanly through the spectral moonlight in a grotesque, malignant saraband of fantastic nightmare. And some of them had tall tiaras of that nameless whitish-gold metal...and some were strangely robed...and one, who led the way, was clad in a ghoulishly humped black coat and striped trousers, and had a man's felt hat perched on the shapeless thing that answered for a head....[31]

Olmstead escapes, but his tale is not over. After a much-needed rest, he continues to pursue genealogical research, and finds appalling evidence that he may himself be related to the Marsh family in a fairly direct way. He learns of a cousin locked in a madhouse in Canton, and an uncle who committed suicide because he learned something nameless about himself. Strange dreams of swimming underwater begin to afflict him, and gradually he breaks down. Then one morning he awakes to learn that he has acquired "the Innsmouth look." He thinks of shooting himself, but "certain dreams deterred me."[32] Later he comes to his decision:

> I shall plan my cousin's escape from that Canton madhouse, and together we shall go to marvel-shadowed Innsmouth. We shall swim out to that brooding reef in the sea and dive down through black abysses to Cyclopean and many-columned Y'ha-nthlei, and in that lair of the Deep Ones we shall dwell amidst wonder and glory for ever.[33]

This nearly flawless tale of insidious regional horror requires volumes of commentary, but we can only touch upon a few notable features here. To begin most mundanely, let us specify the location of Innsmouth. The name had been invented in so early a tale as "Celephaïs" (1920), but was clearly located in England; Lovecraft resurrected the name for the eighth sonnet ("The Port") of the *Fungi from Yuggoth* (1929-1930), where the setting is not entirely clear, although a New England locale is likely. In any event, can we simply say—based on Lovecraft's report that his visit to Newburyport inspired the tale—that Innsmouth itself is Newburyport? In one sense this is true: Newburyport does (or, rather, did, before its recent restoration as a yuppie resort town) have that atmosphere of civic decay that Lovecraft sought to reproduce in Innsmouth, and certain landmarks in the tale are clearly based upon places in Newburyport. But in another sense Newburyport cannot possibly be the *location* for Innsmouth; for, as Will Murray has pointed out,[34] Innsmouth and Newburyport are postulated in the tale as separate communities. If the narrator's bus trip from Newburyport to Innsmouth is duplicated today, one would actually end up in the town of Gloucester, and indeed Lovecraft has clearly drawn upon both the topography of the town and some specific features in it for Innsmouth: the Order of Dagon Hall, for example, is unmistakably modelled upon the American Legion Hall that still stands in a square in the old section of Gloucester. As is the case, then, with Arkham and Dunwich, Innsmouth proves to be a fusion of impressions taken from several different locations—with, of course, a bountiful admixture of pure imagination.

"The Shadow over Innsmouth" is Lovecraft's greatest tale of degeneration; but the causes for that degeneration here are quite different from what we have seen earlier. In such tales as "The Lurking Fear" and "The Dunwich Horror," unwholesome inbreeding within a homogeneous community has caused a descent upon the evolutionary scale; in "The Horror at Red Hook" it is merely said that "modern people under lawless conditions tend uncannily to repeat the darkest instinctive patterns of primitive half-ape savagery,"[35] and all we can perhaps infer is that the breeding of foreigners amongst themselves has resulted in the wholesale squalor we now see in Red Hook. "The Shadow over Innsmouth" is, however, clearly a cautionary tale on the ill effects of *miscegenation*, or the sexual union of different races, and as such may well be considered a vast expansion and subtilization of the plot of "Facts concerning the Late Arthur Jermyn and His Family" (1920). It is, accordingly, difficult to deny a suggestion of racism running all through the story. Lovecraft, who always favored the strictest color line between blacks and whites, and who even in his later years sought for racial or cultural homogeneity rather than heterogeneity ("a real friend of civilisation wishes merely to make the Germans *more German*, the French *more French*, the Spaniards *more Spanish*, and so on,"[36] occasionally betrays his own paranoia through that of his narrator: during his escape from Innsmouth, Olmstead hears "horrible croaking voices exchanging low cries in what was certainly not English,"[37] as if a foreign language is in itself a sign of aberration. All through the tale the narrator expresses—and expects us to share—his revulsion at the physical grotesqueness of the Innsmouth people, just as in his own life Lovecraft frequently comments on the "peculiar" appearance of all races but his own.

This racist interpretation is not refuted by the suggestion made by Zadok Allen that human beings are ultimately related to the fish-frogs; for this has an entirely different implication. Zadok declares:

"Seems that human folks has got a kind o' relation to sech water-beasts—that everything alive come aout o' the water onct, an' only needs a little change to go back agin."[38] Forget for the nonce that Lovecraft had, in *At the Mountains of Madness*, supplied an entirely different account of the emergence of humanity: the intent here and in that story is the same—the complete denigration of human importance by the suggestion of a contemptible and degrading origin of our species.

An examination of the literary influences upon the story can clarify how Lovecraft has vastly enriched a conception that was by no means his own invention. There can little doubt that the use of hybrid fishlike entities was derived from at least two prior works—Irvin S. Cobb's "Fishhead" (which Lovecraft read in the *Cavalier* in 1913 and praised in a letter to the editor) and Robert W. Chambers's "The Harbor-Master," a short story later included as the first five chapters of the episodic novel *In Search of the Unknown* (1904). But in both these stories we are dealing with a *single* case of hybridism, not an entire community or civilization; it is only the latter that can create the sense of worldwide menace that we find in "The Shadow over Innsmouth." What is more, there is no guarantee that human beings will prevail in any future conflict with the fish-frogs; for, loathsome as they are, they nevertheless possess—as do the fungi from Yuggoth and the Old Ones—qualities that raise them in many ways above our species. Aside from their near-immortality (Olmstead in a dream meets his great-great-grandmother, who has lived for 80,000 years), they clearly possess aesthetic skills of a high order (that tiara "belonged to some settled technique of infinite maturity and perfection"), and in fact are allowing human beings to dwell on the earth on *their* sufferance: as Zadok says, "they cud wipe aout the hull brood o' humans ef they was willin' to bother."[39] And, although they are damaged by the destruction of the town in 1927-1928 when Olmstead calls in Federal authorities after his experience, they are by no means extirpated; Olmstead ponders ominously at the very end: "For the present they would rest; but some day, if they remembered, they would rise again for the tribute Great Cthulhu craved. It would be a city greater than Innsmouth next time."[40]

As for the lengthy chase scene that occupies the fourth of the five chapters of the story, I must confess that it strikes me as more and more ridiculous the oftener I read it. Will Murray's interesting conjecture[41] that this episode suggests that Lovecraft wrote the story in part with Harry Bates's *Strange Tales* in mind must at the moment remain unproven in the absence of any documentary evidence to this effect. To be sure, *Strange Tales* (which paid 2¢ a word, better than the 1¢ or 1½¢ Lovecraft received from *Weird Tales*) wished "action" stories, and this passage is otherwise uncharacteristic of Lovecraft; but if *Strange Tales* was the contemplated market, it is odd that Lovecraft did not actually submit the tale there (or anywhere), forcing Murray to conclude that Lovecraft was so dissatisfied with the story when he finished it that he did not wish to submit it to a professional market. This makes Murray's theory incapable either of proof or refutation—barring, of course, the unlikely emergence of a statement by Lovecraft in a letter during the writing of the tale that *Strange Tales* was the market he had in mind. As it happens, Lovecraft did not himself submit the story to *Weird Tales* at all, but August Derleth did so, without Lovecraft's knowledge, around 1933; it was rejected.

The chase scene is certainly engaging enough reading, if only in order to witness the customarily staid and mild-mannered Lovecraftian protagonist battering through doors, leaping out windows, and fleeing along streets or railway tracks. It is, of course, typical that he does not engage in any actual fisticuffs (he is naturally far outnumbered by his enemies), and he reverts to the Lovecraftian norm by fainting as he cowers in a railway cut and watches the loathsome phalanx of hybrids rush by him. More seriously, this notion of *seeing* horrors go by is of some significance in augmenting the atmosphere of nightmarish terror Lovecraft is clearly wishing to achieve; as he wrote in a letter:

> I believe that—because of the foundation of most weird concepts in dream-phenomena—the best weird tales are those in which the narrator or central figure remains (as in actual dreams) largely passive, & witnesses or experiences a stream of bizarre events which—as the case may be—flows past him, just touches him, or engulfs him utterly.[42]

As for Zadok Allen's monologue—which occupies nearly the entirety of the third chapter—it has been criticized for excessive length, but Lovecraft was writing at a time when the use of dialect for long stretches was much commoner than now. The dialogue portions of John Buchan's enormously long novel *Witch Wood* (1927) are almost entirely in Scots dialect, as is the whole of Robert Louis Stevenson's "Thrawn Janet." Zadok's speech is undeniably effective in both supplying the necessary historical backdrop of the tale and in creating a sense of insidious horror. Zadok occupies a structurally important place in the narrative: because he has witnessed, at first hand, the successive generations of Innsmouth folk become increasingly corrupted by the Deep Ones, his account carries irrefutable weight, in spite of Olmstead's harried attempt to dismiss it as the ravings of a senile toper. Olmstead could not possibly have come by this information in any other way, even by some laborious course of historical research. And some of Zadok's words are both hideous and poignant:

> "Hey, yew, why dun't ye say somethin'? Haow'd ye like to be livin' in a town like this, with everything a-rottin' an' a-dyin', an' boarded-up mon-

> sters crawlin' an' bleatin' an' barkin' an' hoppin' araoun' black cellars an' attics every way ye turn? Hey? Haow'd ye like to hear the haowlin' night arter night from the churches an' Order o' Dagon Hall, *an' know what's doin' part o' the haowlin'*? Haow'd ye like to hear what comes from that awful reef every May-Eve an' Hallowmass? Hey? Think the old man's crazy, eh? Wal, Sir, *let me tell ye that ain't the wust!*"[43]

But it is Olmstead around whom the entire story revolves—unusually so for the cosmically oriented Lovecraft; and yet, in this tale Lovecraft succeeds brilliantly both in making Olmstead's plight inexpressibly tragic and poignant and also in hinting at the awesome horrors that threaten the entire planet. It is his greatest union of internal and external horror. The many mundane details that lend substance and reality to Olmstead's character are in large part derived from Lovecraft's own temperament and, especially, from his habits as a frugal antiquarian traveller. Olmstead always "seek[s] the cheapest possible route,"[44] and this is usually—for Olmstead as well as for Lovecraft—by bus. His reading up on Innsmouth in the library, and his systematic exploration of the town by way of the map and instructions given him by the grocery youth, parallel Lovecraft's own thorough researches into the history and topography of the places he wished to visit and his frequent trips to libraries, chambers of commerce, and elsewhere for maps, guidebooks, and historical background.

Even the ascetic meal Olmstead eats at a restaurant—"A bowl of vegetable soup with crackers was enough for me"[45]—echoes Lovecraft's very parsimonious diet both at home and on his travels. But it does more than that. Although Lovecraft's characters have frequently but inanely been criticized for their failure to eat, go to the bathroom, or indulge in long-winded conversation, it should be evident by now that this type of mundane realism is not what he was interested in. Even in his novelettes and short novels, Lovecraft's prime concern—beyond even verisimilitude and topographical realism—was a rigid adherence to Poe's theory of unity of effect; that is, the elimination of any words, sentences, or whole incidents that do not have a direct bearing on the story. Accordingly, a character's eating habits are wholly dispensed with because they are inessential to the *dénouement* of a tale and will only dilute that air of tensity and inevitability which Lovecraft is seeking to establish. It is significant that the only two characters in Lovecraft who do eat—Olmstead and Wilmarth (in "The Whisperer in Darkness")—do so for reasons that are critical to the development of the plot: Wilmarth because Lovecraft wishes to hint at the unsuccessful attempt to drug him with coffee, and Olmstead because he is forced to spend the evening in Innsmouth and this frugal meal contributes to the psychological portrait of a tourist increasingly agitated by his sinister surroundings.

But it is Olmstead's spectacular conversion at the end—where he not merely becomes reconciled to his fate as a nameless hybrid but actually embraces it—that is the most controversial point of the tale. Does this mean that Lovecraft, as in *At the Mountains of Madness*, wishes to transform the Deep Ones from objects of horror to objects of sympathy or identification? Or rather, are we to imagine Olmstead's change of heart as an augmentation of the horror? I can only believe that the latter is intended. There is no gradual "reformation" of the Deep Ones as there is of the Old Ones in the earlier novel: our revulsion at their physical hideousness is not mollified or tempered by any subsequent appreciation of their intelligence, courage, or nobility. Olmstead's transformation is the climax of the story and the pinnacle of its horrific scenario: it shows that not merely his physical body but his mind has been ineluctably corrupted.

This transformation is achieved in many ways, subtle and obvious; one of the most subtle is in the simple use of descriptives. The title, "The Shadow over Innsmouth," is not chosen by accident; for throughout the tale it is used with provocative variations. We first encounter it when Olmstead, after hearing the account of the ticket agent, states: "That was the first I ever heard of shadowed Innsmouth."[46] This mildly ominous usage then successively becomes "rumour-shadowed Innsmouth,"[47] "evil-shadowed Innsmouth,"[48] and other coinages that bespeak Olmstead's increasing sense of loathing at the town and its inhabitants; but then, as he undergoes his "conversion," we read at the very end of "marvel-shadowed Innsmouth" and the even greater marvels of Y'ha-nthlei, where he shall "dwell amidst wonder and glory for ever"—an utterance that, in its hideous parody of the Twenty-Third Psalm, ineffably unites Olmstead's sense of triumph and the reader's sense of utter horror.

In the end, "The Shadow over Innsmouth" is about the inexorable call of heredity; it is one more meditation on that poignant utterance, "The past is *real*—it is *all there is.*"[49] For Lovecraft, the future was essentially unknown in its unpredictability; the present, conversely, was nothing but the inevitable result of all antecedent and circumjacent events of the past, whether we are aware of them or not. Throughout the story Olmstead is secretly guided by his heredity, but is entirely oblivious of the fact. His ambivalent utterance when he sees Zadok Allen and decides to question him—"It must have been some imp of the perverse—or some sardonic pull from dark, hidden sources"[50]—neatly conveys this point, for that "sardonic pull" is nothing other than the past, embodied by his own heredity, that is inexorably leading him to Innsmouth and causing him to undergo what he believes to be a merely fortuitous series of unrelated events. In a sense, too, that utterance reflects Lovecraft's understanding of the workings of destiny (determinism): he knows that "destiny rules inexorably,"[51] but that there are still "proximate...bases...by which human puppets are moved."[52] Olmstead's "imp of the perverse" is only the proximate base of his actions, but the "sardonic pull" is the true source—destiny, embodied here by heredity—that is leading him step by step to the inevitable outcome.

Lovecraft never achieved a greater atmosphere of insidious decay than in "The Shadow over Innsmouth": one can almost smell the overwhelming stench of fish, see the physical anomalies of the inhabitants, and perceive the century-long dilapidation of an entire town in the story's evocative prose. And once again he has produced a narrative that progresses from first word to last without a false note to a cataclysmic conclusion—a conclusion, as noted before, that simultaneously focuses on the pitiable fate of a single human being and hints tantalizingly of the future destruction of the entire race. The cosmic and the local, the past and the present, the internal and the external, and self and the other are all fused into an inextricable unity. It is something that Lovecraft had never achieved before and would never achieve again save—in a very different way—in his last major story, "The Shadow out of Time."

What Lovecraft did produce immediately after "The Shadow over Innsmouth," in February 1932, was "The Dreams in the Witch House." Here we are on a very different level. The story's working title—"The Dreams of Walter Gilman"—actually tells the whole story. A mathematics student at Miskatonic University named Walter Gilman who lives in a peculiarly angled room in the old Witch House in Arkham begins experiencing bizarre dreams filled with sights, sounds, and shapes of an utterly indescribable cast; other dreams, much more realistic in nature, reveal a huge rat with human hands named Brown Jenkin, who appears to be the familiar of the witch Keziah Mason, who once dwelt in the Witch House. Meanwhile Gilman, in his classwork, begins to display a remarkable intuitive grasp of hyperspace, or the fourth dimension. But then his dreams take an even weirder turn, and there are indictions that he is sleepwalking. Keziah seems to be urging him on in some nameless errand ("He must meet the Black Man, and go with them all to the throne of Azathoth at the centre of ultimate Chaos."[53] Then in one very clear dream he sees himself "half lying on a high, fantastically balustraded terrace above a boundless jungle of outlandish, incredible peaks, balanced planes, domes, minarets, horizontal discs poisoned on pinnacles, and numberless forms of still greater wildness."[54] The balustrade is decorated with curious designs representing ridged, barrel-shaped entities (*i.e.*, the Old Ones from *At the Mountains of Madness*); but Gilman wakes screaming when he sees the living barrel-shaped entities coming toward him. The next morning the barrel-shaped ornament—which he had broken off the balustrade *in the dream*—is found in his bed.

Things seem rapidly to be reaching some hideous culmination. A baby is kidnapped and cannot be found. Then, in a dream, Gilman finds himself in some strangely angled space with Keziah, Brown Jenkin, and the baby. Keziah is going to sacrifice the child, but Gilman knocks the knife out of her hand and sends it clattering down some nearby abyss. He and Keziah engage in a fight, and he manages to frighten her momentarily by displaying a crucifix given to him by a fellow tenant; when Brown Jenkin comes to her aid, he kicks it down the abyss, but not before it has made some sort of sacrificial offering with the baby's blood. The next night Gilman's friend Frank Elwood witnesses a nameless horror: he sees some ratlike creature literally eat its way through Gilman's body to his heart. The Witch House is rented no more, and years later, when it is torn down, an enormous pile of human bones going back centuries is discovered, along with the bones of some huge ratlike entity.

One can agree wholeheartedly with Steven J. Mariconda's labelling of this story as "Lovecraft's Magnificent Failure."[55] In a sense, "The Dreams in the Witch House" is the most cosmic story Lovecraft ever wrote: he has made a genuine, and very provocative, attempt actually to visualize the fourth dimension:

> All the objects—organic and inorganic alike—were totally beyond description or even comprehension. Gilman sometimes compared the inorganic masses to prisms, labyrinths, clusters of cubes and planes, and Cyclopean buildings; and the organic things struck him variously as groups of bubbles, octopi, centipedes, living Hindoo idols, and intricate Arabesques roused into a kind of ophidian animation.[56]

The imaginative scope of the novelette is almost unbearably vast; but it is utterly confounded by slipshod writing and a complete confusion as to where the story is actually going. Lovecraft here lapses into hackneyed and overblown purple prose that sounds almost like a parody of his own style: "Everything he saw was unspeakably menacing and horrible;...he felt a stark, hideous fright."[57] There are countless unresolved elements in the tale. What is the significance of the sudden appearance of the Old Ones in the story? To what purpose is the baby kidnapped and sacrificed? How can Lovecraft the atheist allow Keziah to be frightened off by the sight of a crucifix? Why does Nyarlathotep appear in the conventional figure of the Black Man? In the final confrontation with Keziah, what is the purpose of the abyss aside from providing a convenient place down which to kick Brown Jenkin? How does Brown Jenkin subsequently emerge from the abyss to eat out Gilman's heart? Lovecraft does not seem to have thought out any of these issues, concentrating instead merely on rambling and repetitious accounts of Gilman's dreams. It is as if he were aiming merely for a succession of startling images without bothering to think of their logical sequence or coherence.

Nevertheless, the "cosmic" portions of "The Dreams in the Witch House" almost redeem the many flaws in the tale. "Dreams" is really the critical term here; for this story brings to a culmination all Lovecraft's previous ruminations on the "occasionally titanic significance of dreams,"[58] as he commented in "Beyond the Wall of Sleep." Gilman's are not, indeed, ordinary dreams—"faint and fantastic reflections of our waking experiences"[59]—but avenues toward other realms of entity normally inaccessible to human beings. This point is made perhaps a little too obviously by the appearance of the balustrade-ornament from hyperspace into our world.

"The Dreams in the Witch House" is also Lovecraft's ultimate modernization of a conventional myth (witchcraft) by means of modern science. Fritz Leiber, who has written the most perspicacious essay on the tale, notes that it is "Lovecraft's most carefully worked out story of hyperspace-travel. Here (1) a rational foundation for such travel is set up; (2) hyperspace is visualized; and (3) a trigger for such travel is devised."[60] Leiber elaborates keenly on these points, noting that the absence of any mechanical device for such travel is vital to the tale, for otherwise it would be impossible to imagine how a "witch" of the seventeenth century could have managed the trick; in effect, Keziah simply applied advanced mathematics and "thought" herself into hyperspace.

Lovecraft's hints that Keziah's hyperspace-travel is a secret type of knowledge that is only now coming to light in the work of advanced astrophysicists (Planck, Heisenberg, Einstein, and Willem de Sitter are mentioned by name)[61] make for one more "updating" of an older Lovecraftian conception. When Gilman boldly maintains that "Time could not exist in certain belts of space"[62] and goes on to justify this view, we are cast back to the early story "The White Ship" (1919), in which the narrator remarks: "In the Land of Sona-Nyl there is neither time nor space, neither suffering nor death; and there I dwelt for many aeons."[63] Granting the difference between a Dunsanian fantasy and a quasi-science fiction tale, the greater intellectual rigor now underlying Lovecraft's fiction is manifest.

Nevertheless, "The Dreams in the Witch House" overall is indeed a failure, and is one of the most disappointing of his later tales. As with "The Shadow over Innsmouth," the story was submitted surreptitiously to *Weird Tales* by August Derleth, where it was accepted. But Lovecraft seems to have known that it was perhaps a step backward in his fictional development, and he never ranked it high amongst his works.

The remainder of 1932 and much of 1933 was taken up with revision (mostly the tales of Hazel Heald), collaboration ("Through the

Gates of the Silver Key" with E. Hoffmann Price), and moving from 10 Barnes Street to 66 College Street in May 1933. Finally, in August, Lovecraft wrote another original tale—"The Thing on the Doorstep," in a frenetic four days between the 21st and the 24th. This entire period was, however, the most difficult of Lovecraft's entire career: he was suffering a severe sense of discouragement at his own work, and was seeking out ways to remedy the problem by taking fresh stock of himself and of the entire weird tradition. Perhaps inspired by his revision of "Supernatural Horror in Literature" for the *Fantasy Fan* in the fall of 1933, Lovecraft began a systematic re-examination of the history, theory, and technique of the weird tale, producing several interesting documents: the still unpublished "Weird Story Plots," in which he jotted down the plots of significant horror stories with a view to analyzing their merits; "Notes on Writing Weird Fiction"; and several lists printed as the first part of the *Notes and Commonplace Book* (1938)—"Elements of a Weird Story"; "Types of Weird Story"; "A List of Certain Basic Underlying Horrors Effectively Used in Weird Fiction"; and "List of Primary Ideas Motivating Possible Weird Tales." Fragmentary and sketchy as some of these are, taken together they provide an enormously suggestive fund of theoretical and practical analysis of weird fiction.

And yet, it does not appear as if this research helped Lovecraft much in the short term, for "The Thing on the Doorstep" is likewise one of his poorest later efforts. The tale, narrated in the first person by Daniel Upton, tells of Upton's young friend Edward Derby, who since boyhood has displayed a remarkable aesthetic sensitivity toward the weird, in spite of the overprotective coddling he receives from his parents. Derby frequently visits Upton, using a characteristic knock—three raps followed by two more after an interval—to announce himself. Derby attends Miskatonic University and becomes a moderately recognized fantaisiste and poet. When he is thirty-eight he meets Asenath Waite, a young woman at Miskatonic, about whom strange things are whispered: she has anomalous hypnotic powers, creating the momentary impression in her subjects that they are in her body looking across at themselves. Even stranger things are whispered of her father, Ephraim Waite, who died under very peculiar circumstances.

In spite of his father's opposition, Derby marries Asenath—who is one of the Innsmouth Waites—and settles in a home in Arkham. They seem to undertake very recondite and perhaps dangerous occult experiments. Moreover, people observe curious changes in both of them: whereas Asenath is extremely strong-willed and determined, Edward is flabby and weak-willed; but on occasion he is seen driving Asenath's car (even though he did not previously know how to drive) with a resolute and almost demonic expression, and conversely Asenath is seen from a window looking unwontedly meek and defeated. One day Upton receives a call from Maine: Derby is there in a crazed state, and Upton has to fetch him because Derby has suddenly lost the ability to drive. On the trip back Derby tells Upton a wild tale of Asenath forcing him out of his body, and going on to suggest that Asenath is really Ephraim, who forced out the mind of his daughter and placed it in his own dying body. Abruptly Derby's ramblings come to an end, as if "shut off with an almost mechanical click":[64] Derby takes the wheel away from Upton and says in an utterly uncharacteristic way that Upton should pay no attention to what he may just have said.

Some months later Derby visits Upton again. He is in a tremendously excited state, claiming that Asenath has gone away and that he will seek a divorce. Around Christmas of that year Derby breaks down entirely. He cries out: "My brain! My brain! God, Dan—it's tugging—from beyond—knocking—clawing—that she-devil—even now—Ephraim...."[65] He is placed in a mental hospital, and shows no signs of recovery until one day he suddenly seems to be better; but, to Upton's disappointment and even latent horror, Derby is now in that curiously "energised" state such as he had been during the ride back from Maine. Upton is in an utter turmoil of confusion when one evening he receives a phone call. He cannot make out what the caller is saying—it sounds like "glub...glub"[66]—but a little later someone knocks at his door. The creature is wearing one of Derby's old coats, which is clearly too big for it. It hands Upton a sheet of paper which explains the whole story: Derby had killed Asenath as a means of escaping her influence and her plans to switch bodies with him altogether; but death has not put an end to Asenath/Ephraim's mind, for it has emerged from the body, thrust itself into the body of Derby, and hurled his mind into the decaying corpse of Asenath. Upton promptly goes to the madhouse and shoots the thing that is in Edward Derby's body; this account is his confession and attempt at exculpation.

"The Thing on the Doorstep" has many flaws: first, the obviousness of the basic scenario and the utter lack of subtlety in its execution; second, poor writing, laden (as with "The Dreams in the Witch House") with hyperbole, stale idioms, and dragging verbosity; and third, a complete absence of cosmicism in spite of the frequent dropping of the *word* "cosmic" throughout the tale ("some damnable, utterly accursed focus of unknown and malign cosmic forces."[67] The story was clearly influenced by H. B. Drake's *The Shadowy Thing* (1928), a poorly written but strangely compelling novel about a man who displays anomalous powers of hypnosis and mind-transference. An entry in the commonplace book (#158) records the plot-germ:

> Man has terrible wizard friend who gains influence over him. Kills him in defence of his soul—walls body up in ancient cellar—BUT—the dead wizard (who has said strange things about soul lingering

> in body) *changes bodies with him*...leaving him a conscious corpse in cellar.

This is not exactly a description of the plot of *The Shadowy Thing*, but rather an imaginative extrapolation based upon it. In Drake's novel, a man, Avery Booth, does indeed exhibit powers that seem akin to hypnosis, to such a degree that he can oust the mind or personality from another person's body and occupy it. Booth does so on several occasions throughout the novel, and in the final episode he appears to have come back from the dead (he had been killed in a battle in World War I) and occupied the body of a friend and soldier who had himself been horribly mangled in battle. Lovecraft has amended this plot by introducing the notion of *mind-exchange*: whereas Drake does not clarify what happens to the ousted mind when it is taken over by the mind of Booth, Lovecraft clearly envisages an exact transference whereby the ousted mind occupies the body of its possessor. Lovecraft then adds a further twist by envisioning what might happen if the occupier's body were killed and a dispossessed mind was thrust into it. It turns out, then, that in "The Thing on the Doorstep" there are actually *two* supernatural phenomena at work: first, the mind-exchange practised by Ephraim/Asenath Waite; and second, the ability of Edward Derby to lend a sort of hideous animation to the dead body of Asenath purely by the strength of his own mind. (It is scarcely to be wondered at that the sexually reserved Lovecraft has nothing at all to say about the potentially intriguing gender-switching implied by this mind-exchange.)

The significant difference between the story and the plot-germ as recorded in the commonplace book is that the "wizard friend" has become the man's wife; indeed, it is at this point—and only at this point—that the story gains some interest, if only from a biographical perspective. For it is transparently clear that Lovecraft is, in some fashion, supplying a twisted version of his own marriage here, as well as of certain aspects of his childhood. Like Lovecraft, Derby "had organic weaknesses which startled his doting parents and caused them to keep him closely chained to their side"; and it was this that led to Derby's (and Lovecraft's) "private education and coddled seclusion." "All this doubtless fostered a strange, secretive inner life in the boy, with imagination as his one avenue of freedom."[68] Derby's mother died when he was thirty-four, Lovecraft's when he was almost thirty-one; "and for months he was incapacitated by some odd psychological malady.... Afterward he managed to feel a sort of grotesque exhilaration, as if of partial escape from some unseen bondage."[69] This single sentence betrays Lovecraft's awareness of the severe psychological trauma his mother caused him; and it makes us think of the one (and only) occasion when he admitted to his wife that his mother's attitude toward him had been "devastating."[70]

But there are some anomalies in the portrayal of the youthful Edward Derby that need to be addressed. Derby was "the most phenomenal child scholar I have ever known":[71] would Lovecraft write something like this about a character who was modelled upon himself? It seems unlikely, given his characteristic modesty; and this makes me think that Derby is an amalgam of several individuals. Consider this remark on Alfred Galpin: "He is intellectually *exactly like me* save in degree. In degree he is immensely my superior";[72] elsewhere he refers to Galpin—who was only seventeen when Lovecraft first came in touch with him in 1918—as "the most brilliant, accurate, steel-cold intellect I have ever encountered."[73] However, Galpin never wrote "verse of a sombre, fantastic, almost morbid cast"[74] as Derby did as a boy; nor did he publish a volume, *Azathoth and Other Horrors*, when he was eighteen. But did not Clark Ashton Smith create a sensation as a boy prodigy when he published *The Star-Treader and Other Poems* in 1912, when he was nineteen? And was Smith not a close colleague of George Sterling, who—like Justin Geoffrey in the tale—died in 1926 (Sterling by suicide, Geoffrey of unknown causes)? On a more whimsical note, Lovecraft's mention that Derby's "attempts to grow a moustache were discernible only with difficulty"[75] recalls his frequent censures of the thin moustache Frank Belknap Long attempted for years to cultivate in the 1920s.

But if Derby's youth and young manhood are an amalgam of Lovecraft and some of his closest associates, his marriage to Asenath Waite brings certain aspects of Lovecraft's marriage to Sonia H. Greene clearly to mind. In the first place there is the fact that Sonia was clearly the more strong-willed member of the couple; it was clearly from her initiative that the marriage took place at all and that Lovecraft uprooted himself from Providence to come to live in New York. On one occasion Frank Belknap Long told me that Sonia was a very "domineering" woman, a description that manifestly suits Asenath Waite. The objections of Derby's father to Asenath—and specifically to Derby's wish to marry her—may dimly echo the apparently unspoken objections of Lovecraft's aunts to his marriage to Sonia.

Aside from these points of biographical interest, however, "The Thing on the Doorstep" is crude, obvious, lacking in subtlety of execution or depth of conception, and histrionically written. One of its few memorable features is the hideous and grisly conclusion, where we witness Edward—who, trapped in Asenath's decaying body, displays more will and determination than he ever had in his own body—resolutely attempting to call Upton over the phone and, finding that his decomposing body is incapable of enunciating words, actually animating the corpse, writing a note to Upton, and bringing it to him before dissolving on his doorstep in "mostly liquescent horror."[76] In a sense this story is a reprise of *The Case of Charles Dexter Ward*, although actual mind-exchange does not occur there as it does here; but the attempt by

Asenath (in Derby's body) to pass herself off as Edward in the madhouse is precisely analogous to Joseph Curwen's attempts to maintain that he is Charles Dexter Ward. In this case, however, it cannot be said that Lovecraft has improved on the original.

The year 1933 seems to have been an especially difficult one for Lovecraft as a writer. He was clearly attempting to capture on paper various ideas clamoring for expression, but seemed unable to do so. At least two other works of fiction may have been written at this time; one of them is the fragment entitled (by R. H. Barlow) "The Book." The exact date of the fragment is not known, but in a letter of November 1933 Lovecraft writes as follows:

> I am at a sort of standstill in writing—disgusted at much of my older work, & uncertain as to avenues of improvement. In recent weeks I have done a tremendous amount of experimenting in different styles & perspectives, but have destroyed *most* [my italics] of the results.[77]

If "The Book" was one of the things Lovecraft was writing at this time, it could well qualify as a piece of experimentation; for it appears to be nothing more than an attempt to write out the *Fungi from Yuggoth* in *prose*.[78] The first three sonnets of the cycle do indeed form a connected narrative; and the fact that the story fragment peters out into inconclusive vagueness after this point may further suggest that there is no "continuity"—certainly not on the level of plot—in the sonnet sequence.

The other item that was probably written in 1933 is "The Evil Clergyman." This is nothing more than an account of a dream written up in a letter to Bernard Austin Dwyer; the excerpt was made and a title ("The Wicked Clergyman") supplied by Dwyer; it was first published in *Weird Tales* (April 1939), and retitled "The Evil Clergyman" by Derleth. Lovecraft remarks in a letter to Clark Ashton Smith of 22 October 1933 that "Some months ago I had a dream of an evil clergyman in a garret full of forbidden books,"[79] and it is likely that the account of the dream was written up in a letter to Dwyer at this time or earlier; Derleth's dating of the item to 1937 seems entirely unfounded.

It is hardly worth discussing "The Evil Clergyman"[80] as a story, since it was never meant to stand as a discrete and self-contained narrative. Some of the imagery and atmosphere are reminiscent of "The Festival," although the dream clearly takes place in England. Unlike "The Thing on the Doorstep" and other tales, this dream-fragment does not involve *mind*-transference but transference of a very physical sort: because the protagonist has unwisely handled a small box that he was specifically told not to touch, he has summoned the "evil clergyman" and somehow effected an exchange of external features with him, while yet retaining his mind and personality. It is difficult to say how Lovecraft would have developed this curiously conventional supernatural scenario in light of his later quasi-science fictional work.

Yet another minor item, formerly dated to 1934, which we can concern ourselves with here is the "fragment" known as "The Thing in the Moonlight." This has now been conclusively proven to be spurious. The central portion of this "fragment" is indeed taken from a Lovecraft letter to Donald Wandrei (24 November 1927) in which he recounts a dream about a train conductor who metamorphoses into a hideous cone-headed creature; but the opening and concluding paragraphs were supplied by J. Chapman Miske, editor of *Bizarre* (where the item was first published in the issue for January 1941), "in order to do away with some of the otherwise fragmentary effect of the piece," as Miske admitted in a letter to Derleth.[81] Miske was, perhaps, not intentionally attempting to pass off the item as a hoax, but he was certainly culpable in not explaining to his readers the impure state of this "fragment"; but Derleth is still more culpable in that, although Miske told him of the matter after the piece had been published in *Marginalia* (1944), he nevertheless republished it in subsequent editions of Lovecraft's fiction.

Given all the difficulties Lovecraft was experiencing in capturing his ideas in fiction, it is not surprising that his next tale, "The Shadow out of Time," had a genesis of at least four months (November 1934 to February 1935) and went through two or perhaps three entire drafts. Before examining the painful birth of the story, let us gain some idea of its basic plot.

Nathaniel Wingate Peaslee, a professor of political economy at Miskatonic University, suddenly experiences some sort of nervous breakdown on May 14, 1908, while teaching a class. Awaking in the hospital after a collapse, he appears to have suffered an amnesia so severe that it has affected even his vocal and motor faculties. Gradually he relearns the use of his body, and indeed develops tremendous mental capacity, seemingly far beyond that of a normal human being. His wife, sensing that something is gravely wrong, obtains a divorce, and only one of his three children, Wingate, continues to have anything to do with him. Peaslee spends the next five years conducting prodigious but anomalous research at various libraries around the world, and also undertakes expeditions to various mysterious realms. Finally, on September 27, 1913, he suddenly snaps back into his old life: when he awakes after a spell of unconsciousness, he believes he is still teaching the economics course he had done in 1908.

From this point on Peaslee is plagued with dreams of increasing bizarrerie. He thinks that his mind has been placed in the body of an alien entity shaped like a ten-foot-high rugose cone, while this entity's mind occupies his own body. These creatures are called the Great Race "because it alone had conquered the secret of time"[82]: they have perfected a technique of mind-exchange with almost any other life-form throughout the universe and at any point in time—past, present, or future. The Great Race had established a colony on this planet in Australia 150,000,000 years ago; their minds had previously occupied the bodies of another race, but had left them because of some impending cataclysm; later they would migrate to other bodies after the cone-shaped beings were destroyed. They had compiled a voluminous library consisting of the accounts of all the other captive minds throughout the universe, and Peaslee himself writes an account of his own time for the Great Race's archives.

Peaslee believes that his dreams of the Great Race are merely the product of his esoteric study during his amnesia; but then an Australian explorer, having read some of Peaslee's articles on his dreams in psychological journals, writes to him to let him know that some archaeological remains very similar to the ones he has described as the city of the Great Race appear to have been recently discovered. Peaslee accompanies this explorer, Robert B. F. Mackenzie, on an expedition to the Great Sandy Desert, and is horrified to find that what he took to be dreams may have a real source. One night he leaves the camp to conduct a solitary exploration. He winds his way through the now underground corridors of the Great Race's city, increasingly unnerved at the *familiarity* of all the sites he has traversing. He knows that the only way to confirm whether his dreams are only dreams or some monstrous reality is to find that account he had written for the Great Race's archives. After a laborious descent he comes to the place, finds his own record, and opens it:

> No eye had seen, no hand had touched that book since the advent of man to this planet. And yet, when I flashed my torch upon it in that frightful megalithic abyss, I saw that the queerly pigmented letters on the brittle, aeon-browned cellulose pages were not indeed any nameless hieroglyphs of earth's youth. They were, instead, the letters of our familiar alphabet, spelling out the words of the English language in my own handwriting.[83]

But because he loses this record on his maniacal ascent to the surface, he can still maintain, with harried rationalization: "There is reason to hope that my experience was wholly or partly an hallucination."[84]

The cosmic scope of this work—second only to *At the Mountains of Madness* in this regard—allows "The Shadow out of Time" to attain a very high place in Lovecraft's fictional work; and the wealth of circumstantial detail in the history, biology, and civilization of the Great Race is as convincing as in *At the Mountains of Madness*, but perhaps still better integrated into the story. Once again, it is cosmicism of both space and time that is at work here; this is made especially clear in a piquant passage in which Peaslee meets other captive minds of the Great Race:

> There was a mind from the planet we know as Venus, which would live incalculable epochs to come, and one from an outer moon of Jupiter six million years in the past. Of earthly minds there were some from the winged, star-headed, half-vegetable race of palaeogean Antarctica; one from the reptile people of fabled Valusia; three from the furry pre-human Hyperborean worshippers of Tsathoggua; one from the wholly abominable Tcho-Tchos; two from the arachnid denizens of earth's last age; five from the hardy coleopterous species immediately following mankind, to which the Great Race was some day to transfer its keenest minds en masse in the face of horrible peril; and several from different branches of humanity.[85]

That mention of the "hardy coleopterous species" (*i.e.*, beetles) again points to an undercurrent that we have already seen in other tales—the denigration of human self-importance. Lovecraft is, of course, on entirely solid ground scientifically in believing that insects will in all likelihood survive humanity on this planet; but he adds a further dryly cynical twist by maintaining that beetles will not only outlast us but become the dominant *intellectual* species on the planet, so much that the Great Race will deign to occupy their bodies when the cone-shaped bodies face peril. Shortly afterwards Peaslee adds a harrowing note: "I shivered at the mysteries the past may conceal, and trembled at the menaces the future may bring forth. What was hinted in the speech of the post-human entities of the fate of mankind produced such an effect on me that I will not set it down here."[86] Of course, it is the Great Race that become the centerpiece of the story, in such a way that they—like the Old Ones of *At the Mountains of Madness*—come to seem like the "heroes" of the tale. Much is told of their history and civilization; but, unlike the Old Ones, they have suffered scarcely any decline from the prodigious intellectual and aesthetic heights they have achieved, perhaps because their goal is not so much the acquisition of territory and the establishment of colonies but the pure exercise of thought.

The Great Race are a true utopia, and in his description of their political and economic framework Lovecraft is manifestly offering his view as to the future of mankind:

> The Great Race seemed to form a single loosely knit nation or league, with major institutions in com-

> mon, though there were four definite divisions. The political and economic system of each unit was a sort of fascistic socialism, with major resources rationally distributed, and power delegated to a small governing board elected by the votes of all able to pass certain educational and psychological tests....
>
> Industry, highly mechanised, demanded but little time from each citizen; and the abundant leisure was filled with intellectual and aesthetic activities of various sorts.[87]

This and other passages are virtually identical to those in Lovecraft's later letters on the subject, and especially in his essay, "Some Repetitions on the Times" (1933), where again he speaks of the need to spread economic wealth to the many but to restrict political power (*i.e.*, the vote) to the few. The note about "highly mechanised" industry is important in showing that Lovecraft has at last—as he had not done when he wrote "The Mound" (1929-1930) and even *At the Mountains of Madness*—fully accepted mechanization as an ineradicable aspect of modern society, and has devised a social system that will accommodate it. His solution, expressed briefly here and in copious detail in essays and letters, is the artificial restriction of working hours for each individual so that every capable person can secure employment; the resulting abundance of leisure time thereby accruing could then be spent in intellectual and aesthetic activity. Lovecraft sadly underestimated the rationality of the average human being, who is not likely to spend his time in intellectual and aesthetic pursuits when cruder joys are to be had; and the fact that his Great Race functions smoothly as a "fascistic socialism" is perhaps an unwitting admission that only a super-race can adopt such a sensible socioeconomic system.

One of the few flaws in the tale, perhaps, is Lovecraft's imprecision—indeed, his complete silence—on the matter of exactly *how* the Great Race effect their mind-exchanges, especially across gulfs of time. When the mind of one of the Great Race is about to vacate Peaslee's body, it sets up a device made up of "a queer mixture of rods, wheels, and mirrors, though only about two feet tall, one foot wide, and one foot thick";[88] in some fashion this device effects the exchange, although there is absolutely no indication of how it does so. There is a later reference to "suitable mechanical aid"[89] that somehow permits a mind to go forward in time and displace the mind of some entity, but this is again the only clue we ever receive of this procedure; and the mention of "mind-casting outside the recognised senses" and "extra-sensory" methods used by the Great Race stretches Lovecraft's mechanistic materialism to the very limit.

But this is a small blemish in a tale that opens up tremendous cosmic vistas and, as with *At the Mountains of Madness*, succeeds triumphantly in displacing humanity from center stage and enthroning fabulously alien entities there instead. The spectacular concluding *tableau*—a man finding a document he must have written 150,000,000 years ago—must be one of the most *outré* moments in all literature. As Peaslee himself reflects, "If that abyss and what it held were real, there is no hope. Then, all too truly, there lies upon this world of man a mocking and incredible shadow out of time."[90]

The basic mind-exchange scenario of the tale has been taken from at least three sources: first, of course, "The Thing on the Doorstep"; second, Henri Béraud's obscure novel *Lazarus* (1925), which Lovecraft had in his library and which presents a man who suffers a long amnesia and during this period develops a personality very different from that of his usual self; and the film *Berkeley Square* (1933), which enraptured Lovecraft by its portrayal of a man whose mind somehow drifts back into the body of his ancestor in the eighteenth century.[91] The latter two sources in particular may have been critical, for they seem to have supplied Lovecraft with suggestions on how he might embody his long-held belief (expressed in "Notes on Writing Weird Fiction") that "*Conflict with time* seems to me the most potent and fruitful theme in all human expression."[92] Lovecraft had, to be sure, suggested the vast gulfs of time in *At the Mountains of Madness*, but he does so here in a particularly *intimate* way that effects a powerful fusion between internal and external horror. Although Peaslee is emphatic (and correct) in believing that "What came, came from *somewhere else*,"[93] the moment when, in his dream, he sees himself to be in the body of one of the alien entities is as chilling an instance of existential horror as one is likely to find. Peaslee comments poignantly, "it is not wholesome to watch monstrous objects doing what one had known only human beings to do."[94] In a sense, it could be thought that this notion of "possession" by an extraterrestrial being harks back all the way to "Beyond the Wall of Sleep" (1919); but the monumentally expanded and subtilized expression of the idea in "The Shadow out of Time" makes one realize the enormous strides Lovecraft had made as a writer in a mere fifteen years.

It is now time to return to the difficulties Lovecraft experienced in capturing the essence of this story on paper. The core of the plot had already been conceived as early as 1930, emerging out of a discussion between Lovecraft and Clark Ashton Smith regarding the plausibility of stories involving time-travel. Lovecraft properly noted: "The weakness of most tales with this theme is that they do not provide for the recording, in history, of those inexplicable events in the past which were caused by the backward time-voyagings of persons of the present & future."[95] He had already mapped out the cataclysmic ending at this time: "One baffling thing that could be introduced is to have a modern man discover, among documents exhumed from some prehistoric buried city, a mouldering papyrus or parchment *written in English, & in his own handwriting*."[96]

Lovecraft began the actual writing of the story in late 1934. He announces in November: "I developed that story *mistily and allusively* in 16 pages, but it was no go. Thin and unconvincing, with the climactic revelation wholly unjustified by the hash of visions preceding it."[97] What this sixteen-page version could possibly have been like is almost beyond conjecture. The disquisition about the Great Race must have been radically compressed (Lovecraft suggests as much when he notes "an occasional plethora of *visibly explanatory* matter" in his tales and the possibility of replacing it with "*brief implication or suggestion*,"[98] and this is what clearly dissatisfied Lovecraft about this version; for he came to realize that this passage, far from being an irrelevant digression, was actually the heart of the story. What then occurred is a little unclear: is the second draft the version we now have? If so, why does Lovecraft at a still later date say that the final version of "The Shadow out of Time" was "itself the 3d complete version of the same story"?[99] Whether there were two or three entire versions must remain uncertain; but clearly this tale, scribbled harriedly in pencil in a small notebook later given to R. H. Barlow, was one of the most difficult in genesis of any of Lovecraft's tales.

Sadly enough, the history of the tale after publication was also unhappy. It was accepted, through the informal offices of Donald Wandrei, by *Astounding Stories* and appeared in that magazine for June 1936. Although Lovecraft repeatedly declares in letters that this story was not intentionally butchered as *At the Mountains of Madness* had been, there is nonetheless clear evidence of fairly severe textual tampering. A one-page manuscript of the tale (probably a section of the original manuscript recopied by Lovecraft for Barlow, who was surreptitiously typing it) survives, and it indicates that the paragraphing of the text as published in *Astounding Stories* has been extensively altered. Happily, the autograph manuscript of the story has now surfaced, and is safely housed in the John Hay Library of Brown University. It shows that the text was indeed seriously altered in its first publication, especially as regards paragraphing. Other errors—such as the omission or mistranscription of some passages, and the removal of italics from selected phrases—can be ascribed either to Barlow's poor typing or to deliberate changes by the *Astounding* editors. It is to be hoped that a corrected text can soon be published.

Lovecraft's last original story, "The Haunter of the Dark," came about almost as a whim. Robert Bloch had written a story, "The Shambler from the Stars," in the spring of 1935, in which a character—never named, but clearly meant to be Lovecraft—is killed off. Lovecraft was taken with the story, and when it was published in *Weird Tales* (September 1935), a reader wrote to the editor suggesting that Lovecraft repay the favor by writing a story killing off Bloch. Lovecraft did so, telling of one Robert Blake who ends up a glassy-eyed corpse staring out his study window.

But the flippancy of the genesis of "The Haunter of the Dark" should not deceive us; it is one of Lovecraft's more substantial tales. Robert Blake, a young writer of weird fiction, comes to Providence for a period of writing. Looking through his study window down College Hill and across to the far-away and vaguely sinister Italian district known as Federal Hill, Blake becomes fascinated by one object in particular—an abandoned church "in a state of great decrepitude."[100] Eventually he gains the courage actually to go to the place and enter it, and he finds all sort of anomalous things within. There are copies of strange and forbidden books; there is, in a large square room, an object resting upon a pillar—a metal box containing a curious gem or mineral—that exercises an unholy fascination upon Blake; and, most hideously, there is the decaying skeleton of an old newspaper reporter whose notes Blake reads. These notes speak of the ill-regarded Starry Wisdom church, whose congregation gained in numbers throughout the nineteenth century and was suspected of satanic practices of a very bizarre sort, until finally the church was shut down by the city in 1877. The notes also mention a "Shining Trapezohedron" and a "Haunter of the Dark" that cannot exist in light. Blake concludes that the object on the pillar is the Shining Trapezohedron, and in an "access of gnawing, indeterminate panic fear"[101] he closes the lid of the object and flees the place.

Later he hears anomalous stories of some lumbering object creating havoc in the belfry of the church, stuffing pillows in all the windows so that no light can come in. Things come to a head when a tremendous electrical storm on August 8-9 causes a blackout for several hours. A group of superstitious Italians gathers around the church with candles, and they sense some enormous dark object appearing to fly out of the church's belfry:

> Immediately afterward an utterly unbearable foetor welled forth from the unseen heights, choking and sickening the trembling watchers, and almost prostrating those in the square. At the same time the air trembled with a vibration as of flapping wings, and a sudden east-blowing wind more violent than any previous blast snatched off the hats and wrenched the dripping umbrellas of the crowd. Nothing definite could be seen in the candleless night, though some upward-looking spectators thought they glimpsed a great spreading blur of denser blackness against the inky sky—something like a formless cloud of smoke that shot with meteor-like speed toward the east.[102]

Blake's diary tells the rest of the tale. He feels that he is somehow losing control of his own sense of self ("My name is Blake—Robert Harrison Blake of 620 East Knapp Street, Milwaukee, Wisconsin.... I am on this planet"); and still later: "I am it and it is I";[103] his perspective is all confused ("far is near and near is far"); finally he sees some nameless object approaching him ("hell-wind—titan blur—black wings—Yog-Sothoth save me—the three-lobed burning eye...."[104]). The next morning he is found dead—of electrocution, even though his window was closed and fastened.

What, in fact, has happened to Blake? His poignant but seemingly cryptic diary entry "Roderick Usher" tells the whole story. Just as in "Supernatural Horror in Literature" Lovecraft analyzed Poe's "The Fall of the House of Usher" as a tale which "displays an abnormally linked trinity of entities at the end of a long and isolated family history—a brother, his twin sister, and their incredibly ancient house all sharing a single soul and meeting one common dissolution at the same moment,"[105] so in "The Haunter of the Dark" we are led to believe that the entity in the church—the Haunter of the Dark, described as an avatar of Nyarlathotep—has possessed Blake's mind, but, at the moment of doing so, is struck by lightning and killed, and Blake dies as well. Just as, in "The Call of Cthulhu," the accidental sinking of R'lyeh saves the world from a monstrous fate, so here a random bolt of electricity is all that prevents a creature of spectacular power from being let loose upon the planet.

Many of the surface details of the plot were taken directly from Hanns Heinz Ewers's "The Spider," which Lovecraft read in Dashiell Hammett's *Creeps by Night* (1931). This story involves a man who becomes fascinated with a strange woman he sees through his window in a building across from his own, until finally he seems to lose hold of his own personality ("My name—Richard Bracquemont, Richard Bracquemont, Richard—oh, I can't get any farther...."[106]). It is not entirely clear that Lovecraft has improved on Ewers here.

"The Haunter of the Dark" does not involve any grand philosophical principles—Lovecraft does not even do much with the basic symbolism of light and dark as parallel to good and evil or knowledge and ignorance—but it is simply an extremely well-executed and suspenseful tale of supernatural horror. There are only hints of the cosmic, especially in Blake's diary ("What am I afraid of? Is it not an avatar of Nyarlathotep, who in antique and shadowy Khem even took the form of man? I remember Yuggoth, and more distant Shaggai, and the ultimate void of the black planets"[107]), but otherwise the tale is notable chiefly for its vivid evocation of Providence.

Many of the landmarks described in the story are manifestly based upon actual sites. The view from Blake's study, as is well known, is nothing more than a poignant description of what Lovecraft saw out of his own study at 66 College Street:

> Blake's study...commanded a splendid view of the lower town's outspread roofs and of the mystical sunsets that flamed behind them. On the far horizon were the open countryside's purple slopes. Against these, some two miles away, rose the spectral hump of Federal Hill, bristling with huddled roofs and steeples whose remote outlines wavered mysteriously, taking fantastic forms as the smoke of the city swirled up and enmeshed them.[108]

A passage almost identical to this can be found in Lovecraft's letters to Bloch and others as he moved into 66 College Street in May 1933. Moreover, this exact view can be seen today from such a vantage point as Prospect Terrace on the brow of College Hill.

The church that figures so prominently in the tale is also real: it is St. John's Catholic Church on Atwell's Avenue in Federal Hill (recently condemned and partially destroyed, although efforts are being made to save at least its belfry). This church is in fact situated on a raised plot of ground, as in the story, although there is no metal fence around it. It was, in Lovecraft's day, very much a going concern, being the principal Catholic church in the area. The description of the interior and belfry of the church is quite accurate. Lovecraft heard that the steeple had been destroyed by lightning during the summer of 1935 (he was not there at the time, being in Florida visiting Barlow), and this incident no doubt started his imagination working.

"The Haunter of the Dark" is a compact, cumulatively suspenseful, and richly textured tale; it is by no means an unfitting end to Lovecraft's output of fiction (he wrote no original tales in 1936 or 1937), and it is simply unfortunate that increasing ill-health, the press of revisory and other work, and other factors prevented his writing more stories. Lovecraft frequently admitted that he had not used more than a fraction of the ideas in his commonplace book, to the extent that he would actually lend the book to others so that they might write up some of the plot-germs. (August Derleth carried this practice to absurd and contemptible lengths when he pillaged the commonplace book for stories and passed them off as "posthumous collaborations" with Lovecraft.) One cannot possibly predict what fiction Lovecraft might have written had he lived—especially if he had witnessed the second world war—just as one cannot say how his philosophical views might have changed; that they would have changed, and would consequently have affected the type of fiction he wrote, is without question.

There is no clear distinction between the tales of Lovecraft's last five years of active fiction-writing and the four years preceding it: his work since "The Call of Cthulhu" (1926) reveals an ever-increasing grasp of the technical requirements of the novelette form, an ever-enlarged philosophical and aesthetic perspective, and an increasingly provocative approach to weird fiction. Lovecraft was manifestly intent on producing a fusion of the traditional horror tale and the burgeoning tale of "scientifiction"; and although he had great contempt for the actual examples of science fiction appearing in the pulps (as he makes clear in his trenchant essay "Some Notes on Interplanetary Fiction" [1934]), he had read enough of Verne, Wells, and Stapledon to realize that there were clear aesthetic possibilities in this new mode of fiction. Although his early death seems to have cut him off in his prime—"The Shadow out of Time," in spite of his profound doubt as to its quality, is one of his towering achievements—by the time he laid down his pen he had conclusively effected this union of the weird and the scientific, producing an amalgam that rested not upon the ever-decreasing efficacy of traditional myth but upon the boundless and potentially terrifying realms opened up by the sciences of physics, astronomy, biology, and chemistry. There were, of course, a few lapses in this development—"The Dreams in the Witch House" is fascinating in conception but poorly written, while "The Thing on the Doorstep" is both poorly written and disappointingly conventional in its basic supernatural phenomenon—but on the whole Lovecraft continued to produce one great masterwork after another, each very different from what preceded or followed. It is curious to note that Lovecraft's deservedly high reputation in the field of weird fiction may rest upon no more than a dozen tales, although his lesser stories are always of interest and add significant nuances to his great works. One only wishes for Lovecraft a greater personal success in his own lifetime: one wishes that the pulp markets were not so stodgily conventional and aesthetically timid, one wishes that book publishers were more receptive to collections of short stories rather than to novels, and above all one simply wishes that Lovecraft could have shed some of his excessive modesty and even the pessimism and depression that overtook him in his later years and come to realize the triumphant brilliance of his best tales. But, given all we know about Lovecraft, it is not surprising that his success had to be posthumous; in some senses it is surprising that he had any success at all.

VII.

REVISIONS AND COLLABORATIONS

Lovecraft's career as professional literary revisionist was a slightly more regular source of income than his original fiction, although revisory jobs also fluctuated over time. Indeed, it was the lack of revision clients during his New York period (in spite of an ad placed in the *New York Times*), as well as his wife's inability to establish a private millinery business, that resulted in the financial downfall of Lovecraft's marriage; and late in life, when his fiction was becoming both increasingly sporadic and increasingly remote from conventional pulp standards, the gradual drying up of revision work caused severe financial distress.

There were several reasons for the meager financial returns in this line of work. Chiefly, Lovecraft far undersold himself. In 1933 he quotes a rate of $2.25 per page for "Rewriting from old MS., synopsis, plot-notes, idea-germ, or mere suggestion—*i.e.*, 'ghost-writing'. Text in full by reviser—both language & development. Rough draught longhand";[1] for 25¢ more Lovecraft would undertake the (for him) arduous task of typing such a ghostwritten work. This very charitable rate resulted frequently in Lovecraft's getting less than a quarter of what an original story would have fetched: when he revised Zealia Bishop's "The Curse of Yig," he charged $17.50,[2] whereas he would have received at least $90.00 from *Weird Tales* for an original story of similar length. The difference was, of course, that the ghostwriting deal was a sure thing—he would get his payment whether the resulting story sold or not—whereas the selling of original fiction was always a matter of chance.

Moreover, Lovecraft did not market his services very well. A somewhat grotesque ad for the "Crafton Service Bureau" (a revision service jointly run by Lovecraft and James Ferdinand Morton), appearing in the amateur journal *L'Alouette* for September 1924, offers "the expert assistance of a group of highly trained and experienced specialists in the revision and typing of manuscripts of all kinds, prose or verse, at reasonable rates" (of course, the "group" consisted only of Lovecraft and Morton); they also offered to "prepare and supervise courses of home study or reading in any field, and to furnish expert confidential advice with reference to personal problems." It does not appear that this ad brought in much business. Lovecraft was never a good businessman, and his failings in this regard are revealed with especial clarity in his chosen profession.

It cannot be too strongly emphasized that the bulk of Lovecraft's revisory work did not involve ghostwriting—much less the writing of fiction, weird or otherwise—but what would nowadays be termed copy editing. This work ranged from poetry to novels to all manner of nonfiction treatises, from Leon Burr Richardson's *History of Dartmouth College* (1932) to Anne Tillery Renshaw's *Well Bred Speech* (1936). It is sad to think of Lovecraft spending hour after hour revising the wretched poetry of the itinerant preacher and pop psychologist David Van Bush; but Bush paid well and regularly ($1.00 per 8 lines in 1922),[3] and Lovecraft could not afford to scorn him. Some of this general revision work would be of considerable interest if it could be identified: Lovecraft speaks in the 1930s of revising (how extensively is not made clear) a novel, but he never mentions the author or the title of the work (perhaps, however, it was never published); and Lovecraft's exhaustive work (without charge) on his friend Maurice W. Moe's never-published *Doorways to Poetry* in 1928-1929 makes this manuscript a highly significant document, but it is now lost and perhaps no longer exists. Lovecraft's back-breaking work in 1936 on *Well Bred Speech*, a wretched manual of English usage by an old amateur journalism acquaintance, probably contributed in a small way to his death, for on one occasion in September he worked for sixty hours without sleep to finish the treatise on time.[4] To add insult to injury, Renshaw ended up excising much of Lovecraft's work in the published version, in particular several whole chapters that still survive in manuscript. One such chapter is the essay published as "Suggestions for a Reading Guide."

Of course, for the general reader it is those tales of weird fiction that Lovecraft revised, ghostwrote, or collaborated on that are of greatest interest. It is, in fact, a little surprising that more would-be weird writers did not use Lovecraft's services; of his actual paying revision clients, we can number only Adolphe de Castro, Zealia Brown Reed Bishop, and Hazel Heald. Once again, this is probably because Lovecraft did not market his services sufficiently. The following ad, jointly taken out by Lovecraft and Frank Belknap Long, did appear in a 1928 issue of *Weird Tales*:

Frank Belknap Long, Jr.—H. P. Lovecraft
Critical and advisory service for writers of prose and verse;
literary revision in all degrees of extensiveness.
Address Frank B. Long, Jr., 230 West 97th St., New York, N.Y.

Again it is not clear how much actual work this brought in.

Several weird tales were revised for friends or acquaintances in exchange for other services (*e.g.*, C. M. Eddy, Jr., who typed Lovecraft's manuscripts for him) or were done without charge for young colleagues whom Lovecraft wished to encourage in their nascent fiction-writing (R. H. Barlow, Duane W. Rimel, Kenneth Sterling). On two occasions Lovecraft collaborated with professional writers; in one instance ("Through the Gates of the Silver Key" with E. Hoffmann Price) he signed his name, in the other ("The Trap" with Henry S. Whitehead) he did not. Similarly, he revised at least one story for his future wife Sonia H. Greene ("The Horror at Martin's Beach") but refused a joint byline.

The formal distinction between a revision and a collaboration boils down to the simple issue of whether Lovecraft signed his name to the work in print or not. This distinction, in terms of the extent or nature of Lovecraft's work on the item, may occasionally seem arbitrary, but one can usually ascertain the reasons behind it. Hence, the two collaborations with Winifred Jackson ("The Green Meadow" and "The Crawling Chaos") and the one with Anna Helen Crofts ("Poetry and the Gods") bore Lovecraft's name probably because he knew they would only appear in the amateur press (and in fact all three tales appeared under pseudonyms); whereas Sonia Greene's tale was submitted to (and accepted by) *Weird Tales*, and Lovecraft (although he surely did not charge her for it) probably allowed her to publish it under her name alone in order to encourage her and because the original inspiration and preliminary draft had been hers. Lovecraft was in fact very scrupulous in preserving anonymity in revision work for which he had accepted payment. Although he would frequently tell friends in private correspondence about his revision of a given story in *Weird Tales*, he strenuously objected to F. Lee Baldwin's wish to reveal such facts in a planned biographical article:

> It would be violating the confidence of clients to reveal that their alleged work isn't theirs, & if it became known that I 'gave away' those who employ my services, I wouldn't be employed any more!...When I accept pay for a revision or ghost-writing job, I naturally sell all rights which I might otherwise possess. The editorial remuneration & auctorial credit alike belong to the one who has bought the rights—& if I publicly 'tell on him' I am robbing him of something he has paid for.[5]

And yet, toward the end of Lovecraft's life this revisory work—especially in the realm of weird fiction—had become so well known amongst his associates that they frequently assumed Lovecraft's hand in tales which he had not in fact revised, but which were only written in imitation of his style (*e.g.*, various tales by Robert Bloch and Henry Kuttner).

The central issue in regard to Lovecraft's revisions and collaborations, from both a biographical and critical perspective, is to ascertain the precise degree of Lovecraft's actual contribution to the work. Did he write it wholesale from a plot-germ? did he merely touch up an existing manuscript? was his revision work later rewritten by the original client? Various combinations of all these scenarios appear to have occurred, and it takes considerable research amongst Lovecraft's papers and correspondence to arrive at even partial or approximate answers on this matter, since in only a very few instances (notably the tales revised for R. H. Barlow) do actual manuscripts survive. I have elsewhere outlined the evidence for Lovecraft's hand in his revisions,[6] and in the following discussion shall only allude to this evidence where relevant.

Lovecraft's three collaborative stories in the amateur press—the two stories written with Winifred Virginia Jackson and "Poetry and the Gods" (1920), written with Anna Helen Crofts—are among the most peculiar examples of this body of work. It is certainly strange that, of the five Lovecraft tales bearing a joint byline (the others are "Through the Gates of the Silver Key" and "In the Walls of Eryx"), three were collaborations with women. The two Jackson tales—rather similar in general tone and even in certain particulars of plot—were both based on dreams by Jackson; Lovecraft reports that, being primarily a poet, she had little experience with prose,[7] so that most or all the prose can be assumed to be Lovecraft's. The tales are very slight, and the use of the phrase "Crawling Chaos" (usually an attribute of Nyarlathotep) as a title for one of them seems particularly arbitrary, since Nyarlathotep makes no appearance in the story.

"Poetry and the Gods" is also slight, but presents a biographical mystery in that almost nothing is known about Anna Helen Crofts aside from the fact that she was a member of the UAPA living in the far northwest corner of Massachusetts; how Lovecraft came in touch with her, and how and why they collaborated on this very peculiar but mediocre tale, are wholly unknown. Lovecraft never mentions the work or the collaborator in any correspondence I have seen. This tale presents, with apparent seriousness, a long bit of imagistic free verse; given Lovecraft's own hostility to this avant-garde form, one might perhaps imagine that this at least was the contribution of Crofts, but this is a pure conjecture, since I have found no poetry by Crofts in the amateur press.

Little time need be wasted upon the insignificant "Horror at Martin's Beach" by Sonia H. Greene, which was inspired by a visit to the cliffs of Magnolia, Massachusetts, in the summer of 1922. It is a conventional sea-monster tale that does little to vivify this old horrific trope. A second tale by Greene, "Four O'Clock," appears to have been written only at Lovecraft's suggestion;[8] and although Lovecraft perhaps touched up the prose here and there, the tale does not seem to belong within his revisory corpus.

The four tales revised for C. M. Eddy, Lovecraft's Providence associate, have their entertaining moments. The first of them, "Ashes" (1923), is, however, such a shriekingly awful tale—with a nauseating romance element that must have made Lovecraft writhe—that no one would have suspected Lovecraft's hand in it had he not admitted it himself.[9] The other three tales—"The Ghost-Eater" (1923), "The Loved Dead" (1923), and "Deaf, Dumb, and Blind" (1924)—are of somewhat greater interest. The first is a routine ghost story that requires little comment; while "Deaf, Dumb, and Blind," a strange tale of a deaf, dumb, and blind man who records in a typed diary the incursion of some nebulous entity into his lonely cottage, gains a curious power in spite of its stilted prose. "The Loved Dead" is, conversely, one of Lovecraft's unheralded *comic* masterpieces; for there can scarcely be a doubt that this wild and flamboyant tale of a necrophile was meant as a riotous self-parody, in exactly the same way as "The Hound" and the latter parts of "Herbert West—Reanimator" were. Consider the final paragraph:

> Warm, fresh blood spatters grotesque patterns on dingy, decrepit slabs...phantasmal hordes swarm over the rotting graves...spectral fingers beckon me... ethereal fragments of unwritten melodies rise in celestial crescendo...distant stars dance drunkenly in demoniac accompaniment...a thousand tiny hammers beat hideous dissonances on anvils inside my chaotic brain...gray ghosts of slaughtered spirits parade in mocking silence before me...scorching tongues of invisible flame sear the brand of Hell upon my sickened soul...I can—write—no—more...[10]

Some parts of the tale are remarkably explicit for their time, as when an undertaker finds the narrator, his assistant, "stretched out upon a cold slab deep in ghoulish slumber, my arms wrapped about the stark, stiff, naked body of a foetid corpse!"[11] It was probably such passages that caused the issue of *Weird Tales* in which it appeared (May-June-July 1924) to be banned in the state of Indiana.

That same issue of *Weird Tales* contained a story entitled "Imprisoned with the Pharaohs" published as by Harry Houdini; the work was actually ghostwritten by Lovecraft under the title "Under the Pyramids." It is a remarkably fine tale that can stand comparison with his original fiction. J. C. Henneberger, owner of *Weird Tales*, wished Lovecraft to write up an account Houdini had told him: on a trip to Egypt, he had been bound by Arabs and left in some deep chamber of Campbell's Tomb in the valley of the pyramids. Houdini was attempting to pass off this adventure as a true occurrence, but Lovecraft's subsequent research established that the story was largely fictitious. As such, Lovecraft allowed his imagination free rein, transferring the setting to the Temple of the Sphinx but otherwise retaining many of the details of the narrative as related by Houdini.

It is true that the opening portions of "Under the Pyramids" read somewhat like a guidebook to Egyptian antiquities; no doubt Lovecraft was exhuming the knowledge he had gained both from first-hand exploration of the superb Egyptian wing of the Metropolitan Museum of Art in New York and from various handbooks on the subject published by the museum, some of which were in his library. But as the narrative—told in the first person as if by Houdini—gets underway and reaches the point where Houdini, bound hand and foot, is left for dead in some inconceivably deep cavern of the Temple of the Sphinx, the atmosphere of the tale (derived, perhaps, in part from Théophile Gautier's great novelette of Egyptian horror, "One of Cleopatra's Nights") becomes hypnotically compelling.

Amidst the narrator Houdini's various adventures—which include (as perhaps a lampoon of one of the most physically robust individuals of his day) several fits of fainting—he gradually comes to believe that the most harrowing issue is not the spectacularly grotesque hybrid entities he sees in the underground chamber ("*Hippopotami should not have human hands and carry torches...men should not have the heads of crocodiles*"[12] but an idle question he had asked himself at the beginning: "*what huge and loathsome abnormality was the Sphinx originally carven to represent*?"[13] But what does this question have to do with the loathsome creature to whom nameless offerings are being made by the hybrid entities?

> It was something quite ponderous, even as seen from my height; something yellowish and hairy, and endowed with a sort of nervous motion. It was as large, perhaps, as a good-sized hippopotamus, but very curiously shaped. It seemed to have no neck, but five separate shaggy heads springing in a row from a roughly cylindrical trunk; the first very small, the second good-sized, the third and fourth equal and largest of all, and the fifth rather small, though not so small as the first. Out of these heads darted curiously rigid tentacles which seized ravenously on the *excessively great* quantities of unmentionable food placed before the aperture.[14]

What can this five-headed monster be but "*that of which it is the merest fore paw*"?[15] This spectacular conclusion, anticipating the "titan *elbow*" of the entity in "The Shunned House," may perhaps be one of the relatively few genuine "surprise" endings in Lovecraft's work, and suddenly transmutes what would otherwise be merely a tale of grotesque physical horrors into one of stupendously cosmic implications. "Under the Pyramids" is a much undervalued tale, for its convincing Egyptian setting, intentionally overheated prose and atmosphere, and startling conclusion make it one of the better stories of Lovecraft's early period; but its foreign conception—Lovecraft would probably not have written a tale exactly of this kind on his own, certainly not with Houdini as the narrator—compels us to segregate it, however slightly, from his original work.

"Two Black Bottles," a tale revised for Wilfred Blanch Talman, is a mediocre story whose chief feature is the resentment inspired in Talman by Lovecraft's rather heavy-handed attempt to improve the tale. Talman had sent the manuscript to Lovecraft merely for examination, but the latter, as was his wont, took it upon himself to rewrite the tale considerably. Talman, becoming angered, appears to have removed much of Lovecraft's prose and restored his own in the final version, although he has admitted that much of the dialogue (in Dutch dialect) is Lovecraft's.

The two tales ("The Last Test" and "The Electric Executioner") revised for Adolphe de Castro, an elderly German who collaborated with Ambrose Bierce on *The Monk and the Hangman's Daughter* (1892), are of interest purely from a biographical perspective; for they represent perhaps the nadir of Lovecraft's revisions. Both stories are exhaustive revisions of tales published in de Castro's collection, *In the Confessional and The Following* (1893). The original versions are, of course, still worse than Lovecraft's rewrites, but nevertheless the basic skeletons of both tales have been maintained in the revised version. "The Last Test" (1927) in particular suffers from Lovecraft's inability to draw realistic characters; the protagonists are all rendered in a wooden and mechanical fashion, and the scientist Alfred Clarendon is a stock mad scientist of the sort that Lovecraft had already parodied in "Herbert West—Reanimator." Lovecraft remarks of the original story (entitled "A Sacrifice to Science") that "I nearly exploded over the dragging monotony of [the] silly thing,"[16] but his own version is still longer and more plodding.

In "The Electric Executioner" (1929) Lovecraft has transformed de Castro's "The Automatic Executioner" into a *comic* horror story just on this side of self-parody: the protagonist, trapped in a train car with an apparent madman who wishes to test a helmetlike electrocution device, finds all sorts of ridiculous ways to delay putting on the contraption, and finally convinces the lunatic to put it on himself so that he can draw a picture of it for the press. The character of the madman was loosely based on a rather more harmless person whom Lovecraft met on a train in 1929.

Lovecraft's three tales revised for Zealia Bishop—"The Curse of Yig" (1928), "The Mound" (1929-1930), and "Medusa's Coil" (1930)—are, along with the Hazel Heald revisions, among the most notable works of this type; "The Mound" at least need fear no comparison with even the best of his own tales. It is in these tales that Lovecraft begins in earnest to incorporate elements of his own developing myth-cycle (he had inserted certain whimsical references in the de Castro stories purely for fun), and as a result these works need to be consulted by those interested in tracing the development of that myth-cycle.

"The Curse of Yig" is a relatively conventional supernatural tale rendered distinctive by its clever surprise ending and its introduction of the serpent-god Yig, presented as a prototype of Quetzalcoatl. Bishop was at this time a resident of Oklahoma, and both "The Curse of Yig" and "The Mound" convincingly utilize that region as a setting; Lovecraft, of course, having never visited the area, had asked Bishop to fill out a questionnaire so that he would not make geographical or other mistakes.[17] Yig does not actually appear in any subsequent tales (and, indeed, he only appears by implication in this one), but he becomes one of the many names that are dropped in catalogues or litanies of imagined gods and places.

Of "The Mound" it is difficult to speak in small compass. It is itself, at 25,000 words, the lengthiest of Lovecraft's revisions of a weird tale, and is comparable in length to "The Whisperer in Darkness." That it is entirely the work of Lovecraft can be gauged by Bishop's original plot-germ, as recorded by R. H. Barlow: "There is an Indian mound near here, which is haunted by a headless ghost. Sometimes it is a woman."[18] Lovecraft found this idea "insufferably tame & flat,"[19] and fabricated an entire novelette of underground horror, incorporating many conceptions of his myth-cycle—including Cthulhu (under the variant form Tulu)—as well as Clark Ashton Smith's recent creation, Tsathoggua.

"The Mound" concerns a member of Coronado's expedition of 1541, Panfilo de Zamacona y Nuñez, who leaves the main group and conducts a solitary expedition to the mound region of what is now Oklahoma. There he hears tales of an underground realm of fabulous antiquity and (more to his interest) great wealth, and finds an Indian who will lead him to one of the few remaining entrances to this realm, although the Indian refuses to accompany him on the actual journey. Zamacona comes upon the civilization of Xinaian (which he pronounces "K'n-yan"), established by quasi-human creatures who (implausibly) came from outer space. These inhabitants have developed remarkable mental abilities, including telepathy and the power of dematerialization—the process of dissolving themselves and selected objects around them to their component atoms and recombining them at some other location. Zamacona initially expresses wonder at this civilization, but gradually finds that it has declined both intellectually and morally from a much higher level and has now become corrupt and decadent. He attempts to escape, but suffers a horrible fate. A manuscript that he had written of his adventures is unearthed in modern times by an archaeologist, who paraphrases his incredible tale.

This skeletonic plot outline cannot begin to convey the textural richness of the story, which—although perhaps not as carefully written as many of Lovecraft's original works—is successful in depicting vast gulfs of time and in vivifying with a great abundance of detail the underground world of K'n-yan. What should also be evident is that "The Mound"—written a full year before *At the Mountains of Madness*—is the first of Lovecraft's tales to utilize an alien civilization as a transparent metaphor for certain phases of human (and, more specifically, Western) civilization. Initially, K'n-yan seems a Lovecraftian utopia: the people have conquered old age, have no poverty because of their relatively few numbers and their thorough mastery of technology, use religion only as an aesthetic ornament, practise selective breeding to ensure the vigor of the "ruling type,"[20] and pass the day largely in aesthetic and intellectual activity. Lovecraft makes no secret of the parallels he is drawing to contemporary Western civilization:

> The nation [had] gone through a period of idealistic industrial democracy which gave equal opportunities to all, and thus, by raising the naturally intelligent to power, drained the masses of all their brains and stamina.... Physical comfort was ensured by an urban mechanisation of standardised and easily maintained pattern.... Literature was all highly individual and analytical.... The modern tendency was to feel rather than to think....[21]

Lovecraft even notes that in "bygone eras...K'n-yan had held ideas much like those of the classic and renaissance outer world, and had possessed a natural character and art full of what Europeans regard as dignity, kindness, and nobility."[22] But as Zamacona continues to observe the people, he begins to notice disturbing signs of decadence. Consider the state of literature and art at the time of his arrival:

> The dominance of machinery had at one time broken up the growth of normal aesthetics, introducing a lifelessly geometrical tradition fatal to sound expression. This had soon been outgrown, but had left its mark upon all pictorial and decorative attempts; so that except for conventionalised religious designs, there was little depth or feeling in any later work. Archaistic reproductions of earlier work had been found much preferable for general enjoyment.[23]

The similarity of these remarks to those on modern art and architecture as found in "Heritage or Modernism: Common Sense in Art Forms" (1935) is manifest:

> They [the modernists] launch new decorative designs of cones and cubes and triangles and segments—wheels and belts, smokestacks and stream-lined sausage moulders—problems in Euclid and nightmares from alcoholic orgies—and tell us that these things are the only authentic symbols of the age in which we live.... When a given age has no new *natural* impulses toward change, is it not better to continue building on the established forms than to concoct grotesque and meaningless novelties out of thin academic theory?
>
> Indeed, under certain conditions is not a policy of frank and virile antiquarianism—a healthy, vigorous revival of old forms still justified by their relation to life—infinitely sounder than a feverish mania for the destruction of familiar things and the laboured, freakish, uninspired search for strange shapes which nobody wants and which really mean nothing?[24]

But the problems of K'n-yan spread beyond aesthetics. Science was "falling into decay";[25] history was "more and more neglected";[26] and gradually religion was becoming less a matter of aesthetic ritual and more a sort of degraded superstition: "Rationalism degenerated more and more into fanatical and orgiastic superstition...and tolerance steadily dissolved into a series of frenzied hatreds, especially toward the outer world."[27] The narrator concludes: "It is evident that K'n-yan was far along in its decadence—reacting with mixed apathy and hysteria against the standardised and time-tabled life of stultifying regularity which machinery had brought it during its middle period."[28] How can one fail to recall Lovecraft's condemnation of the "machine-culture" dominating his own age and its probable outcome?

> We shall hear of all sorts of futile reforms and reformers—standardised culture-outlines, synthetic sports and spectacles, professional play-leaders and study-guides, and kindred examples of machine-made uplift and brotherly spirit. And it will amount to just about as much as most reforms do! Meanwhile the tension of boredom and unsatisfied imagination will increase—breaking out with increasing frequency in crimes of morbid perversity and explosive violence.[29]

These dour (and sadly accurate) reflections point to the fundamental difference between "The Mound" and such later tales as *At the Mountains of Madness* and "The Shadow out of Time": Lovecraft has not yet developed his later political theory of "fascistic socialism" whereby the spreading of economic wealth among the many and the restricting of political power to the few will (to his mind) produce a genuine utopia of useful citizens who work only a few hours a week and spend the rest of their time engaging in wholesome intellectual and aesthetic activity. That pipe-dream only emerged around 1931, as the depression became increasingly severe and forced Lovecraft wholly to renounce both democracy (in which he had never believed) and laissez-faire capitalism. The civilization of K'n-yan is, perhaps a little surprisingly, said to be "a kind of communistic or semi-anarchical state";[30] but we have already seen that there is a "ruling type" which had "become highly superior through selective breeding and social evolution,"[31] so that in reality K'n-yan is an aristocracy of intellect where "habit rather than law determin[ed] the daily order of things."[32] There is no mention of socialism, and the notion that a "period of idealistic industrial democracy" had been "passed through"[33] bespeaks Lovecraft's hope against hope that mechanization could somehow be overcome or tamed in order to leave traditional aesthetics and modes of behavior relatively unscathed. The fact that this proves not to be the case makes one aware that Lovecraft, for whatever reasons ("The Mound" was begun two months after the stock market crash of October 1929), was very pessimistic about the ultimate fate of Western culture.

After the intellectual richness of "The Mound," Lovecraft's third revision for Zealia Bishop—"Medusa's Coil" (1930)—comes as a vast disappointment. This lengthy tale is as confused, bombastic, and just plain silly a work as anything in Lovecraft's entire corpus. Like some of his early tales, it is ruined by a woeful excess of supernaturalism that produces complete chaos at the end, as well as a lack of subtlety in characterization that (as in "The Last Test") cripples a tale based fundamentally on a conflict of characters.

"Medusa's Coil" tells of a young man, Denis de Russy, who falls in love with a mysterious Frenchwoman, Marceline Bedard, marries her, and brings her back to his family estate in Missouri. It transpires that Marceline is in fact some sort of ancient entity whose hair is animate, and she ultimately brings death and destruction upon all persons concerned—Denis, his father (the narrator of the bulk of the story), the painter Frank Marsh (who tries to warn Denis of the true horror of his wife), and herself. But for Lovecraft, the real climax—the horror that surpasses all the other horrors of the tale—is the revelation that Marceline was, "though in deceitfully slight proportion...a negress."[34] This fatuous racism is a fittingly inept conclusion to a tale one fervently wishes Lovecraft had never written.

Lovecraft's revisory hand in Henry S. Whitehead's "The Trap" (1932) is a relatively recent discovery, but Lovecraft states clearly in a letter that he wrote the entire central section of the tale.[35] "The Trap" is a moderately entertaining supernatural adventure story in which a boy inadvertently enters a strange-dimensioned realm by pressing his hand on an old mirror. Whitehead probably offered Lovecraft coauthorship on this work, but one suspects that Lovecraft out of courtesy refused it. Another tale by Whitehead, "Bothon" (referred to by Lovecraft in letters as "The Bruise"), also has some contributions by Lovecraft; but I believe that he did no more than prepare a synopsis for the story, which Whitehead then presumably wrote up; Lovecraft only says that a new ending was "suggested and mapped out by myself."[36] Indeed, it is a matter of some doubt whether Whitehead did in fact write the story himself, as he and Lovecraft were working on it just prior to his death in late 1932; there has been speculation that "Bothon" (which was not published until 1946) was actually written up from Lovecraft's synopsis by August Derleth, but this conjecture has not been verified.

In October 1932 E. Hoffmann Price essentially railroaded Lovecraft into another collaboration—the celebrated "Through the Gates of the Silver Key." Price was so taken with "The Silver Key" (1926) that he wrote his own extraordinarily inept and stilted sequel, "The Lord of Illusion";[37] Lovecraft, ever the gentleman, felt obligated to do something with the piece, and after a period of seven months (October 1932-April 1933) managed to produce the version we have. He has totally rewritten Price's tale, increasing it in length at least twice to three times over, but nevertheless maintaining some of Price's conceptions (especially the mathematical portions concerning the interrelationship of time, space, and dimension) and even some of his prose.

In spite of Norm Gayford's interesting speculation that "Through the Gates of the Silver Key" is necessary to "complete" the Randolph Carter cycle,[38] it is difficult to deny that the story itself is clumsy and extravagant. Whereas "The Silver Key" is a poignant reflection of some of Lovecraft's innermost sentiments and beliefs, the sequel is nothing more than a fantastic adventure story with awkward and labored mathematical and philosophical interludes. Here we find that Carter, having returned to boyhood, continued on to pass through a succession of "Gates" into some realm "outside time and the dimensions we know,"[39] led by a "Guide" (the capitals are in the original) who proves to be 'Umr at-Tawil, the Prolonged of Life. This guide eventually leads Carter to the thrones of the Ancient Ones—who, following the demythologizing of Lovecraft's later period, are nothing more than the dreaded cosmic entities feared in such tales as "The Dunwich Horror" and "The Whisperer in Darkness." At one point Carter ruminates upon "the vast conceit of those who had babbled of the *malignant* Ancient Ones, as if They could pause from their everlasting dreams to wreak a wrath upon mankind. As well, he thought, might a mammoth pause to visit frantic vengeance upon an angleworm."[40] Interestingly, this passage is taken almost verbatim from Price's "The Lord of Illusion." In any event, Carter learns that there are "archetypes" for every entity in the universe, and that each person's entire ancestry is nothing more than a facet of the single archetype; Carter learns that he himself is a facet of the "SUPREME ARCHETYPE," whatever that means. Then, in some mysterious fashion, Carter finds himself in the body of a fantastically alien being, Zkauba the Wizard, on the planet Yaddith. His efforts to return to his own form comprise the remainder of the story.

It can be seen from this that the philosophical speculations in the tale are scarcely less extravagant than the actual incidents, and are marred by a schoolroom atmosphere very much out of tune with "The Silver Key." Lovecraft recognized this flaw in Price's original sequel, but has failed to rectify it properly. The haphazardness of the plot, the imprecision of the philosophical passages, and the unconvincing atmosphere of the whole condemns "Through the Gates of the Silver Key" to a low place in Lovecraft's canon.

We now come to the five stories by Hazel Heald—"The Man of Stone," "The Horror in the Museum," "Winged Death," "Out of the Æons," and "The Horror in the Burying-Ground." Although published over a several-year period (1932-1937), the evidence from Lovecraft's letters suggests that most if not all the stories were written in 1932-1933. What is also curious is that they nearly all utilize fundamentally the same supernatural conception: the idea of a living brain trapped in a dead or otherwise immobilized body. One suspects that all five stories were wholly written by Lovecraft from plot-germs or synopses by Heald; Heald has maintained that she had herself prepared a draft of "The Man of Stone,"[41] but the likelihood is that Lovecraft revised this story nearly as much as he did the others.

Only two or three of the Heald stories actually amount to much. "The Man of Stone" is in the end a conventional story about Daniel "Mad Dan" Morris, who finds in his ancestral copy of the *Book of Eibon* a formula to turn any living creature into a stone statue. Morris admits that the formula "depends more on plain chemistry than on the Outer Powers," and that "What it amounts to is a kind of petrification infinitely speeded up."[42] He successfully turns the trick on Arthur Wheeler, a sculptor who Morris believes had been making overtures to his wife Rose, but when he attempts it on Rose herself, she tricks him and turns him into stone. Here again, aside from the implausible nature of the supernatural or pseudo-scientific mechanism, Lovecraft's inability at characterization betrays him: his depiction of the love triangle is hackneyed and conventional, and Mad Dan's diary is written in an entirely unconvincing colloquialism. Of course, Lovecraft is hampered by the nature of the basic plot he was given to revise: he himself would never have chosen this scenario for a tale of his own.

The flaws in "Winged Death," however, seem largely of Lovecraft's own making. This preposterous story tells of a scientist, Thomas Slauenwite, who has discovered a rare insect in South Africa whose bite is fatal unless treated with a certain drug; the natives call this insect the "devil-fly" because after killing its victim it purportedly takes over the deceased's soul or personality. Slauenwite kills a rival scientist, Henry Moore, with this insect, but is later haunted by an insect that seems uncannily to bear tokens of Moore's personality. The tale ends ridiculously: Slauenwite himself is killed, his soul enters the body of the insect, and he writes a message on the ceiling of his room by dipping his insect body in ink and walking across the ceiling. This grotesque and unintentionally comic conclusion—which Lovecraft admitted was his own invention—is clearly intended to be the acme of horror, but ends up being merely bathetic.

Conversely, "The Horror in the Museum" must be read as a conscious parody—in this case, a parody of Lovecraft's own myth-cycle. Here we are introduced to a new "god," Rhan-Tegoth, which the curator of a waxworks museum, George Rogers, claims to have found on an expedition to Alaska. Rogers's skeptical friend Stephen Jones looks at a photograph of the entity:

> To say that such a thing could have an *expression* seems paradoxical; yet Jones felt that that triangle of bulging fish-eyes and that obliquely poised proboscis all bespoke a blend of hate, greed, and sheer cruelty incomprehensible to mankind because mixed with other emotions not of the world or this solar system.[43]

The extravagance of this utterance points clearly to parody. Indeed, "The Horror in the Museum" could be read as a parody of both "Pickman's Model" and "The Call of Cthulhu." Consider the absurdity of the scenario: it is not a mere representation of a god that is secreted in a crate in the cellar of the museum, but *the actual god itself!* The utterances of the raving Rogers as he madly seeks to sacrifice Jones to Rhan-Tegoth are grotesque:

> "Iä! Iä!" it [Rogers] was howling. "I am coming, O Rhan-Tegoth, coming with the nourishment. You have waited long and fed ill, but now you shall have what was promised.... You shall crush and drain him, with all his doubts, and grow strong thereby. And ever after among men he shall be shewn as a monument to your glory. Rhan-Tegoth, infinite and invincible, I am your slave and high-priest. You are hungry, and I provide. I read the sign and have led you forth. I shall feed you with blood, and you

> shall feed me with power. Iä! Shub-Niggurath! The Goat with a Thousand Young!"[44]

Later Rogers spouts such oaths as "Spawn of Noth-Yidik and effluvium of K'thun! Son of the dogs that howl in the maelstrom of Azathoth!"[45] Long before his talentless disciples and followers unwittingly reduced the "Cthulhu Mythos" to absurdity, Lovecraft himself had consciously done so.

"Out of the Æons" is perhaps the only genuinely successful Heald revision, although it too contains elements of extravagance that border on self-parody. This tale concerns an ancient mummy housed in the Cabot Museum of Archaeology in Boston and an accompanying scroll in indecipherable characters. Finally the scroll is translated with the assistance of the *Black Book* or *Nameless Cults* of Von Junzt (a title and author invented by Robert E. Howard), and tells the bizarre tale of the god Ghatanothoa,

> ...whom no living thing could behold...without suffering a change more horrible than death itself. Sight of the god, or its image...meant paralysis and petrification of a singularly shocking sort, in which the victim was turned to stone and leather on the outside, while the brain within remained perpetually alive....[46]

This idea is, of course, suspiciously like the drug utilized in "The Man of Stone." The scroll tells of an individual named T'yog who attempts to scale Mount Yaddith-Gho on the lost continent of Mu, where Ghatanotha resides, and to "deliver mankind from its brooding menace";[47] he is protected from Ghatanothoa's glance by a magic formula, but at the last minute the priests of Ghatanothoa steal the parchment on which this formula is written and substitute another one for it. The antediluvian mummy in the museum, therefore, is T'yog, petrified for millennia by Ghatanothoa.

It is manifestly obvious that Heald's sole contribution to this tale is the core notion of a mummy with a living brain; all the rest—Ghatanothoa, T'yog, the setting on Mu, and, of course, all the prose of the tale—are Lovecraft's. The tale is substantial, but it too is written with a certain flamboyance and lack of polish that bar it from taking its place with Lovecraft's own best tales. It is, however, of interest in uniting the atmosphere of his early "Dunsanian" tales with that of his later "Mythos" tales: T'yog's ascent of Yaddith-Gho bears thematic and stylistic similarities with Barzai the Wise's scaling of Ngranek in "The Other Gods," and the entire subnarrative about Mu is narrated in a style analogous to that of Dunsany's tales and plays of gods and men.

"The Horror in the Burying-Ground," on the other hand, returns us to earth very emphatically. Here we are in some unspecified rustic locale where the village undertaker, Henry Thorndike, has devised a peculiar chemical compound that, when injected into a living person, will simulate death even though the person is alive and conscious. Thorndike attempts to dispose of an enemy in this fashion, but in so doing is himself injected with the substance. The inevitable occurs: although the undertaker pleads not to be entombed, he is pronounced dead and buried alive.

Much of the story is narrated in a backwoods patois reminiscent—and perhaps a parody—of that used in "The Dunwich Horror." Other in-jokes—such as the use of the character names Akeley (from "The Whisperer in Darkness"), Zenas (from "The Colour out of Space"), Atwood (from *At the Mountains of Madness*), and Goodenough (referring to Lovecraft's amateur colleague Arthur Goodenough)—suggest that the story is meant, if not as an actual parody, at least as an instance of graveyard humor; and as such it is relatively successful.

Lovecraft appears to have examined and revised several manuscripts by the young Duane W. Rimel, who at the age of nineteen came into contact with Lovecraft in 1934. Perhaps three of them—the stories "The Tree on the Hill" (1934) and "The Disinterment" (1935) and the poem cycle "Dreams of Yith" (1934)—contain sufficient Lovecraft prose to count as legitimate revisions. (The story "The Sorcery of Aphlar" [1934], previously believed to be a Lovecraft revision, was probably only lightly touched up by him.) "The Tree on the Hill" is undistinguished: it is clearly the work of a beginning writer attempting to produce a tale in the Lovecraftian mode, and this is perhaps why Lovecraft charitably (if a little high-handedly) decided to supply an entirely new third and last segment to the story. Lovecraft also, evidently, supplied the lengthy quotation from the mythical *Chronicle of Nath* by Rudolf Yergler (presumably invented by Rimel).

"The Disinterment" (1935) is, however, a very different proposition. This tale—very similar in atmosphere to some of Lovecraft's early macabre stories, especially "The Outsider"—is either wholly written by Lovecraft or a remarkably faithful imitation of Lovecraft's style and manner. Correspondence between Lovecraft and Rimel—especially the former's enthusiastic initial response to the story—leads one to believe that "The Disinterment" really is largely the work of Rimel, Lovecraft acting only as a polisher; but if so, it is odd that Rimel subsequently wrote nothing even remotely as fine (or, at any rate, as Lovecraftian) as this tale.[48] Rimel (or Lovecraft) has taken the hackneyed "mad doctor" trope and shorn it of its triteness and absurdity by a very restrained portrayal, one that suggests far more than it states; and although the "surprise" ending is hardly a surprise to the alert reader, it follows the lead of many Lovecraft stories in which the narrator cannot bring himself to state, unequivocally and definitively, the hideous truth until the very last line.

Several of the tales on which Lovecraft and his future literary executor R. H. Barlow informally collaborated are mere squibs and *jeux d'esprit*, although very entertaining ones: "The Battle That Ended the Century" (1934), a vast in-joke citing dozens of Lovecraft's colleagues under parodic names (*e.g.*, Frank Belknap Long as Frank Chimesleep Short); "Collapsing Cosmoses" (1935), a never-completed parody of the space-opera brand of science fiction in which Lovecraft and Barlow wrote roughly every other paragraph; and other, lesser pieces both in prose and in poetry. Three additional pieces deserve notice here. The earliest has only recently been discovered: "The Hoard of the Wizard-Beast" (1933) is a pseudo-Dunsanian story that Lovecraft exhaustively revised, but it was never published in either the amateur press or the fantasy fan magazines. Lovecraft's revisions of the story are extensive, but it nonetheless remains merely the work of an apprentice. The second item, "'Till A' the Seas'" (1935), is a standard "last man" tale in which the extinction of human life as the earth dries up from its increasing approach toward the sun is depicted somewhat clumsily and amateurishly. The survival of Barlow's typed draft, revised by Lovecraft, allows us to pinpoint exactly the nature and extent of the latter's revisions: the tale remains mediocre simply because Lovecraft, feeling obliged to retain at least some of Barlow's own prose, could only do what amounts to an exhaustive rewrite.

Of the precise degree of Lovecraft's contribution to Barlow's "The Night Ocean" (1936) there will always be doubt, since the manuscript has now perished. All we are left with are various remarks in letters by Lovecraft and certain other documents. Lovecraft tells Hyman Bradofsky (who published the tale in the Winter 1936 issue of the *Californian*) that he "ripped the text to pieces in spots";[49] but in a letter to Duane W. Rimel upon publication of the work, he waxes eloquent about its merits: "The kid is coming along—indeed, the N.O. is one of the most truly artistic weird tales I've ever read."[50] It would be uncharacteristic of Lovecraft so to praise a story in which he had had a very large hand; and he was in any event correct that Barlow had been "coming along," as his "A Dim-Remembered Story" (*Californian*, Summer 1936) is a superbly crafted tale, but one that does not seem to bear any revisory hand by Lovecraft at all. Accordingly, it is quite likely that Lovecraft and Barlow contributed at least equally to "The Night Ocean."

Whatever the exact nature of the collaboration may have been, "The Night Ocean" is one of the most pensively atmospheric tales in the Lovecraft canon. It comes very close—closer, perhaps, than any of Lovecraft's own works with the exception of "The Colour out of Space"—to capturing the essential spirit of the weird tale, as Lovecraft wrote of some of Blackwood's works in "Supernatural Horror in Literature": "Here art and restraint in narrative reach their very highest development, and an impression of lasting poignancy is produced without a single strained passage or a single false note.... Plot is everywhere negligible, and atmosphere reigns untrammelled."[51] The plot of "The Night Ocean"—an artist occupies a remote seaside bungalow for a vacation and senses strange but nebulous presences on the beach or in the ocean—is indeed negligible, but the artistry is in the telling: the avoidance of explicitness—one of the besetting sins of Lovecraft's later works—is the great virtue of the tale, and at the end all the narrator can conclude is that

> ...a strangeness...had surged up like an evil brew within a pot, had mounted to the very rim in a breathless moment, had paused uncertainly there, and had subsided, taking with it whatever unknown message it had borne.... I had come frighteningly near to the capture of an old secret which ventured close to man's haunts and lurked cautiously just beyond the edge of the known. Yet in the end I had nothing.[52]

"The Night Ocean" is a richly interpretable story that produces new insights and pleasures upon each rereading.

The transition from "The Night Ocean" to William Lumley's "The Diary of Alonzo Typer" (1935) is a descent from the sublime to the ridiculous. Lumley, a nearly illiterate individual who had read voluminously in the strange and occult, had produced a hopeless draft of the tale and sent it to Lovecraft, who, feeling sorry for the old codger, rewrote the story wholesale while still preserving as much of Lumley's conceptions and even his prose as possible. The result, however, is still a dismal failure. We are here taken to some spectral house in upstate New York (Lumley was a resident of Buffalo) where strange forces were called up by the Dutch family that had resided there. The narrator, an occult explorer, attempts to fathom the mysteries of the place, only to be seized by a monster at the end while heroically (or absurdly) writing in his diary: "Too late—cannot help self—black paws materialise—am dragged away toward the cellar...."[53]

Somewhat more respectable is the science fiction tale "In the Walls of Eryx" (1936), written with Kenneth Sterling. Sterling—who at the time was a high-school student in Providence and much impressed Lovecraft with his scientific knowledge and familiarity with the science fiction fan world—has stated that the idea of the invisible maze was his, and it is certainly likely that Sterling produced a preliminary draft that Lovecraft revised. The authors have made the tale amusing by devising nasty in-jokes on certain mutual colleagues (*e.g.*, farnoth-flies = Farnsworth Wright of *Weird Tales*; effjay weeds = Forrest J Ackerman), but the narrative turns into a *conte cruel* when the hapless protagonist, trapped in the invisible maze whose opening he can no longer locate, reveals his deteriorating mental and physical condition in the diary he writes as he vainly seeks to escape. The already hackneyed use of Venus as a setting for the tale is perhaps its one significant drawback.

Some general remarks on Lovecraft's revisions are perhaps now in order. It can be seen that the role played by his collaborators or revision-clients varies widely; but in nearly every case the actual genesis, nucleus, or idea for the story is not Lovecraft's. In many instances, both early and late, an actual draft—coherent or otherwise—was provided by the collaborator, and Lovecraft either wrote his corrections directly upon it or rewrote it entirely, while still retaining at least a few phrases from the original. Not infrequently there is more of the original retained than one might initially have supposed, and all credit for the excellencies of a particular tale must not be indiscriminately attributed to Lovecraft.

The most significant pattern we notice in the revisions and collaborations is this: whereas the title, general setting, characters, and other formal details were provided by the collaborator, in nearly every instance the development, motivation, and portrayal of characters were supplied by Lovecraft. In other words, Lovecraft is contributing those features or elements of a tale that are the most difficult for a beginning writer to provide; his sure grasp of short-story technique allowed him instantly to identify deficiencies of this kind and to supply them as best he could, given the need to adhere at least nominally to the subject-matter and framework he was given. Where the revisions fail is exactly in those cases where vivid characterization is required; Lovecraft's lack of skill in this regard (to be studied more detailedly in the Conclusion) renders such works as "The Last Test" and "Winged Death" unwitting caricatures of the stories they might have been.

It is manifest that Lovecraft himself would have written very few of these tales on his own initiative. In particular, we note that the great diversity of settings—California in "The Last Test"; Oklahoma in "The Curse of Yig" and "The Mound"; South Africa in "Winged Death"—derives not from Lovecraft but from his revision clients, since he was loath to set tales in locales he did not know either through first-hand experience (New England) or through exhaustive research (England, Antarctica). Indeed, the C. M. Eddy tales develop their own imaginary New England topography in the recurrent use of such mythical cities as Fenham, Mayfair, Glendale, and Bayboro. My feeling is that Eddy is responsible for these names, since they lack the resonance and specifically New England "feel" of Lovecraft's own Arkham, Kingsport, Dunwich, and Innsmouth. Several of Duane W. Rimel's tales employ recurring characters and settings, but these seem clearly to be Rimel's invention.

While Lovecraft frequently incorporated elements of his own myth-cycle into the revisions—in many cases merely for fun, but at least in "The Mound" and "Out of the Æons" for more serious purposes—it is remarkable that he almost never cited in his own work certain of the pseudomythological elements created in the revisions. Ghatanothoa is mentioned only in "Out of the Æons"; Rhan-Tegoth is mentioned only in "The Horror in the Museum"; Yig is one of the few exceptions to the rule, having been cited in a litany of mythical names in "The Whisperer in Darkness" but otherwise appearing only in "The Curse of Yig," "The Mound," and other revisions. As such, we are perhaps justified in referring to a "Revision Mythos"[54] running parallel to Lovecraft's own myth-cycle.

Many of the revisions were consciously written for the pulp magazines, and are no better or worse than the average run of such material; in general, of course, they lack the philosophical and aesthetic substance that raises Lovecraft's works to levels scarcely to be imagined by pulp standards. It has been said that Lovecraft could have augmented his income by pseudonymously grinding out such hackwork for money while preserving his artistic sincerity in tales bearing his own name; but two arguments militate against this seemingly plausible theory. First, Lovecraft was psychologically incapable of practising this sort of literary dualism, and he expressed repeated amazement at August Derleth's ability to maintain a high aesthetic standard in his serious work (sensitive regional novels and tales) while being a factory of hackwork for the horror and detective pulps. For Lovecraft to have consciously written work below his own high standards would have been a travesty of all that writing meant for him. Second, it is not even clear that Lovecraft would have been successful in this business had he attempted it: several of the Heald revisions took years to land, and other revisions and collaborations did not appear in print until after Lovecraft's death. No doubt he was wryly amused when a reader of *Weird Tales* commented that "even Lovecraft" could scarcely have written the bang-up conclusion to "The Horror in the Museum";[55] but such popular success was rare, and in many cases the revisions sold no better than his original stories.

Lovecraft's revisions are certainly an unique body of work—no other writer seems to have engaged in exactly this sort of activity, at least not to this extent—and a number of them are important and meritorious works in their own right. Once the varying degree of Lovecraft's contribution to each work is ascertained (if, indeed, it is possible to do so), then these tales can be used to augment our understanding of Lovecraft's own work and of the place they occupy in his literary corpus. As noted earlier, in many ways revision was perhaps the worst career Lovecraft could have chosen for himself: it was too similar to original writing to leave him time or energy for work of his own, and it was too time-consuming and poorly paying to be a viable source of income. Lovecraft seems to have relied on a small band of "regular" clients—whether it be writers like Zealia Bishop or Hazel Heald or small-press publishers like the Kenyon Press in Wisconsin or the Stephen Daye Press in Vermont—for most of his business; and even these clients came to him largely by word of mouth or from the recommendations of friends and colleagues. Toward the end of his life revision work seems to have dried up, and this conjoined with his ever-dwindling sale of original fiction made his financial situation extremely precarious. As a gentleman of courtesy and generosity, he performed much revision—for youngsters like Rimel and Barlow, or for mediocre elderly poets like Elizabeth Toldridge—for no pay. One fervently wishes that Lovecraft could have obtained some clerical or other non-literary salaried position that brought in the $10 to $15 a week he needed, but his lack of job training in youth and his lack of business acumen conspired to keep him in increasing poverty as he advanced into middle age. Whether even such distinctive works as "The Mound," "Out of the Æons," and "The Night Ocean" are worth the hardships Lovecraft endured to produce them is a question only he could answer; all we can do is to appreciate them and other such works for their very real merits.

VIII.

ESSAYS

It is not generally known that Lovecraft's essays fill twice the space of his fiction, that his poetry occupies nearly half the bulk of his fiction, and that his correspondence dwarfs, in sheer size, all the rest of his work to complete insignificance. Lovecraft's fiction bulks small indeed in his collected works, although he eventually came to value his tales as the highest artistic products from his pen. In the end this judgment is probably correct, but it is conceivable that his letters may ultimately grant Lovecraft a more secure place in literary history than even his stories. Some mention must therefore be made of these other bodies of his work.

Lovecraft's essays can for convenience be divided into six broad categories: science, philosophy, literary criticism, writings on amateur journalism, travel, and autobiography. It should be pointed out that the overwhelming number of his essays were written in the first phase of his amateur period (1914-1925) and appeared extensively in the amateur press, so that many of them could classify as "amateur" work; and, in all honesty, many of them are also "amateur" in being sketchy, insubstantial, stiff, and a little pompous. But they were of great formative value in allowing Lovecraft, after his hermitry of 1908-1913, to address philosophical, political, and literary concerns and in perfecting his style into the rich, fluent medium we know from the mature stories and letters. They provide insights on many of Lovecraft's early views and interests, and on occasion they are of significant value in themselves.

Much of Lovecraft's scientific writing must be classified as juvenilia, since it was the direct product of his discovery of chemistry in 1898 and astronomy in 1902. It is fascinating to think of Lovecraft the boy working alternately on scientific treatises and dime novels; eventually he would fuse these two aspects of his intellectual and imaginative personality in the powerful works of quasi-science fiction of his last decade. But in his youth scientific writing far outweighed fiction or poetry, at least in quantity. His discovery of chemistry led to the creation of the *Scientific Gazette*, initially a *daily* paper concerned with his chemical experiments; the first issue (4 March 1899), notes laconically: "There was a great explosion in the Providence Laboratory this afternoon. While experimenting some potassium blew up causing great damage to everyone."[1] Later this paper devolved into a weekly (a total of thirty-two issues currently survive), and with the onset of the weekly *Rhode Island Journal of Astronomy* in 1903 it seemed to lose steam, so that in 1905 Lovecraft actually turned the paper over to another boy (Arthur Fredlund) whom he had taken under his wing. (Fredlund's editorship does not appear to have lasted very long.) Lovecraft's chemical interests led also to the writing of separate and by now virtually illegible miniature treatises on the subject, including a six-volume *Chemistry* (of which four volumes survive).

But it was astronomy that led to a tremendous outburst of writing, including separate treatises ("My Opinion as to the Lunar Canals" [1903]; the nine-volume *Science Library* [1904]) and magazines such as the *Rhode Island Journal* and other, more short-lived periodicals, including the *Planet* (1903) and *Astronomy* (later combined with the *Monthly Almanack*) (1903-1904). Of these, the *Rhode Island Journal* is clearly the most substantial, and some enterprising publisher ought to issue the surviving sixty-nine issues in facsimile—if, indeed, it is still possible to produce legible reproductions of the now fading hectographic copies. An average issue of the journal would contain a number of different columns, features, and charts, along with news notes, advertisements (for works by Lovecraft, for items from his collection, for products by his friends, or even for commercial firms), and fillers. They make wholly entertaining reading. Consider the first part of a serial, "How to Become Familiar with the Constellations," beginning with the issue of 10 January 1904:

> Familiarity with the constellations is an utmost requisite for astronomers.
>
> There are many treatises that take up the subject in a masterful manner, but they are beyond the reach of many, so this article had better be read carefully by those who wish to gain a knowledge of the constellations.

Lovecraft's desire to act as tutor to those less well-educated than he—something we find in abundance in his letters, especially those written to the many teenage correspondents of his later years—was already making itself evident before he himself had entered high school.

Lovecraft's earliest publications were astronomy articles in various local papers, among them the *Pawtuxet Valley Gleaner* (1906-1908?), the *Providence Tribune* (morning, evening, and Sunday editions) (1906-1908), the *Providence Evening News* (1914-1918), and the *Asheville* [N.C.] *Gazette-News* (1915). None of these, it must be confessed, are of any overwhelming intrinsic interest, although the *Gleaner* articles, being among his earliest works expressly written for publication, have a certain naive charm as Lovecraft soberly debates several popular controversies regarding the heavens. It is clear that this series is meant to raise public awareness of astronomical phenomena: Lovecraft has intentionally chosen topics of interest to the layman—can the moon be reached by man? Is Mars an inhabited planet? Are there planets in the solar system beyond Neptune?—in the hope that his readers will be inclined learn the truth about these provocative issues and free themselves from myths and misconceptions. Lovecraft is not shy about disputing the leading scientific authorities of his day (Percival Lowell, William Pickering, Giovanni Schiaparelli) on these questions, and on the whole he takes a position of neutrality and skepticism. He thinks it "not only possible, but even probable" that the Martian canals are arti-ficial; he does not believe in an intra-Mercurial planet (commonly called Vulcan), but thinks trans-Neptunian planets do exist; he suspects that man may one day reach the moon, but not "within the lifetime of anyone who now reads these pages."[2]

The *Providence Tribune* articles are less interesting because they are merely chronicles of the notable celestial phenomena for the month, and—like the later *Evening News* articles—become mechanical and repetitive after a time. Their chief interest is the appearance of hand-drawn star-charts for nearly every column, one of the few times that illustrations by Lovecraft were published in his lifetime.

The fifty-three *Providence Evening News* pieces are certainly the most voluminous astronomical articles he ever wrote, but their interest is only intermittent, for reasons just outlined: being accounts of each month's celestial phenomena, they rapidly become tedious if read in succession; after a year nearly all the phenomena recur, and Lovecraft does not make much of an effort to render them any more distinctive. What he does do after a time is again to educate the public, but in a different way: he provides sometimes lengthy elucidations of the myths behind some of the classical names for the stars and constellations. The boy who read Bulfinch's *Mythology* has now become the young man who will himself act as a humble Bulfinch to those not as classically trained as he. Consider this charming account of the "dog days" (*dies caniculares*):

> The traditions surrounding the Dies Caniculares are very interesting and very ancient. In Egyptian times the appearance of Sirius in the morning twilight, preceding the rising of the Nile, counselled the farmers to sow their grain. From this important function, the star acquired a religious significance, and was the object of much worship. Seven ruined temples have been discovered which were so built that the beams of Sirius, heliacally rising, should strike the great altars. Even the name "Sirius" is thought by some students to

> be derived from "Osiris," the name of the greatest of the Egyptian gods. In Asia, the heliacal rising of Sirius was regarded as the source of the extreme heat of late summer, a belief to which Virgil more than once alludes; whilst among the Romans a dog was each year sacrificed to the star at this season.[3]

But on the whole the *Evening News* articles—most of which are nearly 2000 words in length, making a total of more than 100,000 words—are certainly not to be read in quick succession. They were, of course, scarcely designed to be so read, and they eminently fulfill their purpose of reporting the celestial highlights of each month.

In the fall of 1914 Lovecraft found himself embroiled in a controversy. An astrologer had published an article, "Astrology and the European War," in the *Evening News* for 4 September 1914, only three days after Lovecraft's own column for the month and in the exact space his column usually occupied. The author, one Joachim Friedrich Hartmann (1848-1930), deploring the "vulgar prejudice against the noble science of astrology by otherwise learned men," gave a series of astrological predictions for the coming year. This was just the sort of thing to make Lovecraft see red; but his initial response—a sober if somewhat intemperate article entitled "Science versus Charlatanry" (9 September 1914)—did not have its intended effect, for Hartmann struck back with unexpected vigor. Lovecraft was therefore compelled to resort to satire, writing several pseudo-astrological articles himself under the pseudonym Isaac Bickerstaffe, Jr.—a name derived from Jonathan Swift, who parodied the astrologer Partridge with pseudonymous articles of this sort in the early eighteenth century. The hapless Hartmann, not realizing that Bickerstaffe and Lovecraft were the same person, finally withdrew from the fray. The Bickerstaffe pieces are certainly a delight, even if their satire is a trifle obvious; one of the last ones speaks of the destruction of the earth in the year 4954, but the salvation of a portion of the human race on a comet's tail to dwell "for evermore...in peace and plenty" on Venus. Not everyone, however, emerges unscathed:

> I find to my extreme regret that several fragments from the terrestrial explosion of 4954 will strike the planet Venus, there creating much damage, and causing grave injuries to Señor Nostradamo Artmano, a lineal descendant of our talented Prof. Hartmann. Señor Artmano, a wise astrologer, will be hit in the cranial region by a large volume of astronomy, blown from the Providence Public Library, and his mind will be so affected by the concussion that he will no longer be able to appreciate the divine precepts of astrology.[4]

We need not make much of the entire Lovecraft-Hartmann debate: clearly Lovecraft was moved to such vituperation precisely because the false science of astrology threatened to confuse readers whom he was so carefully nurturing in the true science of astronomy. Lovecraft here, as elsewhere, may perhaps be open to charges of intellectual fascism for his lack of confidence in his readers' ability to sort truth from charlatanry; but much of human history appears to justify his skepticism on this point.

In 1915 Lovecraft was given the opportunity to write a more unified series of atronomy articles, in what would essentially be a serialized manual of elementary astronomy. The *Asheville Gazette-News* (no doubt at the instigation of Lovecraft's boyhood friend Chester Pierce Munroe, who had settled in Asheville, North Carolina) asked Lovecraft for a series of fourteen articles, although only thirteen have come to light. They are an orderly and workmanlike series discussing, in sequence, the solar system (including specific discussions of the sun and each of the planets), comets and meteors, the stars, clusters and nebulae, the constellations, and telescopes and observatories. They contain few of the historical or anthropological asides that vivify the *Evening News* pieces, although occasionally some of Lovecraft's favorite topics—notably cosmicism—make an appearance. In speaking of the possibility that the farthest known star may be 578,000 light-years away, Lovecraft notes:

> Our intellects cannot adequately imagine such a quantity as this.... Yet is it not probable that all the great universe unfolded to our eyes is but an illimitable heaven studded with an infinite number of other and perhaps vastly larger clusters? To what mean and ridiculous proportions is thus reduced our tiny globe, with its vain, pompous inhabitants and arrogant, quarrelsome nations![5]

As with the *Evening News* articles, Lovecraft gradually introduces larger cosmological conceptions such as the nebular hypothesis and entropy. Otherwise the *Gazette-News* articles are dry and undistinguished. Toward the end of his life Lovecraft dug them up from his files; "their obsoleteness completely bowled me over."[6] If anything, they—and his amateur journalism work in general—show that Lovecraft had still not realized where his true literary strengths lay: it would be two years before he would recommence the writing of fiction.

Later scientific work needs little comment. "The Truth about Mars" (1917) announces ponderously that "LIVING BEINGS OF SOME SORT MAY DWELL UPON THE SURFACE OF MARS."[7] "The Cancer of Superstition" (1926) is biographically interesting in that it was to have been a book written by Lovecraft and C. M. Eddy, Jr., for Harry Houdini; but Houdini's death in late 1926 confounded the plans. The few pages that survive are a routine exposition of the anthropological basis for superstition, and no one need regret that this work was never completed. A work by Lovecraft published under the title "Some Backgrounds of Fairyland" (1932), dealing similarly with the anthropological origin of fairy-myths, is in fact a portion of a letter to Wilfred B. Talman.

Lovecraft's surviving scientific writing makes one somewhat relieved that he never attended college and gained a degree in astronomy or chemistry; for no one would wish him to have been the author of dry but competent scientific manuals rather than the author of *At the Mountains of Madness*. For all his prodigious self-acquired learning and his obvious enthusiasm for the sciences of astronomy, physics, chemistry, biology, and anthropology—sciences whose revolutionary developments in the first four decades of this century he followed avidly—Lovecraft's literary talents would have been wasted had he restricted himself to such work; instead, he eventually learned to use science and philosophy as a strong backbone for his later cosmic weird tales.

Lovecraft's relatively few formal philosophical essays are also on the whole undistinguished, largely because most of them were written in his early years, when he was laboring under the multiple handicaps of excessive dogmatism, bookishness, sequestration, and in general a simple ignorance of the world. This is especially the case for his early political writings (most of them written for the *Conservative*), which treat such subjects as the European war, Anglo-American relations, temperance, and racial purity with wearying bombast. Even the purely philosophical "Idealism and Materialism—A Reflection" (c. 1919) is not as interesting as many of his later philosophical letters.

There is, however, a startling exception in the series of three papers now titled *In Defence of Dagon* (1921). These essays—which simultaneously defend his aesthetic of weird fiction and his mechanistic materialism—were written in the course of Lovecraft's involvement with the Transatlantic Circulator, a group of amateur journalists in the United States, Canada, and England who exchanged manuscripts of stories, poems, or essays and commented upon them. Some of the adverse comments on Lovecraft's stories—in particular "Dagon" and "The White Ship"—forced him to unearth the Wilde-derived "no artist is ever morbid" tag, while at the same time the attacks by one Mr. Wickenden on his atheistic materialism resulted in scintillating destructions of Wickenden's naive theism, anti-Darwinism, and horror at the prospect of oblivion after death. It is this last issue that Lovecraft treats in one of the noblest passages in his entire *oeuvre*:

> No change of faith can dull the colours and magic of spring, or dampen the native exuberance of perfect

> health; and the consolations of taste and intellect are infinite. It is easy to remove the mind from harping on the lost illusion of immortality. The disciplined intellect fears nothing and craves no sugar-plum at the day's end, but is content to accept life and serve society as best it may. Personally I should not care for immortality in the least. There is nothing better than oblivion, since in oblivion there is no wish unfulfilled. We had it before we were born, yet did not complain. Shall we then whine because we know it will return? It is Elysium enough for me, at any rate.[8]

There is every reason to believe that Lovecraft led his life largely on these tenets.

Very few philosophical or political essays were written in the 1920s—his voluminous discussions of these issues were now confined to correspondence—but in his final five or six years Lovecraft occasionally broached some of these topics again, although in some cases he appears to have made no effort to publish the articles in question. The very curious "Some Causes of Self-Immolation" (1931) is one such piece. I have not been able to ascertain why this essay was written, and no publication of it in Lovecraft's lifetime has come to light; indeed, it survives only in a handwritten manuscript, and one suspects that Lovecraft did not even circulate it amongst his own colleagues. Consider also the subtitle and byline:

> Motives for Voluntary Self-Subjection to Unpleasant Conditions by Human Beings
>
> by L. Theobald, Jun., N.G., A.S.S., Professor of Satanism and Applied Irreverence in Philistine University, Chorazin, Nebraska; Mencken Lecturer on Theology in Holy Roller College, Hoke's Four Corners, Tennessee.

This would certainly lead us to think the work a parody of some sort, and yet it reads as a very sober and seemingly straightforward discussion of human psychology; if it is truly a parody (of, say, academic scholarship), then it is one of the most deadpan parodies ever written.

Less ambiguous is "Some Repetitions on the Times" (1933), a brilliant encapsulation of Lovecraft's later fascistic-socialist political views, written a few weeks before the inauguration of Franklin D. Roosevelt. This essay—also evidently not prepared for publication—is an earnest, almost harried plea for fundamental political and economic change in light of the depression, advocating such policies as old age pensions, unemployment insurance, and—most controversially—the artificial limiting of working hours so that all able-bodied persons could be gainfully employed. On the political side, the need to restrict the vote only to the intellectually qualified was no doubt a pipe-dream (and Lovecraft probably knew it), but the arguments advanced in its favor are compelling. We are ourselves all too aware of the ability of clever politicians to manipulate the minds, emotions, and votes of ill-educated citizens. Again, one wonders why Lovecraft did not send this paper to the *Atlantic Monthly*, *Harper's*, or any other such magazine where it might have been welcomed.

As a pure literary critic Lovecraft cannot claim much standing except in the realm of weird fiction. Once again, most of his critical articles were written during his initial amateur period, when he was wholly under the influence of a somewhat mechanical classicism that despised everything not based upon Graeco-Roman thought or expression. The mere fact that Lovecraft could spend so much time arguing about rhyme and meter ("Metrical Regularity" [1915]; "The Allowable Rhyme" [1915]) or the value of pastoral poetry ("The Despised Pastoral" [1918]) shows how out of touch he was with contemporary literary movements. But these movements finally began to obtrude upon his consciousness: initially he reacted with extreme hostility, attacking free verse ("The Vers Libre Epidemic" [1917]) and simple spelling ("The Simple Spelling Mania" [1918]) with unrestrained violence; but as his classicism shifted to Decadence in the early 1920s, his essays became somewhat more tolerant of modernity. That Lovecraft would in 1924 declare that Joyce's *Ulysses* and Cabell's *Jurgen* were "significant contributions to contemporary art" ("The Omnipresent Philistine")[9] is remarkable enough in itself, even though he later admitted that he never actually read *Ulysses*. As stated before, Lovecraft found in Decadence a means of becoming "modern" without wholly abandoning his earlier principles: he could salvage the central tenets of classicism (purity of expression, striving for beauty, harmony, and restrained elegance), and also attack the most freakish extremes of modernism (stream-of-consciousness, brutal realism, free verse) as being beyond the pale of art altogether. In a sense Lovecraft has been vindicated: the radicalism of the 1920s did not affect subsequent prose literature in any significant or permanent way, while the lax, colloquial, and wholly prosaic "poetry" of today has fallen totally and deservedly out of the intellectual lives of even well-educated people.

A late essay on the aesthetics of art and architeture, "Heritage or Modernism: Common Sense in Art Forms" (1935), has been cited in the previous chapter. It is a notable and even courageous piece of work, keenly pointing out the sterility of much modern art and "functional" architecture and its lack of vital connection either with the past or with the imaginative and emotional lives of most people. Here, as in his strictures against free verse, Lovecraft's views have by no means prevailed amongst the intelligentsia; but this by no means proves him to have been "wrong" on these issues, and in fact his advocacy of a vigorous conservatism in matters of art may once again show him to have been "right": how many of us find any aesthetic value in the freakishness of modern art, and how many of us actually utilize the most extreme examples of "functional" architecture in our own homes?

As a pioneering critic of weird fiction Lovecraft cannot be praised too highly, especially when one considers the paucity of both theoretical and practical criticism of the horror tale prior to his day. Dorothy Scarborough's *The Supernatural in Modern English Fiction* (1917) is more a sort of thematic catalogue of weird tropes than it is a theoretical study, while Edith Birkhead's *The Tale of Terror* (1921)—a landmark analysis of the early Gothic novel which Lovecraft clearly used as a reference for the earlier chapters of "Supernatural Horror in Literature"—similarly fails, for all its acuteness as an historical treatise, to provide a justification for weird writing or an analysis of the nature of the appeal of horror fiction. It is exactly in these areas that Lovecraft's work—first in *In Defence of Dagon*, then in "Supernatural Horror in Literature," "Notes on Writing Weird Fiction" (1933?), and voluminous discussions in letters—gains its importance. In his emphasis on atmosphere rather than plot, his distinction between the genuinely weird tale and the *conte cruel* or tale of psychological suspense, and in his sure grasp of the historical development of the field—with Poe serving as the pivotal figure in the transformation of stale Gothic conventions into viable new forms based on psychological realism and original horrific conceptions—Lovecraft's writing on weird fiction is of lasting value, laying the theoretical foundations upon which much later work has been built. Lovecraft of course has his biases: his emphasis on the supernatural may perhaps have led him to undervalue psychological horror, and his rather casual readings of Le Fanu, Oliver Onions, and a few others resulted in lukewarm appreciations of very able writers; but his designation of Machen, Dunsany, Blackwood, and M. R. James as the "modern masters" of the weird tale has been resoundingly confirmed by subsequent criticism. "Notes on Writing Weird Fiction" is an invaluable guide to Lovecraft's own principles and methods of fiction-writing; "Some Notes on Interplanetary Fiction" (1934) is a salutary exposé of the inferiority of much contemporary pulp science fiction; and the *Commonplace Book* deserves deep study as a mine of sources, ideas, and images utilized in both his fiction and his poetry.

Lovecraft's copious writings on specific topics in amateur journalism are perhaps of interest only to the specialist; but they clearly display his abiding devotion to the cause that helped to rescue him from a stultifying hermitry in 1914, and to which he remained loyal to the end of his life in spite of the many controversies, feuds, and political contretemps in which he was involved. What Lovecraft found (or, rather, liked to believe) in amateur journalism was its practising the ideal of "self-expression" for its own sake, rather than for the sake of fame or for monetary gain; this is a view that harmonized both with his early belief in writing as an elegant diversion of refined aristocrats and with his later "art for art's sake" stance. It is perfectly encapsulated in "For What does the United Stand?" (1920):

> ...the United now aims at the development of its adherents in the direction of purely artistic literary perception and expression; to be effected by the encouragement of writing, the giving of constructive criticism, and the cultivation of correspondence friendships among scholars and aspirants capable of stimulating and aiding one another's efforts. It aims at the revival of the uncommercial spirit; the real creative thought which modern conditions have done their worst to suppress and eradicate. It seeks to banish mediocrity as a goal and standard; to place before its members the classical and the universal and to draw their minds from the commonplace to the beautiful.[10]

Whether or not amateur journalism as a whole had such lofty ambitions, it is clear that Lovecraft himself did so and that he attempted with unflagging energy for at least eleven years (1914-1925) to make them a reality in the UAPA. He was ultimately forced to admit defeat, or at best an incomplete success, but it was certainly not through lack of effort. One must read the entirety of Lovecraft's amateur essays to gain a true sense of his development as a writer and as a human being from the "eccentric recluse" of 1914 to the titan of the amateur cause of 1921 to the respected veteran of 1935. Year by year his views broaden, his dogmatism is sloughed off, opinions dismissed in scorn are reconsidered and adopted. In 1921 Lovecraft, already an elder statesman in the amateur world, could affect modesty in speaking of "What Amateurdom and I Have Done for Each Other": "After all, these remarks form a confession rather than a statement, for they are the record of a most unequal exchange whereby I am the gainer. What I have given Amateur Journalism is regrettably little; what Amateur Journalism has given me is—life itself."[11] And yet, in spite of its false modesty, perhaps there is much truth to that statement.

Lovecraft's travel writings are a wholly different proposition. Almost without exception they were written for no audience but himself and his closest colleagues, so that he could be completely unrestrained in the expression of his personal and stylistic idiosyncrasies. Most of these documents—some of which are among the longest works he ever wrote, including "Observations on Several Parts of America" (1928), "Travels in the Provinces of America" (1929), "An Account of Charleston" (1930), and *A Description of the Town of Quebeck* (1930-

1931)—are written in an exquisite and flawless re-creation of eighteenth-century diction, fittingly for works describing Lovecraft's tireless search for colonial remains up and down the east coast of the North American continent, from Québec to Key West, from Vermont to New Orleans, from Washington, D.C., to Natchez. The historical disquisitions found in these travelogues—the result of Lovecraft's diligent research at the public libraries of the cities he visited—and his detailed walking tours, derived from local guidebooks and his own unflagging pedestrian rambles, make these accounts a delight to anyone familiar with the locales in question.

The essays are by no means lacking in wry humor as well. In "Travels in the Provinces of America" Lovecraft speaks of the early history of Jamestown: "In 1619 wives were sent out for the colonists, and in the same year the first cargo of African blacks arriv'd—proving that troubles never come singly."[12] "An Account of Charleston"—a lavish 15,000-word essay that Lovecraft condensed and wrote in modern English in 1936 for H. C. Koenig, who then published it as *Charleston*—contains an unforgettable passage condemning the modern age, written parodically in frenetic stream-of-consciousness:

> Against all the inherited folkways which alone give us enough of the illusion of interest and purpose to make life worth living for men of our civilization, there now advances a juggernaut of alien and meaningless forms and feelings which cheapens and crushes everything fine and delicate and individual which may lie in its path. Noise—profit—publicity—speed—time-table convict regularity—equality—ostentation—size—standardisation—herding.... Values evaporate, perspectives flatten, and interests grow pale beneath the bleaching acid of ennui and meaninglessness. Emotions grow irrelevant, and art ceases to be vital except when functioning through strange forms which may be normal to the alien and recrystallised future, but are blank and void to us of the dying Western civilization. James Joyce...Erik Dorn...Marcel Proust...Brancusi...Picasso...*The Waste Land*...Lenin...Frank Lloyd Wright...cubes and cogs and circles...segments and squares and shadows...wheels and whirring, whirring and wheels... purring of planes and click of chronographs...milling of the rabble and raucous yells of the exhibitionist..."comic" strips... Sunday feature headings...advertisements...sports... tabloids...luxury...Palm Beach..."sales talk"...rotogravures...radio...Babel...Bedlam....[13]

One of the most curious items in Lovecraft's entire body of work is "European Glimpses" (1931), a travelogue written for his ex-wife Sonia based on accounts and guidebooks she herself supplied on her European tour of the summer of 1931. This essay naturally lacks the immediacy of those written from personal experience, and Sonia's failure to go beyond conventional tourist sites in England, France, and Germany—or to gain any distinctive impressions of these standard landmarks—makes for rather ponderous reading; but perhaps it allowed Lovecraft to fantasize about visiting the Old Continent himself, something his poverty never allowed him to do.

Since Lovecraft's travelogues are among the most personal documents he ever wrote, it is a short step from them to his actual autobiographical essays. These too are relatively few in number—once again we must go to his thousands of letters for his true autobiography—but a number of them supply significant insights. "A Confession of Unfaith" (1922) is a bold statement on his shedding of religious belief as a youth; Lovecraft liked the essay so well that he cribbed much of it for the autobiographical letter he wrote to Edwin Baird, editor of *Weird Tales*, on February 3, 1924. His most sustained autobiographical statement, "Some Notes on a Nonentity" (1933), was commissioned by William L. Crawford for *Unusual Stories* but never appeared there. In the space of less than 3000 words Lovecraft manages to touch upon nearly all the central incidents in his life (with the notable exception of his marriage, which is not mentioned at all) and the core of his philosophic and aesthetic views.

A *Diary* that Lovecraft kept for 1925 is of course not a formal essay, but could serve as the basis for an entire volume on Lovecraft's New York period. The entries—written in a notebook that allowed only a few lines for each day—are extremely brief, sometimes to the point of incomprehensibility, but they provide fascinating glimpses into Lovecraft's surprisingly busy social life at this time. Here is a random entry:

> [April 11:] up early—eat breakfast—S[onia] H[aft] G[reene] left—write—message to see S H off 12:30—did so & return—write—meet boys down town—pet store with R[heinhart] K[leiner] & S[amuel] L[oveman]—Downing St.—back to 169 [Clinton St.]—bathe & dress—write—prepare to depart for Wash[ingto]n—WRITE L[illian] D C[lark]////down to station with Boys—wait—S L & R K farewell—train start—[14]

Quite unclassifiable is the piquant "Cats and Dogs" (1926), written for a meeting of the Blue Pencil Club in Brooklyn which Lovecraft could not attend in person because he had already returned to

Providence. In spite of its whimsical tone, it supplies keen arguments on the aesthetic supremacy of cats over dogs while at the same time underscoring Lovecraft's secular, aristocratic, and anti-democratic outlook. The following passage may not sit comfortably with many today, but in spite of its half-flippant tone it was deeply felt by Lovecraft:

> Dogs are the hieroglyphs of blind emotion, inferiority, servile attachment, and gregariousness—the attributes of commonplace, stupidly passionate, and intellectually and imaginatively undeveloped men. Cats are the runes of beauty, invincibility, wonder, pride, freedom, coldness, self-sufficiency, and dainty individuality—the qualities of sensitive, enlightened, mentally developed, pagan, cynical, poetic, philosophic, dispassionate, reserved, independent, Nietzschean, unbroken, civilised, master-class men. The dog is a peasant and the cat is a gentleman.[15]

His later brief memoirs of deceased colleagues—"In Memoriam: Henry St. Clair Whitehead" (1932) and "In Memoriam: Robert Ervin Howard" (1936)—unite a depth of feeling at the passing of a friend with a critical analysis of the author's work.

Wide-ranging as Lovecraft's essays are in subject-matter, tone, and import, they all reveal that striving for clarity, logic, and rationality which Lovecraft found in the eighteenth-century essayists he admired, and they confirm the statement he made early in his career—"I suppose I picked up my peculiar style from Addison, Steele, Johnson, and Gibbon"[16]—a statement, however, made prior to his resumption of fiction writing in 1917. But if there is any unifying trait to his essays, it is in their employment of *rhetoric* in its widest and most fundamental sense—the manipulation of arguments, tropes, and word-choice for the purpose of persuasion. There is, indeed, a certain hectoring tone to many of Lovecraft's essays, as if he does not have much confidence in his readers and is keen on making sure they properly understand the points being made. Perhaps this is not such an odd thing, since many of his views early and late were by no means fashionable then or now, and require compelling arguments to overcome a reader's skepticism. A definitely didactic tone can also be traced in many of the early essays, especially those designed for the amateur press: Lovecraft's lack of a college education prevented him from becoming a professor, but his obvious intellectual superiority to many in the amateur movement endowed him with the natural tools to be a tutor and guide.

A good many of the essays written in the last decade of his life were not designed for publication, and several appear to have met no other eye than his own; truly this was "self-expression" or "art for art's sake" in its purest form, embodying the idea that the act of creation can have no other goal than the satisfaction of its creator. In this sense many of his essays really become fragments of his autobiography: like the letters they embody some of his most personal views, but unlike the letters they did not reach—and perhaps were not meant to reach—even a single reader.

In the end Lovecraft will never be remembered solely or largely as an essayist; but many of his essays are important adjuncts to his fiction, and all of them were formative influences of the most significant sort, allowing Lovecraft to hone his style into the powerful and fluid weapon we know from the later fiction. It is no accident that description and exposition occupy so large a place in his fiction: in exemplifying his theory that a weird tale must be a sort of "hoax."[17] that will convey an impression of truth through the painstaking accumulation of realistic detail, Lovecraft's stories fundamentally abolish the formal distinction between fiction and nonfiction, so that *At the Mountains of Madness* and "The Shadow out of Time" read like the scientific treatises they purport to be. It could then be said that his tales subsume the best features of his essays—and, indeed, of his poetry as well, in their rich use of metaphor, symbolism, and verbal magic—so that these other bodies of his work are rendered aesthetically subordinate. But a few of his essays will always deserve reading on their own account, and even the least of them contains some small insight into the man and writer that no other document could provide.

IX.

POETRY

The judgment on Lovecraft's poetry has been severe. Winfield Townley Scott, although himself only a minor poet, declared, in tones of magisterial doom, that the bulk of Lovecraft's verse is "eighteenth-century rubbish."[1] After all is said and done, this verdict must stand. Curiously enough, Lovecraft himself came close to uttering a similar judgment. In 1929 he articulated perhaps the soundest evaluation of his verse-writing career that it is possible to give:

> In my metrical novitiate I was, alas, a chronic & inveterate mimic; allowing my antiquarian tendencies to get the better of my abstract poetic feeling. As a result, the whole purpose of my writing soon became distorted—till at length I wrote only as a means of re-creating around me the atmosphere of my 18th century favorites. Self-expression as such sank out of sight, & my sole test of excellence was the degree with which I approached the style of Mr. Pope, Dr. Young, Mr. Thomson, Mr. Addison, Mr. Tickell, Mr. Parnell, Dr. Goldsmith, Dr. Johnson, & so on. My verse lost every vestige of originality & sincerity, its only care being to reproduce the typical forms & sentiments of the Georgian scene amidst which it was supposed to be produced. Language, vocabulary, ideas, imagery—everything succumbed to my own intense purpose of thinking & dreaming myself back into that world of periwigs & long s's which for some odd reason seemed to me the normal world.[2]

To this analysis very little need be added. What it demonstrates is that Lovecraft utilized poetry not for *aesthetic* but for *psychological* ends: as a means of tricking himself into believing that the eighteenth century still existed—or, at the very least, that he was a product of that century and had somehow been transported into an alien and repulsive era.

Lovecraft was, indeed, thoroughly read in the seventeenth- and eighteenth-century poets—from the great (Dryden, Pope, Gray, Johnson) to the near-great (Chatterton, Collins, Cowper, Thomson) to the mediocre (Shenstone, Crabbe, Beattie). And in spite of his repeated assertions that Pope was his principal poetic model, his verse really comes closer in tone and rhythm to the looser and more informal verse of Dryden; much as he admired the *Dunciad* and the *Essay on Criticism*, Lovecraft could not hope to match Pope's scintillating and tightly knit poetic rhetoric. And yet, it should be noted that Lovecraft rarely resorted to outright imitation of his favorite Augustans. The one case of clear imitation that I have found (and even this may be unconscious) is the first stanza of "Sunset" (1917):

> The cloudless day is richer at its close;
>   A golden glory settles on the lea;
> Soft, stealing shadows hint of cool repose
>   To mellowing landscape, and to calming sea.[3]

No reader can fail to recall the opening of Gray's *Elegy*:

> The Curfew tolls the knell of parting day,
> The lowing herd wind slowly o'er the lea,
> The plowman homeward plods his weary way,
> And leaves the world to darkness and to me.[4]

Lovecraft's poetry falls into a number of groupings differentiated generally by subject-matter. The bulk of his verse must be classified under the broad rubric of occasional poetry; this class includes such things as poems to friends and associates, seasonal poems, poems on amateur affairs, imitations of classical poetry (especially Ovid's *Metamorphoses*), and other miscellaneous verse. There is, at least up to about 1919, a large array of political or patriotic verse, almost entirely worthless. Satiric poetry bulks large in Lovecraft's early period, and this is perhaps the most consistently meritorious of his metrical output. Weird verse does not become extensive until 1917, but toward the end of his life nearly all his verse is weird. These categories of course overlap: some of the satiric poetry is directed toward colleagues or individuals in the amateur circle, or is on political subjects.

The quantity of Lovecraft's verse also undergoes fluctuations over the course of his career. By far the majority of his 250 to 300 poems were written in the period 1914-1920; in other words, during the period of his most extensive involvement in amateur journalism. It sometimes appears as if Lovecraft is writing poetry merely to keep the various journals well stocked with material; in some cases he published several poems in a single issue, each poem appearing under a different pseudonym. (Most of Lovecraft's dozen or so pseudonyms were utilized for his verse, and they form an interesting study in themselves; but the issue is not of sufficient importance to treat here.[5] In the period

1921-1929 relatively few poems were written, and one can only conjecture why. It seems clear that his creative energies were being redirected toward fiction, but this in itself does not seem an entirely satisfactory explanation. A comment made as early as 1920 is suggestive: "The flight of imagination, and the delineation of pastoral or natural beauty, can be accomplished as well in prose as in verse—often better. It is this lesson which the inimitable Dunsany hath taught me."[6] Certainly Lovecraft's own Dunsanian fantasies employ all those elements—word-painting, imagery, metaphor, symbolism, and the like—that are customarily the domain of poetry, and these elements gradually sift into his realistic horror tales as well. Perhaps yet another cause of Lovecraft's surcease of poetry is his encounter with Clark Ashton Smith in 1922: here was a superlative poet who, although by no means a modernist, was showing by example how poetry of great beauty and power could be written in a vigorous and generally contemporary mode. Lovecraft could scarcely fail to realize the abysmal inferiority of his own verse in comparison to such things as "The Star-Treader" and *The Hashish-Eater.* Lovecraft's poetical muse revived fleetingly in 1929-1930, and I shall have more to say of this presently.

In terms of form Lovecraft always remained wedded to the most traditional and restrictive modes of English poetry: the heroic couplet (rhyming pentameters), the quatrain (following the model of Thomas Gray), the sonnet (although the *Fungi from Yuggoth* does not precisely follow the rules of either the Italian or the Shakespearean sonnet form), and occasional forays into trimeter (using Samuel "Hudibras" Butler, Jonathan Swift, or Edgar Allan Poe as guides) or internally rhyming verse (as in his very first poem, "The Poem of Ulysses" [1897], modelled metrically upon Coleridge's *Rime of the Ancient Mariner*). So wedded was Lovecraft to rhyme that he used even so conservative a meter as pentameter blank verse relatively rarely, although when he did so he produced some notable effects. As stated previously, he expressed quick disdain for almost all the departures from tradition occurring in the poetry of the early decades of the century, in particular Imagism and free verse. The pendulum of taste has now swung so far in this direction that Lovecraft's verse, already archaic for its time, now seems doubly remote; but his later poetry, in which he sloughs off most of the archaisms that deadened his previous work, can hold its own among other such conservative poets as Rupert Brooke, Walter de la Mare, and Ralph Hodgson.

Of Lovecraft's occasional poetry in general it is difficult to speak kindly. In many instances one quite is literally at a loss to wonder what he was attempting to accomplish with such verse. These poems appear frequently to have served merely as the equivalents of letters. Indeed, Lovecraft once confessed that "In youth I scarcely did any letter-writing—thanking anybody for a present was so much of an ordeal that I would rather have written a two-hundred-fifty-line pastoral or a twenty-page treatise on the rings of Saturn."[7] Thankfully for us, the following was not 250 lines, but it served the same purpose:

> Dear Madam (laugh not at the formal way
> Of one who celebrates your natal day):
> Receive the tribute of a stilted bard,
> Rememb'ring not his style, but his regard.
> Increasing joy, and added talent true,
> Each bright auspicious birthday brings to you;
>
> May they grow many, yet appear but few!

This poem—"To an Accomplished Young Gentlewoman on Her Birthday, Decr. 2, 1914"—is of course an acrostic. I am not certain who Dorrie M. is. This poem was not published, so far as I know, in Lovecraft's lifetime. In any event, poems of this sort are lamentably common in his early work, many of them much longer and more tedious than this.

Some of the occasional verse addressed to his associates have some interest from a biographical perspective. "To Samuel Loveman, Esquire, on His Poetry and Drama, Writ in the Elizabethan Style" (1915), is a tribute to an old-time amateur with whom Lovecraft was not at this time acquainted. Later, of course, Loveman would become one of his closest friends. "To Mr. Kleiner, on Receiving the Poetical Works of Addison, Gay, and Somerville" (1918) is a thank-you note to Kleiner for the receipt of a book and also a delightful impressionistic account of the three Augustan authors in question. Regrettably, however, almost all of Lovecraft's elegies for friends or relatives—among them "An Elegy on Franklin Chase Clark" (1915), "Elegy on Phillips Gamwell" (1917), "Helene Hoffman Cole: The Club's Tribute" (1919), and "Ave Atque Vale" (1927; on the death of Jonathan E. Hoag)—are lamentably wooden and devoid of genuine feeling. There is no question that Lovecraft in fact felt deep emotion at the passing of these individuals; but he was utterly incapable of expressing it in his verse.

Of the seasonal poems very little can be said. There are poems on almost every month of the year, as well as each of the individual seasons; but all are trite, mechanical, and conventional. It is perhaps possible to conjecture the influence of James Thomson's exquisite *The Seasons* (1727), but Lovecraft's own work is wholly lacking in the delicate philosophical and moral reflections that Thomson skillfully interweaves with his descriptions of seasons and landscapes. Lovecraft himself once wrote: "Impromptu verse, or 'poetry' to order, is easy only when approached in the coolly *prosaic* spirit. Given something to say, a *metrical mechanic* like myself can easily hammer the matter into technically correct verse, substituting formal poetic diction for real inspiration of thought."[8] One early poem, "A Mississippi Autumn" (1915), was actually signed "Howard Phillips Lovecraft, Metrical Mechanic."

One heroic work—in more ways than one—that requires some consideration is "Old Christmas" (1917), a 332-line monstrosity that is Lovecraft's single longest poem. Actually, if one can accept the premise of this poem—a re-creation of a typical Christmas night in the England of Queen Anne's time—then one can derive considerable enjoyment from its resolutely wholesome and cheerful couplets. Occasionally Lovecraft's desire to maintain sprightliness to the bitter end leads him astray, as when he depicts the family gathered in the old manor house:

> Here sport a merry train of young and old;
> Aunts, uncles, cousins, kindred shy and bold;
> The ample supper ev'ry care dispels,
> And each glad guest in happy concord dwells.

This could only have been written by one who has not attended many family gatherings. Nevertheless, the sheer geniality of the poem eventually wins one over if one can endure the antiquated diction. At times self-parodic humor enters in ("Assist, gay gastronomic Muse, whilst I / In noble strains sing pork and Christmas pie!"); and even when Lovecraft pays an obligatory tribute—which he clearly did not feel—to Christianity ("An age still newer blends the heathen glee / With the glad rites of Christ's Nativity"), he gently dynamites it by depicting the guests anxious to begin the feast ("Th' impatient throng half grudge the pious space / That the good Squire consumes in saying grace"). The pun on "consumes" is very nice.

Years later this poem received some very welcome praise from an Anglo-Canadian associate of Lovecraft's, John Ravenor Bullen. Commenting on the work in the Transatlantic Circulator, Bullen remarked that the poem was "English in every respect" and went on to say about Lovecraft's poetry generally:

> May I point out that poets of each period have forged their lines in the temper and accent of their age, whereas Mr Lovecraft purposefully "plates over" his poetical works with "the impenetrable rococo" of his predecessors' days, thereby running geat risks. But it may be that his discerning eyes perceive that many modern methods are mongrel and ephemeral. His devotion to Queen Anne style may make his compositions seem artificial, rhetorical descriptions to contemporary critics, but the ever-growing charm of eloquence (to which assonance, alliteration, ono-

> matopoeic sound and rhythm, and tone colour contribute their entrancing effect) displayed in the poem under analysis, proclaims Mr Lovecraft a genuine poet, and "Old Christmas" an example of poetical architecture well-equipped to stand the test of time.[9]

This is, indeed, a very charitable assessment, but on the whole it is an accurate one. In later years Lovecraft produced some of his most unaffectedly delightful verse by writing original Christmas poems to friends and family; these poems, brief and humble as they are meant to be, contain some of his most heart-warming metrical work.

Among the more delightful of Lovecraft's occasional poems are those that focus around books and writers. Here Lovecraft is in his element, for in his early years books were his life and his life was books. "The Bookstall" (1916), dedicated to Rheinhart Kleiner, is one of the earliest and best of these. Casting off the modern age, Lovecraft's "fancy beckons me to nobler days":

> Say, waking Muse, where ages best unfold,
> And tales of times forgotten most are told;
> Where weary pedants, dryer than the dust,
> Like some lov'd incense scent their letter'd must;
> Where crumbling tomes upon the groaning shelves
> Cast their lost centuries about ourselves.

Lovecraft uses this poem to cite some of the curiouser books in his own library: "With Wittie's aid to count the Zodiac host" (referring to Robert Wittie's *Ouronoskopia; or, A Survey of the Heavens* [1681], one of the oldest books in his library), "O'er Mather's prosy page, half dreaming, pore" (referring to his ancestral copy of the first edition of Cotton Mather's *Magnalia Christi Americana* [1702]), and, most delightful of all, "Go smell the drugs in Garth's Dispensary!" (referring to his copy of Sir Samuel Garth's *The Dispensary* [1699]). That last line is worth nearly all his other archaistic verse put together. And how can we not be touched by the little paean to the cat?

> Upon the floor, in Sol's enfeebled blaze,
> The coal-black puss with youthful ardour plays;
> Yet what more ancient symbol may we scan
> Than puss, the age-long satellite of Man?
> Egyptian days a feline worship knew,
> And Roman consuls heard the plaintive mew:
> The glossy mite can win a scholar's glance,
> Whilst sages pause the watch a kitten prance.

Two facets of Lovecraft's poetry that must be passed over in merciful brevity are his classical imitations and his philosophical poetry. Lovecraft seemed endlessly fond of producing flaccid imitations of Ovid's *Metamorphoses*—his first poetic love, let us recall, read in translation at the age of eight—including such things as "Hylas and Myrrha: A Tale" (1919), "Myrrha and Strephon" (1919), and several others. Of the early philosophical poetry, only two are notable. "Inspiration" (1916) is a delicate two-stanza poem on literary inspiration coming to a writer at an unexpected moment. "Brotherhood" (1916) is a genuinely meritorious poem and a surprising one for Lovecraft at this stage of his career to have written. One can find many instances of Lovecraft's social snobbery both in his life and his fiction, so that it is no surprise that this poem begins:

> In prideful scorn I watch'd the farmer stride
>   With step uncouth o'er road and mossy lane;
> How could I help but distantly deride
>   The churlish, callous'd, coarse-clad country swain?

The narrator determines that he is "no kin to such as he"; but then he is taken aback to observe the farmer delicately avoiding stepping on the flowers in his path, and concludes:

> And while I gaz'd, my spirit swell'd apace;
>   With the crude swain I own'd the human tie;
> The tend'rest impulse of a noble race
>   Had prov'd the boor a finer man than I!

How sincere Lovecraft is in this poem is another matter; it would take him a long time to renounce distinctions of class and breeding, and in some ways—even as a socialist—he never did so. But "Brotherhood" is a poignant poem nonetheless.

As the years passed, it became evident to Lovecraft's readers in the amateur press (as it was always evident to Lovecraft himself) that in his poetry he was a self-consciously antiquated fossil with admirable technical skill but no real poetical feeling. Even W. Paul Cook, who so ardently encouraged Lovecraft the fiction-writer, said of his poetry in 1919: "I cannot fully appreciate Mr. Lovecraft as a poet...To me, most of his verse is too formal, too artificial, too stilted in phraseology and form."[10] Eventually Lovecraft began to poke fun at himself on this score; one of the most delightful of such specimens is "On the Death of a Rhyming Critic" (1917). The satire here is emphatically double-edged. Speaking of the death of one Macer, the narrator of the poem remarks in tripping octosyllabics (the meter of choice of Samuel Butler and Swift, and also of Rheinhart Kleiner and Lovecraft's old *Argosy* opponent John Russell):

A curious fellow in his time,
Fond of old books and prone to rhyme—
A scribbling pedant, of the sort
That scorn the age, and write for sport.
A little wit he sometimes had,
But half of what he wrote was bad;
In metre he was very fair;
Of rhetoric he had his share—
But of the past so much he'd prate,
That he was always out of date!

This and a later passage ("His numbers smooth enough would roll, / But after all—he had no soul!") show once again that Lovecraft was fully cognizant of his own deficiencies as a poet; but toward the end of the poem things take an unexpected turn. Lovecraft now plays upon his skill as a corrector of bad poetry—he had probably already by this time commenced his occupation as literary revisionist—by having the poem's narrator stumble incompetently at the last. He must write an elegy on Macer for the *Morning Sun*; but who will help him with it? The poem literally disintegrates:

So many strugglers he befriended,
That rougher bards on him depended:
His death will still more pens than his—
I wonder where the fellow is!
He's in a better land—or worse—
(I wonder who'll revise this verse?)

A later poem, "The Dead Bookworm" (1919), deals somewhat with the same subject. Here the subject of mock-eulogy is someone simply named Bookworm—a "Temp'rance crank—confounded ass!," and one who "never seemed to thrive / I guess he was but half alive."

Well, now it's over! (Hello, Jack!
Enjoy your trip? I'm glad you're back!)
Yes—Bookworm's dead—what's that? Go slow!
Thought he was dead a year ago?

And so on. The sprightliness and colloquialism of this poem are highly unusual for Lovecraft, and may bespeak the influence of the *vers de société* of Rheinhart Kleiner, an unjustly forgotten master of this light form.

This brings us to Lovecraft's satiric poetry, which not only ranges over a very wide array of subject-matter but is clearly the only facet of his poetry aside from his weird verse that is of any account.

Kleiner made this point in "A Note on Howard P. Lovecraft's Verse" (1919), the first critical article on Lovecraft:

> Many who cannot read his longer and more ambitious productions find Mr. Lovecraft's light or humorous verse decidedly refreshing. As a satirist along familiar lines, particularly those laid down by Butler, Swift and Pope, he is most himself—paradoxical as it seems. In reading his satires one cannot help but feel the zest with which the author has composed them. They are admirable for the way in which they reveal the depth and intensity of Mr. Lovecraft's convictions, while the wit, irony, sarcasm and humour to be found in them serve as an indication of his powers as a controversialist. The almost relentless ferocity of his satires is constantly relieved by an attendant broad humour which has the merit of causing the reader to chuckle more than once in the perusal of some attack levelled against the particular person or policy which may have incurred Mr. Lovecraft's displeasure.[11]

This analysis is exactly on target. Lovecraft himself remarked in 1921: "Whatever merriment I have is always derived from the satirical principle...."[12]

In many cases colleagues are the objects of either mild or pungent satire. Of the former sort is a whole array of poems written around the frivolous amours of the young Alfred Galpin ("Damon and Delia, a Pastoral" [1918], "To Delia, Avoiding Damon" [1918], etc.), culminating in the verse play *Alfredo* (1918), in which Galpin, Rheinhart Kleiner, Maurice W. Moe, and others (including Lovecraft himself) appear in thinly disguised form as figures in the court of Renaissance Spain. A spectacular culminating scene in which nearly every character is killed off brings this vast in-joke to an appropriately absurd conclusion. Much more bitter are such things as "The Isaacsonio-Mortoniad" (1915), a vicious poem responding to Charles D. Isaacson's and James F. Morton's attacks on Lovecraft in Isaacson's amateur journal, *In a Major Key* (Lovecraft's poem does not appear to have been published in his lifetime—a fortunate thing, perhaps, else it might have jeopardized his later close friendship with Morton), and "Medusa: A Portrait" (1921), a satire on a female amateur worthy of Juvenal.

Literary faults or literary modernism (much the same thing to Lovecraft) are also the target of many satires. When Isaacson in *In a Minor Key* championed Walt Whitman as the "Greatest American Thinker," Lovecraft responded with a sizzling rebuttal in prose entitled "In a Major Key" (1915) in which he included an untitled poem on Whitman:

Behold great *Whitman*, whose licentious line
Delights the rake, and warms the souls of swine;
Whose fever'd fancy shuns the measur'd place,
And copies Ovid's filth without his grace.

And so on. Whitman was the perfect anathema for Lovecraft at this time, not only in his scornful abandonment of traditional meter but in his frank discussions of both homosexual and heterosexual sex. "The State of Poetry" (1915) is an attack on bad (but not necessarily modern) poetry which has some clever bits. False rhymes are skewered wittily:

How might we praise the lines so soft and sweet,
Were they not lame in their poetic feet!
Just as the reader's heart bursts into flame,
The fire is quenched by rhyming "gain" with "name,"
And ecstasy becomes no easy task
When fields of "grass" in Sol's bright radiançe "bask"!

"The Magazine Poet" (1915) is an amusing squib on hack writing:

The modern bard restrains poetic rage,
To fit his couplets to a quarter-page.
Who now regards his skill, or taste, or strength,
When verse is writ and printed for its length?
His soaring sentiment he needs must pinch,
And sing his Amaryllis by the inch.

But Lovecraft's greatest poem in this regard is "Amissa Minerva" (1919). After supplying a highly condensed history of poetry from Homer to Swinburne, Lovecraft launches upon a systematic attack on modern poetry, mentioning Amy Lowell, Edgar Lee Masters, Carl Sandburg, and others by name. Here is an excerpt:

Yet see on ev'ry hand the antic train
That swarm uncheck'd, and gibber o'er the plain.
Here Librist, Cubist, Spectrist forms arise;
With foetid vapours cloud the crystal skies;
Or led by transient madness, rend the air
With shrieks of bliss and whinings of despair.

The subject-matter of modern poetry offends Lovecraft ("Exempt from wit, each dullard pours his ink / In odes to bathtubs, or the kitchen sink") as much as its abandonment of traditional rhyme and meter.

Lovecraft's political poems make painful reading, not only for their wooden and stilted diction but for their racism, militarism, and a bombastic earnestness that produces bathos rather than heartfelt emotion. Naturally the course of the world war—and especially America's avowed neutrality during the first three years of it—led Lovecraft to endless fulminations in both prose and verse; with the result that we have such forgettable pieces as "The Crime of Crimes" (1915; on the sinking of the *Lusitania*), "The Peace Advocate" (1917), "Pacifist War Song—1917" (1917), and any number of tributes to England ("1914" [1915]; "An American to Mother England" [1916]; "The Rose of England" [1916]; "Britannia Victura" [1917]; "An American to the British Flag" [1917]). With the end of the war all this verse comes to an abrupt and thankful end.

If Lovecraft's verse in general cannot escape being branded as "eighteenth-century rubbish," then much of his weird verse must similarly be termed "Poe-esque rubbish." What this means is that Lovecraft, while developing the knack of imitating Poe's meter and rhythm-patterns ably enough, found little of his own to say in most of this body of work. And yet, as with so much of Lovecraft's inferior work—and it is perhaps this that distinguishes him from most other writers—it is possible to find things to note and even enjoy in nearly all his weird poetry.

"The Poe-et's Nightmare" (1916)[13] is one of the most remarkable of Lovecraft's poems, and is certainly the most significant work of fantasy poetry aside from *Fungi from Yuggoth*. R. Boerem has already written a thoughtful and detailed study of this poem,[14] and I shall add only a few notes. In the first place, the structure of the poem is peculiar: we have a lengthy introductory section and a concluding section in heroic couplets, with a long central portion in pentameter blank verse (the meter of *Paradise Lost* and *The Seasons*). I am not sure that this structure is very felicitous, for the outer sections, comic in nature, tend to subvert the point of the cosmic centerpiece; and yet, we know that Lovecraft's genuine views are embedded in this middle section. By attributing the "nightmare" of Lucullus Languish to overeating and excessive reading of Poe, especially in such lines as

> He feels his aching limbs, whose woeful pain
> Informs his soul his body lives again,
> And thanks his stars—or cosmoses—or such—
> That he survives the noxious nightmare's clutch.

...the cosmic vistas revealed in the nightmare are made the butt of jest. This is probably why, when in 1936 R. H. Barlow wished to include "The Poe-et's Nightmare" in a proposed collection of Lovecraft's fantastic verse, Lovecraft advised dropping the comic framework.[15] This in fact was done when *Weird Tales* published the poem posthumously (July 1952) under the title of the central portion, *Aletheia Phrikodes* (The Frightful Truth).

What is most interesting about "The Poe-et's Nightmare" is its mere existence. This is really the first instance of Lovecraft's artistic expression of cosmicism, written a year before his resumption of fiction writing with "Dagon" (itself only marginally cosmic) and years before Lovecraft's crystallization of cosmicism in "The Call of Cthulhu" (1926), *At the Mountains of Madness* (1931), and "The Shadow out of Time" (1934-1935). And yet, it would be difficult to find a more concentrated expression of cosmicism than in "The Poe-et's Nightmare":

> Alone in space, I view'd a feeble fleck
> Of silvern light, marking the narrow ken
> Which mortals call the boundless universe.
> On ev'ry side, each as a tiny star,
> Shone more creations, vaster than our own,
> And teeming with unnumber'd forms of life;
> Tho' we as life would recognise it not,
> Being bound to earthly thoughts of human mould.

More importantly, we learn that this cosmicism is derived not from literature but from philosophy and science. Such lines as

> ...whirling ether bore in eddying streams
> The hot, unfinish'd stuff of nascent worlds

...make clear the dominant literary influence on the central section—Lucretius. And although Lucretius does not find terror but only awe and wonder and majesty in the contemplation of infinite space, both poets see in the vastness of the cosmos a refutation of human self-importance. In this sense "The Poe-et's Nightmare" is a clue to the development of Lovecraft's whole cosmic philosophy. Although he later remarked that he derived much of the philosophy (or, at least, the fictional representation of it) from Dunsany, the fact that this poem precedes Lovecraft's reading of Dunsany by three years points to the conclusion that his cosmicism was not literarily influenced but taken first from his study of astronomy in 1902 and then from his early readings in the atomic philosophy of Democritus, Epicurus, and Lucretius, tempered by nineteenth-century advances in biology, chemistry, and astrophysics.

And yet, it is a sad fact that many of Lovecraft's weird poems seek to convey merely a shudder, with no overriding philosophical or aesthetic purpose. "The Rutted Road" (1917) concludes ponderously: "What lies ahead, my weary soul to greet? / *Why is it that I do not wish to know?*"[16] But the preceding hints of what lie beyond the rutted road are too vague and insubstantial to be effective. Even the celebrated "Nemesis" (1917) suffers from this flaw. Lovecraft remarks in a letter that the poem "presents the conception...that nightmares are the punishment meted out to the soul for sins committed in previous incarnations—perhaps millions of years ago!"[17] But such a conception is too extravagant to serve as the basis of a purportedly serious poem, and "Nemesis" defeats its own purpose by lapsing into bombast and obscurity.

Other poems, however, are somewhat more successful in their expression of philosophical or moral concerns through horrific imagery. In "The Eidolon" (1918)[18] the narrator seeks to find some redeeming token in the dreary landscape in which he finds himself, and thinks he sees it in "the living glory—Man!" But, as the day dawns, an even more loathsome sight greets his eyes:

> Now on the streets the houses spew
> A loathsome pestilence, a crew
> Of things I cannot, dare not name,
> So vile their form, so black their shame.

In its way "The Eidolon" is as nihilistic as "The Poe-et's Nightmare," although lacking its cosmic scope. What is more interesting is the notion that knowledge (here symbolized by the light of day) is in itself a source of horror and tragedy. This same conception is found in another fine poem, "Revelation" (1919). "Despair" (1919),[19] whose immediate inspiration was the shock of his mother's institutionalization at Butler Hospital in 1919, is a ferociously pessimistic poem in which the narrator, seeking to banish the "Damn'd daemons of despair," sums up the fate of humanity:

> Thus the living, lone and sobbing,
> In the throes of anguish throbbing,
> With the loathsome Furies robbing
>   Night and noon of peace and rest.
> But beyond the groans and grating
> Of abhorrent Life, is waiting
> Sweet Oblivion, culminating
>   All the years of fruitless quest.

One long weird poem that may be worth a little consideration is "Psychopompos: A Tale in Rhyme" (1918).[20] Unlike the bulk of Lovecraft's weird verse written up to this time, the apparent influence on this 312-line poem—the second-longest single poem Lovecraft ever wrote, just shorter than "Old Christmas" and just longer than "The Poe-et's Nightmare"—is not Poe but the ballads of Sir Walter Scott, although I have not found any single work in Scott exactly analogous to "Psychopompos." This surprisingly effective narrative of werewolves or shapeshifters is, in fact, the only instance in which Lovecraft wrote about a conventional myth; and the general medieval setting makes

"Psychopompos" a sort of versified Gothic tale. I am not clear what the significance of the title is: psychopomps (from the Greek *psychopompos*, "conveyer of the dead" [*i.e.*, to the underworld]) are used in some later tales, but werewolves have never been so regarded. Interestingly, Lovecraft himself classified the work among his prose tales, as it is found on several lists of his short stories. Regardless of its literary influences and the intentional obviousness of its plot, "Psychopompos" is a triumph, full of deft and subtle touches. The poem moves crisply and smoothly, slyly hinting at the hideous truth behind the seemingly innocuous events without ever actually stating it; and it builds to a satisfying climax as Sieur De Blois seeks revenge on the death of his wife by leading a band of werewolves to the humble cottage of the bailiff Jean and his family one stormy night. The narrative opens as if in sympathy with the reclusiveness of the noble Sieur and Dame De Blois: it is natural that evil legends would accrue against people who (like Lovecraft) were not conventionally religious and kept to themselves:

> So liv'd the pair, like many another two
> That shun the crowd, and shrink from public view.
> They scorn'd the doubts by ev'ry peasant shewn,
> And ask'd but one thing—to be let alone!

The otherwise curious use of the cross as the ultimate defense against the supernatural wolves is merely a bow to weird tradition.

The remarkable outburst of poetry, most of it fantastic, in late 1929 is a phenomenon parallel to Lovecraft's tremendous surge of fiction writing in late 1926 and early 1927. But while the cause for the latter—his euphoric return to Providence after two traumatic years in New York—is scarcely in doubt, the cause of the former is more difficult to ascertain. Now that the supposed influence of Edwin Arlington Robinson, suggested independently by Winfield Townley Scott and Edmund Wilson, has been exploded (there is no evidence that Lovecraft had read Robinson at this time), the matter does not seem attributable to merely literary influences. David E. Schultz has put forward Lovecraft's extensive work on Maurice W. Moe's never-published book, *Doorways to Poetry*, but I think this factor must be taken in conjunction with an anomalous hiatus in Lovecraft's fiction writing.

Between the completion of "The Dunwich Horror" in the summer of 1928 and the commencement of "The Whisperer in Darkness" in February 1930, Lovecraft wrote no fiction—except the admittedly significant ghost-written novelette "The Mound" (late 1929-early 1930). Even here we note that by the fall of 1929 it had been a full year since Lovecraft had written any fiction at all; perhaps he felt that horrific poetry would help to revive his fictional powers. It was also an appropriate time for Lovecraft to implement some new theories on poetry writing: gone was the desire to imitate the eighteenth-century poets, Lovecraft urging instead—both to himself and to such of his correspondents as Elizabeth Toldridge—a modern idiom shorn of hackneyed inversions and poeticisms. The results are such things as "The Ancient Track," "The Messenger," and *Fungi from Yuggoth*. Although, with the exception of the last, the poetry of this period lacks any sort of philosophical underpinning, it is by far the most evocative and well-crafted verse he ever wrote. "The Messenger" is as flawless a horrific sonnet as was ever written by Clark Ashton Smith or Donald Wandrei (whose *Sonnets of the Midnight Hours*, read by Lovecraft in 1927,[21] were a clear influence on the *Fungi*). "The Ancient Track" is an inexpressibly poignant and chilling poem, and "The Wood" contains that imperishable line: "Forests may fall, but not the dusk they shield."[22]

Much has recently been written about the *Fungi from Yuggoth*,[23] but it seems difficult to deny that the dominant feature of this sonnet cycle is utter randomness of tone, mood, and import. Unlike Wandrei's *Sonnets of the Midnight Hours*, unified by the fact that they are all derived from Wandrei's dreams and by their narration in the first person, in Lovecraft's sonnet series we have miniature horror stories ("The Well") cheek by jowl with autobiographical vignettes ("Expectancy," "Background"), pensive philosophy ("Continuity"), apocalyptic cosmicism ("Nyarlathotep"), and versified nightmares ("Night-Gaunts"). Various recent claims that the *Fungi* yield a "continuity" of some sort seem strained. *Thematic* resonances within the cycle do not establish "continuity" of plot or structure any more than the analogous resonances within Lovecraft's stories make them one large "novel" or something of the sort. I have earlier pointed out that, around 1933, Lovecraft attempted to rewrite the *Fungi* into prose, in the fragment called "The Book"; he seems to have got as far as the first three sonnets (which are indeed a connected narrative), but beyond this his inspiration appears—not surprisingly—to have flagged. Even if we assume that the first three sonnets are a sort of framing device and that the other thirty-three are vignettes derived from the book the narrator has discovered (and even this is a very implausible interpretation), it is difficult to conceive of the cycle as an unified whole. It seems more likely that Lovecraft looked upon the *Fungi* as an opportune means of crystallizing various conceptions, types of imagery, and fragments of dreams that would otherwise not have found creative expression—an imaginative housecleaning, as it were. The degree to which Lovecraft embodied items from his commonplace book in the sonnets supports this conclusion; in effect, the *Fungi from Yuggoth* could be read as a sort of versified commonplace book.

In the final analysis, Lovecraft's weird poetry clearly stands out as the most significant subclass of his verse as a whole; but even this subclass gains its greatest value not intrinsically but for the light it sheds on Lovecraft's fiction. The early weird verse is perhaps worth further study, since so much of it was written before his fiction writing really got underway; and the *Fungi* are inexhaustible sources for details and conceptions found in tales early and late. It is, however, fortunate that Lovecraft came to the conclusion that he was principally a "*prose realist*";[24] for if he had written nothing but poetry he would not be much remembered today, nor deserve to be. This is because Lovecraft never really found a distinctive voice as a poet. It is true that his early fiction bears—sometimes too strongly—the marks of his reading of Poe, Dunsany, Machen, Blackwood, and others; but ultimately his fiction became uniquely his own. This his poetry never achieved, or did so only fleetingly toward the end. And yet, his poetry refuses to fade away, and commands our attention if only for its skill, precision, and occasionally an unforgettable line, conception, or image.

X.

LETTERS

The publication of the five volumes of Lovecraft's *Selected Letters* (1965-1976) could be said to have singlehandedly initiated a newer, deeper trend in Lovecraft studies; for before the 2000 pages of this series emerged, few were aware of the many different sides of Lovecraft the man and writer, and few had any perception to what degree his correspondence in sheer bulk dwarfs all the rest of his work—fiction, poetry, essays, revisions—combined. The 930 letters published in the *Selected Letters* were in almost every case abridged—indeed, in one anomalous instance,[1] only the greeting and the closing were printed, and the body of the letter entirely excised—and only a relatively small proportion of the surviving correspondence was published. And yet, the editing of these 930 letters took nearly forty years—August Derleth began collecting letters from correspondents almost upon Lovecraft's death in 1937—and the tireless work of three editors, Derleth, Donald Wandrei, and James Turner. The audacity of Arkham House in publishing the letters—initially planned for one volume, then augmented respectively to three and five volumes[2]—may be lost on some of us now, since Lovecraft's greatness as an epistolarian is taken for granted by all scholars and many enthusiasts; yet it must be remembered that no figure in fantasy or science fiction has been accorded this treatment save Poe, Bierce, Machen, John W. Campbell, Philip K. Dick, Robert E. Howard, and Clark Ashton Smith. At a time when T. S. Eliot's and W. B. Yeats's letters have yet to be published in a definitive format, five volumes of Lovecraft's letters is a miraculous achievement.

And yet, how small is even this amount when compared to the whole of Lovecraft's surviving correspondence, or—even more unthinkable—his total correspondence, surviving and destroyed. How many letters did Lovecraft write? The exact number has been hotly debated and of course can never be truly ascertained, but the most likely figure still seems to be the 100,000 arrived at (probably by sheer guesswork) by L. Sprague de Camp. Lovecraft variously gave his daily output of letters at anywhere between five and fifteen; if we assume a middle ground of eight to ten, we reach some 3500 letters a year; over a twenty-three year period (1914-1936) we already reach 80,500 at what is probably a conservative estimate. Of these, it is my belief that no more than 10,000 now survive. We know that such correspondents as Alfred Galpin and—most tragically for us—his wife Sonia Davis destroyed all or many of their letters from Lovecraft;[3] and many other letters have surely been lost or destroyed by time and carelessness. The whereabouts of important letter files to Samuel Loveman,[4] Rheinhart Kleiner, Maurice W. Moe, James F. Morton, and many others are unknown.

Now if those 930 letters in the *Selected Letters* were published complete (and the abridgments in some instances have been radical), they could easily have taken up twice the space they now occupy. This means that every 100 letters of Lovecraft would fill an average (400 p.) volume. The 10,000 surviving letters would then fill 100 volumes! And the putative 100,000 letters, if they survived, would fill 1000 volumes!

In practical terms, of course, it would be impossible to publish Lovecraft's complete correspondence in the near future; but this does not mean that the abridgments, mistranscriptions, and generally shoddy editorial method of the *Selected Letters* (especially the first three volumes) need go uncorrected. The logical method of publishing Lovecraft's letters is to arrange them by correspondent; and this is the method now being utilized by David E. Schultz and myself in the issuance of groups of Lovecraft's letters from Necronomicon Press and other publishers. Only a study of these unabridged letters will reveal the true greatness of Lovecraft as epistolarian.

As R. Alain Everts has pointed out,[5] most of Lovecraft's letters were not the treatise-length works which have excited our wonder, but were short, one- or two-page letters written on the front and back of a single sheet of paper. And yet, those long letters are clearly in evidence—thirty, forty, fifty, and even seventy handwritten pages. One can only wonder at the reaction of Lovecraft's correspondents at receiving novella-length letters of this sort. How did they answer them? Did they try to do so? Or did they merely imitate some of Lovecraft's protagonists and lapse into a merciful fit of fainting?

Lovecraft was, curiously enough, at first a very reluctant letter-writer. It was, apparently, his cousin Phillips Gamwell (1898-1916) whose stimulating correspondence, around 1910, fostered Lovecraft's letter-writing habit; but it was his joining the amateur journalism movement in 1914 which really impelled his voluminousness in this regard. As an official of the United Amateur Press Association (at various times Chairman of the Department of Public Criticism, Vice-President, President, and Official Editor) Lovecraft wrote much official correspondence, some of which might be of considerable interest. Each year the UAPA selected several important literary figures to be Laureate Judges to select prize-winning stories, articles, and poems published in that year, and at one point Lovecraft notes his intention of writing to the poets Vachel Lindsay and Harriet Monroe to offer them the post.[6] Whether he did so or nor I do not know, but it would have been one of the few times when Lovecraft came into contact with literary figures outside the narrow world of amateurdom and fantasy fiction.

That the bulk of his total correspondence was with amateur writers—or, at least, with associates whom he first met in amateurdom—is easy to see from the vast number of letters evidently written to such figures as Rheinhart Kleiner, Maurice W. Moe, Alfred Galpin, James F. Morton, Frank Belknap Long, and many others. The various round-robin correspondence cycles in which Lovecraft participated—the Kleicomolo, the Gallomo, and others—are too well known to require description. It was tragically short-sighted of Derleth and Wandrei to have failed to publish many of the early letters dealing with Lovecraft's complex and multifaceted involvement with amateurdom; interested as they were only in his relations with the fantasy field, Derleth and Wandrei did not realize that amateurdom was a lifelong pursuit of Lovecraft's and one that may well have been more important to him—certainly one that shaped more of his attitudes—than the tiny realm of pulp fiction. If Lovecraft had ever corresponded with some of the contemporary giants of weird fiction—he just missed corresponding with Bierce, and felt too diffident to write to Machen, Blackwood, or Dunsany—this emphasis may have had slightly greater justification; but, in truth, his correspondence with such figures as, say, Seabury Quinn, Henry S. Whitehead, or even Derleth himself is of much less significance than that with Moe, Kleiner, Galpin, and Morton.

And yet, it is this amateur correspondence that either has been largely lost or is still unpublished and even unknown. Recently a correspondence cycle from Lovecraft to Arthur Harris (the Welsh amateur who issued Lovecraft's first pamphlet, "The Crime of Crimes," in 1915) has come to light; and who knows how many other Lovecraft letters may lurk undiscovered in forgotten trunks in someone's dusty attic? Lovecraft corresponded with almost all important—and many unimportant—amateurs of the day, and many must surely have kept at least some of these letters. If unearthed and published, they would shed valuable light on a crucial period of his life given short shrift in the *Selected Letters*.

Of course, when Lovecraft began publishing his stories in *Weird Tales*, many fans and writers came into contact with him through the magazine: in this way Lovecraft began to correspond with the nineteen-year-old J. Vernon Shea, the eighteen-year-old Donald Wandrei, the seventeen-year-old August Derleth, the sixteen-year-old Robert Bloch, the thirteen-year-old R. H. Barlow, and more established writers like Henry S. Whitehead, E. Hoffmann Price, and Robert E. Howard. Needless to say, many of these correspondents were very important to Lovecraft: Barlow became, at nineteen, Lovecraft's literary executor (perhaps because Lovecraft saw in him that same incandescent brilliance which, a decade earlier, had impressed him in Alfred Galpin; and in this he may not have been far wrong), Derleth and Wandrei his posthumous editors, and Howard a close associate whose own voluminous replies to Lovecraft's letters would lend themselves ideally to combined publication, as has been done with other figures—notably Alexander Pope and Horace Walpole—where both sides of a correspondence cycle survive. In its own way the Lovecraft-Howard correspondence rivals the Pope-Swift correspondence of the early eighteenth century, and would perhaps be of as much importance to fantasy scholars as the latter is to students of the Augustan age.

As Lovecraft became the fountainhead of the fantasy fandom movement of the 1930s, his correspondents in almost every instance were eager youths—Barlow, Duane W. Rimel, F. Lee Baldwin, Donald A. Wollheim, Kenneth Sterling, William Frederick Anger, Willis Conover, and others—who all looked up to him as a mentor and teacher. Lovecraft naturally slipped into this role, for it finally made real his wistful dream of being a "grandpa" surrounded by excited young children. The Grand Old Man at last had his respectful audience.

And this raises a matter of utmost importance in considering Lovecraft's letters: the varying tones he adopted when dealing with different correspondents. Far from showing Lovecraft as insincere and hypocritical, this adaptation of tone and matter to the individual reveals the consideration and courtesy that were fundamental components of his gentlemanly behavior. Nothing could exemplify this aspect of Lovecraft better than the correspondence to Elizabeth Toldridge, a disabled would-be poet[7] in Washington, D.C., with whom Lovecraft corresponded faithfully for eight years, until his death. Even the voluminous published correspondence to Toldridge does not tell the whole story: only the unabridged, unpublished letters show how carefully and tactfully Lovecraft answered each point raised by his correspondent, tirelessly gave kind and constructive advice on her insipid poetry (much of which was saved by Lovecraft and still survives in manuscript in the John Hay Library), acknowledged the newspaper "cuttings" she sent him, and in general adopted a patient, interested, but by no means patronizing tone in all his correspondence to her. Hypocrisy? Hardly: Lovecraft was merely trying to bring a few moments' pleasure into an invalid's drab existence; and the fact that the correspondence ceased only with his death suggests that he must have been successful in the attempt.

Other correspondence cycles reveal analogous shifts in tone: tongue-in-cheek archaism to Rheinhart Kleiner (himself a polished poet adhering to older standards in prose and poetry); ludicrous slang and colloquialism to James F. Morton (a Harvard graduate and learned curator of a museum); playfully horrific greetings to Clark Ashton Smith; studied—perhaps excessive—politeness to Helen Sully (to the point that she became eventually infuriated that Lovecraft continued to address her as "Miss Sully" instead of as "Helen"); and the like. The correspondence differs, of course, in substance as well, depending on the interests of the correspondent. The letters to Derleth are primarily about weird fiction or regional/historical matters, in accordance with Derleth's literary work; the letters to E. Hoffmann Price are almost solely—indeed, rather monotonously—about the aesthetic foundations of weird fiction (Price's own letters, which Lovecraft retained, are surprisingly vigorous defenses of his "professionalism," just as Lovecraft's own letters defend his amateur status; they ought to be jointly published); the letters to R. H. Barlow are remarkably revelatory about Lovecraft's personal beliefs, perhaps because the inveterately curious Barlow repeatedly interrogated Lovecraft on the particulars of his life and work; heavily philosophical is the surviving correspondence to Galpin (in his youth as fervent a Nietzschean as Lovecraft), Moe (a religious idealist who formed the perfect counterweight to Lovecraft the atheistic materialist), Morton (an atheist even more extreme than Lovecraft until he converted to the Bahai faith), and, to a degree, with Robert E. Howard: to no one else could Lovecraft have written the lengthy and stalwart defenses of civilization over barbarism than to the creator of Conan. It is not certain that Lovecraft got the better of this argument. The correspondence to Wandrei is also primarily literary, but not restricted narrowly to horror fiction as it is to Derleth and Price; rather, Wandrei, holding many of the same philosophical and aesthetic attitudes as Lovecraft, elicited from his correspondent some very profound statements of his literary theory, and it is unfortunate that Wandrei allowed only parts of ten letters (out of the seventy-five letters and 101 postcards he received from Lovecraft) to be published in the *Selected Letters*.

Three correspondence cycles perhaps stand apart, and may represent the pinnacle of Lovecraft's epistolary art: the letters to James F. Morton, Frank Belknap Long, and Clark Ashton Smith. The letters to Smith, of course, also center primarily on weird fiction; but they do so in such a way as to reveal volumes about Lovecraft's aesthetic theory. Lovecraft confided in Smith much more than he did, say, in Derleth: Smith shared Lovecraft's "cosmic" viewpoint, as Lovecraft knew Derleth (the "self-blinded earth-gazer"[8] did not; as a result, Lovecraft had much less difficulty communicating his sense of "cosmic outsideness" and "adventurous expectancy" to Smith. Long and Lovecraft corresponded for some seventeen years, and they let their hair down completely in their letters, talking about everything from eroticism to cosmicism, amateur affairs to weird fiction, colonial architecture to aesthetic sincerity to the decline of the West to Greek philosophy to Anglo-Catholicism. And because they both shared many attitudes and disagreed vehemently on key issues of philosophy, art, and politics, Long elicited from Lovecraft some of his greatest argumentative letters. One massive letter (February 27, 1931)[9] contains more philosophical substance and rhetorical flourishes than any story he ever wrote, and ought to stand next to "The Colour out of Space" and *At the Mountains of Madness* as one of his towering literary achievements. One lengthy excerpt—in which Lovecraft refutes Long's equation of science with technology—will be sufficient:

> Listen, young man. Forget all about your books & machine-made current associations. Kick the present dying parody on civilisation out the back door of consciousness. Shelve the popular second-hand dishings-up of Marxian economic determinism—a genuine force within certain limits, but without the widest ramifications ascribed to it by the fashionable *New Republic* & *Nation* clique. For once in your life, live up to your non-contemporary ideal & do some thinking without the 1930-31 publishers' sausage-grist at your elbow! Get back to the Ionian coast, shovel away some 2500 years, & tell Grandpa who it is you find in a villa at Miletus studying the properties of loadstone & amber, predicting eclipses, explaining the moon's phases, & applying to physics & astronomy the principles of research he learned in Egypt. Thales—quite a boy in his day. Ever hear of him before? He wanted to *know* things. Odd taste, wasn't it? And to think, he never tried to manufacture rayon or form a joint-stock company or pipe oil from Mesopotamia or extract gold from sea-water! Funny old guy—wanted to know things, yet never thought of a collectivist state...leaving this last for the unctuous windbag Plato, upon whom the moustacheletted little Chestertons of a later aera were to dote. Bless me, but *do* you suppose he actually had the normal human instinct of *curiosity* & simply wanted knowledge to satisfy that elemental urge? Perish such an un-modern & un-Marxian thought...yet one has dim suspicions.... And then this bozo Pythagoras. What did he want to bother with that old "what-is-anything" question for? And Heraclitus & Anaxagoras & Anaximander & Democritus & Leucippus & Empedocles? Well—if you take the word of your precious old satyr-faced pragmatist Socrates, these ginks merely wanted to know things for the sake of knowing! According to this beloved super-Babbitt of yours, who brought down philosophy from the clouds to serve among men—serve useful ends in a civically acceptable fashion—the old naturalists & sophists were a sorry

> lot. Your dear Plato agreed. They were not social-minded or collectivistic. Tut, tut—they were actually selfish individualists who gratified the personal human instinct of cosmic curiosity for its own sake. Ugh! take them away! Moustacheletted young Platonists want nothing to do with such outlawed & unregimented pleasure-seekers. They simply *couldn't* have been real "scientists," since they didn't serve big business or have altruistic or bolshevistic motivations. Practically & Marxianly speaking, there simply weren't any such people. How could there be? "Science" is (they print it in books) the servant of the machine age. Since ancient Ionia had no machine age, how could there be "Science"?[10]

But the letters to Morton—at least 160 in number, of which more than 110 were published (abridged) in *Selected Letters*—may be the single greatest set of correspondence Lovecraft ever wrote. Morton was one of the few colleagues who was, relatively speaking, Lovecraft's intellectual equal: having secured a B.A. and M.A. from Harvard at the age of twenty-two, Morton went on to do much pamphleteering for such causes as secularism, free speech, race prejudice, and many other issues; along the way he became Vice-President of the Esperanto Association of America and curator of the Paterson (N.J.) Museum. Lovecraft, could, therefore, discuss virtually every academic subject with Morton, and he did so with a verve and vigor unrivalled in any of his other letters; as with Long, the fact that Morton disagreed significantly with Lovecraft on many of these subjects only added spice to the correspondence.

It is now, of course, scarcely to be denied that Lovecraft's letters have significant literary merit, but Lovecraft was the first to disavow the claim:

> Nobody expects anything of a letter, or judges any man's style by one. Even when I write one by hand I pay no attention to rhetorick, but just sail along at a mile-a-minute pace.... If you were to analyse the language of this letter you would find it shot all to hell with solecisms and bad rhythms.[11]

This passage tells us many things. When Lovecraft wrote, early in his career, that "my reading of publish'd letters hath largely been confined to those of 18th century British authors"[12] along with Cicero and Pliny the Younger, he should have added an important qualification: his letters—those written, at any rate, in his prime—are leagues away from the labored pomposity of Pope's or Johnson's correspondence (the former consciously wrote with the expectation that his letters would one day be published), but resemble instead the easy grace and fluency of Gray or Cowper. And in spite of the "mile-a-minute" rate, there are in fact few solecisms in Lovecraft's letters[13]—and this is one more reason why Lovecraft's letters are one of his greatest accomplishments, for the obvious rapidity with which most of his correspondence was written by no means excludes some dazzling rhetorical strokes: we have the bizarre "stream-of-consciousness" letters[14] where Lovecraft free-associates for pages on end; we have devastating destructions of his opponents' arguments (as in the early letter to Moe on the subject that "the Judaeo-Christian mythology is NOT TRUE"),[15] using not only logic but satire, colloquialism, and *reductio ad absurdum*; and there is unexpected poignancy as Lovecraft records important episodes in his life, such as his return to Providence from New York in 1926 ("HOME—UNION STATION—*PROVIDENCE!!!!*"[16] or the death of Robert E. Howard ("But it is damn hard to realise that there's no longer any R E H at Lock Box 313!"[17] It is certainly not the case that Lovecraft "paid no attention to rhetorick"; rather, that rhetorical instinct—in the best sense of the term, as the ability to express each idea in the language best suited to it—was so imbued in Lovecraft from an early age that it emerged in even the most hastily written epistle.

J. Vernon Shea was one of several who suggested that there were many potential essays buried in the letters,[18] and such is indeed the case. Lovecraft actually did make attempts to create essays out of letters, but only sporadically and half-heartedly. Posthumously, of course, Lovecraft's letters have been mined for essay material: "Some Backgrounds of Fairyland" (in *Marginalia*) is part of a letter to Wilfred B. Talman, as are the two Lovecraft items in *The Occult Lovecraft* (1975); even the "Observations on Several Parts of America" (1928; printed, with erroneous title, in *Marginalia*) began life as a letter to Maurice W. Moe, but Lovecraft found that his summary of his travels of 1928 might be of interest to many correspondents, so he typed up the letter with few modifications and circulated it as a travelogue. He did the same thing for "Travels in the Provinces of America," written the following year. It is, in fact, unfortunate that Lovecraft did not seriously try to market letter-excerpts as essays, for if published in important magazines of the day—*Atlantic Monthly*, *Harper's*, *Scribner's*—they might have led to Lovecraft's developing a reputation as a man of letters instead of merely as as a pulp fictionist.

Conversely, sometimes Lovecraft's lengthy letters were planned out as carefully as any story or essay. For Lovecraft's "last" letter (dated in the *Selected Letters* as March 1937, but obviously begun earlier, perhaps months earlier) we have been given a brief series of notes and topics to be covered in the letter, and Lovecraft confessed that this was a frequent practice of his; an unpublished document in the John Hay Library entitled "Objections to Orthodox Communism" (1936) is nothing more than the outline of a letter on that subject written to C. L. Moore (19 June 1936).[19] And yet, one of the most engaging aspects of Lovecraft's longer letters is their almost kaleidoscopic shift from one topic to the other, a shift determined only by the course of the argument or by the various points raised by the correspondent. In a magnificent letter to Woodburn Harris (prefaced by the very sensible caveat: "*WARNING!* Don't try to read this all at once!"[20] Lovecraft proceeds from the collapse of American culture to a comparison of the Greek tragedians with Shakespeare to the growth of the machine-culture to the notion of love to styles of discourse in debates to democracy to the nature of the human psyche, with asides about Joseph Wood Krutch and Havelock Ellis; and this is merely the portion of the letter—obviously abridged—published in the *Selected Letters*.

Indeed, one could cull an entire volume of pithy utterances from the letters; here is a sample from Volume I alone:

> Peace is the ideal of a dying nation.[21]
>
> Our philosophy is all childishly *subjective*.[22]
>
> Frankly, I cannot conceive how any thoughtful man can really be happy.[23]
>
> Truth-hunger is a hunger just as real as food-hunger.[24]
>
> Possibly it is better to be near-sighted and orthodox like Mo[e], trusting all to a Divine Providence, R.I.[25]
>
> *Entity* precedes morality.[26]
>
> Adulthood is hell.[27]
>
> Success is a relative thing—and the victory of a boy at marbles is equal to the victory of an Octavius at Actium when measured by the scale of cosmic infinity.[28]
>
> I have today not a single well-defined wish save to die or to learn facts.[29]
>
> The cosmos is a mindless vortex; a seething ocean of blind forces, in which the greatest joy is unconsciousness and the greatest pain realisation.[30]
>
> The one sound power in the world is the power of a hairy muscular right arm![31]

> Honestly, my hatred of the human animal mounts by leaps and bounds the more I see of the miserable vermin.[32]

> A gentleman shouldn't write all his images down for a plebeian rabble to stare at.[33]

> The aeons and the worlds are my sport, and I watch with calm and amused aloofness the anticks of planets and the mutations of the universe.[34]

And who can forget the imperishable, "What is anything?"[35]

We can learn more about Lovecraft's development as a stylist from reading his letters than from reading either his stories or his poems or his essays; for his letters both document and exemplify the gradual modification—and mastery—of his style in his stories, poems, and essays. Lovecraft's first published work was, as I have noted, a letter to the editor of the *Providence Sunday Journal* (published 3 June 1906), on a point of astronomy. This indicates the dominance of science in Lovecraft's literary output in his early years, when he was writing many more scientific treatises than stories or poems. The shift toward literature came around 1911, and shortly thereafter we see Lovecraft don the ill-fitting cloak of eighteenth-century diction in stories, letters, and poems alike. The verse letter *Ad Criticos*, which initiated a literary controversy in the *Argosy*, shows Lovecraft to have mastered the rococo externals—but, alas! not the inner fire or living music—of Dryden's and Pope's great satires, and it is not surprising that much of his prose had also adopted the "ineffably pompous and Johnsonese"[36] style he was later to condemn in his early story "The Beast in the Cave" (1905). Lovecraft's characterization of his style in 1915—"I suppose I picked up my peculiar style from Addison, Swift, Johnson, and Gibbon"[37]—is exactly right for this stage of his career. Indeed, throughout much of his early writing there is a curious cleavage between his fiction and poetry on the one hand, full of eighteenth-century affectations, and his scientific and philosophical works, written in a forceful, direct, uncluttered prose reminiscent of Swift or Thomas Henry Huxley. His early letters mirror the split; in remarking on his literary preferences, he writes in a letter of 1918 (addressed as from "Will's Coffee House / Russell Street, Covent-Garden, London"):

> I like the novels of J. Fenimore Cooper and of N. Hawthorne, and the verse of O. W. Holmes. The critical dissertations of J. R. Lowell likewise gratify my taste.... On second perusal, I find Mr. Emerson not altogether wanting in good sense, tho' I much prefer my older friend Mr. Addison.[38]

Pure eighteenth century! It is all very clever, but one can never be quite certain whether Lovecraft in fact is writing with tongue in cheek or is somehow actually trying—naively and pitiably—to transport himself psychologically to the eighteenth century. But a few months *earlier* than the above, in a heated controversy about religion, Lovecraft could write the following:

> What am I? What is the nature of the energy about me, and how does it affect me? So far I have seen nothing which could possibly give me the notion that cosmic force is the manifestation of a mind and will like my own infinitely magnified; a potent and purposeful consciousness which deals individually & directly with the miserable denizens of a wretched little flyspeck on the back door of a microscopic universe, and which singles this putrid excrescence out as the one spot whereto to send an onlie-begotten Son, whose mission is to redeem these accursed flyspeck-inhabiting lice which we call human beings—bah!! Pardon the "bah!" I feel several "bahs!," but out of courtesy I say only one. But it is all so very childish. I cannot help taking exception to a philosophy which would force this rubbish down my throat. 'What have I against religion?' That is what I have against it![39]

This passage is actually much more rhetorically elaborate than the previous one, but it is so in a plain and straightforward manner, with telling colloquialism ("I feel several 'bahs!'"), parody ("onlie-begotten Son"), piquant compounds ("flyspeck-inhabiting lice"), and rhetorical questions. It is as if Lovecraft, when spurred into arguments about issues important to him, sheds his archaism like a cloak and writes with the vigor and force we know from the later fiction.

As the years progress Lovecraft's letters become longer and more involved, filled with lengthy philosophical, historical, and literary disquisitions. But more importantly, the split between his fiction and his essays narrows and finally disappears, so that in a story like "The Shadow out of Time" (1934-1935) the bulk of the narrative has the same forceful directness as his letters, except as the climax approaches and Lovecraft gradually modulates the tempo of the story and raises the tone to a higher pitch, introducing emotive words to prepare the reader for the cataclysmic conclusion.

It is by now clear that Lovecraft's letters contain a mine of information; and before concluding with some observations on the place of Lovecraft's letters in his work it may be well to give a broad idea of their manifold importance to Lovecraft studies. Without the letters we would not know of Lovecraft's hand in the overwhelming bulk of his revisions, from C. M. Eddy's "Ashes" to Hazel Heald's "Out of the Aeons"; in recent years it is consultation of unpublished letters that has resulted in the addition of several "new" revisions—"Ashes," Duane W. Rimel's "The Tree on the Hill" and "The Disinterment," Henry S. Whitehead's "The Trap," R. H. Barlow's "The Night Ocean"—to the Lovecraft corpus. We learn countless details about his writing—dates of stories, poems, and essays; publications of works not otherwise known; sources and origins of works—as well as incalculable details about the particulars of his life. It would, for example, be possible to write an entire book on Lovecraft's two years (1924-1926) in New York solely from the approximately 200,000 words of letters written to his aunt Lillian.

But more importantly, we learn of Lovecraft's keenness as a thinker: his absorption of ancient philosophy, of the philosophy of Nietzsche and the Social Darwinists, of Spengler's *Decline of the West* and Bertrand Russell's *Our Knowledge of the External World*; his powerful materialist stance—expressed in his letters much more cogently than in essays such as "Idealism and Materialism—A Reflection" (c. 1919)—and the modifications of that stance in the light of Einstein, Planck, and the astrophysicists; his towering condemnations of conventional religion; his aesthetic theory, founded upon Poe and the Decadents and constantly refined into the doctrine of non-commercial "self-expression"; the increasing attention given in his later years to the problems of the world economy and of government, to the point that Lovecraft became a socialist who wished FDR to be yet bolder in his reforms. All these things we would know dimly and perhaps not at all without the letters: the long digressions on the political and economic system of the Old Ones and the Great Race in *At the Mountains of Madness* and "The Shadow out of Time" suddenly make sense, given Lovecraft's later interests; the glancing allusions to Einstein and to "intra-atomic action" in "The Shunned House" and "The Dreams in the Witch House" dimly mirror Lovecraft's reconciliation of materialism to modern indeterminacy; and, more profoundly, the increasingly cosmic scope of his later fiction is an echo of the expansion of his thought from his early absorption in the prettiness of the Queen Anne poets to his later interests in the nature of the world and the universe.

What, then, did Lovecraft's letters mean to him—and what do they mean to us? The first branch of the question is easier to answer than the second, for Lovecraft was unequivocal about the fact that correspondence was essentially a substitute for conversation. Both early and late in his career he testified to the importance of correspondence to him:

> As to letters, my case is peculiar. I write such things exactly as easily and rapidly as I would utter the same topics in conversation; indeed, epistolary expression

> is with me largely replacing conversation, as my condition of nervous prostration becomes more and more acute. I cannot bear to talk much now, and am becoming as silent as the Spectator himself! My loquacity extends itself on paper.[40]

> As a person of very retired life, I met very few different sorts of people in youth—and was therefore exceedingly narrow and provincial. Later on, when literary activities brought me into touch with widely diverse types by mail—Texans like Robert E. Howard, men in Australia, New Zealand, &c., Westerners, Southerners, Canadians, people in old England, and assorted kinds of folk nearer at hand—I found myself opened up to dozens of points of view which would otherwise never have occurred to me. My understanding and sympathies were enlarged, and many of my social, political, and economic views were modified as a consequence of increased knowledge. Only correspondence could have effected this broadening; for it would have been impossible to have visited all the regions and met all the various types involved, while books can never talk back or discuss.[41]

Many critics seem to detect, in this use of correspondence as vicarious conversation, one more indication of Lovecraft's eccentricity, as if he could not conduct a personal relationship except on paper. But with whom could he have discussed such philosophical and literary matters amongst his known acquaintances in Providence? Surely C. M. Eddy was not as stimulating as Clark Ashton Smith or Robert E. Howard, and Lovecraft's New York period—with the heyday of the Kalem Club and its regular meetings full of variegated discussion and "nights out on the town"—belies the picture of Lovecraft as tight-lipped recluse. Lovecraft's mind simply required the diverse stimulus of correspondence with all manner of associates, each of very different character and interests.

The only disadvantage in all this was that Lovecraft almost never corresponded with his intellectual equal, so that his own arguments and rebuttals—occasionally superficial or fallacious—can appear triumphs of logical reasoning. It was pitifully easy for Lovecraft to destroy Maurice W. Moe's or his opponent Wickenden's idealism (the latter in the *In Defence of Dagon* essay-letters); only James F. Morton, Alfred Galpin, Robert E. Howard, and especially the little-known but brilliant amateur Ernest A. Edkins could hold a candle to Lovecraft intellectually. One cannot help wishing that Lovecraft could have corresponded with a true authority in some of the fields—philosophy, colonial history, general literature—on which he held forth with such apparent erudition. Certainly, in his later years, when most of his correspondents could have been his sons, he had little trouble dispensing with the occultist leanings of Nils H. Frome, the incredibly erroneous views on sex of Woodburn Harris, or the elementary historical errors of Bernard Austin Dwyer. He might have had a little more trouble with T. E. Hulme's mysticism, and Bertrand Russell might not have been quite as sanguine about Lovecraft's modified late materialism (which involved a fundamental misunderstanding of quantum theory) as Lovecraft himself was.

To the charge—made frequently in recent years—that Lovecraft "wasted his time" writing so many letters we must respond more critically. The charge carries the hidden premise that, since Lovecraft is currently best known for his stories, he should have written more of them and fewer letters. This premise is questionable on several grounds. Lovecraft is certainly well known for his fiction now, but who is to say that that attention will persist in the future? The current literary status of Horace Walpole rests not upon *The Castle of Otranto* or his other fictions (now of only historical importance), but upon the thousands of letters he wrote in his career: it is those letters that have been lavishly and painstakingly edited in a landmark forty-eight-volume edition from Yale University Press. Thomas Gray is heralded equally as a poet and as an epistolarian, and William Cowper's letters now considerably outshine his conventional poetry in critical esteem. Moreover, it is by no means certain that Lovecraft would have written more stories even had he curtailed his correspondence, for his fiction-writing was always a sporadic thing dependent upon mood, inspiration, and many other personal factors.

But even if Lovecraft continues to hold the attention of future generations with his tales (as, indeed, is very likely and entirely justified, as there are complexities and profundities in the fiction which scholars are only now probing), the claim that Lovecraft "wasted his time" in his correspondence implies that we know better than Lovecraft what he should have done with his life. But he led his life to suit himself, not us, and it is very clear that correspondence was very important to him. If he had never written any stories but only letters, it would certainly be our loss, but it would have been his prerogative.

The world of Lovecraft's letters is almost inassimilably rich; one can reread the letters indefinitely and find new things each time. The publication of his complete correspondence may be an unrealizable dream, but it is one worth keeping in our minds. The image of hundreds of bound volumes of letters, dwarfing to insignificance the dozen or so volumes of what would be his collected fiction, poetry, and essays, will make us comprehend the full literary and personal achievement of H. P. Lovecraft, the man who lived to write and wrote to live.

XI.

CONCLUSION

Now that we have examined in some detail the whole of Lovecraft's fiction and have a general overview of his life, thought, and literary career, we are in a position to study certain broad aspects of his work, in particular his style and structure, the themes in and development of his fiction writing, and his place in the history of weird fiction. Few of these matters are without controversy, and some of them—in particular his style—engender very diverse responses among different readers and critics. If my own analysis tends, as it were, to take Lovecraft's side on these matters, it is because I wish to look at them from his perspective and to ascertain whether he himself achieved the literary goals he had set for himself. Lovecraft himself, in the *In Defence of Dagon* essays, asked his critics to adopt such a view when he wrote: "I ask only that my reviewers observe the basic law of their craft; a comparison between design and achievement."[1] This is a quite outmoded critical methodology, but it is one that may still yield fruitful results when utilized properly.

1. Style and Structure

At the most fundamental level, one either likes Lovecraft's style or one doesn't. His lush, florid, richly textured prose adheres to a long-standing tradition of what, in classical rhetoric, is termed the "Asianic" style, in contrast to the reserved, restrained, understated manner known as the "Attic" style. In ancient literature, it is the contrast between Demosthenes and Lysias, between Cicero and Caesar; in modern literature, we find such writers as Addison and Swift adhering to the Attic style while Samuel Johnson and Edward Gibbon wrote in the Asianic. In the early twentieth century—especially under the influence of Sherwood Anderson and Ernest Hemingway—an extreme version of the Attic style, almost entirely shorn of adjectives and adverbs and emphasizing plain statement as a means toward greater realism, came so much into vogue that the Asianic style was not merely rendered obsolete but considered intrinsically inferior or a hallmark of "bad" writing. In the last three decades this modernist style has waned, at least to the degree that such Asianic writers as Thomas Pynchon, Gore

Vidal, and Robertson Davies have been praised—or, at any rate, not criticized—for the density of their prose. We are, therefore, perhaps ready to treat Lovecraft rather more leniently on this issue.

For the true crux of the matter is not whether Lovecraft's style is "good" or "bad" intrinsically, but whether it *works*: whether, in other words, it succeeds in conveying what Lovecraft wished to convey. In the broadest terms, Lovecraft's prose unites two seemingly contrasting manners: scientific *precision* (derived from his early scientific studies and later readings in history, philosophy, and *belles lettres*) and lush *prose-poetry* (derived from Johnson, Gibbon, Poe, Dunsany, Machen, and others). Of course, in his early work he does not always seem quite in control of his style, and pieces like "The Outsider" or "From Beyond" are "overwritten" in ways that leave him open to conventional criticisms of flamboyance and extravagance; even some later works—"The Dreams in the Witch House," "The Thing on the Doorstep"—are open to this charge. But by and large, Lovecraft had by 1924 harnessed his style to the aesthetic purposes he had set for himself—specifically, the creation of atmosphere and the maintenance of a mood of ever-increasing cumulative horror.

It is in these respects that his style must be pronounced an overwhelming success. Few writers in all literature had a better sense of narrative *pacing* than Lovecraft. In all his great tales the narrative flow proceeds inexorably from the first word to the last, with rarely a false note and with a constantly accumulating sense of awe, wonder, and terror. It is only toward the latter parts of a tale that Lovecraft unleashes what has derisively been termed his "adjectivitis"; but he justifies this procedure in "Notes on Writing Weird Fiction":

> Inconceivable events and conditions have a special handicap to overcome, and this can be accomplished only through the maintenance of a careful realism in every phase of the story *except* that touching on the one given marvel. This marvel must be treated very impressively and deliberately—with a careful emotional "build-up"—else it will seem flat and unconvincing.[2]

"The Rats in the Walls" is only the first of many tales to exemplify this dictum. It would be easy to take a passage toward the *end* of the story out of context and label it flagrantly overwritten:

> God! those carrion black pits of sawed, picked bones and opened skulls! Those nightmare chasms choked with the pithecanthropoid, Celtic, Roman, and English bones of countless unhallowed centuries! ...What, I thought, of the hapless rats that stumbled

> into such traps amidst the blackness of their quests in this grisly Tartarus?[3]

But one must realize that this passage occurs only after a 7000-word "build-up" that largely resembles an historical narrative:

> Exham Priory had remained untenanted, though later allotted to the estates of the Norrys family and much studied because of its peculiarly composite architecture; an architecture involving Gothic towers resting on a Saxon or Romanesque substructure, whose foundation in turn was of a still earlier order or blend of orders—Roman, and even Druidic or native Cymric, if legends speak truly.[4]

It is only in those tales where such a "build-up" has not occurred that Lovecraft's style seems *unjustifiably* overwrought and adjective-laden. This is also why Lovecraft's greatest tales are, by and large, his novelettes or short novels, for in these cases the build-up can occur for ten, twenty, or even thirty thousand words before the style unleashes itself for the final revelation.

Some words should be devoted to Lovecraft's actual diction and vocabulary. It is one of the most persistent myths about his writing that his mature style is *archaic*. Anyone who reads the *Spectator* and "The Shadow out of Time" in succession will be in no doubt as to which was written in the eighteenth century and which in the twentieth. There is very little archaism of style, sentence structure, syntax, or word-choice in the tales of the post-1921 period. *Density* of style must not be confused with archaism. Lovecraft, of course, was not writing for fools; and the difficulty in reading him comes both from his remarkable *compression* (derived, ultimately, from Poe's strictures regarding the need for every word of a narrative to be of some relevance to the climax) and his assumption on the part of his readers of wide knowledge in the realms of biology, chemistry, geology, astronomy, art, architecture, literature, mythology, and other disciplines. In the above passages from "The Rats in the Walls," readers unaware of what Romanesque architecture or Tartarus is are at a disadvantage both in comprehending the sense of the text and in absorbing its horrific implications. It is a truism that Lovecraft must on occasion be read with a dictionary; but in reality, an encyclopaedia would be more useful. An annotated edition of his tales would save readers considerable effort in this regard. Lovecraft himself addressed this issue in a slightly different context, defending a person who uses "big words" in conversation or letters:

> If he uses a "five-dollar word," it is merely because that word expresses something real & important *more briefly & accurately than it could otherwise be expressed.* To avoid the use of the "highbrow jawbreaker," it would be necessary to beat around the bush in a clumsy & verbose way involving *far more pose & artificiality* than the concise, clear-cut, straightforward use of the exactly right word.[5]

Hence, for example, Lovecraft's use of "ensilage" in "The Rats in the Walls"[6]—defined by the *Oxford English Dictionary* as "The process of preserving green fodder in a silo or pit, without having previously dried it"—so exactly suits the context that no other word could possibly have been used here without laborious circumlocution.

It is also not the case that Lovecraft was limited in the range of moods and emotions he could express. Even if we discount his avowedly humorous pieces ("A Reminiscence of Dr. Samuel Johnson," "Sweet Ermengarde," "Ibid"), we find delightful instances of self-parody or buffoonery in "Herbert West—Reanimator," "The Hound," and other tales. Poignancy and horror are combined in "The Outsider" and in Nahum Gardner's ineffably tragic dying utterance in "The Colour out of Space"; the spectacular cosmicism of *At the Mountains of Madness* and "The Shadow out of Time" is balanced by horror inspired by loathsome individuals in "The Picture in the House," *The Case of Charles Dexter Ward*, and others; and, of course, pure fantasy is the focus of the "Dunsanian" tales. Lovecraft was, perhaps, not very successful when writing in other idioms than formal prose, and his attempts at colloquialism in "In the Vault" and "Pickman's Model" are infelicitous at best; but his use of New England dialect—even when carried to such lengths as Zadok Allen's speech in "The Shadow over Innsmouth"—powerfully augments the horror of the scenario by conveying a crude, ignorant, but perhaps more intuitive individual's perception of the "frightful truth."

There is, perhaps, less controversy over Lovecraft's mastery of structure. Long ago Peter Penzoldt declared: "Though often slightly too long, Lovecraft's tales are nearly always perfect in structure."[7] In an earlier essay[8] I identified four basic structural patterns in Lovecraft's longer tales: 1) strict chronology (*i.e.*, the incidents are narrated from beginning to end without a break in chronological sequence); 2) flashback; 3) double or multiple climax; and 4) narrative within narrative. The first two are really outgrowths of the short story; many of Lovecraft's shorter tales are nominally flashbacks in that they begin with a narrator briefly, and usually somewhat harriedly, reflecting upon the events that have occurred to him (thereby piquing our curiosity as to the cause of his disturbance) and then relating the events in sequence. Strict chronology is used rarely in the longer stories because it tends to result in an excessively simple and straightforward narration, without flashback or foreshadowing. It was, of course, used by design in *The Dream-Quest of Unknown Kadath* to convey a sense of wonder and amazement at the successive encounters with odd beings and events; the lack of chapter divisions in this short novel enhances this effect.

As Lovecraft refined the flashback method, he would open the tale not with some frenzied narrator on the brink of madness but with a pensive philosophical reflection uttered by a character not only because he has been through the events he is about to narrate but also because he realizes their staggering implications. In the most famous such opening, that of "The Call of Cthulhu," the narrator states that "The most merciful thing in the world, I think, is the inability of the human mind to correlate all its contents,"[9] only because he himself *has* correlated the contents of his mind and has pieced together "dissociated knowledge" that may indeed cause him personally to "go mad from the revelation," and may, if disseminated throughout the world, result in the "peace and safety of a new dark age."

Tales involving multiple climax are more interesting because of the increasing complexity of design required to produce a final climax that supersedes all previous subsidiary ones. Indeed, Lovecraft's poor opinion of "Herbert West—Reanimator" and "The Lurking Fear" rested largely on his belief that the artificial climaxes he was forced to tack on to each episode were all of equal emotional impact; although perhaps he was being overly harsh, for in both cases the final climax is indeed rather more powerful than its predecessors and does bring each tale to proper closure. Lovecraft went to the other extreme in "The Call of Cthulhu," where there is really no climax to speak of at the end of the first two segments; only with the actual sight of Cthulhu do we encounter a true climax, and even this is not the actual end of the story—there are several more paragraphs of reflection by the narrator as he ponders the fate of the planet now that the very existence of Cthulhu is known.

"The Dunwich Horror" is the prototypical tale of a double climax. The death of Wilbur Whateley is certainly a climax of sorts, but those readers who are puzzled at the lengthy clinical description of Whateley's body as it decays in death—a description that objectifies the horror and renders it more remote—should realize that the true horror is the death of his twin at the end of the story. This same type of climax—where one set of alien entities is described very detailedly but a second set of entities are depicted nebulously, as the true horrors of the tale—is evident in both *At the Mountains of Madness* (the Old Ones vs. the shoggoths) and "The Shadow out of Time" (the Great Race vs. the whistling wind-creatures). As for "The Shadow over Innsmouth," far from adopting L. Sprague de Camp's unfortunate belief that Lovecraft erred by "putting the climax in the middle,"[10] we should be aware that the lengthy chase scene is only a subsidiary climax to the real horror of the tale, in which the narrator realizes that he himself is related to the creatures from whose clutches he had fled so energetically.

The narrative within narrative technique is perhaps the most interesting of all because of its still greater complexity and the difficulty in ensuring that the subnarrative does not destroy the unity of the tale as a whole. Lovecraft was, as a critic, aware of the aesthetic problems entailed by an improper or bungling use of the narrative within a narrative; of Maturin's *Melmoth the Wanderer* he remarks in "Supernatural Horror in Literature" that the subnarrative of John and Moncada "takes up the bulk of Maturin's four-volume book; this disproportion being considered one of the chief technical faults of the composition."[11] (Lovecraft expresses himself here in this rather tentative way because he himself never read the entirety of *Melmoth* but only excepts of it in an anthology.) The means to avoid structural awkwardness is to integrate the subsidiary narrative with the main narrative, specifically by allowing the protagonist of the main narrative to become intimately involved in the subsidiary one in some fashion or other. In one of the simplest examples, the modern explorer of "The Mound" (1929-1930) finds the document written by Zamacona and paraphrases it; but this subnarrative is so long—it occupies four of the seven chapters of the tale—that by the time it is concluded and the principal narrator returns abruptly ("When I looked up from my half-stupefied reading..."),[12] we have almost forgotten his existence.

Nevertheless, "The Mound" typifies an interesting pattern exhibited by the narrative-within-narrative tales: the emergence of a character in the subsidiary narrative who develops a personality of his own and becomes the focus of the reader's sympathy (or, at the very least, interest). In "The Mound" it is of course Zamacona who fulfills this function. In "The Lurking Fear" (1922), the earliest example of this technique, although on a rather limited scale, the third segment tells the tale of Jan Martense, whose attempts to escape the horrors of the Martense mansion end in his death. In *At the Mountains of Madness* the subnarrative of the Old Ones' arrival upon and settlement of the earth is vividly told, and they gradually become highly sympathetic figures in contrast to the loathsome shoggoths; similarly, in "The Shadow out of Time" the Great Race's history is narrated in a long narrative. In all these instances it should be noted that the subsidiary narrative is so well integrated into the general framework of the story—principally by means of the main narrator's repeated presence as commentator upon the events or (in the case of "The Shadow out of Time") as an actual participant in them—that it becomes difficult even to speak of a subsidiary narrative at all. It should also be noted that all these subsidiary narratives involve a *reaching backward through time*—a technique Lovecraft uses even in tales technically outside this specific group (*e.g.*, "The Rats in the Walls," "Facts concerning the Late Arthur Jermyn and His Family," and even so early a tale as "The Alchemist"). We have already suggested the importance of the past to such a writer and thinker as Lovecraft (and shall do so again below), so that such a pattern is no surprise.

"The Call of Cthulhu" presents the greatest structural complexity of any of Lovecraft's tales—a remarkable fact given that it is by no means the longest of his narratives. Here we have a main narrator (Francis Wayland Thurston) paraphrasing the notes of a subsidiary narrator (George Gammell Angell) who himself paraphrases two accounts, that of the artist Wilcox and that of Inspector Legrasse, who paraphrases yet another subsidiary account, the tale of Old Castro; Thurston then comes upon a newspaper article and the Johansen narrative, items that confirm the truth of Angell's accounts. This entire sequence can be depicted by the following chart of narrative voices:

Thurston
  Angell
    Wilcox
    Legrasse
      Castro
  newspaper item
  Johansen

This structure never becomes clumsy because we are always aware of the presence of the principal narrator, who has both assembled the various other narratives and repeatedly comments upon them. It should be noted that the most "sensational" part of the story—Castro's wild tale of the Great Old Ones—is *three times* removed from the principal narrative: Thurston—Angell—Legrasse—Castro. This is narrative "distance" with a vengeance! When Lovecraft commented in later years that he felt the story was "cumbrous,"[13] he was perhaps referring to this structural complexity—a complexity, however, that is undeniably effective in conveying with power and verisimilitude what is to be conveyed.

If I regard *The Case of Charles Dexter Ward*—which, with its lengthy subnarrative about Joseph Curwen and its many inserted letters, newspaper articles, and other documents—as fundamentally less complex than "The Call of Cthulhu," it is because we are dealing essentially with a fairly elementary narrative-within-narrative device; the various documents in both the principal and the subsidiary narrative do not produce *structural complexity* so much as *tonal variation.* Here again a descent into the past is the hallmark of the subnarrative; but, interestingly, when the main narrative (the tale of Charles Dexter Ward in the early twentieth century) resumes after the long digression about Curwen, we find the "past" (embodied, literally, in Curwen) making anomalous and troubling incursions into the present, as his centuries-old resurrected body creates increasing havoc in contemporary Providence. We find this same pattern in *At the Mountains of Madness*, where the resumption of the narrative of Dyer and Danforth after the subnarrative about the Old Ones makes it very clear that the millennia-frozen star-headed entities have revived in the present day.

Fritz Leiber has identified two related structural devices at work in a wide variety of Lovecraft's tales—the principle of "confirmation" (as opposed to revelation) and, as a corollary, the "terminal climax"—that is, "where the high point and the final sentence coincide."[14] This latter device has been ridiculed by superficial critics who point to the supposed frequency with which Lovecraft's tales end in italicized final lines, even though only four or five stories are open to this indictment. But the fact is that this technique requires an enormously elaborate and convoluted structure whereby all the explanatory matter is supplied in advance of the conclusion, so that the "high point" can in fact coincide with the final line. What is more, in most cases there is really no "surprise" in this final line: this is where the notion of "confirmation" comes in. Lovecraft boldly departed, in his best work, from cheap jack-in-the-box "surprise" endings: he knew that such a thing was one of the hackneyed conventions of the pulp or popular fiction which he sedulously wished to escape. In his greatest works, one knows almost from the beginning what the outcome is going to be; but the tales nevertheless gain increasing fascination and suspense as we wait for the protagonists finally to "confirm" what both we and they know to be true but which remains undeclared up to the very end. This device also enhances the psychological portrayal of the protagonists, who are seen by the reader to be rationalizing with increasing desperation as a means of shielding themselves from the dreadful facts of the matter, until finally the cumulative weight of evidence forces them to yield and accept the true state of affairs.

David E. Schultz has felicitously described this entire process as a painterly device. Speaking on a panel discussion, Schultz maintained:

> I think Lovecraft's stories are like paintings in that they are static: there's no motion in them, no linear getting from one place to another. At the beginning of the story, you have a pretty sketchy idea of what will happen throughout the story as revealed in the ending...And so what happens is that in the beginning he sketches out what's going to happen in the story, and then he proceeds to fill in things in more detail, so when you get to the end you now have his complete vision.[15]

It may perhaps be inaccurate to say that there is "no motion" in Lovecraft's tales; but Schultz's point—that Lovecraft keeps going over the same territory over and over again, successively filling in more and more details—is well taken. "The Shadow over Innsmouth" is perhaps the clearest example: the narrator first learns sketchily of the history of Innsmouth from the ticket agent, then learns a little more from the grocery youth, then finally gains the full story from Zadok Allen and from his own subsequent investigations. Each time, previously obscure events not merely are clarified, but take on increasingly alarming overtones as their true nature is learned. Hence, what is believed by the outside world to have been a mere plague or epidemic in Innsmouth in 1846 proves to have been a hideous battle between humans and aliens over the control of the town.

The emphasis Lovecraft put on the structure of a tale is made clear in "Notes on Writing Weird Fiction," where he recommends the preparation of *two* synopses, one detailing the events of the tale in order of *chronological occurrence*, the other in order of *narration*. It is clear that these two synopses can be widely different; indeed, the degree of their difference is an indication of the relative structural complexity of the story. Lovecraft once went so far as to say that "*the synopsis is the real heart of the story*";[16] and it is unfortunate that we have the notes or synopses for so few of his major tales. While appreciating the prose style, imagery, and philosophical substance of his tales, it is proper to find an almost architectural beauty in the structure of Lovecraft's narratives.

2. Themes and Development

It is impossible to speak of the development of Lovecraft's fictional work over the two decades of his career as short story writer without speaking of the themes embodied in his tales; for, as I have frequently noted, Lovecraft appears to have had a relatively small number of basic ideas, themes, and scenarios which he utilized over and over again, each time refining them and imbuing them with greater power and effectiveness. There is nothing to regret or criticize in this; for it is exactly the paucity of his conceptions and their incessant recurrence that lend a singular coherence and unity to his work.

Psychic possession is a theme we find in the earliest of Lovecraft's tales—"The Tomb," "Polaris," "Beyond the Wall of Sleep." What we notice as this theme is developed—and what we will notice in regard to many of Lovecraft's themes—is not merely an increasing subtlety in its execution but, in accordance with his later aesthetic theory of "non-supernatural cosmic art,"[17] an increasing manipulation of the theme in such a way as to be highly credible in light of advanced science. "The Shunned House" (1924)—with its attempt (nebulous and obscure as it may be) to link a psychic vampirism with relativity and quantum theory—is a landmark in this regard. In "The Call of Cthulhu," Cthulhu's power to influence dreams is a sort of psychic possession, and the theme is now broadened to a cosmic—or, at least, a worldwide—scale.

One of the most complicated and debatable instances of psychic possession is *The Case of Charles Dexter Ward.* As we have seen, a superficial reading of the tale suggests that Curwen's spirit has possessed the body of his descendant Charles Dexter Ward; but this in fact is not what has happened. Instead, Ward has resurrected Curwen's body but is himself killed by Curwen when he proves too "squeamish" to carry out Curwen's plans. And yet, there is perhaps psychic possession of a subtler sort. Curwen writes in a letter: "*And of ye Seede of Olde shal One be borne who shal looke Back, tho' know'g not what he seeks*";[18] later, in a memo, he writes: "I am Hopeful ye Thing is breed'g Outside ye Spheres. It shall drawe One who is to Come."[19] Whether this "Thing" is Yog-Sothoth or not, perhaps it is responsible for casting some sort of psychic spell over Ward so that he becomes fascinated with his ancestor and performs all those actions that ultimately lead to Curwen's resurrection.

"The Thing on the Doorstep" seems to represent a lapse in the development of the psychic possession idea, for the notion is presented too obviously and without any sort of rationale save the anomalous mental powers of Asenath (or Ephraim) Waite. But in "The Shadow out of Time" the theme reaches its pinnacle both in force of expression and in plausibility. Indeed, Lovecraft has deftly escaped the myriad paradoxes involved in conventional time-travel by appealing to the mind-transference abilities of the Great Race. It may be true that there is no very compelling pseudo-scientific account of these abilities; but the rich background details Lovecraft provides cause this flaw to pass almost unnoticed.

Degeneration in many different forms is also a frequently used theme in Lovecraft's fiction. It is tempting—and, indeed, highly plausible—to link this theme both to Lovecraft's racism and to what can only be called his sexual repressions or inhibitions. His vicious portrayals of ignorant and decadent backwoods denizens—from Joe Slater in "Beyond the Wall of Sleep" to the Dunwich residents in "The Dunwich Horror"—may superficially seem merely the contempt of a refined city-dweller for unwashed countryfolk; but it becomes clear that Lovecraft's disgust is manifested both by what he perceives to be a descent upon the evolutionary scale and by sexual license. Indeed, in "The Lurking Fear" there are two such groups of people: the squatters around the Martense mansion are a relatively benign case of social decay, whereas the degenerate descendants of the Martense family have suffered a spectacular decline precisely because of their violation of the most basic sexual taboo—incest. "The Horror at Red Hook" has been seen to be a wild racist fantasy about the threat of numberless "foreigners"—who in their decadence have reverted to the level of "beasts"[20]—overrunning a formerly American terrain. The degeneration theme reaches its culmination—and in doing so clearly betrays both its racial and sexual foundations—in "The Shadow over Innsmouth," which is obviously a cautionary tale about miscegenation between races. It might be thought that "The Dunwich Horror" is analogous: here we have interbreeding between a human woman and an extraterrestrial god; but the scenario is so preposterous (and in any case is derived directly from Machen's "The Great God Pan") that any symbolic or sociocultural interpretation of it becomes implausible. On the other hand, "The Rats in the Walls" is not precisely a case of degeneration but rather one of pure atavism.

The notion of alien races dwelling on the underside of civilization may perhaps be an outgrowth of the degeneration theme—and it too was in part influenced by Machen, this time his several tales of the "Little People"—but this theme is not always racist in its implications. Indeed, in its first, tentative exposition—the undersea realm of "The Temple"—there is a clear suggestion that this ancient race was significantly superior to the human race in intellectual and aesthetic capacity. This becomes a dominant motif, and most of Lovecraft's other alien civilizations are endowed with several features—principally pure intellect—that elevate them above the supposed masters of the planet.

What becomes gradually evident as this theme develops is that the conception is increasingly broadened so that it unites with—or becomes an instantiation of—what is really the central theme in all Lovecraft's work, cosmicism. In other words, the merely terrestrial alien races of "The Temple" and "The Nameless City" become the awesome extraterrestrials of "The Call of Cthulhu," "The Whisperer in Darkness," *At the Mountains of Madness*, and "The Shadow out of Time." Accordingly, the danger posed by these races no longer affects merely a single individual (in each case the protagonist of the tale in question) but all human civilization. In speaking of the radical shift in scope represented by "The Call of Cthulhu," Stefan Dziemianowicz writes:

> By drawing a parallel between Thurston's personal experience and the fate of the human race, Lovecraft makes it clear that Thurston is not merely a character in a horror story. He is a symbol for mankind itself, alone in the void, piecing together random bits of information in an effort to find greater meaning. Thus, Thurston's internal alienation reflects humanity's greater external alienation as a consciousness aware of its own insignificance in the cosmic scheme of things.[21]

It is at this point that we must study Lovecraft's portrayal of character. His presumed "inability" to draw lifelike character has been much discussed, but without a proper understanding of the goals and direction of his work as a whole. If cosmicism—and its ethical corollary, the insignificance of the human race—is indeed the central focus of his tales, would not strong and distinctive characters be entirely contrary to this purpose? Consider a statement made late in life:

> Individuals and their fortunes within natural law move me very little. They are all momentary trifles bound from a common nothingness toward another common nothingness. Only the cosmic framework itself—or such individuals as symbolise principles (or defiances of principles) of the cosmic framework—can gain a deep grip on my imagination and set it to work creating. In other words, the only "heroes" I can write about are *phenomena*.[22]

It may well be the case that Lovecraft was incapable of drawing lifelike characters: certainly, the many wooden and stereotyped characters we have noted in the revisions seem to bear this out, although judging any aspect of Lovecraft's work on the sole basis of his revisions is a dangerous undertaking. But all that Lovecraft was hoping for was to make his characters *representative*.

And yet, there can nevertheless be traced a certain evolution in Lovecraft's depiction of character. The protagonists of his early tales—clearly derived from Poe—are oftentimes highly eccentric if not actually mad; but in later tales they become increasingly less peculiar in their mental traits and more like everyman figures. David E. Schultz has analyzed this shift with precision:

> Lovecraft's early stories are focused inward; that is, the narrators' attentions are turned nearly exclusively on themselves and their stories are the culmination of their reflections upon their condition. Lovecraft's "outsider" might be considered the typical figure in stories written before 1925.... But the outsiders of the early 1920s have no parallel in Lovecraft's later stories. The jaded, self-absorbed, decadent thrillseekers of "The Hound" and "The Loved Dead" are not seen again. Lovecraft's narrators are no longer self-indulgent "sensitive" types, but respected professionals—not gregarious fellows by any means but sympathetic, caring men who interact daily with others.[23]

The transition is perfectly captured by the replacement of the early "mad scientists" (Crawford Tillinghast in "From Beyond," Herbert West in "Herbert West—Reanimator") with the scientists and professors of "The Whisperer in Darkness" and *At the Mountains of Madness*. The reader is, to be sure, far more concerned with the fate of these latter individuals than with the sundry lunatics, hysterics, and "thrillseekers" of the early tales; but our concern for their specific fate is far overshadowed by our concern for the dismal fate of our species at large. It scarcely requires comment, of course, that Lovecraft's later narrators are intellectuals very largely in order to facilitate the verisimilitude of the narrative: because they are highly educated men who are not likely to be taken in by imposture or be given to hallucinations, their soberly narrated accounts impel reader belief even as the tale becomes increasingly fantastic and bizarre.

Lovecraft's mention of characters who embody "principles (or defiances of principles) of the cosmic framework" is of relevance in studying those tales that are not openly cosmic in their implications. Joseph Curwen is preeminently an individual who has "defied" Nature by prolonging his life through alchemy; and in spite of the random mentions in *The Case of Charles Dexter Ward* of "Outside Spheres" and other pseudo-cosmic suggestions, the novel is really a purely terrestrial story of the Faustian quest for unholy knowledge. There are many such "old men" in Lovecraft's fiction, from as early as "The Alchemist" to as late as Ephraim Waite in "The Thing on the Doorstep"; the hideous backwoodsman of "The Picture in the House" is perhaps the sole instance of a character who defies the natural bounds of human life not through knowledge but merely by an accidental discovery of the life-extending effects of cannibalism.

The theme of forbidden knowledge is perhaps related to cosmicism—or perhaps is a means of conveying it—in that most of the knowledge that is deemed "forbidden" in Lovecraft's tales is the knowledge of our insignificant position in the cosmos. Knowledge itself is a very complicated issue in Lovecraft: one of his earliest utterances—"To the scientist there is the joy in pursuing truth which nearly counteracts the depressing revelations of truth"[24]—is a neat encapsulation of both the fascination of the pursuit of knowledge ("Truth-hunger is a hunger just as real as food-hunger"[25] and its potentially devastating psychological effects; and we find exactly this ambivalence in the resounding openings of "Arthur Jermyn" and "The Call of Cthulhu." Lovecraft may, indeed, have had an exaggerated belief in the power of thought to affect human behavior—something perfectly understandable in one who himself preeminently led the life of the mind, but perhaps not so plausible when applied to the public at large. Recall another early statement: "All rationalism tends to minimize the value and importance of life, and to decrease the sum total of human happiness. In many cases the truth may cause suicidal or nearly suicidal depression."[26] In the fiction it is the realization of human insignificance that shatters the protagonists' psychological well-being, to the point that the narrator of "The Call of Cthulhu" declares at the end: "I have looked upon all that the universe has to hold of horror, and even the skies of spring and the flowers of summer must ever afterward be poison to me."[27] Is this really a viable emotional reaction? The tenacity with which many otherwise intelligent people cling to the outmoded myths of religion—perhaps in fear of being "alone in the universe"—may lend more credence to Lovecraft's view than one might otherwise have thought.

Credible or not, the reaction of the narrator of "The Call of Cthulhu" to the existence of Cthulhu should help to shatter another misconception about Lovecraft's fiction—that it is psychologically vacuous in its depiction of purely "external" horrors. The hapless protagonist of "The Outsider" is only one of many characters who learns the devastating truth about himself and is emotionally crippled thereby; "The Shadow over Innsmouth" similarly becomes a powerful rumination on the horrors of *self-knowledge*, and many other such instances could be found. In effect, horror in Lovecraft is never purely "external": the mere existence upon this earth of incalculably powerful monsters, from whatever depths of space they may have come, always has a jarring psychological impact on those pitiable few who come to be aware of them and come also to realize humanity's suddenly tenuous hold upon the planet. "The Shadow out of Time"—in which a spectacularly alien intelligence actually occupies the body of the narrator and passes for him for years—is as exquisite a union of external and internal horror as could possibly be imagined.

Cosmicism as such was curiously slow in manifesting itself in Lovecraft's stories, in spite of his declaration at a very early stage in his career that it was the prime focus of his fictional work. In early works cosmicism is conveyed somewhat crudely and superficially by the mere size of some monster or other, as in "Dagon" (this device would still be utilized, although in a vastly subtler way, in "The Call of Cthulhu"—"A mountain walked or stumbled."[28] But already in "The Colour out of Space"—which Lovecraft was probably correct in declaring his greatest success at depicting *outsideness*—cosmicism is broached merely by the extreme bizarrerie and nebulousness of the extraterrestrial incursion. What exactly is the meteorite in this story? Does it house a single creature or many? Why do they seem to violate the most fundamental scientific laws governing phenomena in our universe? We have only the cloudiest answers to any of these questions at the end of the tale, and it is principally this very lack of knowledge on the reader's part—more than the purely physical horrors on display—that is the true source of horror.

Later stories emphasize cosmicism not so much in terms of space as in terms of time. The vast gulfs of time suggested in *At the Mountains of Madness* and "The Shadow out of Time" make these tales among the most breathlessly evocative in all Lovecraft's work, and it is also no surprise that they are considered classics of science fiction.

Lovecraft was, in effect, forced to stress temporal cosmicism in these tales because his alien entities became, as it were, domesticated (as they do not in "The Colour out of Space" and "The Whisperer in Darkness") and actually come to be representative of the human race.

It is by no means the case that Lovecraft's work evinces a continuous improvement from beginning to end. "The Rats in the Walls," for all its relatively limited scope, is as technically flawless a tale as he ever wrote; while such a later tale as "The Dreams in the Witch House," in spite of its vastly larger scope, is marred by poor writing and flaws in conception. "The Thing on the Doorstep" is also a disappointing later tale. Nevertheless, the systematic, and in many ways radical, improvement Lovecraft made from "The Tomb" to "The Shadow out of Time" within a period of two decades is remarkable and unprecedented. All too often in the realm of weird fiction—as is the case with Arthur Machen, Algernon Blackwood, and even lesser writers such as Robert W. Chambers—an author will do his greatest work early in his career only to peter out in harmless mediocrity at the end. Lovecraft's career, of course, was considerably shorter than that of many of his predecessors and contemporaries, but his exponential development— in refinement of style, breadth of conception, and philosophic and aesthetic depth—is singular in this field and perhaps in any other field of literature.

3. Lovecraft's Legacy

When Lovecraft died in 1937, only one true book bearing his name had been published (the wretched Visionary Press *Shadow over Innsmouth* [1936]). His early essays and poetry had already achieved oblivion in forgotten amateur journals, and some of his most significant work—notably the two short novels, *The Dream-Quest of Unknown Kadath* and *The Case of Charles Dexter Ward*—had not been published at all. But the devotion that Lovecraft could inspire even through correspondence seized many of his friends, especially his literary executor Robert Hayward Barlow (who travelled from Kansas to Providence to organize Lovecraft's effects and to donate his papers to the John Hay Library of Brown University) and August Derleth, who with Donald Wandrei initially attempted to market an omnibus of Lovecraft's fiction with major publishers and, when rebuffed, decided to found their own publishing company, Arkham House, for the sole purpose of publishing Lovecraft.

There is now no need to tell the story of Lovecraft's literary resurrection: Derleth and Wandrei's publication of *The Outsider and Others* (1939) and *Beyond the Wall of Sleep* (1943); the reprints of his work by Victor Gollancz of London and in paperback by Bartholomew House, Avon, and the Editions for the Armed Services; the slow but steady translation of his tales into French, Spanish, German, Japanese, and other languages; the emergence of critical analysis with Fritz Leiber and George T. Wetzel; Wetzel's early and invaluable bibliographic work; and on up to the present day with the revolution of scholarship in the 1970s and 1980s and the republication of his work by Arkham House in corrected texts in the 1980s. What does need to be addressed is Lovecraft's precise position in the history of weird fiction, both as the inheritor of older traditions and the founder of new ones.

Peter Penzoldt's somewhat unkind remark that Lovecraft was "too well read"[29] does nevertheless point to the fact that he had a thorough grasp of the history of weird fiction and was indeed influenced by a large number of his predecessors, although in most instances this influence affected only superficial details of plot and imagery. I myself have elsewhere suggested that Lovecraft in many ways "took the best features" of some of his predecessors and made them his own—"Machen's notion of evil cults lurking on the underside of civilization; Dunsany's artificial pantheon and cosmicism; Blackwood's sense of transcendent awe; James's structural complexity and verisimilitude; and Bierce's cynicism, concision, and narrative tensity."[30] But this too is perhaps unjust in suggesting that Lovecraft is only the sum total of his literary antecedents. Where, then, does his fundamental originality lie?

Lovecraft's greatest distinction is in developing a very carefully worked out philosophy of life and embodying it in tales of immense power and richness. This philosophy—whose basic tenets included mechanistic materialism, cosmicism, atheism, respect for science, concern for the state of civilization, and even a certain misanthropy or "indifferentism" in regard to conventional human relations, emotions, and values—does not on the surface seem like a very promising basis for literature, but Lovecraft performed the trick. In doing so, what he achieved was a new type of weird tale—one that incorporated important elements from the nascent field of science fiction to produce an inextricable fusion of the two, especially in such features as scientific justification for supernormal events and transposition of the locus of fear from the mundane world to the boundless cosmos. That Lovecraft emphatically influenced such later writers of science fiction as John W. Campbell, Fritz Leiber, Philip K. Dick, Gene Wolfe, and many others proves—in spite of the hostility with which many science fiction critics have regarded him—that his union of horror and science fiction was a highly felicitous one.

One major objection to according Lovecraft a place in the realm of science fiction is that his vision appears to be backward-looking rather than forward-looking. Maurice Lévy perhaps expressed this objection best:

> Lovecraft's art...is essentially regressive, oriented toward a fabulous past and rooted in myth. In this it is an authentically fantastic art, forever belonging to

> the realm of chimeras and the unverifiable. We might even be tempted to say that the fantastic is, on the axis of the imagination, rigorously opposed to science fiction.[31]

This is very persuasive, but perhaps some words can be said on the other side. To be sure, Lovecraft had little good to say about the present or future, and his antiquarianism certainly led him to see himself as living in an age of decline and imminent barbarism. The fact that even many of his avowedly science fictional tales—notably *At the Mountains of Madness* and "The Shadow out of Time"—are oriented backward (the Old Ones and the Great Race came to earth millennia ago and established flourishing civilizations, from which there has merely been an aesthetic and intellectual falling off) is certainly indicative of Lovecraft's orientation. But we must also realize that his renunciation of pure supernaturalism in his later work manifestly links him with science fiction, and in his later years he even seemed to gain a certain optimism regarding the cultural benefits that might accrue through socialism. As for his use of myth (a remarkably complex phenomenon about which it is difficult to speak in small compass) I reiterate David E. Schultz's conception of Lovecraft's pseudomythology as an "anti-mythology"—in other words, a mythology that parodies or confutes the purpose of most conventional mythologies in such matters as the divine creation of the human race, human relations with the gods, and the centrality of human beings in the cosmic sphere—something that could only have been devised by a scientific rationalist who had renounced all religious belief as well as the value of any conventional myth to sustain human culture. It is in the realms of science, philosophy, and politics that Lovecraft shows himself to be most "forward-looking"; although, since these aspects of his thought were not commonly known until the publication of his letters, they have not yet been of any significant influence upon subsequent literature.

It is, indeed, an unfortunate fact that Lovecraft's most obvious influence has been in that tiny subgenre of weird fiction known as the "Cthulhu Mythos." This is unfortunate because Lovecraft had the bad luck to attract a very mediocre group of self-styled "disciples" and followers—from August Derleth to C. Hall Thompson to Brian Lumley to the legions of dismal "fan" writers, each intent on creating a spanking new god or book or place—who failed utterly to grasp the philosophical essence of Lovecraft's pseudomythology and instead found a childish pleasure in imitating its flamboyant externals. That most of these writers produced unwitting parodies of their mentor's work passed wholly beyond their consciousness; but the result was that, through no fault of his own, Lovecraft's own name and work became tainted by these inferior and half-baked imitations, to the point that careless critics such as Damon Knight failed to take the effort to distinguish between the real

Lovecraft and the cheap spinoffs. One would like to think that this "Cthulhu Mythos" writing is on the wane; certainly, none of the various anthologies of such work—Derleth's *Tales of the Cthulhu Mythos*, either in its original (1969) or its revised (1990) edition; the thoroughly mediocre *Lovecraft's Legacy* (1990); Robert M. Price's pretentiously titled assemblage of barrel-scrapings, *Tales of the Lovecraft Mythos* (1992)—does anything to suggest that the "Cthulhu Mythos" is a viable literary form.

It is only a seeming paradox that Lovecraft's influence on weird fiction is actually less significant than his influence on science fiction; for the fact is that post-Lovecraftian weird fiction has veered in directions quite different from those Lovecraft pioneered. The cosmicism that he—as well as Blackwood and Hodgson—emphasized was dropped, as such writers as Ray Bradbury, Richard Matheson, and Shirley Jackson founded their horrific scenarios exactly in those "ordinary people" in whom Lovecraft frankly professed no interest. External horror was replaced by internal horror, the horror of a diseased mentality. It is not my place here to make any blanket judgments on the relative merits of the older or newer weird literature: while it does not seem as if the present age has produced the equals of that remarkable quartet of the early part of the century—Machen, Dunsany, Blackwood, and Lovecraft—the work of Shirley Jackson, Robert Aickman, Ramsey Campbell, T. E. D. Klein, and a few others is by no means to be despised.

Two of these writers—Campbell and Klein—have, of course, been heavily influenced by Lovecraft; Klein's work in particular represents a remarkable melding of influences from Machen, Lovecraft, and perhaps Blackwood, while yet remaining highly original and individual. Campbell's juvenile tales—published in *The Inhabitant of the Lake and Less Welcome Tenants* (1964) and elsewhere—do indeed imitate the "Cthulhu Mythos" rather slavishly, even if with verve; but Campbell has himself admitted that his very next volume, the landmark story collection *Demons by Daylight* (1973), was written in an attempt to be as unlike Lovecraft as possible. And yet, this same collection contained one magnificent tale ("The Franklyn Paragraphs") that toyed with "Mythos" trappings only to produce a chilling and wholly original excursion into Campbellian horror. More recently, Thomas Ligotti's scintillating work consciously harks back to Lovecraft's early "macabre" tales while being as far from pastiche as it is possible to be.

Lovecraft has certainly left his mark on the work of Stephen King, Clive Barker, Whitley Strieber, and others, but much of this influence is sporadic and tangential. Perhaps this is as it should be: any writer who has something of his own to say will not stoop to blatant imitation, but will use another writer's work as a springboard for self-expression. This is exactly what, for example, Colin Wilson did in *The Mind Parasites* (1967), perhaps the only substantial work ever to be written in the "Cthulhu Mythos" tradition. As for those writers who have nothing of their own to say and who find the pinnacle of achievement in copying someone else's vision or modes of expression, it would be merciful if they would simply shut up.

Lovecraft is slowly coming to occupy the place he deserves in weird literature and in general literature. Recognition by the literary and academic mainstream has been slow, but in the last decade or so mentions of Lovecraft in this realm have both increased in number and decreased in condescension. In a brief notice of Donald R. Burleson's *Lovecraft: Disturbing the Universe* (1990), an anonymous reviewer in *American Literature*—the leading academic journal for American writing—stated: "It's getting to where those who still ignore Lovecraft will have to go on the defensive."[32]

Lovecraft is now not likely to fade from the scene: his major work is well preserved in hardcover, has been translated into more than a dozen languages, and is widely available in paperback; his obscure work has been reprinted in the small press; criticism of him both in this country and abroad is abundant, and is appearing in increasingly prestigious venues. And yet, Lovecraft's popular appeal has scarcely lessened over the decades—a remarkable fact given the near-oblivion that has overtaken such of his contemporaries as Machen, Dunsany, Blackwood, Clark Ashton Smith, and so many others. Moreover, there are indications that Lovecraft may benefit from the new adaptations and technologies that have lately been developed—from comic books to role-playing games to CD-interactive media. The worldwide dissemination of the work of a artist who himself died in poverty and obscurity is an irony that has occurred all too often in the history of literature, art, and music; but it is an irony that Lovecraft himself would have appreciated, for he knew that his work was a decidedly acquired taste. Indeed, weird fiction as a whole was, in his view, only meant for a select audience:

> The imaginative writer devotes himself to art in its most essential sense.... He is a painter of moods and mind-pictures—a capturer and amplifier of elusive dreams and fancies—a voyager into those unheard-of lands which are glimpsed through the veil of actuality but rarely, and only by the most sensitive.... He is the poet of twilight visions and childhood memories, but sings only for the sensitive.[33]

It is nice to think that there enough "sensitives" in the world to keep H. P. Lovecraft's work alive.

NOTES

For Lovecraft's shorter stories I do not supply page citations for quoted passages, but I do for the longer tales. Full information on the works cited here can be found in the Primary and Secondary Bibliography.

Chapter One

[1]On this idea see Robert Bloch's significant brief article, "Inside the Outsider," in *Xenophile* 2:6 (October 1975): 4-5.

[2]H. P. Lovecraft. *Selected Letters, 1911-1924* [Volume I]. Sauk City, WI: Arkham House, 1965, p. 110.

[3]John Taylor Gatto. *The Major Works of H. P. Lovecraft*. New York: Monarch Press, 1977, p. 15.

[4]Robert M. Price. "Did Lovecraft Have Syphilis?," in *Crypt of Cthulhu* No. 53 (Candlemas 1988): 25-26.

[5]HPL to J. Vernon Shea, 8 November 1933 (ms.).

[6]HPL to J. Vernon Shea, 19-31 July 1931 (ms., John Hay Library, Brown University).

[7]H. P. Lovecraft. *Selected Letters, 1925-1929* [Volume II]. Sauk City, WI: Arkham House, 1968, p. 109.

[8]The first issue of the *Scientific Gazette* dates to 4 March 1899, and there were perhaps some other trial issues prior to the "new issue" of 1903.

[9]H. P. Lovecraft. "A Confession of Unfaith," in *Miscellaneous Writings*, by H. P. Lovecraft, edited by S. T. Joshi. Sauk City, WI: Arkham House, 1995, p. 536.

[10]*Selected Letters, 1911-1924*, p. 38.

[11]HPL to Lillian D. Clark, 22-23 December 1925 (ms., JHL).

[12]H. P. Lovecraft. *Selected Letters, Volume Four, 1932-1934*, edited by August Derleth and James Turner. Sauk City, WI: Arkham House, 1976, p. 358-359.

[13]*Ibid.*, p. 26.

[14]*Selected Letters, 1911-1924*, p. 40-41.

[15]*Selected Letters, Volume Four, 1932-1934*, p. 172.

[16]*Selected Letters, 1911-1924*, p. 31. See also an ad for "International Correspondence Schools, Scranton, Pa." in the *Scientific Gazette* (January 1909), which is very likely the correspondence course Lovecraft himself took.

[17]For overviews of Lovecraft's early association with the Munsey pulps, see Sam Moskowitz, "Lovecraft and the Munsey Magazines," and Will Murray, "Lovecraft and the Pulp Magazine Tradition."

[18]HPL to Richard F. Searight, 16 April 1935, reproduced in *Letters to Richard F. Searight*, by H. P. Lovecraft, edited by David E. Schultz and S. T. Joshi. West Warwick, RI: Necronomicon Press, 1992, p. 54.

[19]*Miscellaneous Writings*, p. 452.

[20]"Extracts from the Letters to G. W. Macauley" (1938), in *Lovecraft Studies* 1:3 (Fall 1980): 14.

NOTES

[21]Clara L. Hess, "Letter to the Editor," in *Providence Journal* (19 September 1948); reprinted (with additions) in August Derleth's "Addenda to *H.P.L.: A Memoir*," in *Something about Cats and Other Pieces*, by H. P. Lovecraft (Sauk City, WI: Arkham House, 1949).

[22]*Selected Letters, 1911-1924*, p. 138.

[23]*Selected Letters, 1911-1924*, p. 44-49.

[24]*Selected Letters, 1911-1924*, p. 139.

[25]H. P. Lovecraft. *Selected Letters, 1929-1931* [Volume III]. Sauk City, WI: Arkham House, 1971, p. 262.

[26]*Selected Letters, 1929-1931*, p. 8.

[27]*Selected Letters, 1911-1924*, p. 351.

[28]HPL to Lillian D. Clark, 29 March 1926 (ms., JHL).

[29]*Selected Letters, 1925-1929*, p. 46-47.

[30]Maurice Lévy. *Lovecraft: A Study in the Fantastic*. Detroit: Wayne State University Press, 1988, p. 23.

[31]H. P. Lovecraft. *Selected Letters, Volume Five, 1934-1937*, edited by Donald Wandrei and James Turner. Sauk City, WI: Arkham House, 1976, p. 224.

[32]*Ibid.*, p. 363.

[33]For graphic accounts of his final months and days, see: H. P. Lovecraft and Willis Conover, *Lovecraft at Last* (Arlington, VA: Carrollton Clark, 1975); and R. Alain Everts, *The Death of a Gentleman: The Last Days of Howard Phillips Lovecraft* (Madison, WI: The Strange Co., 1987).

[34]*Selected Letters, 1925-1929*, p. 51.

[35]*Selected Letters, 1911-1924*, p. 231.

[36]*Selected Letters, 1925-1929*, p. 266-267.

[37]*Selected Letters, 1929-1931*, p. 228.

[38]*Miscellaneous Writings*, p. 153-154.

[39]*Ibid.*, p. 170-171.

[40]See "A Confession of Unfaith" in *Miscellaneous Writings*, but compare *Selected Letters, 1911-1924*, p. 110-111.

[41]*Selected Letters, Volume Four, 1932-1934*, p. 57.

[42]H. P. Lovecraft. *In Defence of Dagon*, in *Miscellaneous Writings*, p. 165.

[43]*Selected Letters, 1925-1929*, p. 269.

[44]*Ibid.*, p. 310.

[45]*Selected Letters, 1911-1924*, p. 132.

[46]*Miscellaneous Writings*, p. 179.

[47]*Selected Letters, Volume Five, 1934-1937*, p. 241.

[48]*Selected Letters, 1929-1931*, p. 222.

[49]*Selected Letters, 1925-1929*, p. 356-357.

[50]*Ibid.*, p. 288-289.

[51]H. P. Lovecraft. "Nietzscheism and Realism," in *Miscellaneous Writings*, p. 173.

[52]*Selected Letters, 1911-1924*, p. 207.

[53]*Selected Letters, 1925-1929*, p. 305.

[54]*Selected Letters, Volume Five, 1934-1937*, p. 326.

[55]*Ibid.*, p. 397-398.

[56]*Ibid.*, p. 321.

[57]*Selected Letters, 1925-1929*, p. 304.

[58]*Selected Letters, 1929-1931*, p. 50.

[59]*Ibid.*, p. 104.

[60]*Ibid.*, p. 50.

[61]*Selected Letters, 1925-1929*, p. 123.

[62]*Ibid.*, p. 71.

[63]*Miscellaneous Writings*, p. 212.
[64]*Ibid.*, p. 111-112.
[65]HPL to August Derleth, [1929] (ms., State Historical Society of Wisconsin).
[66]*Selected Letters, 1925-1929*, p. 100.
[67]*Selected Letters, 1929-1931*, p. 21.
[68]*Ibid.*, p. 23.
[69]*Selected Letters, 1925-1929*, p. 226.
[70]*Selected Letters, 1929-1931*, p. 20.
[71]*In Defence of Dagon*, in *Miscellaneous Writings*, p. 155.
[72]*Miscellaneous Writings*, p. 147-148.
[73]H. P. Lovecraft. *Dagon and Other Macabre Tales*, edited by August Derleth. Sauk City, WI: Arkham House, 1986, p. 365-366.
[74]*Ibid.*, p. 436.
[75]*Ibid.*, p. 368.
[76]*Miscellaneous Writings*, p. 113.
[77]*Selected Letters, Volume Four, 1932-1934*, p. 417-418.
[78]*Dagon and Other Macabre Tales*, p. 368.
[79]*Selected Letters, 1929-1931*, p. 434.
[80]*Ibid.*, p. 295-296.

Chapter Two

[1]*Selected Letters, 1911-1924*, p. 19.
[2]*Selected Letters, Volume Four, 1932-1934*, p. 360.
[3]HPL to Lillian D. Clark, postcard [c. 15 July 1928] (ms., JHL).
[4]*Dagon and Other Macabre Tales*, p. 327.
[5]*Ibid.*
[6]*Ibid.*, p. 396.
[7]*Selected Letters, 1929-1931*, p. 219.
[8]*Dagon and Other Macabre Tales*, p. 3-13.
[9]HPL to Rheinhart Kleiner, 27 August 1917, in *Uncollected Letters*, by H. P. Lovecraft. West Warwick, RI: Necronomicon Press, 1986, p. 21.
[10]*Dagon and Other Macabre Tales*, p. 400.
[11]William Fulwiler. "'The Tomb' and 'Dagon': A Double Dissection," in *Crypt of Cthulhu* No. 38 (Eastertide 1986): 8-14.
[12]*Dagon and Other Macabre Tales*, p. 14-19.
[13]*Ibid.*, p. 25-35.
[14]*Ibid.*, p. 337-343.
[15]HPL to Duane W. Rimel, 30 October 1934 (ms., JHL).
[16]H. P. Lovecraft. *At the Mountains of Madness and Other Novels*. Sauk City, WI: Arkham House, 1985, p. 299-305.
[17]*Ibid.*, p. 422.
[18]*Dagon and Other Macabre Tales*, p. 59-72.
[19]*Ibid.*, p. 73-82.
[20]H. P. Lovecraft. *The Dunwich Horror and Others*. Sauk City, WI: Arkham House, 1984, p. 116-124.
[21]Colin Wilson. *The Strength to Dream*. Boston: Houghton Mifflin Co., 1962, p. 5.
[22]*Dagon and Other Macabre Tales*, p. 98-110.
[23]*Ibid.*, p. 118-126.
[24]*Ibid.*, p. 90-97.
[25]Hugh Elliot. *Modern Science and Materialism*. London: Longmans, Green, 1919, p. 2-3. See in general my article, "The Sources for 'From Beyond'," in *Crypt of Cthulhu* No. 38 (Eastertide 1986): 15-19.

[26]*Miscellaneous Writings*, p. 31.
[27]*Ibid.*, p. 35-36.
[28]*Ibid.*, p. 32-34.
[29]Will Murray. "Behind the Mask of Nyarlathotep," in *Lovecraft Studies* No. 25 (Fall 1991): 25-29.

CHAPTER THREE

[1]Lord Dunsany. *Patches of Sunlight*. London: William Heinemann, 1938, p. 9.
[2]*Ibid.*, p. 135.
[3]*Selected Letters, 1925-1929*, p. 328.
[4]*Ibid.*
[5]*Selected Letters, 1911-1924*, p. 91-92.
[6]*Dagon and Other Macabre Tales*, p. 20-24.
[7]*Selected Letters, 1925-1929*, p. 120.
[8]*Selected Letters, 1911-1924*, p. 63.
[9]*Ibid.*, p. 62.
[10]*Dagon and Other Macabre Tales*, p. 36-42.
[11]*Ibid.*, p. 43-49.
[12]Lord Dunsany. "In the Land of Time," in *Time and the Gods*, by Lord Dunsany. London: William Heinemann, 1906.
[13]*The Dunwich Horror and Others*, p. 272-275.
[14]*Dagon and Other Macabre Tales*, p. 50-54.
[15]HPL to Alfred Galpin, 29 August 1918 (ms., JHL).
[16]*Selected Letters, 1911-1924*, p. 315.
[17]S. T. Joshi. "'The Tree' and Ancient History," in *Nyctalops* No. 19 (April 1991): 68-71.
[18]*Dagon and Other Macabre Tales*, p. 55-58.
[19]*Ibid.*, p. 83-89.
[20]*Selected Letters, 1911-1924*, p. 106.
[21]*Dagon and Other Macabre Tales*, p. 111-117.
[22]*Ibid.*, p. 127-132.
[23]George T. Wetzel. "The Cthulhu Mythos: A Study" (1972), in *H. P. Lovecraft: Four Decades of Criticism*, edited by S. T. Joshi. Athens, OH: Ohio University Press, 1980, p. 80.
[24]*Dagon and Other Macabre Tales*, p. 429.
[25]*Ibid.*, p. 430.
[26]*Selected Letters, 1911-1924*, p. 93.
[27]Lord Dunsany, Letter to August Derleth (28 March 1952), quoted in *Lovecraft Studies* No. 14 (Spring 1987): 38.

CHAPTER FOUR

[1]*The Dunwich Horror and Others*, p. 46-52.
[2]William Fulwiler. "Reflections on 'The Outsider'," in *Lovecraft Studies* No. 2 (Spring 1980): 3-4.
[3]*Selected Letters, 1929-1931*, p. 379.
[4]I am grateful to Forrest Jackson for this observation. See also Carl Buchanan, "'The Outsider' as a Homage to Poe," in *Lovecraft Studies* No. 30 (Spring 1994): .
[5]Dirk W. Mosig. "The Four Faces of 'The Outsider'," in *Nyctalops* 2:2 (July 1974): 3-10.
[6]*Selected Letters, 1911-1924*, p. 27.

[7]*The Dunwich Horror and Others*, p. 83-91.
[8]Robert M. Price. "Erich Zann and the Rue d'Auseil," in *Lovecraft Studies* No. 22/23 (Fall 1990): 13-14.
[9]*Dagon and Other Macabre Tales*, p. 164-170.
[10]*Ibid.*, p. 28.
[11]Steven J. Mariconda. "H. P. Lovecraft's 'Hypnos': Art, Philosophy, and Insanity" (unpublished paper).
[12]*Selected Letters, 1925-1929*, p. 301.
[13]Steven J. Mariconda. "'The Hound'—A Dead Dog?," in *Crypt of Cthulhu* No. 38 (Eastertide 1986): 3-7.
[14]*Dagon and Other Macabre Tales*, p. 171-178.
[15]*Selected Letters, 1911-1924*, p. 198.
[16]*Dagon and Other Macabre Tales*, p. 357-358.
[17]*Miscellaneous Writings*, p. 37-38.
[18]*Selected Letters, Volume Four, 1932-1934*, p. 170.
[19]*Selected Letters, 1911-1924*, p. 154.
[20]*Ibid.*, p. 158.
[21]*Dagon and Other Macabre Tales*, p. 133-163.
[22]*Miscellaneous Writings*, p. 162.
[23]*Dagon and Other Macabre Tales*, p. 179-199.
[24]*Selected Letters, 1929-1931*, p. 31.
[25]*The Dunwich Horror and Others*, p. 26-45.
[26]Steven J. Mariconda. "Baring-Gould and the Ghouls: The Influence of *Curious Myths of the Middle Ages* on 'The Rats in the Walls'," in *Crypt of Cthulhu* No. 14 (St. John's Eve 1983): 3-7, 27.
[27]*Dagon and Other Macabre Tales*, p. 361.
[28]*Ibid.*, p. 200-207.
[29]*Ibid.*, p. 208-216.
[30]*Selected Letters, 1911-1924*, p. 205-206.
[31]*Selected Letters, 1929-1931*, p. 126.
[32]*At the Mountains of Madness and Other Novels*, p. 232-261.
[33]*Selected Letters, 1929-1931*, p. 295-296.
[34]*Selected Letters, 1925-1929*, p. 20.
[35]*Dagon and Other Macabre Tales*, p. 244-265.
[36]See "The Incantation from Red Hook" (not an article but an excerpt from a letter to Wilfred B. Talman), in *The Occult Lovecraft*, by H. P. Lovecraft. Saddle River, NJ: Gerry de la Ree, 1975.
[37]*Dagon and Other Macabre Tales*, p. 266-276.
[38]*Selected Letters, 1925-1929*, p. 101.
[39]Lévy. *Lovecraft: A Study in the Fantastic*, p. 22.
[40]S. T. Joshi. "Lovecraft and Dunsany's *Chronicles of Rodriguez*," in *Crypt of Cthulhu* No. 82 (Hallowmass 1992): 3-6.
[41]*The Dunwich Horror and Others*, p. 199-207.
[42]Mara Kirk Hart. "Walkers in the City: George Willard Kirk and Howard Phillips Lovecraft in New York City, 1924-1926," in *Lovecraft Studies* No. 28 (Spring 1993): 2-17.
[43]HPL to Henry Kuttner, 29 July 1936, in *Letters to Henry Kuttner*. West Warwick, RI: Necronomicon Press, 1990, p. 21.
[44]Arthur Machen. "The Novel of the White Powder," in *Tales of Horror and the Supernatural*, by Arthur Machen. New York: Alfred A. Knopf, 1948, p. 55.
[45]Edgar Allan Poe. *Collected Works*, edited by T. O. Mabbott. Cambridge, MA: Harvard University Press, 1978, Vol. 3, p. 1243.
[46]*The Dunwich Horror and Others*, p. 3-11.

[47]Donald R. Burleson. "Lovecraft: The Hawthorne Influence," in *Extrapolation* 22:3 (Fall 1981): 262-269.
[48]Jason C. Eckhardt. "The Cosmic Yankee," in *An Epicure in the Terrible: A Centennial Anthology of Essays in Honor of H. P. Lovecraft*, edited by David E. Schultz and S. T. Joshi. Rutherford, NJ: Fairleigh Dickinson University Press, 1991, p. 78-100.

CHAPTER FIVE

[1]W. Paul Cook. *In Memoriam: Howard Phillips Lovecraft*. West Warwick, RI: Necronomicon Press, 1991, p. 11.
[2]Oscar Wilde. "Preface" to *The Picture of Dorian Gray*. London: Ward, Lock, 1891.
[3]H. P. Lovecraft. "Lord Dunsany and His Work," in *Miscellaneous Writings*, p. 37-38.
[4]Peter Cannon. "The Influence of *Vathek* on H. P. Lovecraft's *The Dream-Quest of Unknown Kadath*," in *H. P. Lovecraft: Four Decades of Criticism*, p. 153-157.
[5]*At the Mountains of Madness and Other Novels*, p. 306.
[6]*Ibid.*, p. 400-401.
[7]*Ibid.*, p. 406.
[8]*Ibid.*, p. 354-355.
[9]*Dagon and Other Macabre Tales*, p. 357.
[10]*At the Mountains of Madness and Other Novels*, p. 338.
[11]S. T. Joshi. "The Dream World and the Real World in Lovecraft," in *Crypt of Cthulhu* No. 15 (Lammas 1983): 4-15.
[12]*Selected Letters, 1925-1929*, p. 95.
[13]*At the Mountains of Madness and Other Novels*, p. 408-420.
[14]*Selected Letters, Volume Five, 1934-1937*, p. 354.
[15]*Selected Letters, 1911-1924*, p. 106.
[16]*Selected Letters, 1925-1929*, p. 81-89.
[17]Kenneth W. Faig, Jr. "'The Silver Key' and Lovecraft's Childhood," in *Crypt of Cthulhu* No. 81 (St. John's Eve 1992): 11-47.
[18]*Dagon and Other Macabre Tales*, p. 277-286.
[19]*Selected Letters, 1925-1929*, p. 164.
[20]*Selected Letters, 1929-1931*, p. 433.
[21]S. T. Joshi. "Lovecraft and Dunsany's *Chronicles of Rodriguez*."
[22]*Selected Letters, 1929-1931*, p. 410.
[23]*Ibid.*, p. 212.
[24]*Selected Letters, 1911-1924*, p. 234.
[25]*Selected Letters, 1929-1931*, p. 96.
[26]*Selected Letters, 1925-1929*, p. 100.
[27]*Ibid.*, p. 106.
[28]See HPL to Lillian D. Clark, 8 August 1925 (ms., JHL).
[29]*At the Mountains of Madness and Other Novels*, p. 181-182.
[30]*Ibid.*, p. 234.
[31]*Ibid.*, p. 199.
[32]Barton L. St. Armand. "Facts in the Case of H. P. Lovecraft," in *H. P. Lovecraft: Four Decades of Criticism*, p. 178.
[33]*At the Mountains of Madness and Other Novels*, p. 230.
[34]*Ibid.*, p. 228.
[35]*Ibid.*, p. 166.
[36]HPL to R. H. Barlow, [19 March 1934] (ms., JHL).
[37]*Selected Letters, 1911-1924*, p. 114-115.

[38]See HPL's *Diary* for 12-13 Aug. 1925 (ms., JHL).
[39]For an incisive account of the genesis of the story, see: Steven J. Mariconda. "On the Emergence of 'Cthulhu'," in *Lovecraft Studies* No. 15 (Fall 1987): 54-58.
[40]*The Dunwich Horror and Others*, p. 139.
[41]HPL to August Derleth, 16 May 1931 (ms., State Historical Society of Wisconsin).
[42]*Selected Letters, 1929-1931*, p. 293.
[43]*Selected Letters, 1925-1929*, p. 150.
[44]H. P. Lovecraft. "Some Notes on a Nonentity" (1933), in *Autobiographical Writings*, by H. P. Lovecraft, edited by S. T. Joshi. West Warwick, RI: Necronomicon Press, 1992, p. 36.
[45]David E. Schultz. "The Origin of Lovecraft's 'Black Magic' Quote," in *Crypt of Cthulhu* No. 48 (St. John's Eve 1987): 9-13.
[46]*The Dunwich Horror and Others*, p. 141.
[47]"Some Notes on a Nonentity."
[48]David E. Schultz. "From Microcosm to Macrocosm: The Growth of Lovecraft's Cosmic Vision," in *An Epicure in the Terrible*, p. 199-219.
[49]John Milton. *Paradise Lost*, Vol. I, p. 26.
[50]*The Dunwich Horror and Others*, p. 154.
[51]*Ibid.*, p. 12-25.
[52]*Ibid.*, p. 53.
[53]*Ibid.*, p. 59.
[54]*Ibid.*, p. 64.
[55]*Ibid.*, p. 71.
[56]*Ibid.*, p. 72.
[57]*Selected Letters, 1925-1929*, p. 114.
[58]HPL to Richard Ely Morse, 13 October 1935 (ms., JHL).
[59]*The Dunwich Horror and Others*, p. 53.
[60]*Selected Letters, 1929-1931*, p. 429.
[61]*The Dunwich Horror and Others*, p. 81.
[62]*Ibid.*, p. 66.
[63]Fritz Leiber. "A Literary Copernicus" (1949), in *H. P. Lovecraft: Four Decades of Criticism*, p. 50.
[64]*Miscellaneous Writings*, p. 54-58.
[65]*The Dunwich Horror and Others*, p. 155.
[66]*Ibid.*, p. 160.
[67]*Ibid.*, p. 167.
[68]*Ibid.*, p. 176.
[69]*Ibid.*, p. 185.
[70]*Ibid.*, p. 196.
[71]Letter to Edwin Baird, [c. October 1923], in *Miscellaneous Writings*.
[72]Donald R. Burleson. "The Mythic Hero Archetype in 'The Dunwich Horror'," in *Lovecraft Studies* No. 4 (Spring 1981): 3-9.
[73]*The Dunwich Horror and Others*, p. 170.
[74]*Ibid.*, p. 185.
[75]*Ibid.*, p. 197.
[76]HPL to August Derleth, 3 August 1931 (ms., State Historical Society of Wisconsin).
[77]Will Murray. "An Uncompromising Look at the Cthulhu Mythos," in *Lovecraft Studies* No. 12 (Spring 1986): 26-31.
[78]*The Dunwich Horror and Others*, p. 172.
[79]HPL to Lillian D. Clark, 1 July 1928 (ms., JHL). Donald R. Burleson has relocated the site; see his "Humour Beneath Horror: Some Sources for

'The Dunwich Horror' and 'The Whisperer in Darkness'," in *Lovecraft Studies* No. 2 (Spring 1980): 5-15.

[80]Burleson. "Humour Beneath Horror."

[81]*Selected Letters, 1925-1929*, p. 306.

[82]HPL to Lillian D. Clark, 19 June 1928 (ms., JHL).

[83]Eckhardt. "The Cosmic Yankee."

[84]Steven J. Mariconda, "Tightening the Coil: The Revision of 'The Whisperer in Darkness'," in *Lovecraft Studies* No. 32 (Spring 1995): 12-17.

[85]*The Dunwich Horror and Others*, p. 271.

[86]Frank Belknap Long. "Some Random Memories of H.P.L.," in *Marginalia*, by H. P. Lovecraft. Sauk City, WI: Arkham House, 1944, p. 336.

[87]*The Dunwich Horror and Others*, p. 242.

[88]*Ibid.*, p. 240.

[89]*Ibid.*, p. 243.

[90]H. P. Lovecraft. "Notes on Writing Weird Fiction," in *Miscellaneous Writings*.

[91]*The Dunwich Horror and Others*, p. 260.

[92]*Ibid.*, p. 262.

[93]*Ibid.*, p. 266.

[94]*Ibid.*, p. 256.

[95]*Ibid.*

CHAPTER SIX

[1]*Selected Letters, 1929-1931*, p. 295-296.

[2]*Ibid.*, p. 434.

[3]*The Dunwich Horror and Others*, p. 144.

[4]*At the Mountains of Madness and Other Novels*, p. 14.

[5]*Ibid.*, p. 22.

[6]*Ibid.*, p. 101.

[7]Jason Eckhardt. "Behind the Mountains of Madness: Lovecraft and the Antarctic in 1930," in *Lovecraft Studies* No. 14 (Spring 1987): 31-38.

[8]*At the Mountains of Madness and Other Novels*, p. 18.

[9]*Selected Letters, 1929-1931*, p. 193.

[10]*At the Mountains of Madness and Other Novels*, p. 61.

[11]Leiber. "A Literary Copernicus," p. 57.

[12]*At the Mountains of Madness and Other Novels*, p. 95-96.

[13]*Ibid.*, p. 96.

[14]*Ibid.*, p. 37.

[15]*Ibid.*, p. 86.

[16]*Ibid.*, p. 65.

[17]*Ibid.*, p. 92.

[18]H. P. Lovecraft. "An Account of Charleston" (1930), in *Miscellaneous Writings*.

[19]*At the Mountains of Madness and Other Novels*, p. 75.

[20]*Miscellaneous Writings*, p. 165.

[21]S. T. Joshi. *H. P. Lovecraft: The Decline of the West*. Mercer Island, WA: Starmont House, 1990.

[22]*In Defence of Dagon*, in *Miscellaneous Writings*, p. 166.

[23]*At the Mountains of Madness and Other Novels*, p. 65.

[24]Robert M. Price. "Demythologizing Cthulhu," in *H. P. Lovecraft and the Cthulhu Mythos*, by Robert M. Price. Mercer Island, WA: Starmont House, 1990, p. 76-84.

[25]*At the Mountains of Madness and Other Novels*, p. 59.

[26]*Selected Letters, Volume Five, 1934-1937*, p. 224.
[27]See HPL to Samuel Loveman, 29 April 1923 (ms.).
[28]*Selected Letters, 1929-1931*, p. 435.
[29]*The Dunwich Horror and Others*, p. 305.
[30]*Ibid.*, p. 311.
[31]*Ibid.*, p. 360-361.
[32]*Ibid.*, p. 367.
[33]*Ibid.*
[34]Will Murray. "In Search of Arkham Country," in *Lovecraft Studies* No. 13 (Fall 1986): 54-67.
[35]*Dagon and Other Macabre Tales*, p. 248.
[36]*Selected Letters, Volume Four, 1932-1934*, p. 253.
[37]*The Dunwich Horror and Others*, p. 350.
[38]*Ibid.*, p. 331.
[39]*Ibid.*
[40]*Ibid.*, p. 367.
[41]Will Murray. "Lovecraft and *Strange Tales*," in *Crypt of Cthulhu* No. 74 (Lammas 1990): 3-11.
[42]*Selected Letters, Volume Five, 1934-1937*, p. 236.
[43]*The Dunwich Horror and Others*, p. 339.
[44]*Ibid.*, p. 305.
[45]*Ibid.*, p. 342.
[46]*Ibid.*, p. 305.
[47]*Ibid.*, p. 316.
[48]*Ibid.*, p. 361.
[49]*Selected Letters, 1929-1931*, p. 31.
[50]*The Dunwich Horror and Others*, p. 326.
[51]*Selected Letters, 1911-1924*, p. 132.
[52]H. P. Lovecraft. "Some Causes of Self-Immolation," in *Miscellaneous Writings*.
[53]*At the Mountains of Madness and Other Novels*, p. 272.
[54]*Ibid.*, p. 277.
[55]Steven Mariconda. "Lovecraft's Cosmic Imagery," in *An Epicure in the Terrible*, p. 192.
[56]*At the Mountains of Madness and Other Novels*, p. 267.
[57]*Ibid.*
[58]*Dagon and Other Macabre Tales*, p. 25.
[59]*Ibid.*
[60]Fritz Leiber. "Through Hyperspace with Brown Jenkin," in *The Dark Brotherhood and Other Pieces*, by H. P. Lovecraft and Divers Hands, edited by August Derleth. Sauk City, WI: Arkham House, 1966, p. 171.
[61]*At the Mountains of Madness and Other Novels*, p. 264.
[62]*Ibid.*, p. 285.
[63]*Dagon and Other Macabre Tales*, p. 39.
[64]*The Dunwich Horror and Others*, p. 289-290.
[65]*Ibid.*, p. 296.
[66]*Ibid.*, p. 299.
[67]*Ibid.*, p. 290.
[68]*Ibid.*, p. 277.
[69]*Ibid.*, p. 279.
[70]Sonia H. Davis. "Memories of Lovecraft: I," in *Arkham Collector* No. 4 (Winter 1969): 116.
[71]*The Dunwich Horror and Others*, p. 277.
[72]*Selected Letters, 1911-1924*, p. 128.

[73]*Ibid.*, p. 256.
[74]*The Dunwich Horror and Others*, p. 277.
[75]*Ibid.*, p. 278.
[76]*Ibid.*, p. 302.
[77]*Selected Letters, Volume Four, 1932-1934*, p. 289.
[78]S. T. Joshi. "On 'The Book'," in *Crypt of Cthulhu* No. 53 (Candlemas 1988): 3-7.
[79]*Selected Letters, Volume Four, 1932-1934*, p. 289-290.
[80]*Dagon and Other Macabre Tales*, p. 287-291.
[81]David E. Schultz. "'The Thing in the Moonlight': A Hoax Revealed," in *Crypt of Cthulhu* No. 53 (Candlemas 1988): 12-13.
[82]*The Dunwich Horror and Others*, p. 385.
[83]*Ibid.*, p. 433. The text of this and subsequent passages of "The Shadow Out of Time" have been corrected by consultation of the recently discovered autograph manuscript.
[84]*Ibid.*, p. 368.
[85]*Ibid.*, p. 395.
[86]*Ibid.*, p. 396.
[87]*Ibid.*, p. 399.
[88]*Ibid.*, p. 374.
[89]*Ibid.*, p. 386.
[90]*Ibid.*, p. 433.
[91]Darrell Schweitzer. "Lovecraft's Favorite Movie," in *Lovecraft Studies* Nos. 19/20 (Fall 1989): 23-25, 27.
[92]*Miscellaneous Writings*, p. 113.
[93]*The Dunwich Horror and Others*, p. 370.
[94]*Ibid.*, p. 392.
[95]*Selected Letters, 1929-1931*, p. 217.
[96]*Ibid.*
[97]*Selected Letters, Volume Five, 1934-1937*, p. 71.
[98]*Ibid.*, p. 70.
[99]*Ibid.*, p. 346.
[100]*The Dunwich Horror and Others*, p. 97.
[101]*Ibid.*, p. 104.
[102]*Ibid.*, p. 112.
[103]*Ibid.*, p. 115.
[104]*Ibid.*
[105]*Dagon and Other Macabre Tales*, p. 399.
[106]Hanns Heinz Ewers. "The Spider," in *Creeps by Night*, edited by Dashiell Hammett. New York: John Day Co., 1931, p. 184.
[107]*The Dunwich Horror and Others*, p. 114.
[108]*Ibid.*, p. 94.

CHAPTER SEVEN

[1]See the chart in *Letters to Richard F. Searight*, by H. P. Lovecraft, edited by David E. Schultz and S. T. Joshi. West Warwick, RI: Necronomicon Press, 1992, p. 12.
[2]*Selected Letters, 1925-1929*, p. 233.
[3]*Selected Letters, 1911-1924*, p. 199.
[4]*Selected Letters, Volume Five, 1934-1937*, p. 421-422.
[5]HPL to F. Lee Baldwin, 29 April 1934 (ms., JHL).

[6]S. T. Joshi. "Lovecraft's Revisions: How Much of Them Did He Write?," in *Selected Papers on Lovecraft*, by S. T. Joshi. West Warwick, RI: Necronomicon Press, 1989.
[7]*Selected Letters, 1911-1924*, p. 136.
[8]As Greene herself declares in a letter to Winfield Townley Scott (11 December 1948; ms., JHL).
[9]*Selected Letters, 1911-1924*, p. 257.
[10]H. P. Lovecraft, and others. *The Horror in the Museum and Other Revisions*, edited by August Derleth. Sauk City, WI: Arkham House, 1989, p. 357.
[11]*Ibid.*, p. 353.
[12]*Dagon and Other Macabre Tales*, p. 240.
[13]*Ibid.*, p. 243.
[14]*Ibid.*
[15]*Ibid.*
[16]*Selected Letters, 1925-1929*, p. 207.
[17]*Ibid.*, p. 232.
[18]R. H. Barlow. Ms. note on the typed ms. of "The Mound" (JHL).
[19]*Selected Letters, 1929-1931*, p. 97.
[20]*The Horror in the Museum and Other Revisions*, p. 134.
[21]*Ibid.*, p. 134-136.
[22]*Ibid.*, p. 149.
[23]*Ibid.*, p. 135.
[24]*Miscellaneous Writings*, p. 196-197.
[25]*The Horror in the Museum and Other Revisions*, p. 135.
[26]*Ibid.*, p. 136.
[27]*Ibid.*, p. 149.
[28]*Ibid.*
[29]*Selected Letters, 1925-1929*, p. 309.
[30]*The Horror in the Museum and Other Revisions*, p. 135.
[31]*Ibid.*, p. 134.
[32]*Ibid.*, p. 135.
[33]*Ibid.*, p. 134.
[34]*Ibid.*, p. 200.
[35]HPL to R. H. Barlow, 25 February 1932 (ms., JHL).
[36]*Selected Letters, Volume Four, 1932-1934*, p. 127.
[37]This has been published in *Crypt of Cthulhu* No. 10 (1982): 47-56.
[38]Norm Gayford. "Randolph Carter: An Anti-Hero's Quest," in *Lovecraft Studies* No. 16 (Spring 1988): 3-11; and No. 17 (Fall 1988): 5-13.
[39]*At the Mountains of Madness and Other Novels*, p. 431.
[40]*Ibid.*, p. 433-434.
[41]See August Derleth's note to "The Man of Stone," in *The Horror in the Museum and Other Revisions* (1970 edition), p. 270.
[42]*The Horror in the Museum and Other Revisions* (1989 edition), p. 209.
[43]*Ibid.*, p. 225.
[44]*Ibid.*, p. 232.
[45]*Ibid.*, p. 234.
[46]*Ibid.*, p. 272.
[47]*Ibid.*, p. 274.
[48]See, in general, Will Murray. "Facts in the Case of 'The Disinterment'," in *Lovecraft Studies* No. 17 (Fall 1988): 30-33.
[49]HPL to Hyman Bradofsky, 4 November 1936 (ms.).
[50]HPL to Duane W. Rimel, 20 February 1937 (ms., JHL).
[51]*Dagon and Other Macabre Tales*, p. 428-429.

[52]*The Horror in the Museum and Other Revisions*, p. 449-450.
[53]*Ibid.*, p. 322.
[54]Robert M. Price, "The Revision Mythos," in *H. P. Lovecraft and the Cthulhu Mythos*.
[55]H. P. Lovecraft. *H. P. Lovecraft in "The Eyrie"*, edited by S. T. Joshi and Marc A. Michaud. West Warwick, RI: Necronomicon Press, 1979, p. 37.

CHAPTER EIGHT

[1]All of the juvenile scientific mss. cited here are in JHL.
[2]All the *Gleaner* articles are reprinted in *First Writings: Pawtuxet Valley Gleaner 1906*, by H. P. Lovecraft. West Warwick, RI: Necronomicon Press, 1976; rev. 1986.
[3]H. P. Lovecraft. "The August Sky," in *Providence Evening News* (1 August 1914): 8.
[4]H. P. Lovecraft. *Science Versus Charlatanry*. West Warwick, RI: Necronomicon Press, 1979, p. 30-31.
[5]H. P. Lovecraft. "[The Stars, Part II]," in *Asheville Gazette-News* (23 March 1915): 4.
[6]*Selected Letters, Volume Five, 1934-1937*, p. 422.
[7]H. P. Lovecraft. *To Quebec and the Stars*, edited by L. Sprague de Camp. West Kingston, RI: Donald M. Grant, Publisher, 1976, p. 35.
[8]*Miscellaneous Writings*, p. 166-167.
[9]H. P. Lovecraft. "The Omnipresent Philistine," in *Miscellaneous Writings*, p. 242.
[10]*Miscellaneous Writings*, p. 443.
[11]*Ibid.*, p. 452.
[12]*Ibid.*, p. 336.
[13]*Ibid.*, p. 376.
[14]A manuscript located in the John Hay Library.
[15]*Miscellaneous Writings*, p. 548.
[16]*Selected Letters, 1911-1924*, p. 11.
[17]*Selected Letters, 1929-1931*, p. 193.

CHAPTER NINE

[1]Winfield Townley Scott. "A Parenthesis on Lovecraft as Poet" (1945), in *H. P. Lovecraft: Four Decades of Criticism*, p. 214.
[2]*Selected Letters, 1925-1929*, p. 314-315.
[3]Nearly all of Lovecraft's poetry is included in four volumes: *Collected Poems* (Sauk City, WI: Arkham House, 1963); *A Winter Wish* (Chapel Hill, NC: Whispers Press, 1977); *Saturnalia and Other Poems* (Bloomfield, NJ: Cryptic Publications, 1984); and *Medusa and Other Poems* (Mount Olive, NC: Cryptic Publications, 1986). All Lovecraft's weird verse, except the *Fungi from Yuggoth*, is included in *The Fantastic Poetry* (West Warwick, RI: Necronomicon Press, 1990; rev. 1993). I provide no specific citations of poetry except for items contained in *The Fantastic Poetry*.
[4]Alexander Pope. *Poetical Works*. Oxford: Clarendon Press, 1977, p. 34.
[5]S. T. Joshi. "The Rationale of Lovecraft's Pseudonyms," in *Crypt of Cthulhu* No. 80 (Eastertide 1992): 15-24, 29.
[6]*Selected Letters, 1911-1924*, p. 110.
[7]*Selected Letters, 1929-1931*, p. 369-370.
[8]*Selected Letters, 1911-1924*, p. 12.
[9]Cited in *In Defence of Dagon*, p. 6, 19.

[10]W. Paul Cook. "Howard P. Lovecraft's Fiction," in *Vagrant* (November 1919); cited in Cook's *In Memoriam: Howard Phillips Lovecraft*. West Warwick, RI: Necronomicon Press, 1991, p. 30.
[11]Rheinhart Kleiner. "A Note on Howard P. Lovecraft's Verse," in *United Amateur* 18:4 (March 1919): 76.
[12]*Selected Letters, 1911-1924*, p. 132.
[13]H. P. Lovecraft. *The Fantastic Poetry*. West Warwick, RI: Necronomicon Press, 1993, p. 14-20.
[14]R. Boerem. "A Lovecraftian Nightmare," in *Nyctalops* 2:4/5 (April 1976): 22-24.
[15]HPL to R. H. Barlow, 13 June 1936 (ms., JHL).
[16]*The Fantastic Poetry*, p. 20.
[17]*Selected Letters, 1911-1924*, p. 51-52.
[18]*The Fantastic Poetry*, p. 31-33.
[19]*Ibid*., p. 33-34.
[20]*Ibid*., p. 24-31.
[21]*Selected Letters, 1925-1929*, p. 186.
[22]*The Fantastic Poetry*, p. 54.
[23]Robert H. Waugh. "The Structural and Thematic Unity of *Fungi from Yuggoth*," in *Lovecraft Studies* No. 26 (Spring 1992): 2-14. Also: Dan Clore. "Metonyms of Alterity: A Semiotic Interpretation of *Fungi from Yuggoth*," in *Lovecraft Studies* No. 30 (Spring 1994).
[24]*Selected Letters, 1929-1931*, p. 96.

Chapter Ten

[1]*Selected Letters, 1929-1931*.
[2]A supplementary volume of letters and an index were announced by Arkham House catalogues before Derleth's death in 1971, but copyright disputes evidently derailed these plans. I supplied the index in 1980 through Necronomicon Press.
[3]Galpin reports that "In anguish of conscience and after careful sifting, I destroyed, with other material, the great bulk of my letters from Howard." Galpin, "Memories of a Friendship," in *The Shuttered Room and Other Pieces*, by H. P. Lovecraft and Divers Hands, edited by August Derleth. Sauk City, WI: Arkham House, 1959, p. 200. Only twenty-eight of Galpin's letters now survive.

Sonia Davis states: "I had a trunkful of his letters which he had written me throughout the years but before leaving New York to California I took them to a field and set a match to them." *The Private Life of H. P. Lovecraft*. West Warwick, RI: Necronomicon Press, 1992, p. 24.
[4]Samuel Loveman states: "I have in my possession some 500 folio pages of his letters, generally in his handwriting and one running to as much as sixty pages." "Lovecraft as a Conversationalist," in *Fresco* 8:3 (Spring 1958): 34. Only five letters and postcards to Loveman have come to light thus far.
[5]R. Alain Everts. "Letter to the Editor," in *Fantasy Commentator* 5:3 (Fall 1985): 217.
[6]HPL to Rheinhart Kleiner, 5 May 1918, as cited in *Uncollected Letters*, p. 25.
[7]Actually, as James Turner has pointed out to me, she published two slim books of poetry around 1910, years before ever encountering Lovecraft.
[8]*Selected Letters, 1929-1931*, p. 295.
[9]*Ibid*. The date of the letter is February 27, 1931.
[10]*Ibid*., p. 298-299.

[11]*Ibid.*, p. 337.
[12]*Selected Letters, 1911-1924*, p. 88.
[13]J. Vernon Shea, however, once piqued Lovecraft by pointing out the doubtful usage "three alternatives" in one letter (*Selected Letters, Volume Four, 1932-1934*, p. 99); and there are other solecisms—found also in the stories—such as the use of "data" in the singular and the continual misspelling of "accommodate" (as "accomodate") and "Portuguese" (as "Portugese").
[14]See, for example, letter #454 in *Selected Letters, 1929-1931*.
[15]*Selected Letters, 1911-1924*, p. 60+.
[16]*Selected Letters, 1925-1929*, p. 47.
[17]*Selected Letters, Volume Five, 1934-1937*, p. 277.
[18]*Selected Letters, Volume Four, 1932-1934*, p. 35+.
[19]See letter #856 dated June 19, 1936, in *Selected Letters, Volume Five, 1934-1937.*
[20]*Selected Letters, 1929-1931*, p. 58.
[21]*Selected Letters, 1911-1924*, p. 12.
[22]*Ibid.*, p. 24.
[23]*Ibid.*, p. 26.
[24]*Ibid.*, p. 45.
[25]*Ibid.*, p. 57.
[26]*Ibid.*, p. 63.
[27]*Ibid.*, p. 106.
[28]*Ibid.*, p. 111.
[29]*Ibid.*, p. 135.
[30]*Ibid.*, p. 156.
[31]*Ibid.*, p. 209.
[32]*Ibid.*, p. 211.
[33]*Ibid.*, p. 243.
[34]*Ibid.*, p. 327.
[35]*Selected Letters, 1929-1931*, p. 83.
[36]*Selected Letters, Volume Four, 1932-1934*, p. 360.
[37]*Selected Letters, 1911-1924*, p. 11.
[38]*Ibid.*, p. 73.
[39]*Ibid.*, p. 63-64.
[40]*Ibid.*, p. 52.
[41]*Selected Letters, Volume Four, 1932-1934*, p. 389.

CHAPTER ELEVEN

[1]*Miscellaneous Writings*, p. 148.
[2]*Ibid.*, p. 115.
[3]*The Dunwich Horror and Others*, p. 44.
[4]*Ibid.*, p. 26-27.
[5]*Selected Letters, 1929-1931*, p. 75.
[6]*The Dunwich Horror and Others*, p. 42.
[7]Peter Penzoldt. *The Supernatural in Fiction*. London: Peter Nevill, 1952. Reprinted in *H. P. Lovecraft: Four Decades of Criticism*, p. 69.
[8]S. T. Joshi. "The Structure of Lovecraft's Longer Narratives," in *Selected Papers on Lovecraft.*
[9]*The Dunwich Horror and Others*, p. 125.
[10]L. Sprague de Camp. *Lovecraft: A Biography*. Garden City, NY: Doubleday & Co., 1975, p. 354.
[11]*Dagon and Other Macabre Tales*, p. 382.
[12]*The Horror in the Museum and Other Revisions*, p. 155.

[13]*Selected Letters, 1925-1929*, p. 217.
[14]Leiber, "A Literary Copernicus," p. 50.
[15]David E. Schultz. "What Is the Cthulhu Mythos? A Panel Discussion," in *Lovecraft Studies* No. 14 (Spring 1987): 22.
[16]H. P. Lovecraft. "Suggestions for Writing a Story," in *The Notes & Commonplace Book...*, by H. P. Lovecraft, edited by R. H. Barlow. Lakeport, CA: Futile Press, 1938, p. 5.
[17]*Selected Letters, 1929-1931*, p. 296.
[18]*At the Mountains of Madness and Other Novels*, p. 151.
[19]*Ibid.*, p. 162.
[20]*Dagon and Other Macabre Tales*, p. 265.
[21]Stefan Dziemianowicz. "Outsiders and Aliens: The Uses of Isolation in Lovecraft's Fiction," in *An Epicure in the Terrible*, p. 175.
[22]*Selected Letters, Volume Five, 1934-1937*, p. 19.
[23]David E. Schultz. "From Microcosm to Macrocosm: The Growth of Lovecraft's Cosmic Vision," in *An Epicure in the Terrible*, p. 209.
[24]*Selected Letters, 1911-1924*, p. 27.
[25]*Ibid.*, p. 45.
[26]*Ibid.*, p. 65.
[27]*The Dunwich Horror and Others*, p. 154.
[28]*Ibid.*, p. 152.
[29]Penzoldt. *The Supernatural in Fiction*.
[30]S. T. Joshi. "H. P. Lovecraft: The Decline of the West," in *The Weird Tale*. Austin, TX: University of Texas Press, 1990, p. 228.
[31]Lévy. *Lovecraft: A Study in the Fantastic*, p. 80.
[32]*American Literature* 63 (June 1991): 374.
[33]*In Defence of Dagon*, in *Miscellaneous Writings*, p. 166.

ANNOTATED PRIMARY BIBLIOGRAPHY

A. FICTION

At the Mountains of Madness and Other Novels. Selected by August Derleth. Sauk City, WI: Arkham House, 1964; rev. ed. (by S. T. Joshi), 1985. Contains: *At the Mountains of Madness*, *The Case of Charles Dexter Ward*, "The Shunned House," "The Dreams in the Witch House," "The Statement of Randolph Carter," *The Dream-Quest of Unknown Kadath*, "The Silver Key," "Through the Gates of the Silver Key" (with E. Hoffmann Price).

Dagon and Other Macabre Tales. Selected by August Derleth. Sauk City, WI: Arkham House, 1965; rev. ed. (by S. T. Joshi), 1986. Contains: "The Tomb," "Dagon," "Polaris," "Beyond the Wall of Sleep," "The White Ship," "The Doom That Came to Sarnath," "The Tree," "The Cats of Ulthar," "The Temple," "Facts concerning the Late Arthur Jermyn and His Family," "Celephaïs," "From Beyond," "The Nameless City," "The Quest of Iranon," "The Moon-Bog," "The Other Gods," "Herbert West—Reanimator," "Hypnos," "The Hound," "The Lurking Fear," "The Unnamable," "The Festival," "Under the Pyramids," "The Horror at Red Hook," "He," "The Strange High House in the Mist," "The Evil Clergyman," "In the Walls of Eryx," "The Beast in the Cave," "The Alchemist," "The Transition of Juan Romero," "The Street," "Poetry and the Gods" (with Anna Helen Crofts), "Azathoth," "The Descendant," "The Book" (with R. H. Barlow), "Supernatural Horror in Literature."

The Dunwich Horror and Others. Selected by August Derleth. Sauk City, WI: Arkham House, 1963; rev. ed. (by S. T. Joshi), 1984. Contains: "In the Vault," "Pickman's Model," "The Rats in the Walls" (with Kenneth Sterling), "The Outsider," "The Colour out of Space," "The Music of Erich Zann," "The Haunter of the Dark," "The Picture in the House," "The Call of Cthulhu," "The Dunwich Horror," "Cool Air," "The Whisperer in Darkness," "The Terrible Old Man," "The Thing on the Doorstep," "The Shadow over Innsmouth," "The Shadow out of Time."

The Horror in the Museum and Other Revisions. [Selected by August Derleth.] Sauk City, WI: Arkham House, 1970; rev. ed. (by S. T. Joshi), 1989. Contains: "The Green Meadow" (with Winifred Jackson), "The Crawling Chaos" (with Winifred Jackson), "The Last Test" (with Adolphe de Castro), "The Electric Executioner" (with Adolphe de Castro), "The Curse of Yig" (with Zealia Bishop), "The Mound" (with Zealia Bishop), "Medusa's Coil" (with Zealia Bishop), "The Man of Stone" (with Hazel Heald), "The Horror in the Museum" (with Hazel Heald), "Winged Death" (with Hazel Heald), "Out of the Æons" (with Hazel Heald), "The Horror in the Burying-Ground" (with Hazel Heald), "The Diary of Alonzo Typer" (with William Lumley), "The Horror at Martin's Beach" (with Sonia H. Greene), "Ashes" (with C. M. Eddy, Jr.), "The Ghost-Eater" (with C. M. Eddy, Jr.), "The Loved Dead" (with C. M. Eddy, Jr.), "Deaf, Dumb, and Blind" (with C. M. Eddy, Jr.), "Two Black Bottles" (with Wilfred B. Talman), "The Trap" (with Henry S. Whitehead), "The Tree on the Hill" (with Duane W. Rimel), "The Disinterment" (with Duane W. Rimel), "'Till A' the Seas'" (with Robert H. Barlow), "The Night Ocean" (with Robert H. Barlow).

B. POETRY

Collected Poems. [Selected by August Derleth.] Sauk City, WI: Arkham House, 1963. New York: Ballantine Books, 1971 (as *Fungi from Yuggoth and Other Poems*). Historically important collection, although by no means complete and full of errors.

The Fantastic Poetry. Edited by S. T. Joshi. West Warwick, RI: Necronomicon Press, 1990 (rev. 1993). Complete reprinting of Lovecraft's weird verse except for *Fungi from Yuggoth*.

Fungi from Yuggoth. West Warwick, RI: Necronomicon Press, 1982 (rev. 1993). Most accurate text of Lovecraft's sonnet-cycle.

Medusa and Other Poems. Edited by S. T. Joshi. Mount Olive, NC: Cryptic Publications, 1986. Contains all Lovecraft's unreprinted poetry not contained in *Collected Poems*, *Saturnalia*, or *A Winter Wish*.

Saturnalia and Other Poems. Edited by S. T. Joshi. Bloomfield, NJ: Cryptic Publications, 1984. Contains all Lovecraft's hitherto unpublished poetry.

A Winter Wish. Edited by Tom Collins. Chapel Hill, NC: Whispers Press, 1977. Contains much unreprinted (mostly non-fantastic) poetry. Very unsound textually.

C. LETTERS

Letters to Henry Kuttner. Edited by David E. Schultz and S. T. Joshi. West Warwick, RI: Necronomicon Press, 1990.

Letters to Richard F. Searight. Edited by David E. Schultz and S. T. Joshi. West Warwick, RI: Necronomicon Press, 1992. Unabridged publication of the 35 extant letters to Searight; with annotations.

Letters to Robert Bloch. Edited by David E. Schultz and S. T. Joshi. West Warwick, RI: Necronomicon Press, 1993. (Supplement, 1993.) Unabridged publication of 68 letters to Bloch; with annotations.

Lovecraft at Last. By H. P. Lovecraft and Willis Conover. Arlington, VA: Carrollton-Clark, 1975. Selection of the correspondence between Lovecraft and Conover during 1936-1937; contains much other interesting matter. Already a legend in fine book production.

Selected Letters: 1911-1937. Edited by August Derleth and Donald Wandrei (Vols. I-III), August Derleth and James Turner (Vols. IV-V). Sauk City, WI: Arkham House, 1965-1976. 5 vols. Extensive selection of letters, marred by poor editing, repetition, and lack of an index. Latter deficiency has been supplied by S. T. Joshi, *An Index to the Selected Letters of H. P. Lovecraft* (West Warwick, RI: Necronomicon Press, 1980; rev. ed. 1991).

Uncollected Letters. Edited by S. T. Joshi. West Warwick, RI: Necronomicon Press, 1986. Collection of letters written to *Weird Tales*, *The Fantasy Fan*, and other magazines, along with other groups of previously published letters.

D. ESSAYS AND MISCELLANY

Autobiographical Writings. Edited by S. T. Joshi. West Warwick, RI: Necronomicon Press, 1992. Contains: "A Confession of Unfaith," "Some Notes on a Nonentity," and other autobiographical pieces.

Beyond the Wall of Sleep. Collected by August Derleth and Donald Wandrei. Sauk City, WI: Arkham House, 1943. Almost totally superseded by later publications, but an important landmark in the field.

Commonplace Book. Edited by David E. Schultz. West Warwick, RI: Necronomicon Press, 1987. 2 vols. Definitive text, with exhaustive annotations, of Lovecraft's book of plot-germs.

The Conservative. Edited by Marc A. Michaud. West Warwick, RI: Necronomicon Press, 1976, 1977. Complete reprinting of Lovecraft's amateur journal. The 3rd ed. (1990; ed. S. T. Joshi) contains only a selection of Lovecraft's contributions, but is a superior text with annotations.

The Dark Brotherhood and Other Pieces. [Compiled by August Derleth.] Sauk City, WI: Arkham House, 1966. Contains some previously unpublished matter (*Alfredo*, "Suggestions for a Reading Guide" [with Anne Renshaw], "The Cancer of Superstition" [with C. M. Eddy Jr. as "Houdini"], etc.) and some good essays about Lovecraft.

H. P. Lovecraft in the Argosy: Collected Correspondence from the Munsey Magazines. Edited by S. T. Joshi. West Warwick, RI: Necronomicon Press, 1994. A complete collection of letters by and about Lovecraft (1913-1920) from the *Argosy* and the *All-Story*.

In Defence of Dagon. Edited by S. T. Joshi. West Warwick, RI: Necronomicon Press, 1985. (Rev. ed. forthcoming.) Annotated edition of Lovecraft's three philosophical-literary essays of 1921.

Juvenilia: 1897-1905. Edited by S. T. Joshi. West Warwick, RI: Necronomicon Press, 1984. (Rev. ed. forthcoming.) Corrected texts of Lovecraft's complete juvenile fiction and poetry.

The Lovecraft Collectors Library. Edited by George Wetzel. North Tonawanda, NY: SSR Publications, 1952-55. 7 vols. Madison, WI: Strange Co., 1979 (in 1 vol.). Now obsolete, but contains much obscure matter, especially poetry and essays.

Marginalia. Collected by August Derleth and Donald Wandrei. Sauk City, WI: Arkham House, 1944. Contains some obscure items by Lovecraft and some important essays about him.

Miscellaneous Writings. Edited by S. T. Joshi. Sauk City, WI: Arkham House, 1995. Most extensive collection of Lovecraft's essays ever published; also contains minor fiction not contained in the four-volume Arkham House revised edition of the fiction (see above).

The Notes & Commonplace Book... [Edited by R. H. Barlow.] Lakeport, CA: Futile Press, 1938. West Warwick, RI: Necronomicon Press, 1977. *Commonplace Book* superseded by Schultz's edition (see above), but the "Notes" section contains Lovecraft's lists and notes on weird fiction.

The Shuttered Room and Other Pieces. Compiled by August Derleth. Sauk City, WI: Arkham House, 1959. Almost entirely superseded by later volumes, but with some important essays about Lovecraft.

Something about Cats and Other Pieces. Collected by August Derleth. Sauk City, WI: Arkham House, 1949. Freeport, NY: Books for Libraries Press, 1971. Almost entirely superseded by later volumes, but with some important essays about Lovecraft.

To Quebec and the Stars. Edited by L. Sprague de Camp. West Kingston, RI: Donald M. Grant, 1976. Noteworthy collection of essays, including Lovecraft's complete travelogue of Quebec and other matter.

Uncollected Prose and Poetry. Edited by S. T. Joshi and Marc A. Michaud. West Warwick, RI: Necronomicon Press, 1978-82. 3 vols. Contains much obscure matter, although some items have since been reprinted in other volumes.

Writings in The United Amateur: 1915-1925. Edited by Marc A. Michaud. West Warwick, RI: Necronomicon Press, 1976. Large (but incomplete) collection of writings from *The United Amateur*, reprinted in facsimile.

ANNOTATED SECONDARY BIBLIOGRAPHY

The literature on Lovecraft has now reached titanic proportions; much of it, especially in the last twenty years, is of great value and insight. Listed below are only the most notable general books and articles; citations to additional works can be found in the notes.

A. BIBLIOGRAPHICAL

Joshi, S. T. *H. P. Lovecraft and Lovecraft Criticism: An Annotated Bibliography.* Kent, OH: Kent State University Press, 1981.

___, and L. D. Blackmore. *H. P. Lovecraft and Lovecraft Criticism: An Annotated Bibliography: Supplement 1980-1984.* West Warwick, RI: Necronomicon Press, 1985. Supersedes all previous works.

___, and Marc A. Michaud. *Lovecraft's Library: A Catalogue.* West Warwick, RI: Necronomicon Press, 1980. Rev. ed. forthcoming. Listing of nearly 1000 books in Lovecraft's library. Rev. ed. includes complete contents for many volumes and extensive annotation.

B. BIOGRAPHICAL

Barlow, Robert H. "The Wind That Is in the Grass: A Memoir of H. P. Lovecraft in Florida." In Lovecraft, *Marginalia* (q.v.). Sensitive memoir by Lovecraft's literary executor.

Beckwith, Henry L. P., Jr. *Lovecraft's Providence and Adjacent Parts.* West Kingston, RI: Donald M. Grant, 1979 (rev. 1986). Interesting but sketchy survey of the topographical sites in Providence and Rhode Island known to Lovecraft and cited in his work. See Eckhardt (q.v.) for a more condensed but more reliable guide.

Brobst, Harry K., and Will Murray. "An Interview with Harry K. Brobst." *Lovecraft Studies* Nos. 22/23 (Fall 1990): 24-42, 21. Fascinating interview with a man who met Lovecraft frequently during the last five years of his life.

Cook, W. Paul. *In Memoriam: Howard Phillips Lovecraft: Recollections, Appreciations, Estimates.* North Montpelier, VT: Driftwind Press, 1941. West Warwick, RI: Necronomicon Press, 1977, 1991. Still the best memoir of Lovecraft, concentrating on his early years and his involvement with amateur journalism.

Davis, Sonia H. *The Private Life of H. P. Lovecraft.* Ed. S. T. Joshi. West Warwick, RI: Necronomicon Press, 1985 (rev. 1992). Important if at times unreliable memoir by Lovecraft's wife, extensively discussing his character and life during his "New York Exile."

de Camp, L. Sprague. *Lovecraft: A Biography.* Garden City, NY: Doubleday, 1975. The first full-length biography, full of much useful information but also filled with errors, omissions, and misinterpretations of Lovecraft's ideals and motives.

Derleth, August. *H.P.L.: A Memoir*. New York: Ben Abramson, 1945. Brief biography, now completely superseded by later works but still of historical importance.

___. *Some Notes on H. P. Lovecraft*. Sauk City, WI: Arkham House, 1959. West Warwick, RI: Necronomicon Press, 1982. Random biographical and critical notes. Most of the contents reprinted in Lovecraft, *Dark Brotherhood* (q.v.).

Eckhardt, Jason C. "The Cosmic Yankee." In Schultz and Joshi, *An Epicure in the Terrible* (q.v.), p. 78-100. Thoughtful essay on Lovecraft's New England heritage.

___. *Off the Ancient Track: A Lovecraftian Guide to New-England and New-York*. West Warwick, RI: Necronomicon Press, 1987. Compact illustrated guide to Lovecraftian sites in Providence, Massachusetts, and New York.

Everts, R. Alain. *The Death of a Gentleman: The Last Days of Howard Phillips Lovecraft*. Madison, WI: The Strange Co., 1987. Detailed examination of Lovecraft's final days in the hospital, based upon an interview with Lovecraft's doctor and containing transcriptions of his "Death Diary" made by R. H. Barlow.

Faig, Kenneth W., Jr. *H. P. Lovecraft: His Life, His Work*. West Warwick, RI: Necronomicon Press, 1979. Concise but extensive chronology of Lovecraft's life and the recognition of his work; includes an illuminating interpretation of the man by Faig plus a chronology of Lovecraft's work by S. T. Joshi.

___. "Howard Phillips Lovecraft: The Early Years, 1890-1914." *Nyctalops* 2:1 (April 1973): 3-9; and 2:2 (July 1974): 34-44. Exhaustive study of Lovecraft's early life and writings.

___. *The Parents of Howard Phillips Lovecraft*. West Warwick, RI: Necronomicon Press, 1990. Brilliant and insightful account of Lovecraft's parents and their influence upon their son's life and work.

Hart, Mara Kirk. "Walkers in the City: George Willard Kirk and Howard Phillips Lovecraft in New York City, 1924-1926." *Lovecraft Studies* No. 28 (Spring 1993): 2-17. Valuable account of Lovecraft's relations to Kirk, based largely on letters written by Kirk to his future wife.

Long, Frank Belknap. *Howard Phillips Lovecraft: Dreamer on the Nightside*. Sauk City, WI: Arkham House, 1975. Interesting if insubstantial memoir filled with random memories and sporadic critical comment.

Moskowitz, Sam. "H. P. Lovecraft and the Munsey Magazines." In Moskowitz's *Under the Moons of Mars*. New York: Holt, Rinehart & Winston, 1970. Study of Lovecraft's literary controversy in the *Argosy*, 1913-1920.

Murray, Will. "Lovecraft and the Pulp Magazine Tradition." In Schultz and Joshi, *An Epicure in the Terrible* (q.v.), p. 101-134. Thorough examination of Lovecraft's attempts to achieve publication in the pulps.

Scott, Winfield Townley. "His Own Most Fantastic Creation: Howard Phillips Lovecraft." In Lovecraft, *Marginalia* (q.v.). In Scott's *Exiles and Fabrications*. Garden City, NY: Doubleday & Co., 1961. First biographical study of Lovecraft, still valuable.

Sterling, Kenneth. "Caverns Measureless to Man." *Science-Fantasy Correspondent* 1 (1975): 36-43. Poignant memoir of Lovecraft's later years, concentrating on his scientific rationalism.

C. CRITICAL

Boerem, R. "A Lovecraftian Nightmare." *Nyctalops* 2:4/5 (April 1976): 22-24. In Joshi, *Four Decades* (q.v.). Study of "The Poe-et's Nightmare" and its reflection of Lovecraft's central philosophical principle of cosmicism.

Buhle, Paul. "Dystopia as Utopia: Howard Phillips Lovecraft and the Unknown Content of American Horror Literature." *Minnesota Review* N.S. No. 6 (Spring 1976): 118-131. In Joshi, *Four Decades* (q.v.). Profound essay exploring Lovecraft's philosophical thought, its relation to political and social history, and how it is manifested in his fiction.

Burleson, Donald R. *H. P. Lovecraft: A Critical Study*. Westport, CT: Greenwood Press, 1983. Comprehensive introductory guide to Lovecraft.

___. "H. P. Lovecraft: The Hawthorne Influence." *Extrapolation* 22:3 (Fall 1981): 262-269. Detailed and illuminating treatment of the subject.

___. "Humour beneath Horror: Some Sources for 'The Dunwich Horror' and 'The Whisperer in Darkness.'" *Lovecraft Studies* No. 2 (Spring 1980): 5-15. Exhaustive treatment of the New England historical and topographical sources for the two tales.

___. *Lovecraft: Disturbing the Universe*. Lexington: University Press of Kentucky, 1990. Challenging deconstructionist study of Lovecraft's tales.

___. "The Mythic Hero Archetype in 'The Dunwich Horror.'" *Lovecraft Studies* No. 4 (Spring 1981): 3-9. A mythic study which interprets the Whateley twins as the true "heroes" of the tale.

___. "Prismatic Heroes: The Colour out of Dunwich." *Lovecraft Studies* No. 25 (Fall 1991): 13-18. Mythic interpretation of "The Colour out of Space."

Cannon, Peter. *H. P. Lovecraft*. New York: Twayne, 1989. Fine general overview of Lovecraft's life and work.

___. *"Sunset Terrace Imagery in Lovecraft" and Other Essays*. West Warwick, RI: Necronomicon Press, 1990. Collection of Cannon's wide-ranging essays on Lovecraft the man and writer.

Carter, Lin. "H. P. Lovecraft: The Books." In Lovecraft, *The Shuttered Room* (q.v.). Rev. ed. (by Robert M. Price and S. T. Joshi) in Schweitzer, *Discovering H. P. Lovecraft* (rev. ed.; q.v.). Exhaustive article discussing the use of real and mythical books by Lovecraft and his followers.

___. *Lovecraft: A Look Behind the "Cthulhu Mythos."* New York: Ballantine, 1972. History of the development of Lovecraft's myth-cycle, especially after Lovecraft's death. Full of errors and uncritical assumptions.

Derleth, August. "H. P. Lovecraft: The Making of a Literary Reputation, 1937-1971." *Books at Brown* 25 (1977): 13-25. Traces the publication and recognition of Lovecraft's work.

Dziemianowicz, Stefan. "Outsiders and Aliens: The Uses of Isolation in Lovecraft's Fiction." In Schultz and Joshi, *An Epicure in the Terrible* (q.v.), p. 159-187. Studies the development of the isolation theme from early tales involving the psychological isolation of a single character to later tales suggesting the cosmic isolation of the human race.

Eckhardt, Jason. "Behind the Mountains of Madness: Lovecraft and the Antarctic in 1930." *Lovecraft Studies* No. 14 (Spring 1987): 31-38. Studies Lovecraft's novel in the context of the Antarctic exploration of the period.

Frierson, Meade and Penny, ed. *HPL*. Birmingham, AL: The Editors, 1972, 1975. Interesting collection of essays (especially notable are those by Robert Bloch, R. Alain Everts, George T. Wetzel, J. Vernon Shea, Roger

Bryant, and Richard L. Tierney), plus much fiction and some fine illustrations.

Fulwiler, William. "'The Tomb' and 'Dagon': A Double Dissection." *Crypt of Cthulhu* No. 38 (Eastertide 1986): 8-14. Penetrating study of the themes of and influences upon the two tales.

Gafford, Sam. "'The Shadow over Innsmouth': Lovecraft's Melting Pot." *Lovecraft Studies* No. 24 (Spring 1991): 6-13. Extensive discussion of the many themes in the story.

Gayford, Norm. "Randolph Carter: An Anti-Hero's Quest." *Lovecraft Studies* No. 16 (Spring 1988): 3-11; and No. 17 (Fall 1988): 5-13. Mythic study that sees "Through the Gates of the Silver Key" as a necessary conclusion to the Randolph Carter cycle; quotes extensively from Lovecraft's and Price's letters discussing the story.

Joshi, S. T. "The Development of Lovecraftian Studies, 1971-1982." *Lovecraft Studies* No. 9 (Fall 1984): 62-71; and No. 10 (Spring 1985): 18-28; and No. 11 (Fall 1985): 54-65. Detailed discussion of the publication and criticism of Lovecraft's work during the period.

___, ed. *H. P. Lovecraft: Four Decades of Criticism.* Athens: Ohio University Press, 1980. Large anthology of essays covering many aspects of Lovecraft's work; see individual essays by Boerem, Buhle, Leiber, Mosig, St. Armand, and Wetzel.

___. *H. P. Lovecraft: The Decline of the West.* Mercer Island, WA: Starmont House, 1990. Comprehensive discussion of Lovecraft's philosophical thought (metaphysics, ethics, aesthetics, and politics) and its ramifications in his fiction.

___. "'Reality' and Knowledge: Some Notes on the Aesthetic Thought of H. P. Lovecraft." *Lovecraft Studies* No. 3 (Fall 1980): 17-27. On Lovecraft's aesthetic of weird fiction and its reconciliation with his metaphysical and ethical thought.

___. *Selected Papers on Lovecraft.* West Warwick, RI: Necronomicon Press, 1989. Collection of five lengthy papers on Lovecraft's alien civilizations, the structure of his tales, his revisions, his letters, and other subjects.

Leiber, Fritz. "A Literary Copernicus." In Lovecraft, *Something about Cats* (q.v.). In Joshi, *Four Decades* (q.v.), p. 40-62. Brilliant study discussing how Lovecraft brought the weird tale up to date by transferring the locus of horror from this planet to the unknown cosmos; also studies themes in Lovecraft, his prose style, and his creation of mythical sites and books.

___. "Through Hyperspace with Brown Jenkin: Lovecraft's Contribution to Speculative Fiction." In Lovecraft, *The Dark Brotherhood* (q.v.), p. 164-178. In Joshi, *Four Decades* (q.v.), p. 140-152. Strong article tracing the ideas of hyperspace, space travel, and time travel in Lovecraft's later fiction.

Lévy, Maurice. *Lovecraft ou du fantastique.* Paris: Christian Bourgois (Union Générale d'Éditions), 1972. Translated by S. T. Joshi as *Lovecraft: A Study in the Fantastic.* Detroit: Wayne State University Press, 1988. Perhaps still the best full-length study of Lovecraft, discussing many important themes in his work.

Mariconda, Steven J. "H. P. Lovecraft: Art, Artifact, and Reality." *Lovecraft Studies* No. 29 (Fall 1993): 2-12. Study of Lovecraft's aesthetic theory and of his use of artists and archaeological artifacts in his fiction.

___. "H. P. Lovecraft: Consummate Prose Stylist." *Lovecraft Studies* No. 9 (Fall 1984): 43-51. Landmark study of Lovecraft's prose rhythm.

___. "Lovecraft's Concept of 'Background'." *Lovecraft Studies* No. 12 (Spring 1986): 3-12. Examines how Lovecraft reconciled his cosmicism with his devotion to New England.

___. "Notes on the Prose Realism of H. P. Lovecraft." *Lovecraft Studies* No. 10 (Spring 1985): 3-12. Further study of Lovecraft's prose style.

Mosig, Dirk W. "The Four Faces of 'The Outsider.'" *Nyctalops* 2:2 (July 1974): 3-10. In Schweitzer, *Discovering H. P. Lovecraft* (q.v.), p. 18-41. Interpretation of the tale on autobiographical, psychological, philosophical, and cultural levels.

___. "H. P. Lovecraft: Myth-Maker." *Whispers* 3:1 (December 1976): 48-55. In Joshi, *Four Decades* (q.v.), p. 104-112. Important article revealing August Derleth's misconceptions about Lovecraft's myth-cycle and pointing to cosmicism as the true foundation of his work.

Murray, Will. "The Dunwich Chimera and Others: Correlating the Cthulhu Mythos." *Lovecraft Studies* No. 8 (Spring 1984): 10-24. Extensive treatment of the influence of Greek mythology on Lovecraft's myth-cycle.

___. "In Search of Arkham Country." *Lovecraft Studies* No. 13 (Fall 1986): 54-67. Revolutionary article showing that Lovecraft's mythical New England topography is an amalgam of many previously unidentified locales.

___. "In Search of Arkham Country Revisited." *Lovecraft Studies* Nos. 19/20 (Fall 1989): 65-69. Additions and corrections to the above.

___. "An Uncompromising Look at the Cthulhu Mythos." *Lovecraft Studies* No. 12 (Spring 1986): 26-31. Maintains that Lovecraft lost control of his myth-cycle when he allowed other writers to contribute to it.

Nelson, Dale J. "Lovecraft and the Burkean Sublime." *Lovecraft Studies* No. 24 (Spring 1991): 2-5. Traces the influence of Edmund Burke's aesthetics on Lovecraft's cosmicism.

Onderdonk, Matthew H. "Charon—in Reverse; or, H. P. Lovecraft Versus the 'Realists' of Fantasy." *Fantasy Commentator* 2:6 (Spring 1948): 193-97. *Fresco* 8:3 (Spring 1958): 45-51. *Lovecraft Studies* No. 3 (Fall 1980): 5-10. Philosophical interpretation of Lovecraft's myth-cycle; also touches upon literary influences.

___. "The Lord of R'lyeh." *Fantasy Commentator* 1:6 (Spring 1945): 103-114. *Lovecraft Studies* No. 7 (Fall 1982): 8-17. Strong article showing how Lovecraft reconciled the horror tale with modern science and with his own mechanistic materialist philosophy.

Price, Robert M., ed. *Black Forbidden Things: Cryptical Secrets from the "Crypt of Cthulhu."* Mercer Island, WA: Starmont House, 1992. Contains some useful articles by Murray, Schultz, Joshi, and others.

___. *H. P. Lovecraft and the Cthulhu Mythos*. Mercer Island, WA: Starmont House, 1990. Collection of many of his provocative articles on Lovecraft's myth-cycle.

___, ed. *The Horror of It All: Encrusted Gems from the "Crypt of Cthulhu."* Mercer Island, WA: Starmont House, 1990. Contains some useful articles by Mariconda, Schultz, Joshi, and others.

Schultz, David E. "From Microcosm to Macrocosm: The Growth of Lovecraft's Cosmic Vision." In Schultz and Joshi, *An Epicure in the Terrible* (q.v.), p. 199-219. Traces the development of Lovecraft's work from "macabre" fiction of limited scope to the later cosmic works.

___. "Who Needs the Cthulhu Mythos?" *Lovecraft Studies* No. 13 (Fall 1986): 43-53. Maintains that an excessive concentration on Lovecraft's tales involving his myth-cycle hinders our understanding of the overall unity of his entire work.

___, and S. T. Joshi, ed. *An Epicure in the Terrible: A Centennial Anthology of Essays in Honor of H. P. Lovecraft.* Rutherford, NJ: Fairleigh Dickinson University Press, 1991. Important collection of original essays on Lovecraft by leading scholars in the field.

Schweitzer, Darrell. *The Dream Quest of H. P. Lovecraft.* San Bernardino, CA: Borgo Press, 1978. Simplified and frequently erroneous introduction for the beginner.

___, ed. *Essays Lovecraftian.* Baltimore: T-K Graphics, 1976. Rev. ed. as *Discovering H. P. Lovecraft.* Mercer Island, WA: Starmont House, 1987. 2nd ed. San Bernardino, CA: Borgo Press, 1996. Worthy collection of essays with contributions by Bloch, Leiber, Mosig, Wetzel, and others.

Shreffler, Philip A. *The H. P. Lovecraft Companion.* Westport, CT: Greenwood Press, 1977. Plot outlines and glossary of characters in Lovecraft's fiction.

Sigurdson, Kirk. "A Gothic Approach to Lovecraft's Sense of *Outsideness.*" *Lovecraft Studies* No. 28 (Spring 1993): 22-34. Extensive treatment of Gothic imagery in Lovecraft.

St. Armand, Barton L. "Facts in the Case of H. P. Lovecraft." *Rhode Island History* 31:1 (February 1972): 3-19. In Joshi, *Four Decades* (q.v.), p. 166-185. Discussion of *The Case of Charles Dexter Ward* and its use of local historical data.

___. *H. P. Lovecraft: New England Decadent.* Albuquerque, NM: Silver Scarab Press, 1979. Provocative study of the influence of Puritanism and the French Decadent movement upon Lovecraft. Perhaps overstates its case.

___. *The Roots of Horror in the Fiction of H. P. Lovecraft.* Elizabethtown, NY: Dragon Press, 1977. Extensive if discursive discussion of "The Rats in the Walls."

Tierney, Richard L. "The Derleth Mythos." In Frierson, *HPL* (q.v.). *Crypt of Cthulhu* No. 24 (Lammas 1984): 52-53. Landmark article revealing August Derleth's misinterpretations of Lovecraft's myth-cycle.

Waugh, Robert H. "Documents, Creatures, and History in H. P. Lovecraft." *Lovecraft Studies* No. 25 (Fall 1991): 2-10. Wide-ranging article studying documents, language, and the role of history in Lovecraft's tales.

Wetzel, George T. "The Cthulhu Mythos: A Study." In Frierson, *HPL* (q.v.). In Joshi, *Four Decades* (q.v.). Exhaustive discussion of Lovecraft's myth-cycle and such conceptions as the *Necronomicon*, the ghoul-changeling, ghosts and avatars, and the like. A summation of many of Wetzel's earlier articles.

INDEX

TITLE INDEX

(by Lovecraft unless otherwise noted)

INDEX

INDEX

CHARACTER INDEX

ABOUT S. T. JOSHI

S. T. Joshi, generally considered to be the world's leading scholar on H. P. Lovecraft and his successors, has edited the definitive collections of the master's stories for Arkham House, as well as numerous collections of Lovecraft's letters and anthologies of essays on Lovecraft for Necronomicon Press and others. His *H. P. Lovecraft and Lovecraft Criticism: An Annotated Bibliography* (Kent State, 1981) is the definitive guide to works by and about HPL. He is currently working on a critical guide to *The Modern Weird Tale* for The Borgo Press.

www.ingramcontent.com/pod-product-compliance
Lightning Source LLC
Chambersburg PA
CBHW021217090426
42740CB00006B/260

* 9 7 8 1 8 8 0 4 4 8 6 1 8 *